Lecture Notes in Computer Science   10301

Commenced Publication in 1973
Founding and Former Series Editors:
Gerhard Goos, Juris Hartmanis, and Jan van Leeuwen

More information about this series at http://www.springer.com/series/7408

Iain Phillips · Hafizur Rahaman (Eds.)

Reversible Computation

9th International Conference, RC 2017
Kolkata, India, July 6–7, 2017
Proceedings

 Springer

Editors
Iain Phillips
Imperial College London
London
UK

Hafizur Rahaman
Indian Institute of Engineering Science
    and Technology
Shibpur
India

ISSN 0302-9743   ISSN 1611-3349 (electronic)
Lecture Notes in Computer Science
ISBN 978-3-319-59935-9   ISBN 978-3-319-59936-6 (eBook)
DOI 10.1007/978-3-319-59936-6

Library of Congress Control Number: 2017941548

LNCS Sublibrary: SL2 – Programming and Software Engineering

Printed on acid-free paper

This Springer imprint is published by Springer Nature
The registered company is Springer International Publishing AG
The registered company address is: Gewerbestrasse 11, 6330 Cham, Switzerland

Preface

This volume contains the papers presented at RC 2017, the 9th International Conference on Reversible Computation, held during July 6–7, 2017, in Kolkata (India). The conference was jointly organized by: (a) the Indian Institute of Technology, Kharagpur, (b) the Indian Institute of Engineering Science and Technology, Shibpur, (c) the Indian Statistical Institute, Kolkata, and (d) Jadavpur University, Kolkata.

Reversible computation has a growing number of promising application areas such as low-power design, testing and verification, database recovery, discrete event simulation, reversible specification formalisms, reversible programming languages, process algebras, quantum computation, etc. RC 2017 was the ninth event in a series of annual meetings designed to gather researchers from different scientific disciplines for the discussion and dissemination of recent developments in all aspects of reversible computation. Previous RC events took place in York, UK (2009), Bremen, Germany (2010), Ghent, Belgium (2011), Copenhagen, Denmark (2012), Victoria, Canada (2013), Kyoto, Japan (2014), Grenoble, France (2015), and Bologna, Italy (2016).

The RC 2017 conference included two invited talks, by Kalyan S. Perumalla (abstract included in the front matter of this volume) and Martin Roetteler (invited paper included in this volume). The conference received 47 valid submissions, all of which were reviewed by at least three members of the Program Committee. After careful deliberation, the Program Committee selected 13 full papers and five short papers for inclusion in these proceedings and for presentation at the conference.

We would like to thank everyone who contributed to the success of RC 2017: the authors for submitting the results of their research to RC 2017; our two invited speakers for their inspiring talks and their time; the Program Committee and their co-reviewers for their expert work under tight time constraints, and for their commitment to the quality of the conference; the general chairs, Indranil Sengupta and Rolf Drechsler, for keeping the conference on track and for their help and advice; the organizing chair, Amlan Chakrabarti; the student volunteers for their untiring effort to ensure the smooth running of the conference; and the attendees of the events for their interest in the presentations and the constructive discussions.

We would like to thank our sponsors for supporting this conference: VLSI Society of India, Nucleodyne Systems, USA, and JIS Group Educational Initiatives.

We benefited from using the EasyChair system for the work of the Program Committee and the compilation of the proceedings.

April 2017

Iain Phillips
Hafizur Rahaman

Organization

Program Committee

Bhargab B. Bhattacharya	Indian Statistical Institute, Kolkata, India
Anupam Chattopadhyay	Nanyang Technological University, Singapore
Bob Coecke	University of Oxford, UK
Debesh Das	Jadavpur University, India
Kamalika Datta	National Institute of Technology Meghalaya, India
Gerhard Dueck	University of New Brunswick, Canada
Robert Glück	University of Copenhagen, Denmark
Jarkko Kari	University of Turku, Finland
Martin Kutrib	Universität Giessen, Germany
Ivan Lanese	University of Bologna, Italy and Inria, France
Kazutaka Matsuda	Tohoku University, Japan
Michael Miller	University of Victoria, Canada
Iain Phillips	Imperial College London, UK
Francesco Quaglia	Sapienza Università di Roma, Italy
Hafizur Rahaman	Indian Institute of Engineering Science and Technology (IIEST), Shibpur, India
Ulrik Schultz	University of Southern Denmark, Denmark
Peter Selinger	Dalhousie University, Canada
Indranil Sengupta	Indian Institute of Technology Kharagpur, India
Mathias Soeken	EPFL, Switzerland
Jean-Bernard Stefani	Inria, France
Susmita Sur-Kolay	Indian Statistical Institute, Kolkata, India
Yasuhiro Takahashi	NTT Communication Science Laboratories, Japan
Michael Thomsen	University of Copenhagen, Denmark
Irek Ulidowski	University of Leicester, UK
Robert Wille	Johannes Kepler University Linz, Austria
Shigeru Yamashita	Ritsumeikan University, Japan

Additional Reviewers

Axelsen, Holger Bock	Klimov, Andrei
De Vos, Alexis	Kole, Dipak
Di Sanzo, Pierangelo	Mogensen, Torben Ægidius
Hirvensalo, Mika	Mosca, Michele
Kaarsgaard, Robin	Paler, Alexandru
Kakutani, Yoshihiko	Pellegrini, Alessandro

Pinna, G. Michele
Podlaski, Krzysztof
Qiu, Daowen
Renz, Wolfgang
Salo, Ville

Schordan, Markus
Unno, Hiroshi
Yakaryilmaz, Abuzer
Yokoyama, Tetsuo

Relating the Limits of Computational Reversibility to Emergence (Abstract of Invited Talk)

Kalyan S. Perumalla

Oak Ridge National Laboratory, Oak Ridge, TN, USA
perumallaks@ornl.gov

An interesting aspect of reversible computation is that analyses of the theoretical limits of reversibility can touch metaphysical aspects. An objective treatment in reversible computation has given us the understanding that any expressed finite computation (for example, a Turing program) is effectively reversible by design or by transformation. However, a subjective treatment of reversibility regarding the purpose or meaning of a computation can lead to metaphysical considerations. A stark way this notion arises is in the concept of "emergence." Informally, emergence involves the phenomenon of something (new) arising or coming into view (for example, a leader emerging in a democracy of equals, or new particles spontaneously emerging from sub-atomic particle collisions). We argue that the concept of emergence and the concept of reversibility are disjunctive in any objective treatment. If something emerges (subjective view), it can never be reversed (objective view). If something can be reversed, it cannot have emerged. If the arguments hold, they lead to a strange equivalence class of terms that equates the following words to mean essentially the same thing (or lose meaning together): new, random, (dis)orderly, (in)elegant, (un)interesting, first, spontaneous, abrupt, (un)expected, and so on. When the computation of physics and the physics of computation meet in their limits, the confluence of subjective and objective views with respect to their reversibility opens the counter-intuitive implications of the aforementioned equivalence class. We relax the concept of emergence into three types, the first encompassing the fully reversible objective view, the second capturing the fundamentally irreversible subjective view, and the third bridging the two ends by partial reversibility and proxy randomization.

Contents

Invited Paper

Tools for Quantum and Reversible
Circuit Compilation

Martin Roetteler[✉]

Microsoft Research, One Microsoft Way, Redmond, WA 98052, USA
martinro@microsoft.com

Abstract. We present tools for resource-aware compilation of higher-level, irreversible programs into lower-level, reversible circuits. Our main focus is on optimizing the memory footprint of the resulting reversible networks. We discuss a number of examples to illustrate our compilation strategy for problems at scale, including a reversible implementation of hash functions such as SHA-256, automatic generation of reversible integer arithmetic from irreversible descriptions, as well as a test-bench of Boolean circuits that is used by the classical Circuits and Systems community. Our main findings are that, when compared with Bennett's original "compute-copy-uncompute", it is possible to reduce the space complexity by 75% or more, at the price of having an only moderate increase in circuit size as well as in compilation time. Finally, we discuss some emerging new paradigms in quantum circuit synthesis, namely the use of dirty ancillas to save overall memory footprint, probabilistic protocols such as the RUS framework which can help to reduce the gate complexity of rotations, and synthesis methods for higher-dimensional quantum systems.

Keywords: Quantum circuits · Reversible circuits · Quantum programming languages · Pebble games · Dirty ancillas · Repeat-Until-Success protocols · Ternary systems

1 Introduction

The compilation of quantum algorithms into sequences of instructions that a quantum computer can execute requires a multi-stage framework. This framework needs to be capable of taking higher level descriptions of quantum programs and successively breaking them down into lower level net-lists of circuits until ultimately pulse sequences are obtained that a physical machine can apply. Independent of the concrete realization of the compilation method, one of the key steps is to implement subroutines[1] over the given target instruction set. As often the underlying problem is a classical problem in that the problem specification involves classical data (such as finding the period of a function or searching an assignment that satisfies a given Boolean predicate), the question arises how

---

[1] In quantum computing literature, such subroutines are often implementing "oracles".

© Springer International Publishing AG 2017
I. Phillips and H. Rahaman (Eds.): RC 2017, LNCS 10301, pp. 3–16, 2017.
DOI: 10.1007/978-3-319-59936-6_1

such functions can best be implemented on a quantum computer. Examples are Shor's algorithm for factoring and the computation of discrete logarithms over a finite field [38], Grover's quantum search algorithm [23], quantum walk algorithms [27], the HHL algorithm for solving linear equations [16,25], and quantum simulation methods [8,9]. The field of reversible computing deals with the latter problem and investigates such issues as how to minimize the gate count over a given universal gate set and how to minimize various other resources, such as the circuit depth, the total number of qubits required, and other metrics.

There are many ramifications to this compilation problem. Some stem from the choice of programming language to express the tools that perform the translation. Choices that have been reported in the literature range from C-like languages such as QCL [32] and Scaffold [26] to functional languages such as Quipper [21,22] and LIQ$Ui|\rangle$ [40]. Further choices involve the methods to compile classical, irreversible programs into quantum circuits and several approaches have been taken in the literature. One approach is to hide all classical subroutines in libraries and to provide an optimized collection of functions to implement these. This is the approach taken in several languages and as long as quantum programming remains a very much circuit-centric endeavor, this approach might well be appropriate. On the other hand, tools that allow the translation of classical, irreversible code into, say, networks of Toffoli gates have been developed: in the Haskell-based Quipper language, there is a monadic bind to lift classical computation to reversible circuits. In the LIQ$Ui|\rangle$ there is REVS [34], a tool to perform the task of obtaining reversible networks automatically from a little language that can be used to express classical programs.

The main idea behind REVS is to improve on Bennett's [6] method to make computations reversible: arbitrary computations can be carried out by a computational device in such a way that in principle each time-step can be reversed by first performing a forward computation, using only step-wise reversible processes, then copying out the result, and finally undoing all steps in the forward computation in reverse order. This solves the reversible embedding problem, albeit at the cost of very large memory-requirements as the result from each intermediate process have to be stored. Bennett already pointed out a solution [7] that is applicable in principle to reduce the memory-overhead by studying time-space trade-offs for reversible computation. He introduced the notion of reversible pebble games which allow to systematically study ways to save on scratch space at the expense of recomputing intermediate results. To determine the best pebbling strategy for the dependency graph imposed by actual real-world programs and to automate the process of pebbling in general, however, are non-trivial matters. In the REVS framework, we follow a pragmatic approach: (i) Boolean functions are synthesized directly using various heuristics and optimizations, such as exclusive-sum-of-products (ESOP) based optimization [15,30], (ii) the compiler provides different strategies for making irreversible computations reversible: one is Bennett's method, another is heuristic that computes data dependencies in the source program and tries to uncompute data that is no longer needed as soon as possible.

As a real-world example we consider cryptographic hash-functions such as SHA-256, which is part of the SHA-2 family [1]. This cipher can be thought of as a Boolean function $f : \{0,1\}^N \to \{0,1\}^n$, where $n \ll N$. It has a simple and straightforward classical program for its evaluation that has no branchings and only uses simple Boolean functions such as XOR, AND, and bit rotations. However, it has internal *state* between rounds. The fact that there is state prevents the Boolean function from being decomposed, thereby making purely truth-table or BDD-based synthesis methods useless for this problem.

The basic underlying fault-tolerant architecture and coding scheme determines the universal gate set, and hence by extension also the synthesis problems that have to be solved in order to compile high-level, large-scale algorithms into a sequence of operations that an actual physical quantum computer can then execute. A gate set that arises frequently and that has been oft studied in the literature, but by no means the only conceivable gate set, is the so-called Clifford+T gate set [31]. This gate set consists of the Hadamard gate $H = \frac{1}{\sqrt{2}} \begin{bmatrix} 1 & 1 \\ 1 & -1 \end{bmatrix}$, the phase gate $P = \mathrm{diag}(1, i)$, and the CNOT gate which maps $(x, y) \mapsto (x, x \oplus y)$ as generators of the Clifford group, along with the T gate given by $T = \mathrm{diag}(1, \exp(\pi i/4))$. The Clifford+$T$ gate set is known to be universal [31], i.e., any given target unitary single qubit operation can be approximated to within ε using sequences of length $4 \log_2(1/\varepsilon)$ [28,37] and using an entangling gate such as the controlled NOT gate. Often, only T-gates are counted as many fault-tolerant implementation of the Clifford+T gate set at the logical gate level require much more resources [19] for T-gates than for Clifford gates. We based reversible computations entirely on the Toffoli gate $|x, y, z\rangle \mapsto |x, y, z \oplus xy\rangle$ which is known to be universal for reversible computing [31] and which can be implemented exactly over the Clifford+T gate set, see [36] for T-depth 1 implementation using a total of 7 qubits and [3] for a T-depth 3 realization using a total of 3 qubits.

2   Data Dependency Analysis in Revs

Data dependencies that might be present in a given F# program are modeled in REVS using a data structure called a mutable data dependency graph (MDD). This data structure tracks the data flow during a classical, irreversible computation. MDDs allow to identify parts of the data flow where information can be overwritten as well as other parts where information can be uncomputed early as it is no longer needed. These two techniques of *overwrite*, which are implemented using so-called in-place operations, and *early cleanup*, for which we use a strategy that can be interpreted as a particular pebble game played on the nodes of the data flow graph, constitute the main innovation of the present work. The cleanup methods described here can be thought of as an analog to garbage collection for quantum architectures. REVS outputs a Toffoli network which then can directly imported as an internal representation into LIQ$Ui|\rangle$ and be used as part of another quantum computation.

```
let rippleAdd (a:bool[])(b:bool[])=       CNOT [qs.[0]; qs.[10]]
   let n = Array.length a                 CNOT [qs.[5]; qs.[10]]
   let res = Array.zeroCreate (n)         CCNOT [qs.[0]; qs.[5]; qs.[15]]
   res.[0] <- a.[0] <> b.[0]              CNOT [qs.[15]; qs.[11]]
   let mutable carry = a.[0] && b.[0]     CNOT [qs.[1]; qs.[11]]
   res.[1] <- a.[1] <> b.[1] <> carry     CNOT [qs.[6]; qs.[11]]
   for i in 2 .. n - 1 do                 CNOT [qs.[15]; qs.[17]]
      // compute outgoing carry            CNOT [qs.[6]; qs.[17]]
      carry <- (a.[i-1]                    CCNOT [qs.[1]; qs.[17]; qs.[16]]
               && (carry <> b.[i-1]))      CCNOT [qs.[15]; qs.[6]; qs.[16]]
               <> (carry && b.[i-1])       CNOT [qs[6]; qs.[17]]
      res.[i]  <-  a.[i] <> b.[i]          CNOT [qs.[15]; qs.[17]]
                   <> carry                CNOT [qs.[16]; qs.[12]]
   res                                     ...
```

(a) REVS source program   (b) Segment of the compiled LIQ$Ui|\rangle$ program

Fig. 1. F# program that implements a carry ripple adder using a for-loop and maintaining a running carry.

REVS is an embedded language into the .NET language F# and as such inherits some functions and libraries from its host language. Also, the look-and-feel of a typical REVS program is very similar to that of F# programs. In fact, it is one of our design goals to provide a language that provides different *interpretations* of the same source program, i.e., the same source code can be compiled into (a) an executable for a given classical architecture such as the .NET CLR, (b) a Toffoli network, (c) rendered form of output, e.g., pdf or svg, or (d) an internal representation which can then be simulated efficiently on a classical computer.

The current implementation of the REVS compiler supports Booleans as basic types only. The core of the language is a simple imperative language over Boolean and array (register) types. The language is further extended with ML-style functional features, namely first-class functions and *let* definitions, and a reversible domain-specific construct *clean*. It should be noted also that REVS was designed to facilitate interoperability with the quantum programming language LIQ$Ui|\rangle$ which is also F# based and which provides rich support for expressing and simulating quantum circuits on classical machines, but which also provides support for compiling quantum algorithms for target hardware architectures and abstract quantum computer machine models.

An example REVS program is shown in Fig. 1(a). This example implements a simple carry ripple adder of two n-bit integers. Shown in (b) is one of the possible target intermediate representations, namely LIQ$Ui|\rangle$ code.

At a high level, all compilation strategies that are implemented in REVS proceed start from a classical description of the given function which is then turned into an abstract syntax tree (AST) by a parser. This level might use libraries and further optimizations by the F# compiler. The subsequent levels are domain-specific to the reversible synthesis domain and use the MDD data-structure presented in [34]. See Fig. 2 for an example. The overall compilation can use pre-computed libraries, e.g., for reversible arithmetic and other optimized functions.

It should be noted that possibly the overall compilation can fail, namely in case
the given target strategy cannot be implemented using the given upper bound
on the number of available qubits.

3   An Example at Scale: SHA-256

We implemented the round function of SHA-256 which is a hash function as
specified in the FIPS 180-2 publication [1]. Like many other hash functions,
SHA proceeds in a round-like fashion and uses the current state of a finite state
machine, the next incoming data block, and various constants in order to define
the next state of the finite state machine. In the round function of the cipher
32 bit registers A, B, ..., E are needed. The following Boolean functions are
introduced to describe the round functions:

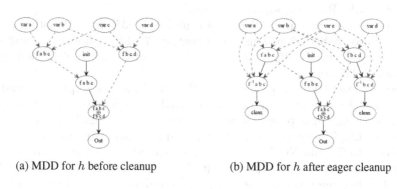

(a) MDD for h before cleanup   (b) MDD for h after eager cleanup

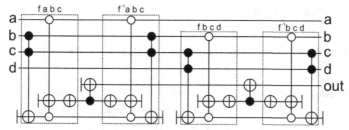

(c) Final resulting Toffoli network implementing the function h.

Fig. 2. Shown in (a) is the mutable data dependency graph (MDD) for the function
$h(a, b, c, d) = f(a, b, c) \oplus f(b, c, d)$ where $f(a, b, c) = a \| (b \& c)$. Shown in (b) is the MDD
that results in applying Eager cleanup (as described in [34]) to the MDD in (a). Shown
in (c) is the final circuit that REVS emits based on the MDD in (b). Qubits that are
initially clean are shown as ⊢, qubits that terminate in a clean state are shown as ⊣.
Overall, the circuit uses a total of 7 qubits to compute the function h. This should
be compared with applying the Bennett cleanup which would result in a much larger
number of qubits, namely 11.

$$Ch(E, F, G) := (E \wedge F) \oplus (\neg E \wedge G)$$
$$Ma(A, B, C) := (A \wedge B) \oplus (A \wedge C) \oplus (B \wedge C)$$
$$\Sigma_0(A) := (A \ggg 2) \oplus (A \ggg 13) \oplus (A \ggg 22)$$
$$\Sigma_1(E) := (E \ggg 6) \oplus (E \ggg 11) \oplus (E \ggg 25).$$

For a given round, the values of all these functions is computed and considered to be 32 bit integers. Further, a constant 32 integer value K_i is obtained from a table lookup which depends on the number i of the given round, where $i \in \{0, \dots, 63\}$ and finally the next chunk of the message W_i is obtained from the message after performing a suitable message expansion is performed as specified in the standard. Finally, H is replaced according to $H \leftarrow H + Ch(E, F, G) + Ma(A, B, C) + \Sigma_0(A) + \Sigma_1(E) + K_i + W_i$ and then the cyclic permutation $A \leftarrow H, B \leftarrow A, \dots, H \leftarrow G$ is performed. The implementation of the entire round function for a given number of rounds n was presented in [34] using the REVS high-level language.

To test the performance of the REVS compiler, in [34] we hand-optimized an implementation of SHA-256. This circuit contains 7 adders (mod 2^{32}). Using the adder from [17] with a Toffoli cost of $2n - 3$ this corresponds to 61 Toffoli gates per adder or 427 per round.

Next, we used REVS to produce Toffoli networks for this cipher, depending on various increments of the number n of rounds. The circuits typically are too large to be visualized in printed form, however, an automatically generated .svg file that the LIQ$Ui|\rangle$ compiler can be navigated by zooming in down to the level of Toffoli, CNOT, and NOT gates. The resource estimates are summarized in Table 1. Shown are the resulting circuit sizes, measured by the total number of Toffoli gates, the resulting total number of qubits, and the time it took to compile the circuit for various numbers of rounds. All timing data in the table

Table 1. Comparison of different compilation strategies for the cryptographic hash function SHA-256.

Rnd	Bennett			Eager			Reference	
	Bits	Gates	Time	Bits	Gates	Time	Bits	Gates
1	704	1124	0.254	353	690	0.329	353	683
2	832	2248	0.263	353	1380	0.336	353	1366
3	960	3372	0.282	353	2070	0.342	353	2049
4	1088	4496	0.282	353	2760	0.354	353	2732
5	1216	5620	0.290	353	3450	0.366	353	3415
6	1344	6744	0.304	353	4140	0.378	353	4098
7	1472	7868	0.312	353	4830	0.391	353	4781
8	1600	8992	0.328	353	5520	0.402	353	5464
9	1728	10116	0.334	353	6210	0.413	353	6147
10	1856	11240	0.344	353	6900	0.430	353	6830

are measured in seconds and resulted from running the F# compiler in Visual Studio 2013 on an Intel i7-3667 @ 2GHz 8 GB RAM under Windows 8.1. The table shows savings of almost $4X$ in terms of the total numbers of qubits required to synthesize the cipher when comparing the simple Bennett cleanup strategy versus the Eager cleanup strategy. The reason for this is that the Bennett cleanup methods allocates new space essentially for each gate whereas the Eager cleanup strategy tries to clean up and reallocate space as soon as possible which for the round-based nature of the function can be done as soon as the round is completed.

Besides SHA-256, and other hash functions such as MD5, this technique has also been applied to SHA-3 [4]. Our findings supports the thesis that it is possible to trade circuit size (time) for total memory (space) in reversible circuit synthesis. To the best of our knowledge, REVS is the first compiler that allows to navigate this trade space and that offers strategies for garbage collection for quantum architectures that go beyond the simple Bennett strategy which generally leads to very poor memory utilization as most of the qubits are idle most of the time.

4   Quantum Computing Software Architecture

REVS is part of a larger framework provided by the LIQ$Ui|\rangle$ software architecture. LIQ$Ui|\rangle$ is a quantum programming language and a high-performance simulator for quantum circuits. LIQ$Ui|\rangle$ is an embedded language into F# which itself is a full .NET language, i.e., F# supports object-oriented, imperative and functional programming, as well as ease of using reflection and pattern matching which helps with walking complex datastructures. LIQ$Ui|\rangle$ can be obtained from https://github.com/StationQ/Liquid. Runtimes supported in LIQ$Ui|\rangle$ are client/server versions, as well as an Azure based cloud service. There are several ways in which LIQ$Ui|\rangle$ code can be executed, e.g., from the command line running the .NET Common Language Runtime, or directly in a Visual Studio interactive session (particularly useful for script files), or in a normal Visual Studio development mode.

The REVS compiler can compile classical, irreversible code into functions that can then be further processed, e.g., by using simulators in LIQ$Ui|\rangle$. An example are Toffoli networks for specific functions such as the SHA-256 example from the previous section. These circuits can then be executed by various simulation backends that are available in LIQ$Ui|\rangle$, e.g., a full functional simulator which can simulate arbitrary circuits on up to 32 qubits using about 32 GB of memory, or a special purpose Toffoli simulator which can be used, e.g., to simulate large Toffoli networks to implement controlled modular multiplication. For the latter see e.g. [24] where simulation of modular multiplication networks have been reported for bit sizes up to 8, 192.

5 Other Paradigms for Quantum and Reversible Synthesis

5.1 Using Dirty Ancillas

By *dirty* ancillas we mean qubits which can be in an unknown state, possibly entangled with other qubits in an unknown way, but which are available as scratch space for other computations. There are not many use cases of this situation and a priori it seems even difficult to imagine any situation where such a "full quantum memory" could be of use at all as any manipulation that uses dirty ancillas without restoring them to their state before they were used, will destroy interferences between computational paths.

So far, we are aware of two specific situations where dirty ancillas help: (i) the implementation of a multiply controlled NOT operation, see [5] and recent improvements [2,29]. The second use case is an implementation of a constant incrementer $|x\rangle \mapsto |x + c\rangle$, where c is an integer that is known at compile time and x an input that can be in superposition. In [24] it was shown that dirty ancillas help to realize this operation using $O(n \log n)$ Toffoli gates and a total of n qubits which are needed to represent x, along with $O(n)$ dirty ancillas. This in turn can be used to implement the entire Shor algorithm using almost entirely Toffoli gates.[2]

Table 2. Costs associated with various implementations of addition $|a\rangle \mapsto |a + c\rangle$ of a value a by a classical constant c.

	Cuccaro et al. [17]	Takahashi et al. [39]	Draper [18]	Häner et al. [24]
Size	$\Theta(n)$	$\Theta(n)$	$\Theta(n^2)$	$\Theta(n \log n)$
Depth	$\Theta(n)$	$\Theta(n)$	$\Theta(n)$	$\Theta(n)$
Ancillas	$n+1$ (clean)	n (clean)	0	$\frac{n}{2}$ (dirty)

Mathematically, the underlying idea how to make use of dirty ancillas can be illustrated in case of an addition "+1" which is an observation due to Gidney [20]: Using the ancilla-free adder by Takahashi [39], which requires no incoming carry, and its reverse to perform subtraction, one can perform the following sequence of operations to achieve an incrementer using n borrowed ancilla qubits in an unknown initial state $|g\rangle$:

$$|x\rangle|g\rangle \mapsto |x - g\rangle|g\rangle \mapsto |x - g\rangle|g' - 1\rangle$$
$$\mapsto |x - g - g' + 1\rangle|g' - 1\rangle \mapsto |x + 1\rangle|g\rangle,$$

---

[2] Indeed, the only non-Toffoli gates in the quantum circuit presented in [24] are single qubit Hadmard gates, single qubit phase rotations, and single qubit measurements. The vast majority of other gates in the circuit form one big circuit component which can be classically simulated and tested.

where g' denotes the two's-complement of g and $g' - 1 = \bar{g}$, the bit-wise complement of g. Notice that $g + g' = 0$ holds for all g and that the register holding the dirty qubits $|g\rangle$ is returned to its initial state.

Table 2 provides a comparison between different ways to implement addition on a quantum computer with the last column being the implementation based on dirty ancillas.

In total, using the standard phase estimation approach to factoring this leads to an $\mathcal{O}(n^3 \log n)$-sized implementation of Shor's algorithm from a Toffoli based in-place constant-adder, which adds a classically known n-bit constant c to the n-qubit quantum register $|a\rangle$, i.e., which implements $|a\rangle|0\rangle \mapsto |a + c\rangle$ where a is an arbitrary n-bit input and $a + c$ is an n-bit output (the final carry is ignored).

5.2   Repeat-Until-Success Circuits

Recently, Paetznick and Svore [33] showed that by using non-deterministic circuits for decomposition, called Repeat-Until-Success (RUS) circuits, the number of T gates can be further reduced by a factor of 2.5 on average for axial rotations, and by a larger factor for non-axial rotations. They emphasized that synthesis into RUS circuits can lead to a shorter *expected* circuit length that surpasses the theoretical lower bound for the length of a purely unitary circuit design. Leveraging the RUS framework, in [12, 13] efficient algorithms were presented to synthesize a non-deterministic Repeat-Until-Success (RUS) circuits for approximating any given single-qubit unitary. Our algorithm runs in probabilistically polynomial classical runtime for any desired precision ε. Our methods demonstrate the power of using ancilla qubits and measurement for quantum circuit compilation.

The general layout of a RUS protocol is shown in Fig. 3. Consider a unitary operation U acting on $n + m$ qubits, of which n are target qubits and m are ancillary qubits. Consider a measurement of the ancilla qubits, such that one measurement outcome is labeled "success" and all other measurement outcomes are labeled "failure". Let the unitary applied to the target qubits upon measurement be V. In the RUS protocol, the circuit in the dashed box is repeated on the $(n + m)$-qubit state until the "success" measurement is observed. Each time a "failure" measurement is observed, an appropriate Clifford operator $W_i^\dagger$ is applied in order to revert the state of the target qubits to their original input state $|\psi\rangle$. The number of repetitions of the circuit is finite with probability 1.

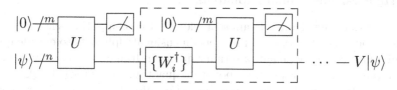

Fig. 3. Repeat-Until-Success (RUS) protocol to implement a unitary V.

In [12,13] efficient algorithms were given to synthesize RUS protocols and so-called fallback protocols which also allow to implement unitary gates using probabilistic circuits. The inputs to the synthesis algorithms are the given unitary U, typically assumed to be a Z-rotation, and a target accuracy ε. Under mild number-theoretic conjectures, the complexity of the compilation method is in $\widetilde{O}(\log(1/\varepsilon))$ and the length of the output, i.e., a sequence of H and T gates that ε-approximates U, scales as $(1+\delta)\log_2(1/\varepsilon)$, where δ can be made arbitrary close to 0. These results demonstrate the power of using ancilla qubits and measurement for quantum circuit compilation as the currently best known deterministic schemes lead to lengths of the resulting circuits that scale as $c\log_2(1/\varepsilon)$, where $3 \leq c \leq 4$, with the actual choice of c depending on various computational and number-theoretic assumptions. See [12,13,28,35,37] for further reading about single qubit unitary decomposition methods. Figure 4 conveys the basic intuition behind RUS based methods: by allowing measurement and, if needed, repetition, it is possible to achieve a much higher density of rotations that can effectively be addressed.

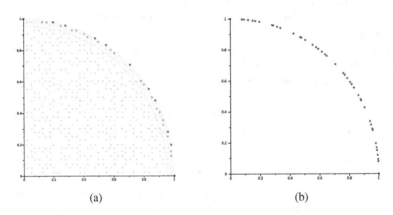

(a)   (b)

Fig. 4. Comparing approximations of z-rotations by (a) unitary $\langle H, T \rangle$ circuits of T-depth at most 8 and (b) RUS protocols with a comparable expected T-depth of at most 7.5. In (a) only 40 circuits are close to any z-rotation (dark red points separated by the outer arc), illustrating a higher density of RUS protocols. In the asymptotic limit for T-depth this ratio tends to 3. (Color figure online)

5.3   Higher-Dimensional Alphabets

It turns out that some fault-tolerant scalable quantum computing schemes underline the importance to work with higher-dimensional alphabets to encode quantum information. In particular, a ternary quantum framework recently emerged from proposals for a metaplectic topological quantum computer (MTQC) which offers native topological protection of quantum information. MTQC creates an inherently ternary quantum computing environment; for example the common binary CNOT gate is no longer a Clifford gate in that environment.

In [11], compilation and synthesis methods for ternary circuits were developed for 2 different elementary gate sets: the so-called Clifford+$R_{|2\rangle}$ basis [10] and the Clifford+P_9 basis [11], where $R_{|2\rangle}$ and P_9 are both non-Clifford single qutrit gate defined as $R_{|2\rangle} = \mathrm{diag}(1, 1, -1)$ and $P_9 = \mathrm{diag}(e^{-2\pi i/9}, 1, e^{2\pi i/9})$.

The Clifford+$R_{|2\rangle}$ basis, also called metaplectic basis, was obtained from a MTQC by braiding of certain metaplectic non-abelian anyons and projective measurement. The gate $R_{|2\rangle}$ is produced by injection of the magic state $|\psi\rangle = |0\rangle - |1\rangle + |2\rangle$. The injection circuit is coherent probabilistic, succeeds in three iterations on average and consumes three copies of the magic state $|\psi\rangle$ on average. The $|\psi\rangle$ state is produced by a relatively inexpensive protocol that uses topological measurement and consequent intra-qutrit projection. This protocol requires only three qutrits and produces an exact copy of $|\psi\rangle$ in 9/4 trials on average. This is much better than any state distillation method, especially because it produces $|\psi\rangle$ with fidelity 1. In [10] effective compilation methods for Clifford+$R_{|2\rangle}$ were developed to compile efficient circuits in the metaplectic basis. In particular, given an arbitrary two-level Householder reflection r and a precision ε, then r is effectively approximated by a metaplectic circuit of $R_{|2\rangle}$-count at most $C \log_3(1/\varepsilon) + O(\log(\log(1/\varepsilon)))$, $C \leq 8$.

The Clifford+P_9 basis is a natural generalization of the binary $\pi/8$ gate. The P_9 gate can be realized by a certain deterministic measurement-assisted circuit given a copy of the *magic state* $\mu = e^{-2\pi i/9}|0\rangle + |1\rangle + e^{2\pi i/9}|2\rangle$, which further can be obtained from the usual magic state distillation protocol. Specifically, it requires $O(\log^3(1/\delta))$ raw magic states of low fixed fidelity in order to distill a copy of the magic state μ at fidelity $1 - \delta$. The paper [11] developed a novel approach to synthesis of reversible ternary classical circuits over the Clifford+P_9 basis. We have synthesized explicit circuits to express classical reflections and other important classical non-Clifford gates in this basis, which we subsequently used to build efficient ternary implementations of integer adders and their extensions.

In [14] further optimizations were given under the assumption of binary-encoded data and applied the resulting solutions to emulating of the modular exponentiation period finding (which is the quantum part of the Shor's integer factorization algorithm). We have performed the comparative cost analysis of optimized solutions between the "generic" Clifford+P_9 architecture and the MTQC architecture (the Clifford+$R_{|2\rangle}$) using magic state counts as the cost measure. We have shown that the cost of emulating the entire binary circuit for the period finding is almost directly proportional to the cost of emulating the three-qubit Toffoli gate and the latter is proportional to the cost of the P_9 gate.

6   Conclusions

We presented REVS, a compiler and programming language that allows to automate the translation of classical, irreversible programs into reversible programs. This language does not constrain the programmer to think in a circuit-centric way. In some cases (e.g., hash functions such as SHA-256) the savings of our method over Bennett-style approaches can even be unbounded. We navigate the PSPACE completeness of finding the optimal pebble game by invoking heuristic strategies that identify parts of the program that are mutable which then can be implemented via in-place operations. In order to manage the arising data dependencies, we introduced MDD graphs which capture data dependencies as well as data mutation. Using an example benchmark suite compiled from classical circuits and systems community, we show that the method can be applied for medium to large scale problems. We also showed that hash functions such as SHA-256 can be compiled into space-optimized reversible circuits.

Also, we highlighted that there are paradigms that break out of the usual framework considered in quantum circuit synthesis: we highlighted that there are concrete case in which the presence of qubits helps, even if they have already been used and are entangled with the rest of the quantum computer's memory. Using such dirty ancillas, it is possible to reduce circuit sizes e.g. for constant incrementers. Next, discussed the power of using probabilistic protocols to implement unitaries, which helps to bring down circuit sizes by a constant factor. In a concrete case, probabilistic protocols such as RUS or fallback schemes help to reduce the cost for single qubit axial rotations from $4\log_2(1/\varepsilon)$ to $\log_2(1/\varepsilon)$. Finally, we mentioned that in some physical systems, ternary alphabets arise very naturally from the way universal operations are performed. We mentioned two such gate sets and gave pointers to method for synthesizing into these gate sets.

References

1. Federal information processing standards publication 180–2, 2002. See also the Wikipedia entry. http://en.wikipedia.org/wiki/SHA-2
2. Abdessaied, N., Amy, M., Drechsler, R., Soeken, M.: Complexity of reversible circuits and their quantum implementations. Theor. Comput. Sci. **618**, 85–106 (2016)
3. Amy, M., Maslov, D., Mosca, M., Roetteler, M.: A meet-in-the-middle algorithm for fast synthesis of depth-optimal quantum circuits. IEEE Trans. Comput. Aided Des. Integr. Circ. Syst. **32**(6), 818–830 (2013)
4. Amy, M., Di Matteo, O., Gheorghiu, V., Mosca, M., Parent, A., Schanck, J.M.: Estimating the cost of generic quantum pre-image attacks on SHA-2 and SHA-3. IACR Cryptol. ePrint Arch. **2016**, 992 (2016)
5. Barenco, A., Bennett, C.H., Cleve, R., DiVincenzo, D.P., Margolus, N., Shor, P., Sleator, T., Smolin, J.A., Weinfurter, H.: Elementary gates for quantum computation. Phys. Rev. A **52**(5), 3457 (1995)
6. Bennett, C.H.: Logical reversibility of computation. IBM J. Res. Dev. **17**, 525–532 (1973)
7. Bennett, C.H.: Time/space trade-offs for reversible computation. SIAM J. Comput. **18**, 766–776 (1989)
8. Berry, D.W., Childs, A.M., Cleve, R., Kothari, R., Somma, R.D.: Exponential improvement in precision for simulating sparse hamiltonians. In: Symposium on Theory of Computing (STOC 2014), pp. 283–292 (2014)
9. Berry, D.W., Childs, A.M., Kothari, R.: Hamiltonian simulation with nearly optimal dependence on all parameters. In: IEEE 56th Annual Symposium on Foundations of Computer Science (FOCS), pp. 792–809 (2015)

10. Bocharov, A., Cui, S.X., Kliuchnikov, V., Wang, Z.: Efficient topological compilation for weakly-integral anyon model. Phys. Rev. A **93**, 012313 (2016)
11. Bocharov, A., Cui, S.X., Roetteler, M., Svore, K.M.: Improved quantum ternary arithmetics. Quantum Inf. Comput. **16**(9&10), 862–884. arXiv preprint (2016). arXiv:1512.03824
12. Bocharov, A., Roetteler, M., Svore, K.M.: Efficient synthesis of probabilistic quantum circuits with fallback. Phys. Rev. A **91**, 052317 (2015)
13. Bocharov, A., Roetteler, M., Svore, K.M.: Efficient synthesis of universal repeat-until-success circuits. Phys. Rev. Lett. **114**, 080502. arXiv preprint (2015). arXiv:1404.5320
14. Bocharov, A., Roetteler, M., Svore, K.M.: Factoring with qutrits: Shor's algorithm on ternary and metaplectic quantum architectures. arXiv preprint (2016). arXiv:1605.02756
15. Chrzanowska-Jeske, M., Mishchenko, A., Perkowski, M.A.: Generalized inclusive forms - new canonical reed-muller forms including minimum esops. VLSI Des. **2002**(1), 13–21 (2002)
16. Clader, B.D., Jacobs, B.C., Sprouse, C.R.: Preconditioned quantum linear system algorithm. Phys. Rev. Lett. **110**, 250504 (2013)
17. Cuccaro, S.A., Draper, T.G., Kutin, S.A., Moulton, D.P.: A new quantum ripple-carry addition circuit. arXiv preprint (2004). arXiv:quant-ph/0410184
18. Draper, T.G.: Addition on a quantum computer. arXiv preprint (2000). arXiv:quant-ph/0008033
19. Fowler, A.G., Mariantoni, M., Martinis, J.M., Cleland, A.N.: Surface codes: towards practical large-scale quantum computation. Phys. Rev. A **86**, 032324 (2012). arXiv:1208.0928
20. Gidney, C.: StackExchange: creating bigger controlled nots from single qubit, toffoli, and CNOT gates, without workspace (2015)
21. Green, A.S., Lumsdaine, P.L.F., Ross, N.J., Selinger, P., Valiron, B.: An introduction to quantum programming in quipper. In: Dueck, G.W., Miller, D.M. (eds.) RC 2013. LNCS, vol. 7948, pp. 110–124. Springer, Heidelberg (2013). doi:10.1007/978-3-642-38986-3_10
22. Green, A.S., Lumsdaine, P.L., Ross, N.J., Selinger, P., Valiron, B.: Quipper: a scalable quantum programming language. In: Proceedings of Conference on Programming Language Design and Implementation (PLDI 2013). ACM (2013)
23. Grover, L.: A fast quantum mechanical algorithm for database search. In: Proceedings of the Symposium on Theory of Computing (STOC 1996), pp. 212–219. ACM Press (1996)
24. Häner, T., Roetteler, M., Svore, K.M. Factoring using $2n+2$ qubits with Toffoli based modular multiplication. arXiv preprint (2016). arXiv:1611.07995
25. Aram, W., Harrow, A.H., Lloyd, S.: Quantum algorithm for linear systems of equations. Phys. Rev. Lett. **103**(15), 150502 (2009)
26. Heckey, J., Patil, S., JavadiAbhari, A., Holmes, A., Kudrow, D., Brown, K.R., Franklin, D., Chong, F.T., Martonosi, M.: Compiler management of communication and parallelism for quantum computation. In: Proceedings of the Twentieth International Conference on Architectural Support for Programming Languages and Operating Systems (ASPLOS 2015), pp. 445–456. ACM (2015)
27. Kempe, J.: Quantum random walks - an introductory overview. Contemporary Phys. **44**(4), 307–327 (2003)
28. Kliuchnikov, V., Maslov, D., Mosca, M.: Practical approximation of single-qubit unitaries by single-qubit quantum Clifford and T circuits. IEEE Trans. Comput. **65**(1), 161–172 (2016)

29. Maslov, D.: On the advantages of using relative phase Toffolis with an application to multiple control Toffoli optimization. Phys. Rev. A **93**, 022311 (2016)
30. Mishchenko, A., Brayton, R.K., Chatterjee, S.: Boolean factoring and decomposition of logic networks. In: Proceedings of the IEEE/ACM International Conference on Computer-Aided Design, pp. 38–44. IEEE Press (2008)
31. Nielsen, M.A., Chuang, I.L.: Quantum Computation and Quantum Information. Cambridge University Press, Cambridge (2000)
32. Oemer, B.: Classical concepts in quantum programming. Int. J. Theor. Phys. **44**(7), 943–955 (2005)
33. Paetznick, A., Svore, K.M.: Repeat-until-success: non-deterministic decomposition of single-qubit unitaries. Quantum Inf. Comput. **4**(15&16), 1277–1301 (2014)
34. Parent, A., Roetteler, M., Svore, K.M.: Reversible circuit compilation with space constraints. arXiv preprint (2015). arXiv:1510.00377
35. Ross, N.J., Selinger, P.: Optimal ancilla-free Clifford+T approximation of z-rotations. arXiv preprint (2014). arXiv:403.2975
36. Selinger, P.: Quantum circuits of T-depth one. Phys. Rev. A **87**, 042302 (2013)
37. Selinger, P.: Efficient Clifford+T approximation of single-qubit operators. Quantum Inf. Comput. **15**(1–2), 159–180 (2015)
38. Shor, P.W.: Polynomial-time algorithms for prime factorization and discrete logarithms on a quantum computer. SIAM J. Comput. **26**(5), 1484–1509 (1997)
39. Takahashi, Y., Tani, S., Kunihiro, N.: Quantum addition circuits, unbounded fan-out. arXiv preprint (2009). arXiv:0910.2530
40. Wecker, D., Svore, K.M.: LIQ Ui|⟩: a software design architecture and domain-specific language for quantum computing. arXiv preprint arXiv:1402.4467

Foundations

Foundations of Generalized
Reversible Computing

Michael P. Frank[(⊠)]

Center for Computing Research, Sandia National Laboratories,
P.O. Box 5800, Mail Stop 1322, Albuquerque, NM 87185, USA
mpfrank@sandia.gov
http://www.cs.sandia.gov/cr-mpfrank

Abstract. Information loss from a computation implies energy dissipation due to Landauer's Principle. Thus, increasing the amount of useful computational work that can be accomplished within a given energy budget will eventually require increasing the degree to which our computing technologies avoid information loss, *i.e.*, are logically reversible. But the traditional definition of logical reversibility is actually more restrictive than is necessary to avoid information loss and energy dissipation due to Landauer's Principle. As a result, the operations that have traditionally been viewed as the atomic elements of reversible logic, such as Toffoli gates, are not really the simplest primitives that one can use for the design of reversible hardware. Arguably, a complete theoretical framework for reversible computing should provide a more general, parsimonious foundation for practical engineering. To this end, we use a rigorous quantitative formulation of Landauer's Principle to develop the theory of *Generalized Reversible Computing* (GRC), which precisely characterizes the minimum requirements for a computation to avoid information loss and the consequent energy dissipation, showing that a much broader range of computations are, in fact, reversible than is acknowledged by traditional reversible computing theory. This paper summarizes the foundations of GRC theory and briefly presents a few of its applications.

Keywords: Landauer's Principle · Foundations of reversible computing · Logical reversibility · Reversible logic models · Reversible hardware design · Conditional reversibility · Generalized reversible computing

1   Introduction

As we approach the end of the semiconductor roadmap [1], there is a growing realization that new computing paradigms will be required to continue improving

M.P. Frank—This work was supported by the Laboratory Directed Research and Development program at Sandia National Laboratories, and by the Advanced Simulation and Computing program under the U.S. Department of Energy's National Nuclear Security Administration (NNSA). Sandia National Laboratories is a multi-program laboratory managed and operated by Sandia Corporation, a wholly owned subsidiary of Lockheed Martin Corporation, for NNSA under contract DE-AC04-94AL85000. Approved for unclassified unlimited release SAND2017-3513 C.

© Springer International Publishing AG 2017
I. Phillips and H. Rahaman (Eds.): RC 2017, LNCS 10301, pp. 19–34, 2017.
DOI: 10.1007/978-3-319-59936-6_2

the energy efficiency (and thus, cost efficiency) of computing technology beyond the expected final CMOS node, when signal energies will reach a minimum practical level due to thermal noise and architectural overheads.[1] Sustained progress thus requires recovering and reusing signal energies with efficiency approaching 100%, which implies we must carry out logically reversible transformations of the local digital state, due to Landauer's Principle [2], which tells us that performing computational operations that are *irreversible* (*i.e.*, that lose information) necessarily generates entropy, and results in energy dissipation. Thus, it's essential for the designers of future computing technologies to clearly and correctly understand the meaning of and rationale for Landauer's Principle, and the consequent requirements, at the logical level, for computational operations to be reversible—meaning, both not information-losing, and also capable of being physically carried out in an asymptotically thermodynamically reversible way.

Although Landauer's Principle is valid, his original definition of what it meant for a computation to be "logically reversible" was not general enough to encompass all of the abstract logical structures that a computation can have while still avoiding information loss and being able to be carried out via (asymptotically) thermodynamically reversible physical processes. It turns out that a much larger set of computational operations can be reversible *at the logical level* than Landauer's traditional definition of logical reversibility acknowledges, which opens up many possibilities for engineering reversible devices and circuits that could never have been understood using the traditional definition, although some of those opportunities were discovered anyway by the designers of historical concepts for hardware implementation of reversible computing, such as Drexler's rod logic ([3], Chap. 12) and Younis and Knight's charge recovery logic [4].

Yet, there remains today a widespread disconnect between standard reversible computing theory and the engineering principles required for the design of efficient reversible hardware. This disconnect has contributed to an ongoing debate (*e.g.*, [5]) regarding the question of whether logical reversibility is really required for physical reversibility. Indeed it is, but *not* if the standard definition of logical reversibility is used. A useful response from the theory side would be to *update* the standard definition of logical reversibility to reflect the *exact* logical-level requirements for physical reversibility. Upon that firmer foundation, we can construct a more general theoretical model for reversible computing, which can then help bridge the historical disconnect between theory and engineering in this field. It is the goal of this paper to develop such a model from first principles, and show exactly why it is necessary and useful.

The rest of this paper is structured as follows. In Sect. 2, we review some physical foundations and derive a general formulation of Landauer's Principle, which we then use in Sect. 3 as the basis for systematically reconstructing reversible computing theory to produce a new theoretical framework that we call

---

[1] Per [1], minimum gate energies are expected to bottom out at around the 40–$80\,k_{\mathrm{B}}T$ (1–2 eV) level (where k_{B} is Boltzmann's constant, and T is operating temperature); while typical total CV^2 node energies (where C is node capacitance, and V is logic swing voltage) may level off at a corresponding higher range of 1–2 keV.

Generalized Reversible Computing (GRC), which formalizes the essential but often-overlooked concept of *conditional reversibility* (previously mentioned in [6]). In Sect. 4, we present a few examples of conditionally-reversible operations that are useful building blocks for reversible hardware design, and are straightforwardly physically implementable. Section 5 briefly discusses why GRC is the appropriate model for asymptotically thermodynamically reversible hardware such as adiabatic switching circuits. Section 6 contrasts GRC's concept of conditional reversibility with existing concepts of conditions for correctness of reversible computations. Section 7 concludes with an outline of directions for future work.

The present version of this paper has been limited to a summary of results, omitting the proofs, due to conference page limits. A longer, more comprehensive version will be published as a journal article at a later time.

2   Formulating Landauer's Principle

Landauer's Principle is essentially the observation that the loss of information from a computation corresponds to an increase in physical entropy, implying a certain associated dissipation of energy to heat in the environment. But, articulating the meaning of and justification for the Principle in a more detailed way will help clarify what *information loss* really means, and under what conditions, precisely, information is lost in the course of carrying out a given computation.

As is standard in modern physics, we assume that any finite, closed physical system has only some finite number N of distinguishable physical states, thus a maximum entropy $\bar{S} = k_B \ln N$. In quantum theory, N is also the dimensionality of the system's Hilbert space, *i.e.*, the cardinality of any basis set of orthogonal (distinguishable) state vectors that spans the space of all possible quantum states of the system. Let Σ denote any such maximal set of distinguishable states; we call this a *physical state space* for the system.

Furthermore, modern physics requires that the physical dynamics relating states at any time $t \in \mathbb{R}$ to the states that they may evolve to (or from) at any later (resp. earlier) time $t + \Delta t \in \mathbb{R}$ is a bijective (one-to-one and onto) functional relation. In quantum physics, this bijective dynamics is given by the unitary time-evolution operator $U(\Delta t) = e^{-iH\Delta t/\hbar}$, where H is the system's Hamiltonian operator (its total-energy observable).[2] Thus, physics is bijective, in the above sense, implying that it is deterministic (meaning, the present state determines the future) and reversible (the present determines the past).

Note that if fundamental physics were irreversible, then the Second Law of Thermodynamics (which states that the change in entropy over time is non-negative, $\Delta S \geq 0$) would be false, because two distinguishable states each with nonzero probability could merge, combining their probabilities, and reducing their contribution to the total entropy. Thus, the reversibility of fundamental physics follows from the empirically-observed validity of the Second Law.

---

[2] Although quantum physics does not yet incorporate a description of gravity, it's expected that even a full theory of quantum gravity would still exhibit unitarity.

In any event, if one accepts the bijectivity of dynamical evolution as a truism of mathematical physics, then, as we will see, the validity of Landauer's Principle follows rigorously from it, as a theorem.

Given a physical state space Σ, a *computational subspace* C of Σ can be identified with a partition of the set Σ. We say that a physical system Π is *in computational state* $c_j \in C$ whenever there is an $s_i \in c_j$ such that the physical state of the system is not reliably distinguishable from s_i. In other words, a computational state c_j is just an equivalence class of physical states that can be considered equivalent to each other, in terms of the computational information that we are intending them to represent. We assume that we can also identify an appropriate computational subspace $C(\Delta t)$ that is a partition of the evolved physical state space $\Sigma(\Delta t)$ at any past or future time $t_0 + \Delta t \in \mathbb{R}$.

Consider, now, any initial-state probability distribution p_0 over the complete state space $\Sigma = \Sigma(0)$ at time $t = t_0$. This then clearly induces an implied initial probability distribution P_1 over the *computational* states at time t_0 as well:

$$P_1(c_j) = \sum_{k=1}^{|c_j|} p_0(s_{j,k}), \tag{1}$$

where $s_{j,k}$ denotes the kth physical state in computational state $c_j \in C$.

For probability distributions p and P over physical and computational states, we can define corresponding entropy measures. Given any probability distribution p over a physical state space Σ, the *physical entropy* $S(p)$ is defined by

$$S(p) = \sum_{i=1}^{N=|\Sigma|} p(s_i) \log \frac{1}{p(s_i)}, \tag{2}$$

where the logarithm can be considered to be an indefinite logarithm, dimensioned in generic logarithmic units.

The bijectivity of physical dynamics then implies the following theorem:

Theorem 1 *Conservation of entropy*. The physical entropy of any closed system, as determined for any initial state distribution p_0, is exactly conserved over time. *I.e.*, if the physical entropy of an initial-state distribution $p_0(s_i)$ at time t_0 is $S(0)$, and we evolve that system over an elapsed time $\Delta t \in \mathbb{R}$ according to its bijective dynamics, the physical entropy $S(\Delta t)$ of its final-state probability distribution $p_{\Delta t}$ at time $t_0 + \Delta t$ will be the exact same value, $S(\Delta t) = S(0)$.

Theorem 1 takes an ideal, theoretical perspective. In practice, entropy from any real observer's perspective increases, because the observer does not have exact knowledge of the dynamics, or the capability to track it exactly. But in principle, the ideal perspective with constant entropy still always exists.

We can also define the entropy of the computational state. Given any probability distribution P over a computational state space C, the *information entropy* or *computational entropy* $H(P)$ is defined by:

$$H(P) = \sum_{j=1}^{|C|} P(c_j) \log \frac{1}{P(c_j)}, \tag{3}$$

which, like $S(p)$, is dimensioned in arbitrary logarithmic units.

Finally, we define the *non-computational entropy* as the remainder of the total physical entropy, other than the computational part; $S_{nc} = S - H \geq 0$. This is the expected physical entropy conditioned on the computational state.

The above definitions let us derive Landauer's Principle, in its most general, quantitative form, as well as another form frequently seen in the literature.

Theorem 2 *Launder's Principle (general formulation).* If the computational state of a system at initial time t_0 has entropy $H_I = H(P_1)$, and we allow that system to evolve, according to its physical dynamics, to some other "final" time $t_0 + \Delta t$, at which its computational entropy becomes $H_F = H(P_F)$ where $P_F = P(\Delta t)$ is the induced probability distribution over the computational state set $C(\Delta t)$ at time $t_0 + \Delta t$, then the non-computational entropy is increased by

$$\Delta S_{nc} = H_I - H_F. \tag{4}$$

Conventional digital devices are typically designed to locally reduce computational entropy, *e.g.*, by erasing or destructively overwriting "unknown" old bits obliviously, *i.e.*, ignoring any independent knowledge of their previous value. Thus, typical device operations necessarily eject entropy into the non-computational form, and so, over time, non-computational entropy typically accumulates in the system, manifesting as heating. But, systems cannot tolerate indefinite entropy build-up without overheating. So, the entropy must ultimately be moved out to some external environment at some temperature T, which involves the dissipation of energy $\Delta E_{diss} = T \Delta S_{nc}$ to the form of heat in that environment, by the definition of thermodynamic temperature. From Theorem 2 together with these facts and the logarithmic identity 1 bit = $(1 \, \text{nat}) / \log_2 e = k_B \ln 2$ follows the more commonly-seen statement of Landauer's Principle:

Corollary 1 *Launder's Principle (common form).* For each bit's worth of computational information that is lost within a computer (*e.g.*, by obliviously erasing or destructively overwriting it), an amount of energy

$$\Delta E_{diss} = k_B T \ln 2 \tag{5}$$

must eventually be dissipated to the form of heat added to some environment at temperature T.

3   Reformulating Reversible Computing Theory

We now carefully analyze the implications of the general Landauer's Principle (Theorem 2) for computation, and reformulate reversible computing theory on that basis. We begin by redeveloping the foundations of the traditional theory of unconditionally logically-reversible operations, using a language that we subsequently build upon to develop the generalized theory.

For our purposes, a computational *device* D will simply be any physical artifact that is capable of carrying out one or more different *computational operations*, by which the physical and computational state spaces Σ, C associated with D's local state are transformed. If D has an associated local computational state space $C_I = \{c_{I1}, ..., c_{Im}\}$ at some initial time t_0, a computational operation O on D that is applicable at t_0 is specified by giving a probabilistic transition rule, *i.e.*, a stochastic map from the initial computational state at t_0 to the final computational state at some later time $t_0 + \Delta t$ (with $\Delta t > 0$) by which the operation will have been completed. Let the computational state space at this later time be $C_F = \{c_{F1}, ..., c_{Fn}\}$. Then, the operation $O : C_I \rightarrow \mathcal{P}(C_F)$ is a map from C_I to probability distributions over C_F; which is characterizable, in terms of random variables c_I, c_F for the initial and final computational states, by a conditional probabilistic transition rule

$$r_i(j) = \Pr(c_F = c_{Fj} | c_I = c_{Ii}) = [O(c_{Ii})](c_{Fj}), \qquad (6)$$

where $i \in \{1, ..., m\}$ and $j \in \{1, ..., n\}$. That is, $r_i(j)$ denotes the conditional probability that the final computational state is c_{Fj}, given that the initial computational state is c_{Ii}.

A computational operation O will be called *deterministic* if and only if all of the probability distributions r_i are single-valued. *I.e.*, for each possible value of the initial-state index $i \in \{1, ..., m\}$, there is exactly one corresponding value of the final-state index j such that $r_i(j) > 0$, and thus, for this value of j, it must be the case that $r_i(j) = 1$, while $r_i(k) = 0$ for all other $k \neq j$. If an operation O is not deterministic, we call it *nondeterministic*.[3] For a deterministic operation O, we can write $O(c_{Ii})$ to denote the unique c_{Fj} such that $r_i(j) = 1$, that is, treating O as a simple transition function rather than a stochastic one.

A computational operation O will be called (unconditionally logically) *reversible* if and only if all of the probability distributions r_i have non-overlapping nonzero ranges. In other words, for each possible value of the final-state index $j \in \{1, ..., n\}$, there is at most one corresponding value of the initial-state index i such that $r_i(j) > 0$, while $r_k(j) = 0$ for all other $k \neq i$. If an operation O is not reversible, we call it *irreversible*.

For a computational operation O with an initial computational state space C_I, a *(statistical) operating context* for that operation is any probability distribution P_I over the initial computational states; for any $i \in \{1, ..., m\}$, the value of $P_I(c_{Ii})$ gives the probability that the initial computational state is c_{Ii}.

A computational operation O will be called *(potentially) entropy-ejecting* if and only if there is some operating context P_I such that, when the operation O is applied within that context, the increase ΔS_{nc} in the non-computational entropy required by Landauer's Principle is greater than zero. If an operation O is not potentially entropy-ejecting, we call it *non-entropy-ejecting*.

---

[3] Note that this is a different sense of the word "nondeterministic" than is commonly used in computational complexity theory, when referring to, for example, nondeterministic Turing machines, which conceptually evaluate all of their possible future computational trajectories in parallel. Here, when we use the word "nondeterministic," we mean it simply in the physicist's sense, to refer to randomizing or stochastic operations; *i.e.*, those whose result is uncertain.

Now, we can derive Landauer's original result stating that only operations that are logically reversible (in his sense) can always avoid ejecting entropy from the computational state (independently of the operating context).

Theorem 3 *Fundamental Theorem of Traditional Reversible Computing.* Non-entropy-ejecting deterministic operations must be reversible. That is, if a given deterministic computational operation O is non-entropy-ejecting, then it is reversible in the sense defined above (its transition relation is injective).

The proof of the theorem involves showing that entropy is ejected when states with nonzero probability are merged by an operation. However, when states having *zero* probability are merged with other states, there is no increase in entropy. This is the key realization that sets us up to develop GRC.

To do this, we define a notion of a *computation* that fixes a specific statistical operating context for a computational operation, and then we examine the detailed requirements for a given computation to be non-entropy-ejecting. This leads to the concept of *conditional reversibility*, which is the most general concept of logical reversibility, and provides the appropriate foundation for GRC.

For us, a *computation* $\mathcal{C} = (O, P_I)$ performed by a device D is defined by specifying *both* a computational operation O to be carried out by that device, *and* a specific operating context P_I under which the operation O is to be performed.

A computation $\mathcal{C} = (O, P_I)$ is called *(specifically) entropy-ejecting* if and only if, when the operation O is applied within the specific operating context P_I, the increase ΔS_{nc} in the non-computational entropy required by Landauer's Principle is greater than zero. If $\mathcal{C}$ is not specifically entropy-ejecting, we call it *non-entropy-ejecting*.

A deterministic computational operation O is called *conditionally reversible* if and only if there is a non-empty subset $A \subseteq C_I$ of initial computational states (the *assumed set* or *assumed precondition*) that O's transition rule maps onto an equal-sized set $B \subseteq C_F$ of final states. That is, each $c_{Ii} \in A$ maps, one to one, to a unique $c_{Fj} \in B$ where $r_i(j) = 1$. We say that B is the *image of A under O*. We also say that O is *(conditionally) reversible under the precondition (that the initial state is in) A*.

It turns out that *all* deterministic computational operations are, in fact, conditionally reversible, under some sufficiently-restrictive preconditions.

Theorem 4 *Conditional reversibility of all deterministic operations.* All deterministic computational operations are conditionally reversible.

A trivial proof of Theorem 4 involves considering precondition sets A that are singletons. However, deterministic operations with any number $k > 1$ of reachable final computational states are also conditionally reversible under at least one precondition set A of size k.

Whenever we wish to fix a *specific* assumed precondition A for the reversibility of a conditionally-reversible operation O, we use the following concept:

Let O be any conditionally-reversible computational operation, and let A be any one of the preconditions under which O is reversible. Then the *conditioned reversible operation* $O_A = (O, A)$ denotes the concept of performing operation O in the context of a requirement that precondition A is satisfied.

Restricting the set of initial states that may have nonzero probability to a specific proper subset $A \subset C_I$ represents a change to the semantics of an operation, so generally, a conditioned reversible version of an arbitrary deterministic operation is, in effect, not exactly the same operation. But we will see that arbitrary computations can still be composed out of these restricted operations.

The central result of GRC theory (Theorem 5, below) is then that a deterministic computation $\mathcal{C} = (O, P_I)$ is specifically non-entropy-ejecting, and therefore avoids any requirement under Landauer's Principle to dissipate any energy $\Delta E_{diss} > 0$ to its thermal environment, if and only if its operating context P_I assigns total probability 1 to some precondition A under which its computational operation O is reversible. Moreover (Theorem 6), even if the probability of satisfying some such precondition only *approaches* 1, this is sufficient for the entropy ejected (and energy dissipation required) to approach zero.

Theorem 5 *Fundamental Theorem of Generalized Reversible Computing.* Any deterministic computation is non-entropy-ejecting if and only if at least one of its preconditions for reversibility is satisfied. *I.e.,* let $\mathcal{C} = (O, P_I)$ be any deterministic computation (*i.e.,* any computation whose operation O is deterministic). Then, part (a): If there is some precondition A under which O is reversible, such that A is satisfied with certainty in the operating context P_I, then $\mathcal{C}$ is a non-entropy-ejecting computation. And, part (b): Alternatively, if no such precondition A is satisfied with certainty, then $\mathcal{C}$ is entropy-ejecting.

Theorem 6 *Entropy ejection vanishes as precondition certainty approaches unity.* Let O be any deterministic operation, and let A be any precondition under which O is reversible, and let $P_{I1}, P_{I2}, \ldots$ be any sequence of operation contexts for O within which the total probability mass assigned to A approaches 1. Then, in the corresponding sequence of computations, the entropy ejected ΔS_{nc} also approaches 0.

A numerical example illustrating how the ΔS_{nc} calculation comes out in a specific case where the probability of violating the precondition for reversibility is small can be found in [7].

It's important to note that in order for real hardware devices to apply Theorems 5 and 6 to avoid or reduce energy dissipation in practice, the device must be designed with implicit knowledge of not only what conditionally-reversible operation it should perform, but also which specific one of the preconditions for that operation's reversibility it should assume is satisfied.

As we saw in Theorem 4, any deterministic computational operation O is conditionally reversible with respect to any given one A of its suitable preconditions for reversibility. For any computation $\mathcal{C} = (O, P_I)$ that satisfies the conditions for reversibility of the conditioned reversible operation O_A with certainty, we can undo the effect of that computation exactly by applying any conditioned reversible operation that is what we call a *reversal* of O_A. The reversal of a conditioned reversible operation is simply an operation that maps the image of the assumed set back onto the assumed set itself in a way that exactly inverts the original forward map.

The above framework can also be extended to work with nondeterministic computations. In fact, adding nondeterminism to an operation only makes it easier to avoid ejecting entropy to the non-computational state, since nondeterminism tends to increase the computational entropy, and thus tends to reduce the non-computational entropy. As a result, a nondeterministic operation can be non-entropy-ejecting (or even entropy-absorbing, *i.e.*, with $\Delta S_{nc} < 0$) even in computations where none of its preconditions for reversibility are satisfied, so long as the reduction in computational entropy caused by its irreversibility is compensated for by an equal or greater increase in computational entropy caused by its nondeterminism. However, we will not take the time, in the present paper, to flesh out detailed analyses of such cases.

4   Examples of Conditioned Reversible Operations

Here, we define and illustrate a number of examples of conditionally reversible operations (including a specification of their assumed preconditions) that comprise natural primitives out of which arbitrary reversible algorithms may be composed. First, we introduce some textual and graphical notations for describing conditioned reversible operations.

Let the computational state space be factorizable into independent *state variables* $x, y, z, ...$, which are in general n-ary discrete variables. A common case will be binary variables ($n = 2$). For simplicity, we assume here that the sets of state variables into which the initial and final computational state spaces are factorized are identical, although more generally this may not be the case.

Given a computational state space C that is factorizable into state variables $x, y, z, ...$, and given a precondition A on the initial state defined by

$$A = \{c_i \in C \mid P(x, y, ...)\}, \tag{7}$$

where $P(x, y, ...)$ is some propositional (*i.e.*, Boolean-valued) function of the state variables $x, y, ...$, we can denote a conditionally-reversible operation O_A on C that is reversible under precondition A using notation like:

$$\texttt{OpName}(x, y, ... \mid P(x, y, ...)) \tag{8}$$

which represents a conditionally-reversible operation named OpName that operates on and potentially transforms the state variables $x, y, ...$, and that is reversible under an assumed precondition A consisting of the set of initial states that satisfy the given proposition $P(x, y, ...)$.

A simple, generic graphical notation for a deterministic, conditionally reversible operation named OpName, operating on a state space that is decomposable into three state variables x, y, z, and possibly including an assumed precondition for reversibility $P(x, y, z)$, is the ordinary space-time diagram representation shown in Fig. 1(a).

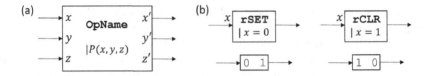

Fig. 1. (a) Generic graphical notation for a deterministic, conditioned reversible operation $\texttt{OpName}(x, y, z \mid P(x, y, z))$ on three state variables x, y, z, with an assumed precondition specified by the propositional function $P(x, y, z)$. (b) Left: Standard graphical notation (top) and simplified symbol (bottom) for the conditioned reversible operation $\texttt{rSET}(x \mid x = 0)$; Right: Likewise for $\texttt{rCLR}(x \mid x = 1)$.

In this representation, as in standard reversible logic networks, time is visualized as flowing from left to right, and the horizontal lines represent state variables. The primed versions x', y', z' going outwards represent the values of the state variables in the final computational state c_F after the operation.

As Landauer observed, operations such as "set to one" and "reset to zero" on binary state spaces are logically irreversible, under his definition; indeed, they constitute classic examples of *bit erasure* operations for which (assuming equiprobable initial states) an amount $k_B \ln 2$ of entropy is ejected from the computational state. However, as per Theorem 4, these operations are in fact conditionally reversible, under suitably-restricted preconditions. A suitable precondition, in this case, is one in which one of the two initial states is excluded. Thus, the initial state is known with certainty in any operating context satisfying such a precondition. A known state can be transformed to any specific new state reversibly. If the new state is different from the old one, such an operation is non-vacuous. Thus, the following conditioned reversible operations are useful.

The deterministic operation $\texttt{rSET}$ (*reversible set-to-one*) on a binary variable x, which (to be useful) is implicitly associated with an assumed precondition for reversibility of $x = 0$, is an operation that is defined to transform the initial state into the final state $x' = 1$; in other words, it performs the operation $x := 1$. Standard and simplified graphical notations for this operation are illustrated on the left-hand side of Fig. 1(b).

By Theorem 5, the conditioned reversible operation $\texttt{rSET}(x \mid x = 0)$ is specifically non-entropy-ejecting in operating contexts where the designated precondition for reversibility is satisfied. It can be implemented in a way that is asymptotically physically reversible (as the probability that its precondition is satisfied approaches 1) using any mechanism that is designed to adiabatically transform the state $x = 0$ to the state $x = 1$.

Similarly, we can consider a deterministic conditioned reversible operation $\texttt{rCLR}(x \mid x = 1)$ (*reversible clear* or *reversible reset-to-zero*) which has an assumed precondition for reversibility of $x = 1$ and which performs the operation $x := 0$, illustrated on the right-hand side of Fig. 1(b).

A very commonly-used computational operation is to copy one state variable to another. As with any other deterministic operation, such an operation is conditionally reversible under suitable preconditions. An appropriate precondition for the reversibility of this $\texttt{rCOPY}$ operation is any in which the initial value of the target variable is known, so that it can be reversibly transformed to the new value. A standard reversal of a suitably-conditioned rCOPY operation, which we can call rUnCOPY, is simply a conditioned reversible operation that transforms the final states resulting from rCOPY back to the corresponding initial states.

Formally, let x, y be any two discrete state variables both with the same arity (number n of possible values, which without loss of generality we may label $0, 1, ...$), and let $v \in \{0, 1, ..., n-1\}$ be any fixed initial value. Then *reversible copy of x onto $y = v$* or

$$\mathtt{rCOPY}_v = \mathtt{rCOPY}(x, y \,|\, y = v) \tag{9}$$

is a conditioned reversible operation O with assumed precondition $y = v$ that maps any initial state where $x = i$ onto the final state $x = i, y = i$. In the language of ordinary pseudocode, the operation performed is simply $y := x$.

Given any conditioned reversible copy operation $\mathtt{rCOPY}_v$, there is a conditioned reversible operation which we hereby call *reversible uncopy of y from x back to v* or

$$\mathtt{rUnCOPY}_v = \mathtt{rUnCOPY}_v(x, y \,|\, y = x) \tag{10}$$

which, assuming (as its precondition for reversibility) that initially $x = y$, carries out the operation $y := v$, restoring the destination variable y to the same initial value v that was assumed by the rCOPY operation.

Figure 2(a) shows graphical notations for $\mathtt{rCOPY}_v$ and $\mathtt{rUnCOPY}_v$.

It is easy to generalize rCOPY to more complex functions. In general, for any function $F(x, y, ...)$ of any number of variables, we can define a conditioned reversible operation $\mathtt{r}F(x, y, ..., z \,|\, z = v)$ which computes that function, and writes the result to an output variable z by transforming z from its initial value to $F(x, y, ...)$, which is reversible under the precondition that the initial value of z is some known value v. Its reversal $\mathtt{rUn}F_v(x, y, ..., z \,|\, z = F(x, y, ...))$ decomputes the result in the output variable z, restoring it back to the value v. See Fig. 2(b).

The F above may indeed be any function, including standard Boolean logic functions operating on binary variables, such as AND, OR, *etc.* Therefore, the above

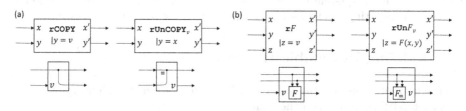

Fig. 2. (a) Left: Reversible copy of x onto $y = v$; Right: Reversible uncopy of y from x back to v. (b) Given any function $F(x, y) = z$ of n (here, $n = 2$) state variables, we can easily convert it to a pair of conditioned reversible operations $\mathtt{r}F(x, y, z \,|\, z = v)$ and $\mathtt{rUn}F_v(x, y, z \,|\, z = F(x, y))$ that are mutual reversals of each other that compute and decompute the value of F by reversibly transforming the output variable z from and to any predetermined value v. Top: standard notation, bottom: simplified symbols.

scheme leads us to consider conditioned reversible operations such as $rAND_0$, $rAND_1$, rOR_0, rOR_1; and their reversals $rUnAND_0$, $rUnAND_1$, $rUnOR_0$, $rUnOR_1$; which reversibly do and undo standard AND and OR logic operations with respect to output nodes that are expected to be a constant logic 0 or 1 initially before the operation is done (and also finally, after doing the reverse operations).

Clearly, one can compose arbitrary n-input Boolean functions out of such primitives using standard logic network constructions, and decompute intermediate results using the reverse (mirror-image) circuits (after rCOPYing the desired results), following the general approach pioneered by Bennett [8]. This results in an embedding of the desired function into a reversible function that preserves only the input and the final output.

One may wonder, however, what is the advantage of using operations such as rAND and rUnAND for this, compared to the traditional unconditionally reversible operation $ccNOT(x, y, z)$ (controlled-controlled-NOT, a.k.a. the Toffoli gate operation [9], $z := z \oplus xy$). Indeed, any device that implements $ccNOT(x, y, z)$ in a physically-reversible manner could be used in place of a device that implements $rAND(x, y, z \mid z = 0)$ and $rUnAND_0(x, y, z \mid z = xy)$, or in place of one that implements $rNAND(x, y, z \mid z = 1)$ and $rUnNAND_1(x, y, z \mid z = \overline{xy})$, in cases where the preconditions of those operations would be satisfied.

But, the converse is not true. In other words, there are devices that can asymptotically physically reversibly carry out $rAND_0$ and $rUnAND_0$ that do not also implement full Toffoli gate operations. Therefore, if what one really needs to do, in one's algorithm, is simply to do and undo Boolean AND operations reversibly, then to insist on doing this using Toffoli operations rather than conditioned reversible operations such as rAND and rUnAND is overkill, and amounts to tying one's hands with regards to the implementation possibilities, leading to hardware designs that can be expected to be more complex than necessary. Indeed, there are very simple adiabatic circuit implementations of devices capable of performing rAND/rUnAND and rOR/rUnOR operations (based on *e.g.* series/parallel combinations of CMOS transmission gates [10]), whereas, adiabatic implementations of ccNOT itself are typically much less simple. This illustrates our overall point that the GRC framework generally allows for simpler designs for reversible computational hardware than does the traditional reversible computing model based on unconditionally reversible operations.

5   Modeling Reversible Hardware

A broader motivation for the study of GRC derives from the following observation (not yet formalized as a theorem):

Assertion 1 *General correspondence between truly, fully adiabatic circuits and conditioned reversible operations.* Part (a): Whenever a switching circuit is operated deterministically in a truly, fully adiabatic way (*i.e.*, that asymptotically approaches thermodynamic reversibility), transitioning among some discrete set of logic levels, the computation being performed by that circuit corresponds to a conditioned reversible operation O_A whose assumed precondition A is (asymptotically) satisfied. Part (b): Likewise, any conditioned reversible operation O_A can be implemented in an asymptotically thermodynamically reversible manner by using an appropriate switching circuit that is operated in a truly, fully adiabatic way, transitioning among some discrete set of logic levels.

Part (a) follows from our earlier observation in Theorem 5 that, in deterministic computations, conditional reversibility is the correct statement of the logical-level requirement for avoiding energy dissipation under Landauer's Principle, and therefore it is a necessity for approaching thermodynamic reversibility in any deterministic computational process, and therefore, more specifically, in the operation of adiabatic circuits.

Meanwhile, part (b) follows from general constructions showing how to implement any desired conditioned reversible operation in an asymptotically thermodynamically reversible way using adiabatic switching circuits. For example, Fig. 3 illustrates how to implement an rCOPY operation using a simple four-transistor CMOS circuit. In contrast, implementing rCOPY by embedding it within an unconditionally-reversible cNOT would require including an XOR capability, and would require a much more complicated adiabatic circuit, whose operation would itself be composed from numerous more-primitive operations (such as adiabatic transformations of individual MOSFETs [11]) that are themselves only conditionally reversible.

In general, the traditional reversible computing framework of unconditionally reversible operations does not exhibit any correspondence such as that of Assertion 1 to any natural class of asymptotically physically-reversible hardware that we know of. In particular, the traditional unconditionally-reversible framework does not correspond to the class of truly/fully adiabatic switching circuits, because there are many such circuits that do not in fact perform unconditionally reversible operations, but only conditionally-reversible ones.

6   Comparison to Prior Work

The concept of conditional reversibility presented here is similar to, but distinct from, certain concepts that are already well known in the literature on the theory of reversible circuits and languages.

First, the concept of a reversible computation that is only semantically correct (for purposes of computing a desired function) when a certain precondition on the inputs is satisfied is one that was already implicit in Landauer's original paper [2], when he introduced the operation now known as the Toffoli gate, as a reversible operation within which Boolean AND may be embedded. Implicit in the description of that operation is that it only correctly computes AND if the control bit is initially 0; otherwise, it computes some other function (in this case, NAND). This is the origin of the concept of *ancilla* bits, which are required to obey certain pre- and post-conditions (typically, being cleared to 0) in order for reversible circuits to be composable and still function as intended. The study

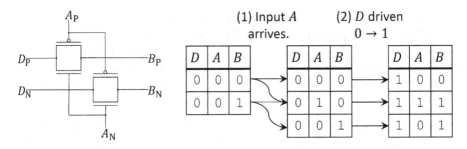

Fig. 3. (Left) A simple adiabatic CMOS circuit capable of carrying out a variant of the rCOPY operation. Here, computational states are represented using dual-rail complementary voltage coding, so that, for example, a logical state $A = 0$ is represented using the voltage assignments $A_P = V_H$, $A_N = V_L$, where V_H, V_L are high and low voltage levels, respectively. The logical state $A = 1$ would be represented using the opposite voltage assignments. The two CMOS transmission gates shown will thus be turned ON (conducting) only when $A = 1$. In this circuit, A is the logic input, B is the output, and D is a driving signal. (Right) Sequence of operation. Assume initially that $D = 0$ and $A = 0$. Normally we would also have $B = 0$ initially, but to illustrate the conditional reversibility of this circuit, we will also consider the case $B = 1$. In step 1, some external circuit adiabatically transforms input A from logic 0 to a newly-computed value (0 or 1) to be copied, then in step 2, the drive signal D is unconditionally transformed adiabatically from logic 0 to 1. Note that, in the course of this operation sequence, if B were 1 initially, then it would be dissipatively sourced to $D = 0$ in step 1 if $A = 1$. Thus, this particular operation sequence implements a conditioned reversible operation rCOPY'$(A, B \mid \overline{AB})$; it is reversible as long as we don't try to copy an input value $A = 1$ onto an initial state where $B = 1$. The prime there after rCOPY is denoting the variant semantics, namely that in the case $\overline{AB}$, the value $A = 0$ is not copied to B.

of the circumstances under which such requirements may be satisfied has been extensively developed, *e.g.* as in [12]. However, any circuit composed from Toffoli gates is *still reversible* even if restoration of its ancillas is violated; it may yield nonsensical outputs in that case, when composed together with other circuits, but at no point is information erased. This distinguishes ancilla-preservation conditions from our preconditions for reversibility, which, when they are unsatisfied, necessarily yield actual (physical) irreversibility.

Similarly, the major historical examples of reversible high-level programming languages such as Janus ([13, 14]), Ψ-Lisp [15], the author's own R language [16], and RFUN ([17, 18]) have invoked various "preconditions for reversibility" in the defined semantics of many of their language constructs. But again, that concept really has more to do with the "correctness" or "well-definedness" of a high-level reversible program, and this notion is distinct from the requirements for actual physical reversibility during execution. For example, the R language compiler generated PISA assembly code in such a way that even if high-level language requirements were violated (*e.g.*, in the case of an if condition changing its truth value during the if body), the resulting assembly code would still execute reversibly, if nonsensically, on the Pendulum processor [19].

In contrast, the notion of conditional reversibility explored in the present document ties directly to Landauer's principle, and to the possibility of the physical reversibility of the underlying hardware. Note, however, that it does not concern the semantic correctness of the computation, or lack thereof, and in general, the necessary preconditions for the physical reversibility and correctness of a given computation may be orthogonal to each other, as illustrated by the example in Fig. 3.

7   Conclusion

In this paper, we presented the core foundations of a general theoretical framework for reversible computing. We considered the case of deterministic computational operations in detail, and presented results showing that the class of deterministic computations that are not required to eject any entropy from the computational state under Landauer's Principle is larger than the set of computations composed of the unconditionally-reversible operations considered by traditional reversible computing theory, because it also includes the set of conditionally-reversible operations whose preconditions for reversibility are satisfied with probability approaching unity. This is the most general possible characterization of the set of classical deterministic computations that can be physically implemented in an asymptotically thermodynamically reversible way.

We then illustrated some basic applications of the theory in modeling conditioned reversible operations that transform an output variable between a predetermined, known value and the computed result of the operation. Such operations can be implemented easily using *e.g.* adiabatic switching circuits, whose low-level computational function cannot in general be represented within the traditional theory of unconditionally-reversible computing. This substantiates that the GRC theory warrants further study.

Some promising directions for future work include: (1) Giving further examples of useful conditioned reversible operations; (2) illustrating detailed physical implementations of devices for performing such operations; (3) further extending the development of the new framework to address the nondeterministic case; and (4) developing further descriptive frameworks for reversible computing at higher levels (*e.g.*, hardware description languages, programming languages) building on top of the fundamental conceptual foundations that GRC theory provides.

Since GRC broadens the range of design possibilities for reversible computing devices in a clearly delineated, well-founded way, its study and further development will be essential for the computing industry to successfully transition, over the coming decades, to the point where it is dominantly utilizing the reversible computing paradigm. Due to the incontrovertible validity of Landauer's Principle, such a transition will be an absolute physical prerequisite for the energy efficiency (and cost efficiency) of general computing technology to continue growing by many orders of magnitude.

References

1. International Technology Roadmap for Semiconductors 2.0, 2015 th edn. Semiconductor Industry Association (2015)

2. Landauer, R.: Irreversibility and heat generation in the computing process. IBM J. Res. Dev. **5**(3), 183–191 (1961)
3. Drexler, K.E.: Nanosystems: Molecular Machinery, Manufacturing, and Computation. Wiley, New York (1992)
4. Younis, S.G., Knight Jr., T.F.: Practical implementation of charge recovering asymptotically zero power CMOS. In: Proceedings of the 1993 Symposium on Research in Integrated Systems, pp. 234–250. MIT Press (1993)
5. López-Suárez, M., Neri, I., Gammaitoni, L.: Sub-$k_B T$ micro-electromechanical irreversible logic gate. Nat. Commun. **7**, 12068 (2016)
6. Frank, M.P.: Approaching the physical limits of computing. In: 35th International Symposium on Multiple-Valued Logic, pp. 168–185. IEEE Press, New York (2005)
7. DeBenedictis, E.P., Frank, M.P., Ganesh, N., Anderson, N.G.: A path toward ultra-low-energy computing. In: IEEE International Conference on Rebooting Computing. IEEE Press, New York (2016)
8. Bennett, C.H.: Logical reversibility of computation. IBM J. Res. Dev. **17**(6), 525–532 (1973)
9. Toffoli, T.: Reversible computing. In: Bakker, J., Leeuwen, J. (eds.) ICALP 1980. LNCS, vol. 85, pp. 632–644. Springer, Heidelberg (1980). doi:10.1007/3-540-10003-2_104
10. Anantharam, V., He, M., Natarajan, K., Xie, H., Frank, M.: Driving fully-adiabatic logic circuits using custom high-Q MEMS resonators. In: Arabnia, H.R., Guo, M., Yang, L.T. (eds.) ESI/VLSI 2004, pp. 5–11. CSREA Press (2004)
11. Frank, M.P.: Towards a more general model of reversible logic hardware. In: Invited talk Presented at the Superconducting Electronics Approaching the Landauer Limit and Reversibility (SEALeR) Workshop. Sponsored by NSA/ARO (2012)
12. Thomsen, M.K., Kaarsgaard, R., Soeken, M.: Ricercar: a language for describing and rewriting reversible circuits with ancillae and its permutation semantics. In: Krivine, J., Stefani, J.-B. (eds.) RC 2015. LNCS, vol. 9138, pp. 200–215. Springer, Cham (2015). doi:10.1007/978-3-319-20860-2_13
13. Lutz, C.: Janus: a time-reversible language. Letter from Chris Lutz to Rolf Landauer (1986). http://tetsuo.jp/ref/janus.pdf
14. Yokoyama, T.: Reversible computation and reversible programming languages. Elec. Notes Theor. Comput. Sci. **253**(6), 71–81 (2010)
15. Baker, H.G.: NREVERSAL of fortune — the thermodynamics of garbage collection. In: Bekkers, Y., Cohen, J. (eds.) IWMM 1992. LNCS, vol. 637, pp. 507–524. Springer, Heidelberg (1992). doi:10.1007/BFb0017210
16. Frank, M.: Reversibility for Efficient Computing. Doctoral dissertation, Massachusetts Institute of Technology. Department of Electrical Engineering and Computer Science (1999)
17. Yokoyama, T., Axelsen, H.B., Glück, R.: Towards a reversible functional language. In: Vos, A., Wille, R. (eds.) RC 2011. LNCS, vol. 7165, pp. 14–29. Springer, Heidelberg (2012). doi:10.1007/978-3-642-29517-1_2
18. Axelsen, H.B., Glück, R.: Reversible representation and manipulation of constructor terms in the heap. In: Dueck, G.W., Miller, D.M. (eds.) RC 2013. LNCS, vol. 7948, pp. 96–109. Springer, Heidelberg (2013). doi:10.1007/978-3-642-38986-3_9
19. Vieri, C.J.: Reversible Computer Engineering and Architecture. Doctoral dissertation, Massachusetts Institute of Technology, Department of Electrical Engineering and Computer Science (1999)

Reversible Nondeterministic Finite Automata

Markus Holzer[✉] and Martin Kutrib

Institut für Informatik, Universität Giessen,
Arndtstr. 2, 35392 Giessen, Germany
{holzer,kutrib}@informatik.uni-giessen.de

Abstract. By former and recent results the model of reversible deterministic finite automata is well understood. On the other hand, reversible nondeterministic finite automata and their accepted languages have not systematically been considered in the literature. Here it turns out that reversible nondeterministic finite automata (REV-NFAs) are more powerful compared to their reversible deterministic counterparts, but still cannot accept all regular languages. Moreover, we compare the family of languages accepted by REV-NFAs to the language families accepted by deterministic and nondeterministic finite state automata with irreversibility degree k. Besides these results on the computational power of REV-NFAs we consider closure properties of the language family induced by these devices.

1 Introduction

Although our experience in the real world tells us that irreversibility is almost everywhere, that is, irreversible events appear on the large scale of things, the fundamental nature of physics behaves differently as supported by the following quote:

> "So far as we know, all the fundamental laws of physics, like Newton's equations, are reversible."
>
> Richard P. Feynman (Lecture 46 "Ratchet and Pawl")

This means that irreversible processes are composed by reversible ones. Viewing physical processes in an abstract way, by representing them in terms of states and transitions between states, links physics with computations. Computational models with discrete internal states are subject to studies in computer science since its beginning. Thus, by its close connection to physics, it is natural to ask, whether abstract computational models are able to obey fundamental principles of physics such as reversibility. For example, reversible Turing machines have been introduced in [5], where it turned out that every Turing machine can be simulated by a reversible one—for improved simulation constructions see [4,15]. There are legions of other computational devices that were studied with respect to the concept of reversibility. One are finite state automata, which are on the other end of the computational spectra compared to Turing machines, since their computational power is very weak.

© Springer International Publishing AG 2017
I. Phillips and H. Rahaman (Eds.): RC 2017, LNCS 10301, pp. 35–51, 2017.
DOI: 10.1007/978-3-319-59936-6_3

For deterministic finite state automata, reversibility can usually be verified by simple inspection of the transition function, ensuring that the induced computation step relation is an injective function on configurations. Injectivity is the least common property of almost all reversible finite state automata models that are considered in the literature. On other aspects such as, for example, the number of initial and final states, these reversible automata differ slightly. In principle the following situations appear in the literature:

1. one initial and one final state (also called *bideterminism*) [2,12],
2. one initial and multiple final states [1,9], and
3. multiple initial and multiple final states [14,16].

Obviously, the third model is the most general one, but it cannot accept all regular languages [16]. For instance, the language a^*b^* is not reversible. It is worth mentioning that finite automata in the sense of [16] may have limited nondeterminism plugged in from the outside world at the outset of the computation, since one of the multiple initial states is guessed. A further generalization that allows nondeterministic transitions even between different strongly connected components of the automaton was introduced in [14]—see also [6]. The corresponding automata are said to be quasi-reversible. However, due to the still restrictive use of the nondeterministic transitions, quasi-reversible finite automata are not more powerful than reversible finite automata in the sense of [16].

Thus, the question arises, what happens if nondeterminism is allowed in general in a reversible finite state automaton? Here we stick to the standard definition of finite automata, that is, one initial state and possibly multiple final states. This is in the line of research on reversible deterministic finite automata started in [1], recently restarted in [9], followed by [3,13]. At a first glance, one may think that languages accepted by reversible nondeterministic finite automata (REV-NFA) are mirror images of languages accepted by deterministic finite automata. However, in general, the reversal of a REV-NFA language is not accepted by a deterministic finite automaton, but by a multiple entry deterministic finite automaton with a sole accepting state, a more or less unexplored model as well. We will not directly focus on this issue, but will use it later in some of our proofs.

The paper is organized as follows. In the next section we introduce the necessary notations for reversible finite automata. Then in Sect. 3 we study the accepting power of REV-NFAs. In Subsect. 3.1 the computational power of REV-NFAs is compared with the power of other reversible devices. In particular, reversible nondeterministic finite automata turn out to be strictly more powerful than their deterministic reversible counterparts, already for unary languages. But REV-NFAs still cannot accept all regular languages—again a^*b^* is such an example. Subsection 3.2 is devoted to study the relationships with language families induced by deterministic and nondeterministic finite state automata with irreversibility degree k—see [3]. Here the irreversibility degree for a regular language is the minimal number of irreversible states necessary in *any* finite automaton accepting the language. As in the case of deterministic finite automata, the irreversibility degree induces a strict and infinite hierarchy on nondeterministic automata as well. Finally, in Subsect. 3.3 we consider the closure properties of the family of languages accepted by REV-NFAs. Although REV-NFAs and REV-DFAs induce different language families, these share the same closure properties. It turns out that both families are intersection closed and are nearly anti-AFLs, except for the positive closure under inverse homomorphisms. Recall, that the AFL operations are union, concatenation, Kleene star, homomorphism, inverse homomorphism, and intersection with regular sets. An anti-AFL is not closed under all of these operations. These closure properties are somehow surprising since we consider language families that are defined *via* a classical automaton model. Due to space constraints some proofs are omitted.

2   Preliminaries

We recall some definitions on formal languages and finite automata as contained, for example, in [8]. An *alphabet* Σ is a non-empty finite set, its elements are called *letters* or *symbols*. We write Σ^* for the *set of all words* over the finite alphabet Σ. In particular, the *empty word* is referred to as λ.

A *nondeterministic finite automaton* (NFA) is a 5-tuple $A = (Q, \Sigma, \delta, q_0, F)$, where Q is the finite set of *internal states*, Σ is the alphabet of *input symbols* or *letters*, $q_0 \in Q$ is the *initial state*, $F \subseteq Q$ is the set of *accepting states*, and $\delta \colon Q \times \Sigma \to 2^Q$ is the partial *transition function*. The *language accepted* by A is

$$L(A) = \{ w \in \Sigma^* \mid \delta(q_0, w) \cap F \neq \emptyset \},$$

where the transition function is recursively extended to $\delta \colon Q \times \Sigma^* \to 2^Q$. A NFA A is *deterministic* if $|\delta(p, a)| \leq 1$, for all states $p \in Q$ and $a \in \Sigma$. In this case we simply write $\delta(p, a) = q$, if $\delta(p, a) = \{q\}$. By $\delta^R \colon Q \times \Sigma \to 2^Q$, with $\delta^R(q, a) = \{ p \in Q \mid q \in \delta(p, a) \}$, we denote the *reverse* transition function of δ. Similarly, also δ^R can be extended to words instead of symbols. A state $p \in Q$ is *accessible* in A if there is a word $w \in \Sigma^*$ such that $\delta(q_0, w) = p$, and it is *productive* if there is a word $w \in \Sigma^*$ such that $\delta(p, w) \in F$. If p is both accessible and productive then we say that p is *useful*. In this paper we only consider automata with all states useful. Two automata A and A' are said to be *equivalent* if they accept the same language, that is, $L(A) = L(A')$. In this case we simply write $A \equiv A'$. An NFA (DFA, respectively) is *minimal* among all NFAs (DFAs, respectively) if there does not exist an equivalent NFA (DFA, respectively) with fewer states. It is well known that minimal DFAs are unique up to isomorphism. Minimal NFAs are not isomorphic in general.

Next we define reversible NFAs and DFAs. Let $A = (Q, \Sigma, \delta, q_0, F)$ be an NFA. A state $r \in Q$ is said to be *irreversible* if there are two distinct states p and q in Q and a letter $a \in \Sigma$ such that $r \in \delta(p, a) \cap \delta(q, a)$. Then an NFA is *reversible* if it does not contain any irreversible state. In this case the automaton is said to be a *reversible* NFA (REV-NFA). A language $L \subseteq \Sigma^*$ is said to be *nondeterministically reversible* if there is a REV-NFA A which accepts the language L. Analogously one defines reversible DFAs (REV-DFA)—alternatively one can define reversibility for DFAs as follows: the DFA A is reversible, if every letter $a \in \Sigma$ induces an *injective partial mapping* from Q to itself *via* the mapping $\delta_a : Q \to Q$ with $p \mapsto \delta(p, a)$. In this case, the reverse transition function δ^R can then be seen as a (partial) injective function $\delta^R : Q \times \Sigma \to Q$. A language is said to be *deterministically reversible* or for short *reversible* if there is a REV-DFA that accepts it. Finally, a REV-NFA (REV-DFA, respectively) is *minimal* among all REV-NFAs (REV-DFAs, respectively) if there is no equivalent REV-NFA (REV-DFA, respectively) with a smaller number of states. Both minimal REV-DFAs and minimal REV-NFAs are not isomorphic in general.

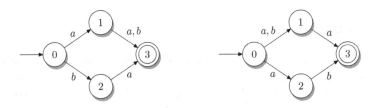

Fig. 1. A minimal NFA (left) and a minimal REV-NFA (right) for the finite language $L = \{aa, ab, ba\}$. Thus, L is a nondeterministically reversible language.

Example 1. Consider the finite language $L = \{aa, ab, ba\}$. A minimal NFA and a REV-NFA for this language are shown in Fig. 1. It is easy to see that the NFA shown is minimal. Obviously, this minimal NFA is *not* reversible, since it contains the irreversible state 3. Observe, that the REV-NFA is of same size as the minimal NFA. This is in contrast to minimal DFAs and REV-DFAs. Whenever the minimal DFA for a reversible language is not reversible, the minimal REV-DFA is of strictly larger size.   ∎

In [9] the following structural characterization of regular languages that can be accepted by REV-DFAs in terms of their minimal DFAs is given. The conditions of the characterization are illustrated in Fig. 2.

Theorem 2. *Let $A = (Q, \Sigma, \delta, q_0, F)$ be a minimal deterministic finite automaton. The language $L(A)$ can be accepted by a reversible deterministic finite automaton if and only if there do not exist useful states $p, q \in Q$, a letter $a \in \Sigma$, and a word $w \in \Sigma^*$ such that $p \neq q$, $\delta(p, a) = \delta(q, a)$, and $\delta(q, aw) = q$.*

3   Nondeterministic Reversible Finite Automata

As mentioned in the introduction, at a first glance, one may think that languages accepted by REV-NFAs are mirror images of languages accepted by deterministic finite automata. But, in general, the reversal of a REV-NFA language is not accepted by a deterministic finite automaton. Here the *reversal* of a language

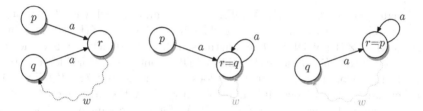

Fig. 2. The "forbidden pattern" of Theorem 2. The states p and q must be distinct, but state r could be equal to state p or state q. The situations where $r = q$ or $r = p$ are shown in the middle and on the right, respectively—here the word w and its corresponding path are grayed out because they are not relevant.

L is defined by $L^R = \{ w^R \in \Sigma^* \mid w \in L \}$, where w^R refers to the *reversal* of w. The mirror image of a word is inductively defined as $\lambda^R = \lambda$ and $(wa)^R = a(w^R)$, for $w \in \Sigma^*$ and $a \in \Sigma$. We find the following situation, where a *multiple-entry* DFA (MeDFA) is a 5-tuple $A = (Q, \Sigma, \delta, Q_0, F)$, with Q, Σ, δ, and F are as for ordinary DFAs and $Q_0 \subseteq Q$ is the set of initial states, and the language accepted by A is $L(A) = \bigcup_{q_0 \in Q_0} L(A_{q_0})$, where $A_q = (Q, \Sigma, \delta, q, F)$. The reversible variant of MeDFAs is referred to as REV-MeDFA.

Lemma 3. *Let $L \subseteq \Sigma^*$. The language L is accepted by a REV-NFA if and only if L^R is accepted by a multiple-entry DFA with a sole final state.* ☐

It is worth mentioning that multiple-entry DFAs were previously investigated in the literature [7,10,11,17], but the additional restriction to a sole final state makes it an almost unexplored automaton model. Next, we investigate the accepting power of REV-NFAs and later the closure properties of the family of all those languages accepted by REV-NFAs.

3.1   Computational Power

We consider the computational power of REV-NFAs compared to ordinary finite state automata. In general, the family of all languages accepted by automata of some type X will be denoted by $\mathscr{L}(X)$. Deterministic finite automata and their reversible variants were already considered in [9,16]. Here we first examine their relationships. Recall that reversible deterministic finite automata with one initial and one final state are called *bideterministic* [2,12]. Let $\mathscr{L}$(Bi-DFA) refer to the family of languages accepted by bideterministic finite automata and REG refer to the family of all regular languages.

Theorem 4. $\mathscr{L}(Bi\text{-}DFA) \subset \mathscr{L}(REV\text{-}DFA) \subset \mathscr{L}(REV\text{-}MeDFA) \subset REG.$

Proof. The inclusions are obvious. For the strictness of the first inclusion we use the characterization that a language L is accepted by a bideterministic finite automaton if and only if the minimal DFA of L is reversible and has a unique final state [16]. The strictness follows from the finite language $L = \lambda + a$. Since every finite language belongs to $\mathscr{L}$(REV-DFA), but the minimal DFA for L, although it is reversible, has two final states, L does not belong to $\mathscr{L}$(Bi-DFA). Thus, $\mathscr{L}$(Bi-DFA) $\subset \mathscr{L}$(REV-DFA). The strictness of the second inclusion is witnessed by the language $a^* + b^*$. Because the minimal DFA contains the forbidden pattern described in Theorem 2, this language does not belong to $\mathscr{L}$(REV-DFA). On the other hand, with a reversible multiple-entry DFA the language $a^* + b^*$ is easily acceptable by using the minimal DFAs for the languages a^* and b^* as sub-components. Therefore $\mathscr{L}$(REV-DFA) $\subset \mathscr{L}$(REV-MeDFA). Finally, in [16] it was shown that the regular language a^*b^* is not member of $\mathscr{L}$(REV-MeDFA). Therefore $\mathscr{L}$(REV-MeDFA) $\subset$ REG.   □

Before we investigate the computational power of REV-NFAs in detail we prove an important property of reversible automata if they accept unary words that are long enough.

Lemma 5. *Let $A = (Q, \Sigma, \delta, q_0, F)$ be an n-state REV-NFA and $a \in \Sigma$. If a unary word a^m, for $m \geq n$, is accepted by A, then it can be written as $a^m = a^i a^{m-i}$ for some $1 \leq i \leq m$ satisfying the conditions (i) $q_0 \in \delta(q_0, a^i)$ and (ii) $q_f \in \delta(q_0, a^{m-i})$ with $q_f \in F$. We may have $q_0 = q_f$, in particular this is the case if $i = m$. The statement remains valid in case A is a REV-DFA.*

Proof. Consider an accepting computation of A on input a^m. Let

$$q_0 = p_0, p_1, \ldots, p_{i-1}, p_i, p_{i+1}, \ldots, p_{k-1}, p_k, p_{k+1}, \ldots, p_{m-1}, p_m = q_f$$

with $q_f \in F$ be the sequence of states during the accepting computation under consideration, where $p_{j+1} \in \delta(p_j, a)$, for $0 \leq j < m$. Since $m \geq n$ at least one state in this sequence appears twice because of the pigeon hole principle. We take the first state p_i, for some $0 \leq i < m$, from the left in the sequence with this property. This means that all states p_j to the left of p_i, that is, $0 \leq j < i$, are different to all other states, that are the states to the right of p_i including state p_i, in the whole sequence. Since p_i appears twice, its counterpart is assumed to be state p_k with $i < k \leq m$.

Let p_i be the initial state q_0. Then we have found a loop pattern in the REV-NFA. This means that the word a^m can be written as $a^m = a^k a^{m-k}$ satisfying $1 \leq k \leq m$ and $q_k \in \delta(q_0, a^k)$ and $q_f \in \delta(q_k, a^{m-k})$ with $q_f \in F$. Note that $q_k = q_0$ by assumption. Now, let $1 \leq i < m$. Then as mentioned above both states p_{i-1} and p_{k-1} are different, but they satisfy $\delta(p_{i-1}, a) \ni p_i = p_k \in \delta(p_{k-1}, a)$, which means that p_i is irreversible. This is a contradiction to our assumption that A is a REV-NFA. Therefore, p_i must be the initial state and we have found the loop pattern as described above.   □

Now we are ready to investigate the computational power of the reversible automata we are interested in. We find the following situation.

Theorem 6. $\mathscr{L}(REV\text{-}DFA) \subset \mathscr{L}(REV\text{-}NFA) \subset REG.$

Proof. All inclusions are obvious by definition. Thus, their strictnesses remains to be shown: (1) For the strictness of the inclusion $\mathscr{L}(\text{REV-DFA}) \subseteq \mathscr{L}(\text{REV-NFA})$ we consider the infinite unary language $L = \{\lambda, a^2, a^3, \ldots\}$, which is the complement of the finite language $\{a\}$. A REV-NFA for the language L is depicted in Fig. 3. Note that in [3] it was shown that the complement of a non-empty finite unary language cannot be accepted by any REV-DFA. Therefore, L is *not* a reversible language. Thus, nondeterminism improves the accepting power of reversible finite state automata and therefore $\mathscr{L}(\text{REV-DFA}) \subset \mathscr{L}(\text{REV-NFA})$. (2) Next we show that the regular language $L = a^*b^*$ is not nondeterministically reversible. Assume in contrast to the assertion that there is a REV-NFA $A = (Q, \{a, b\}, \delta, q_0, F)$ that accepts L. Let n be the number of states of A. Then we apply Lemma 5 for the word a^n in L. Hence we find a loop-structure of the form $q_0 \in \delta(q_0, a^{i_1})$ and $q_{f_a} \in \delta(q_0, a^{n-i_1})$, for some state $q_{f_a} \in F$ and $1 \le i_1 \le n$. Applying Lemma 5 once again, but now for the word b^n, results in a loop-structure $\delta(q_0, b^{i_2})$ and $q_{f_b} \in \delta(q_0, b^{n-i_2})$, for some $1 \le i_2 \le n$ and state $q_{f_b} \in F$. Then we combine the computations of these two loops by first doing the computation on a^{i_1} leading from the initial state to q_0, followed by reading b^{i_2}, which leads us to q_0 again, followed by reading a^{i_1} and b^{n-i_2} which in turn leads to an accepting state q_{f_b} visiting q_0 in between. Hence the word $a^{i_1}b^{i_2}a^{i_1}b^{n-i_2}$ is accepted by A, which is a contradiction since all words in L are of the form a^*b^*. This shows that a^*b^* does not belong to $\mathscr{L}(\text{REV-NFA})$. Therefore, the inclusion $\mathscr{L}(\text{REV-NFA}) \subseteq \mathscr{L}(\text{NFA})$ is strict. $\qquad\square$

It remains to compare the families $\mathscr{L}(\text{REV-NFA})$ and $\mathscr{L}(\text{REV-MeDFA})$.

Fig. 3. A REV-NFA for the infinite unary language $L = \{\lambda, a^2, a^3, \ldots\}$. Thus L is a nondeterministically reversible language.

Theorem 7. *The families $\mathscr{L}(REV\text{-}NFA)$ and $\mathscr{L}(REV\text{-}MeDFA)$ are incomparable.*

Proof. The language $L = a^* + b^*$ belongs to $\mathscr{L}(\text{REV-MeDFA})$ as already argued in the proof of Theorem 4. We show that L cannot be accepted by any REV-NFA. To this end we argue as follows: Assume to the contrary that the language L is accepted by a REV-NFA $A = (Q, \{a, b\}, \delta, q_0, F)$. Let $n = |Q|$. Then we apply Lemma 5 for the word a^n in L. Hence we find a loop-structure of the form $q_0 \in \delta(q_0, a^{i_1})$ and $q_{f_a} \in \delta(q_0, a^{n-i_1})$, for some $1 \le i_1 \le n$ and $q_{f_a} \in F$. Applying Lemma 5 once again, but now for the word b^n, results in a loop-structure $\delta(q_0, b^{i_2})$ and $q_{f_b} \in \delta(q_0, b^{n-i_2})$, for some $1 \le i_2 \le n$ and state $q_{f_b} \in F$. Then we combine the computations of these two loops by first doing the computation on a^{i_1} leading from the initial state to q_0, followed by reading b^{i_2}, which leads us to q_0 again, and finally reading a^{n-i_1} moving to the final state q_{f_a}. Hence the word $a^{i_1} b^{i_2} a^{n-i_1}$ is accepted by A, which is a contradiction since all words in L are either in a^* or b^* only. Thus, $L \notin \mathscr{L}(\text{REV-NFA})$.

For the converse, we consider the language $L = ba + a^+ ba^*$ that is accepted by some REV-NFA. In order to show that L is not a member of $\mathscr{L}(\text{REV-MeDFA})$, a characterization of the languages accepted by reversible multiple-entry DFAs in terms of a forbidden pattern in the minimal DFA given in [16] is utilized. Here the details are omitted.   □

The inclusion structure of the language families accepted by variants of reversible finite automata is summarized in Fig. 4. Observe that $\mathscr{L}(\text{Bi-DFA})$ and FIN are incomparable, which can be seen by the languages a^* and $\lambda + a$.

In the remainder of this subsection we consider unary languages accepted by REV-NFAs in more detail. A unary language is said to be *cyclic* if it can be accepted by a DFA that consists of a loop only. It is known that unary REV-DFAs can only accept finite and

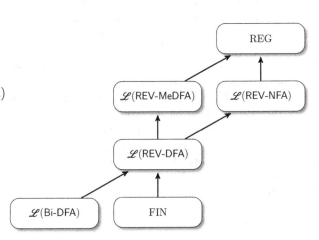

Fig. 4. Inclusion structure of the language families accepted by different variants of reversible finite automata in question. The arrows indicate strict inclusions. Language families not linked by a path are pairwise incomparable. Here FIN is the family of all finite languages and REG the family of all regular languages.

cyclic languages [3]. In particular this means that the complement of a non-empty finite unary language cannot be accepted by any REV-DFA. On the other hand, one can show that complements of unary finite languages are always accepted by REV-NFAs.

Theorem 8. *Let $L \subseteq \Sigma^*$ be a finite language, where Σ is a singleton set. Then the language L and its complement $\Sigma^* \backslash L$ are both accepted by REV-NFAs.*

Proof. Clearly, every finite language L is reversible and thus also nondeterministically reversible. It remains to be shown that $\Sigma^* \backslash L$ is also accepted by a REV-NFA, if Σ is a singleton set. Regardless whether Σ is a singleton set or not, it is easy to see that the language $\Sigma^* \backslash L$ can be written as

$$\Sigma^* \backslash L = \Sigma^{n+1} \Sigma^* \cup S, \tag{1}$$

where $n = \max\{\,|w| \mid w \in L\,\}$ and S is a finite set of words of length at most n. In fact, S is the complement of L with respect to the set Σ^n, that is, $S = \Sigma^n \backslash L$. Now let us assume without loss of generality that $\Sigma = \{a\}$. Let A be the REV-NFA $(Q, \{a\}, \delta, q_0, F)$ with $Q = \{0, 1, \dots, n\} \cup \{1', 2', \dots, (n+1)'\}$, initial state $q_0 = 0$, set of final states

$$F = \{\, i \mid 0 \le i \le n \text{ and } a^i \notin L \,\} \cup \{\, i' \mid 1 \le i \le n+1 \,\},$$

and the transition function

$$\delta(i, a) = \begin{cases} \{i+1\} & \text{if } 0 \le i < n \\ \{0\} \cup \{1'\} & \text{if } i = n \end{cases} \quad \text{and} \quad \delta(i', a) = \{(i+1)'\} \text{ if } 1 \le i < n+1.$$

The REV-NFA is depicted in Fig. 5. By construction all words a^i of length at most n with $a^i \notin L$ are accepted by A. Furthermore all words a^i are accepted by the accepting tail states, where i satisfies the condition

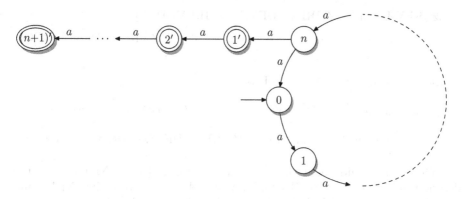

Fig. 5. A REV-NFA for a co-finite unary language that can be written as $\Sigma^{n+1}\Sigma^* \cup S$, where S is a finite set of words that are of length at most n. The loop-state i, for $0 \le i \le n$, is accepting if $a^i \in S$.

$$k \cdot (n+1) + n + 1 = (k+1) \cdot n + (k+1) \le i \le k \cdot (n+1) + n + (n+1) = (k+2) \cdot n + (k+1),$$

for $k \ge 0$. Note that

$$(k+2) \cdot n + (k+2) = ((k+1)+1) \cdot n + ((k+1)+1),$$

for every $k \ge 0$, which means that the described intervals for i are consecutive. Therefore, all unary words of length at least $n+1$ are accepted by the automaton. Hence, A accepts all words according to the description given in Eq. 1. $\square$

Although REV-NFAs are more powerful than REV-DFAs, the former automaton model is not able to accept all unary regular languages.

Theorem 9. *The unary regular language* $L = \{a\} \cup \{\, a^{2i} \mid i \ge 0 \,\}$ *cannot be accepted by any REV-NFA.* $\square$

3.2   On the Degree of Irreversibility

The degree of irreversibility of DFAs was introduced in [3]. For a DFA A the *degree of irreversibility* $d(A)$ is the number of irreversible states that are part of one of the forbidden patterns shown in Fig. 2. Observe, that since the DFAs need not to be complete and only contain useful states, the non-accepting sink state does not count for the degree of irreversibility. The hierarchy on regular languages that is induced by the irreversibility degree was studied in [3] in detail. Let

$$\text{IREV}_k\text{-DFA} = \{\, A \mid A \text{ is a DFA and } d(A) \leq k \,\},$$

for $k \geq 0$. Obviously this notion generalizes to NFAs as well. In this case we refer to the set of all NFAs with irreversibility degree at most k by IREV_k-NFA.

It was shown in [3] that

$$\mathcal{L}(\text{REV-DFA}) = \mathcal{L}(\text{IREV}_0\text{-DFA}) \subset \mathcal{L}(\text{IREV}_1\text{-DFA}) \subset \cdots$$
$$\cdots \subset \bigcup_{k \geq 0} \mathcal{L}(\text{IREV}_k\text{-DFA}) \subset \text{REG},$$

by the separating languages L_k, where

$$L_k = (aa^*bb^*)^{k/2} \quad \text{if } k \text{ is even, and} \quad L_k = (aa^*bb^*)^k aa^* \quad \text{if } k \text{ is odd,}$$

for $k \geq 0$. It turned out that $L_k \in \mathcal{L}(\text{IREV}_k\text{-DFA}) \backslash \mathcal{L}(\text{IREV}_{k-1}\text{-DFA})$, for $k \geq 1$.

What can be said about the language families $\mathcal{L}(\text{IREV}_k\text{-NFA})$? As in the deterministic case we have $\text{IREV}_0\text{-NFA} = \{\, A \mid A \text{ is a reversible NFA} \,\}$ and thus the equality $\mathcal{L}(\text{IREV}_0\text{-NFA}) = \mathcal{L}(\text{REV-NFA})$ holds. Moreover, by definition the inclusion $\text{IREV}_k\text{-NFA} \subseteq \text{IREV}_{k+1}\text{-NFA}$ follows and, therefore, the corresponding language classes satisfy $\mathcal{L}(\text{IREV}_k\text{-NFA}) \subseteq \mathcal{L}(\text{IREV}_{k+1}\text{-NFA})$, for $k \geq 0$. Since a^*b^* is not a member of $\mathcal{L}(\text{REV-NFA})$ which was shown in the proof of Theorem 6 we have

$$\mathcal{L}(\text{REV-NFA}) = \mathcal{L}(\text{IREV}_0\text{-NFA}) \subset \mathcal{L}(\text{IREV}_1\text{-NFA})$$

since already the minimal DFA for the language in question has irreversibility degree one. Next we consider the hierarchy on regular languages induced by the irreversibility degree of NFAs, which is tight and infinite.

Theorem 10. *For all $k \geq 0$, $\mathcal{L}(IREV_k\text{-}NFA) \subset \mathcal{L}(IREV_{k+1}\text{-}NFA)$.*

Proof. The strict inclusion $\mathcal{L}(\text{IREV}_0\text{-NFA}) \subset \mathcal{L}(\text{IREV}_1\text{-NFA})$ is shown above. Now let $k \geq 2$ and define $\Sigma_k = \{a_1, a_2, \ldots, a_k\}$. Now consider the languages L_k over the alphabet Σ_k defined as

$$L_k = a_1^* + a_2^* + \cdots + a_k^*.$$

The language L_k, for $k \geq 2$, is accepted by the DFA $A_k = (Q_k, \Sigma_k, \delta_k, q_0, F)$, with $Q = \{0, 1, \ldots, k\}$, $q_0 = 0$, $F = \{0, 1, \ldots, k\}$, and

$$\delta_k(0, a_i) = i \quad \text{and} \quad \delta_k(i, a_i) = i,$$

for $1 \leq i \leq k$. By construction the DFA A_k has k irreversible states.

In order to prove our statement it remains to be shown that k irreversible states are needed for the language L_k, even when considering NFAs. Assume to the contrary that there is an NFA $B_k = (Q, \Sigma_k, \delta, q_0, F)$, that accepts L_k with strictly less than k irreversible states. Then for every letter a_i in Σ_k we can find a state p of B_k that is different from the initial state and, moreover, is irreversible, and three natural numbers i_1, i_2, i_3 such that (i) $p \in \delta(q_0, a_i^{i_1})$ with $i_1 \geq 1$, (ii) $p \in \delta(p, a_i^{i_2})$ with $i_2 \geq 1$, and (iii) $\delta(p, a_i^{i_3}) \cap F \neq \emptyset$. This is seen as follows: Let n be the number of states of B_k. Consider an accepting computation on the word a^n, for $a \in \Sigma_k$. Let

$$q_0 = p_0, p_1, \ldots, p_{i-1}, p_i, p_{i+1}, \ldots, p_{j-1}, p_j, p_{j+1}, \ldots, p_{n-1}, p_n = q_f$$

with $q_f \in F$ be the sequence of states during the accepting computation under consideration, where $p_{i+1} \in \delta(p_i, a)$, for $0 \leq i < n$. Since $n + 1$ states appear in the sequence, at least one state appears twice. We choose the first state p_i, for some $0 \leq i < n$, from the left in the sequence with this property. Let p_j be a repetition of p_i, that is, $p_j = p_i$. Our choice of p_i means that all states to the left of p_i are different to all other states, that are the states to the right of p_i including state p_i, in the whole sequence. Thus, $p_i \in \delta(q_0, a^i)$, $p_i \in \delta(p_i, a^{j-i})$, and $q_f \in \delta(p_i, a^{n-j})$.

If p_i is the initial state, then the automaton B_k accepts words that do not belong to L_k by first reading letters a until the state p_i is reached (which is the initial state), and then reading some letters different from a. We conclude that state p_i cannot be the initial state of B_k. Thus, $i \geq 1$ and moreover $j - i \geq 1$. This implies that p_i is an irreversible state, since two different states p_{i-1} and p_{j-1} map to p_i by reading the same letter a. Thus, we have found a state p_i and three natural numbers $(i, j - i, n - j)$ satisfying (i) $p_i \in \delta(q_0, a^i)$ with $i \geq 1$, (ii) $p_i \in \delta(p_i, a^{j-i})$ with $j - i \geq 1$, and (iii) $\delta(p_i, a^{n-j}) \cap F \neq \emptyset$.

Since this argumentation applies to all letters from Σ_k, we now have k irreversible states $q_1, q_2, \ldots, q_k$ each of which is associated with three naturals numbers

$$(i_1, j_1, \ell_1,), (i_2, j_2, \ell_2), \ldots, (i_k, j_k, \ell_k)$$

satisfying the above mentioned conditions. Let q_i be the state that is induced by the letter a_i, for $1 \leq i \leq k$. Since B_k has strictly less than k irreversible states, at least two of these states must be the same. Assume without loss of generality that q_1 is the same as q_2. But then the automaton B_k accepts words that do not belong to the language L_k, because the word $a_1^{i_1} a_2^{j_2 + \ell_2}$ with $j_2 \geq 1$ is accepted by the computation $p_1 \in \delta(q_0, a_1^{i_1})$ which is equal to state p_2, continued by $p_2 \in \delta(p_2, a_2^{j_2})$ and finally by $\delta(p_2, a_2^{\ell_2}) \cap F \neq \emptyset$. This is a contradiction to our assumption that B_k has strictly less than k irreversible states and shows $L_k \in \mathscr{L}(\text{IREV}_k\text{-NFA}) \setminus \mathscr{L}(\text{IREV}_{k-1}\text{-NFA})$, for $k \geq 2$. $\qquad\square$

Finally, we consider the relation between languages accepted by deterministic and nondeterministic finite automata with respect to the degree of irreversibility.

Theorem 11. *For all $k \geq 0$, we have*

$$\mathscr{L}(REV\text{-}NFA) \setminus \mathscr{L}(IREV_k\text{-}DFA) \neq \emptyset.$$

Proof. As already mentioned above, the languages L_k where

$$L_k = (aa^*bb^*)^{k/2} \quad \text{if } k \text{ is even, and} \quad L_k = (aa^*bb^*)^k aa^* \quad \text{if } k \text{ is odd,}$$

for $k \geq 0$, separate $\mathscr{L}(\text{IREV}_k\text{-DFA})$ from $\mathscr{L}(\text{IREV}_{k-1}\text{-DFA})$, for $k \geq 1$, [3].

Next we turn to show that L_k, for $k \geq 0$, is accepted by a REV-NFA. Let $A_k = (Q_k, \{a, b\}, \delta_k, q_0, F_k)$ with $Q_k = \{1, 2, \ldots, k+1\}$, $q_0 = 1$, $F_k = \{k+1\}$, and $\delta(i, a) = \{i, i+1\}$ if i is odd and $1 \leq i < k+1$, and $\delta(i, b) = \{i, i+1\}$ if i is even and $1 \leq i < k+1$. By construction the NFA A_k is reversible and accepts the language L_k. This shows that $L_k \in \mathscr{L}(\text{REV-NFA}) \setminus \mathscr{L}(\text{IREV}_k\text{-DFA})$, for $k \geq 1$, and our stated claim follows. $\qquad\square$

As immediate consequence of the previous proof we obtain the following corollary.

Corollary 12. *For all $k \geq 0$, $\mathscr{L}(IREV_k\text{-}DFA) \subset \mathscr{L}(IREV_k\text{-}NFA)$.* $\qquad\square$

Moreover, the levels of irreversibility of deterministic and nondeterministic finite automata which are off by one are incomparable.

Theorem 13. *The families $\mathscr{L}(IREV_{k+1}\text{-}DFA)$ and $\mathscr{L}(IREV_k\text{-}NFA)$ are incomparable, for $k \geq 0$.*

Proof. The fact $\mathscr{L}(\text{IREV}_k\text{-NFA}) \setminus \mathscr{L}(\text{IREV}_{k+1}\text{-DFA}) \neq \emptyset$ is shown in Theorem 11. For $k \geq 1$, the language used in the proof of Theorem 10 shows $\mathscr{L}(\text{IREV}_{k+1}\text{-DFA}) \setminus \mathscr{L}(\text{IREV}_k\text{-NFA}) \neq \emptyset$. For the remaining case $k = 0$ we take the language $a^*b^* \in \mathscr{L}(\text{IREV}_1\text{-DFA}) \setminus \mathscr{L}(\text{IREV}_0\text{-NFA})$. Hence the language families are incomparable. $\qquad\square$

3.3 Closure Properties of REV-NFA Languages

Next we consider the closure properties of the language families accepted by finite automata. Most closure properties of $\mathscr{L}(\text{REV-DFA})$, except for inverse homomorphism, λ-free homomorphism, and intersection with regular sets, were studied in [3] in the context of the degree of reversibility. The results are summarized in Table 1. Interestingly, although $\mathscr{L}(\text{REV-DFA})$ and $\mathscr{L}(\text{REV-NFA})$ are different language families, they share the same closure properties. We start with the union and the concatenation operations. The family $\mathscr{L}(\text{REV-DFA})$ is not closed under both of these operations [3]. The same is true for the nondeterministic variant.

Table 1. Closure properties of the language families $\mathscr{L}$(REV-DFA) and $\mathscr{L}$(REV-NFA). The results on $\mathscr{L}$(REV-DFA), except for inverse homomorphism, λ-free homomorphism, and intersection with regular sets, can be found in [3].

Operation	Language family	
	$\mathscr{L}$(REV-DFA)	$\mathscr{L}$(REV-NFA)
Union	No	No
Intersection	Yes	Yes
Inverse homomorphism	Yes	Yes
λ-free homomorphism	No	No
Intersection with regular sets	No	No
Complementation	No	No
Concatenation	No	No
Kleene star	No	No

Theorem 14. *The language family $\mathscr{L}(REV\text{-}NFA)$ is not closed under union or concatenation.*

Proof. Let $L_1 = a^*$ and $L_2 = b^*$ which are obviously nondeterministically reversible. But neither the union of L_1 and L_2 nor the concatenation of L_1 and L_2 can be accepted by any REV-NFA. The former was shown in the proof of Theorem 7, while the latter was proven in the proof of Theorem 6. Thus, $\mathscr{L}$(REV-NFA) is not closed under union and concatenation. □

Now we draw our attention to the complementation. In [3] it was shown that the complementation of every non-empty unary finite language is *not* accepted by any REV-DFA. This shows the non-closure of $\mathscr{L}$(REV-DFA) under complementation because every finite language is a reversible language. On the other hand, we have already shown in the previous subsection that complements of unary finite languages are always accepted by REV-NFAs. Thus, with these languages one cannot disprove the closure under complementation. In the next theorem we show that $\mathscr{L}$(REV-NFA) is not closed under complementation by using a very simple but non-unary language.

Theorem 15. *The language family $\mathscr{L}(REV\text{-}NFA)$ is not closed under complementation.*

Proof. Consider the language $L = a^*b^*$, which was shown in the proof of Theorem 6 to be *not* accepted by any REV-NFA. The REV-NFA

$$A = (Q, \{a, b\}, \delta, q_0, F)$$

with the set of states $Q = \{0, 1, 2\}$, the initial state $q_0 = 0$, the set of final states $F = \{2\}$, and the transition function $\delta(0, a) = \{0\}$, $\delta(0, b) = \{0, 1\}$, $\delta(1, a) = \{1, 2\}$, and $\delta(2, b) = \{2\}$ accepts the complement of L. This is seen as follows.

The automaton A is depicted on the left of Fig. 6. The DFA built by the powerset construction from A is drawn on the right of Fig. 6. By interchanging accepting and non-accepting states of the DFA one obtains a DFA for the language a^*b^*, which can be easily verified. Thus, the REV-NFA A accepts the complement of the language under consideration. Therefore, the language family $\mathscr{L}$(REV-NFA) is *not* closed under complementation.   □

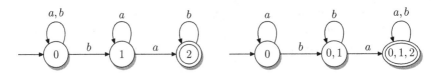

Fig. 6. A REV-NFA (left) and a DFA (right) both accepting the complement of the language a^*b^*. The DFA is built by the powerset construction from the REV-NFA.

Note that the language a^*b^* and its complement cannot be accepted by any REV-DFA, which can easily be seen by applying Theorem 2 to the DFA and its complement from Fig. 6. As an immediate consequence we obtain the non-closure of both $\mathscr{L}$(REV-DFA) and $\mathscr{L}$(REV-NFA) under intersection with regular sets using the reversible language $\{a, b\}^*$ and the regular set a^*b^*.

Corollary 16. *Both families $\mathscr{L}$(REV-DFA) and $\mathscr{L}$(REV-DFA) are not* closed *under intersection with regular sets.*   □

Up to now we have only seen non-closure results. But restricting the intersection to reversible and nondeterministically reversible languages, respectively, we obtain the following result. The intersection closure of $\mathscr{L}$(REV-DFA) was shown in [3].

Theorem 17. *The language family $\mathscr{L}$(REV-NFA) is closed under intersection.*
□

Next we take a closer look on homomorphisms. Since homomorphisms were not covered for REV-DFAs yet, we consider them here as well.

Theorem 18. *The families $\mathscr{L}$(REV-DFA) and $\mathscr{L}$(REV-NFA) are not* closed *under λ-free homomorphisms.*   □

For inverse homomorphisms we obtain the closure under inverse homomorphisms.

Theorem 19. *The families $\mathscr{L}$(REV-DFA) and $\mathscr{L}$(REV-NFA) are closed under inverse homomorphisms.*   □

Finally we consider the Kleene star operation. Again we find a non-closure result. Here we utilize our characterization of REV-NFA languages in terms of multiple-entry DFAs with a sole final state as shown in Theorem 2.

Theorem 20. *The family $\mathscr{L}(REV\text{-}NFA)$ is* not *closed under Kleene star.*

Proof. We consider the language $L = (aa + aaa + bb + bbb)^*$ as witness for the assertion. Since $\{aa + aaa + bb + bbb\}$ is finite, it is accepted by some REV-NFA. So, it remains to be shown that L is not accepted by any REV-NFA.

In contrast to the assertion assume that L belongs to $\mathscr{L}(\text{REV-NFA})$. Since L is closed under reversal, that is, $L = L^R$, by Lemma 3 there exists a multiple-entry DFA with a sole accepting state $A = (Q, \{a, b\}, \delta, Q_0, \{q_f\})$ that accepts L. Since $\lambda \in L$ we conclude that $q_f \in Q_0$. Moreover, since neither a nor b do belong to L, we know that $\delta(q_f, a) \neq q_f$ as well as $\delta(q_f, b) \neq q_f$.

Starting the computation in some initial state on arbitrarily long unary inputs of the form a^+ or b^+ drives automaton A either into loops that do not contain the accepting state q_f, or into loops that do contain state q_f. Since all these unary words longer than one have to be accepted, there are at least one initial state $q_i \in Q_0$ and numbers $k_a, \ell_a \geq 2$ such that $\delta(q_i, a^{k_a}) = q_f$ and $\delta(q_f, a^{\ell_a}) = q_f$. Similarly, there are at least one initial state $q_j \in Q_0$ and numbers $k_b, \ell_b \geq 2$ such that $\delta(q_j, b^{k_b}) = q_f$ and $\delta(q_f, b^{\ell_b}) = q_f$.

Now we consider an infinite sequence of words belonging to L defined as

$$a^{\ell_a+1}, a^{\ell_a+1}b^{\ell_b+1}, a^{\ell_a+1}b^{\ell_b+1}a^{\ell_a+1}, a^{\ell_a+1}b^{\ell_b+1}a^{\ell_a+1}b^{\ell_b+1}, \ldots$$

Let $q \in Q_0$ be an initial state such that A accepts one of these words when starting in q. Then none of the other words are accepted when A starts the computation in q. In order to give evidence of this claim, let w_1 be a word in the sequence such that $\delta(q, w_1) = q_f$. Say that w_1 ends with a^{ℓ_a+1}. Then we consider any longer word in the sequence, say

$$w_2 = w_1(b^{\ell_b+1}a^{\ell_a+1})^i b^{\ell_b+1}, \quad \text{for } i \geq 0, \quad \text{or} \quad w_2 = w_1(b^{\ell_b+1}a^{\ell_a+1})^i, \quad \text{for } i \geq 1.$$

Assume $\delta(q, w_2) = q_f$. Since $\delta(q, w_1) = q_f$ we conclude

$$\delta(q_f, (b^{\ell_b+1}a^{\ell_a+1})^i b^{\ell_b+1}) = q_f \quad \text{or} \quad \delta(q_f, (b^{\ell_b+1}a^{\ell_a+1})^i) = q_f.$$

However, since $\delta(q_f, b^{\ell_b}) = q_f$, we have

$$\delta(q_f, ba^{\ell_a+1}(b^{\ell_b+1}a^{\ell_a+1})^{i-1}b^{\ell_b+1}) = q_f \quad \text{or} \quad \delta(q_f, ba^{\ell_a+1}(b^{\ell_b+1}a^{\ell_a+1})^{i-1}) = q_f,$$

a contradiction since neither b nor a may appear alone in any word of L. So, in order to accept all of the words, an infinite number of initial states would be necessary. This shows that L is not accepted by any multiple-entry DFA with a sole accepting state and, thus, not accepted by any REV-NFA. □

4 Conclusions

We have investigated the accepting power of REV-NFAs. These automata are a straightforward generalization of REV-DFAs, which were recently investigated in [3,9,13]. It turned out that REV-NFAs are strictly more powerful than REV-DFAs. Moreover, their relation to other reversible finite state models are studied. Further aspects such as the degree of irreversibility and closure properties of the language family induced by REV-NFAs is investigated, too. Reversible NFAs are a natural host for further research questions. For instance, can we develop characterization of minimal REV-NFAs? Recently, this task was considered for REV-DFAs in [13], where conditions were found that characterize the class of regular languages that admit several non-isomorphic minimal REV-DFAs.

References

1. Ambainis, A., Freivalds, R.: 1-way quantum finite automata: strengths, weakness and generalizations. In: Motwani, R. (ed.) Foundations of Computer Science (FOCS 1998), pp. 332–341. IEEE Computer Society (1998)
2. Angluin, D.: Inference of reversible languages. J. ACM **29**, 741–765 (1982)
3. Axelsen, H.B., Holzer, M., Kutrib, M.: The degree of irreversibility in deterministic finite automata. In: Han, Y.-S., Salomaa, K. (eds.) CIAA 2016. LNCS, vol. 9705, pp. 15–26. Springer, Cham (2016). doi:10.1007/978-3-319-40946-7_2
4. Axelsen, H.B., Glück, R.: A simple and efficient universal reversible turing machine. In: Dediu, A.-H., Inenaga, S., Martín-Vide, C. (eds.) LATA 2011. LNCS, vol. 6638, pp. 117–128. Springer, Heidelberg (2011). doi:10.1007/978-3-642-21254-3_8
5. Bennett, C.H.: Logical reversibility of computation. IBM J. Res. Dev. **17**, 525–532 (1973)
6. García, P., de Parga, M.V., López, D.: On the efficient construction of quasi-reversible automata for reversible languages. Inform. Process. Lett. **107**, 13–17 (2008)
7. Gill, A., Kou, L.T.: Multiple-entry finite automata. J. Comput. System Sci. **9**, 1–19 (1974)
8. Harrison, M.A.: Introduction to Formal Language Theory. Addison-Wesley, Boston (1978)
9. Holzer, M., Jakobi, S., Kutrib, M.: Minimal reversible deterministic finite automata. In: Potapov, I. (ed.) DLT 2015. LNCS, vol. 9168, pp. 276–287. Springer, Cham (2015). doi:10.1007/978-3-319-21500-6_22
10. Holzer, M., Salomaa, K., Yu, S.: On the state complexity of k-entry deterministic finite automata. J. Autom. Lang. Comb. **6**, 453–466 (2001)
11. Kappes, M.: Descriptional complexity of deterministic finite automata with multiple initial states. J. Autom. Lang. Comb. **5**, 265–278 (2000)
12. Kobayashi, S., Yokomori, T.: Learning approximately regular languages with reversible languages. Theoret. Comput. Sci. **174**, 251–257 (1997)
13. Lavado, G.J., Pighizzini, G., Prigioniero, L.: Minimal and reduced reversible automata. In: Câmpeanu, C., Manea, F., Shallit, J. (eds.) DCFS 2016. LNCS, vol. 9777, pp. 168–179. Springer, Cham (2016). doi:10.1007/978-3-319-41114-9_13
14. Lombardy, S.: On the construction of reversible automata for reversible languages. In: Widmayer, P., Eidenbenz, S., Triguero, F., Morales, R., Conejo, R., Hennessy, M. (eds.) ICALP 2002. LNCS, vol. 2380, pp. 170–182. Springer, Heidelberg (2002). doi:10.1007/3-540-45465-9_16

15. Morita, K., Shirasaki, A., Gono, Y.: A 1-tape 2-symbol reversible Turing machine. Trans. IEICE **E72**, 223–228 (1989)
16. Pin, J.-E.: On reversible automata. In: Simon, I. (ed.) LATIN 1992. LNCS, vol. 583, pp. 401–416. Springer, Heidelberg (1992). doi:10.1007/BFb0023844
17. Veloso, P.A.S., Gill, A.: Some remarks on multiple-entry finite automata. J. Comput. System Sci. **18**, 304–306 (1979)

Capacitive-Based Adiabatic Logic

Ayrat Galisultanov, Yann Perrin, Hervé Fanet, and Gaël Pillonnet$^{(\boxtimes)}$

University Grenoble Alpes, CEA, LETI, 38000 Grenoble, France
gael.pillonnet@cea.fr

Abstract. This paper introduces a new paradigm to implement logic gates based on variable capacitance components instead of transistor elements. Using variable capacitors and Bennett clocking, this new logic family is able to discriminate logic states and cascade combinational logic operations. In order to demonstrate this, we use the capacitive voltage divider circuit with the variable capacitor modulated by an input bias state to the set output state. We propose the design of a four-terminal capacitive element which is the building block of this new logic family. Finally, we build a Verilog-A model of an electrically-actuated MEMS capacitive element and analyze the energy transfer and losses within this device during adiabatic actuation. The proposed model will be used for capacitive-based adiabatic logic circuit design and analysis, including construction of reversible gates.

Keywords: Adiabatic logic · Capacitive-based adiabatic logic · Variable capacitor · Electromechanics · MEMS · NEMS

1   Introduction

Field-effect transistor (FET) scaling is probably not a long-term answer to dramatically increase the energy-efficiency of logical computation. Therefore, a trade-off between the leakage and conduction losses still exists at each CMOS technology node: the energy per operation can be minimized using an appropriate supply voltage and operating frequency. However, despite the nanoscale transistor size, the lowest dissipation per operation is nowadays a few decades higher than the theoretical limit introduced by Landauer [1,2]. Even though Landauer's theory is still being discussed, it is possible to decrease the energy required to implement the logical operation at the hardware level. Adiabatic logic based on FET has been introduced to alleviate this inherent trade-off and reduce the conduction loss [3]. By smoothing transitions between logic states, the charge and discharge of the FET gate capacitance C through the FET channel resistance R of the previous stage is lowered by a factor of $\frac{2RC}{T}$, where T is the ramp duration. But there is still a reduction limit factor due to the FET threshold voltage V_{TH}. This non-adiabatic part of the conduction limit remains equal to $\frac{CV_{TH}^2}{2}$. On the other hand, adiabatic operation reduces the operation frequency and magnifies the FET leakage loss. Even if the energy per operation

© Springer International Publishing AG 2017
I. Phillips and H. Rahaman (Eds.): RC 2017, LNCS 10301, pp. 52–65, 2017.
DOI: 10.1007/978-3-319-59936-6_4

is slightly reduced, by only a factor of ten, there is still a trade-off between the non-adiabatic conduction and leakage loss. This therefore limits the interest of FET-based adiabatic logic.

To suppress the leakage, electromechanical relays have been used in the literature [4]. As they are based on metal-metal contact instead of a semiconductor junction, the leakage becomes almost negligible [5]. The Shockley law, which basically links the on-state resistance and leakage in the off-region, is not valid in relay devices as it is based on electrical contact between two plates [6]. Moreover, the main bottleneck of the relay-based adiabatic logic is the mechanical reliability of devices [7,8]. To overcome these limitations, we propose a new logic family called Capacitive-based Adiabatic Logic (CAL) [9]. By substituting relays with variable capacitors, this approach avoids electrical contact. Mechanical contact between the electrodes is then no longer required. For this reason, CAL could be more reliable compared to electromechanical relays.

The first section of this paper presents an overview of the new logic family, at the gate-level. We focus on buffer, inverter, and AND and OR gates, operated using Bennett clocking. These gates (excluding the NOT gate) are irreversible, but we also suppose that CAL could be used for reversible gates construction. Next, we address the question of the cascadability of CAL gates, and a solution to implement the elementary CAL device based on MEMS technology is proposed. Finally, we analyze the energy transfer and losses within this device.

2   Buffer and Inverter Functions in CAL

CMOS-based adiabatic logic circuits basically operate with two types of architecture: the quasi adiabatic pipeline and Bennett clocking. Power supplies called power clocks (PC's) are quite different for these two architectures. In a pipeline architecture, a four-phase power supply is used. The logic state is received from the previous gate during the evaluate interval, then transmitted to the next gate during the hold interval. In the recovery stage, the electrical energy stored in the capacitor of the next gate is recovered. The symmetrical idle phase is added for reasons of cascadability. In order to guarantee constant output signal from the previous gate during the evaluation stage, a 90° phase shift between subsequent PC's is needed.

The second type of PC is called Bennett clocking. Here, the power supply voltage of the current gate increases and decreases only when the inputs are stable, as presented in Fig. 1(a). In this work, we use Bennett clocking in order to avoid problems with maintaining the signal during the hold interval in the pipeline architecture [2]. The CAL can also be operated in 4-phase PC's, but it is out the scope of this paper.

As the PC provides an AC signal, the resistive elements (transistors) in a voltage divider circuit can be replaced by capacitive ones. In CAL, we keep the FET transistor notations, i.e. the input voltage is applied between the gate (G) and the ground. These two terminals are isolated from the drain (D) and source (S) terminals, which form output with a capacitance C_{DS}. Let us consider the capacitive divider circuit presented in Fig. 1(b). In the first assumption,

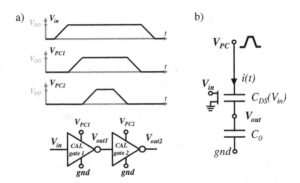

Fig. 1. Schematics depicting (a) the Bennett clocking principle, and (b) the capacitive voltage divider circuit.

$C_{DS}(V_{in})$ is a variable capacitor which depends only on the input voltage V_{in}. The fixed capacitor C_0 is the equivalent load of the next gate(s) and the interconnections. The output voltage is defined by the capacitance ratio and the PC voltage $V_{PC}(t)$ such that:

$$V_{out}(t) = \frac{C_{DS}(V_{in})}{C_0 + C_{DS}(V_{in})} V_{PC}(t). \tag{1}$$

In this and the next section, the voltages are normalized to the maximum voltage reached by the PC, V_{PCmax}, i.e. voltages range from 0 to 1. Two limiting cases emerge which are:

– when $C_{DS} \gg C_0$, the output voltage value is close to one;
– when $C_{DS} \ll C_0$, the output voltage value is close to zero.

Thus, with an appropriate $C_{DS}(V_{in})$ characteristic, the output voltage can be triggered by V_{in}. A particular electromechanical implementation of this variable capacitor will be discussed later.

There are two possible behaviors of capacitance as a function of the input voltage. The curve $C_{DS}(V_{in})$ can have a positive or negative slope, as presented in Fig. 2(a). The former case is called positive variation capacitance (PVC) and the latter, negative variation capacitance (NVC). The low and high-capacitance values are denoted C_L and C_H, respectively. PVC and NVC voltage-controlled capacitors could play the same role in CAL as NMOS and PMOS in FET-based logic. According to (1), the load capacitance C_0 is a critical parameter in the design of cascadable gates. In order to minimize the low logic state and maximize the high logic state, the load capacitance must satisfy the following condition:

$$C_0 = \sqrt{C_L C_H}. \tag{2}$$

For electrical modeling purposes, we assume that the capacitances of PVC and NVC blocks are given by (3) and (4), respectively.

$$C_{DS}(V_{in}) = \frac{C_H + C_L}{2} + \left(\frac{C_H - C_L}{2}\right) \tanh\left(a(V_{in} - V_T)\right) \tag{3}$$

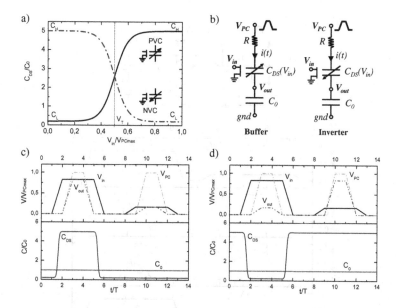

Fig. 2. (a) $C(V)$ characteristics and symbols for PVC (solid line) and NVC (dash-dot line) capacitors. (b) Electrical schematics of simple CAL buffer (left) and inverter (right) circuits. (c-d) Spice-simulated input and output signals (first graph), C_{DS} and C_0 (second graph) of the buffer (c) and inverter (d) gates over time. For (a), (c) and (d), we used the following parameters: $C_L = 0.2$ pF, $C_H = 5$ pF, $C_0 = 1$ pF, $V_{PCmax} = 1$ V, $V_T = 0.5$ V, $a = 10$ V^{-1}, $V_{inmax} = 0.83$ V, $R = 1$ kΩ, $T = 100$ ns.

$$C_{DS}(V_{in}) = \frac{C_H + C_L}{2} - \left(\frac{C_H - C_L}{2}\right) \tanh\left(a(V_{in} - V_T)\right) \qquad (4)$$

In (3) and (4), V_T is the threshold voltage and a is a positive parameter that defines the slope of the $C_{DS}(V_{in})$ curve.

Buffer and inverter logic gates can be implemented using a capacitive voltage divider containing a variable capacitor. CAL buffer and inverter circuits are shown in Fig. 2(b). Relation (1) is true for buffer and inverter circuits only if the voltage drop in the series resistance is small, and generally this is the case in adiabatic logic. The results of electrical simulation of a buffer and an inverter are presented in Fig. 2(c) and (d), respectively. With the set of parameters arbitrarily chosen here, the logic states can easily be identified in the output. In order to imitate the cascade of elements, the high and low values of the input voltage are set equal to the high and low values of the output voltage.

The ratio $\frac{C_H}{C_L}$ needs to be maximized in order to clearly identify the logic states. For example, for a buffer gate with a capacitance ratio of about 25, the minimal output voltage is equal to 0.17 and the maximal output voltage is equal to 0.83 (cf. Fig. 2(c)). With a capacitance ratio of about 4, these voltages become 0.33 and 0.66, respectively.

a)

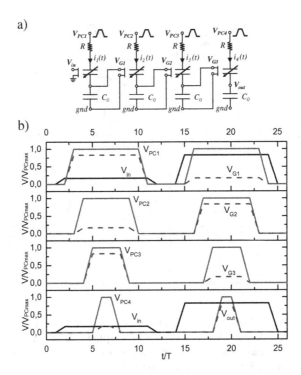

b)

Fig. 3. (a) The cascade of 4 inverters. (b) Spice-simulated: input voltage V_{in}, V_{PC1}, output of the first inverter V_{G1} (first graph), V_{PC2}, output of the second inverter V_{G2} (second graph), V_{PC3}, output of the third inverter V_{G3} (third graph), input voltage V_{in}, V_{PC4}, output voltage of the fourth inverter V_{out} (fourth graph) over time. The model parameters are the same as in Fig. 2.

To prove the ability of CAL to process and transfer logic states through N logic gates, we investigated the cascading of the 4 inverters presented in Fig. 3(a). Here, we use Bennett clocking and assume that the input capacitance of the next gate C_0 is constant. It should be noted that from an energy point of view, this hypothesis is inaccurate as it does not take into account the work of electrical force (see later). The binary input logic word is "0 1". The input voltage levels are the same as in the previous simulation. The results of electrical simulation of the 4 cascaded inverters are shown in Fig. 3(b). We compare the PC signal and the output voltage of each gate. As expected, the input logic word has been transmitted through the 4 inverters. In addition, the amplitude of the output signal is the same as the amplitude of the input signal.

3   Implementation of AND and OR Gates in CAL

The possible realizations of AND and OR gates based on PVC elements are shown in Fig. 4(a). The parameters of the circuits are the same as in the previous calculations. The simulated evolution of the output voltage of an AND gate is given in Fig. 4(b) as a function of the input voltage over time. As expected, the output reaches a high level only if both AND gate inputs are high. However, the third graph of Fig. 4(b) shows that the output voltage for low-low and high-high inputs decreases compared to the case of the buffer examined above. For example, the high level output voltage drops from 0.83 to 0.7. This is due to the decrease of the equivalent capacitance, caused by the series connection of the two variable capacitors C_{DS1} and C_{DS2}.

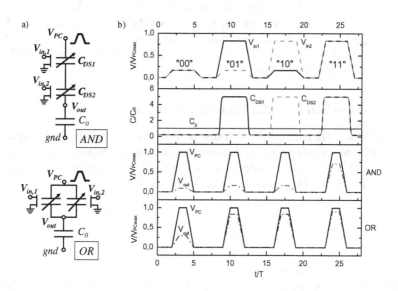

Fig. 4. (a) AND and OR gate circuits. (b) Evolution of the input voltages (first graph), capacitances (second graph), PC and output voltage for AND (third graph) and OR (fourth graph) gates over time.

We now examine the case of an OR gate. The corresponding output voltage is reported in the fourth graph of Fig. 4(b). A high output is reached when one or both inputs are high. In contrast with the case of the AND gate, the output voltage for low-low and high-high inputs is now higher than for the case of the buffer. The low level output voltage for low-low inputs rises from 0.17 to 0.3. This is due to the increase of the equivalent capacitance, caused by the connection in parallel of the two variable capacitors C_{DS1} and C_{DS2}.

Serial and parallel connection of variable capacitors reduces the difference between low and high logic states. This could be an issue for CAL operation. The same limitation applies to the quantity of gates, N, connected to the output, i.e. for fan-out operation. Total value of the load capacitance should be in the range of the variation of the variable capacitor C_{DS}, i.e.:

$$C_L < NC_0 < C_H. \tag{5}$$

4 Electromechanical Model of a Four-Terminal Variable Capacitor Element

The key challenge of CAL development is being able to define the scalable hardware necessary to implement the elementary PVC and NVC devices. The capacitor value can be modulated by the variation of relative permittivity, plate surface and gap thickness. In principle, there are a wide range of available actuators to realize this modulation: magnetic, piezoelectric, electrostatic, etc. For further analysis, we selected electrostatic actuators as electrostatic MEMS relays for scaling with sub-1-volt operation [6], as a possibility for the integration of the MEMS relays in VSLI circuits has already been demonstrated [4]. The basic electromechanical device of CAL consists of the two electrically-isolated and mechanically-coupled capacitors.

4.1 Two-Terminal Parallel Plate Transducer

Let us consider a 1D parallel-plate transducer model of a gap-variable capacitor with an initial air-filled gap g_0, equivalent mass m and equivalent spring constant k. The electromechanical transducer model in up-state position is shown in the left part of Fig. 5(a). The up-state capacitance equals:

$$C_{G\_U} = \frac{\epsilon_0 A_G}{g_{eff}}, \tag{6}$$

where ϵ_0 is the permittivity constant of a vacuum, $g_{eff} = g_0 + t_d/\epsilon_d$ is the effective electrostatic gap, A_G is the electrode area of the gate capacitance, and t_d, ϵ_d are the thickness and relative permittivity of the dielectric layer, respectively.

When V_G is applied to the electrodes, the electrostatic attractive force (7) acting on the piston causes its static displacement z. This displacement is defined by the equilibrium equation related to the restoring force of the spring (8).

$$F_{elG}(z) = \frac{\epsilon_0 A_G V_G^2}{2(g_{eff} - z)^2} \tag{7}$$

$$\frac{\epsilon_0 A_G V_G^2}{2(g_{eff} - z)^2} = kz \tag{8}$$

It can be shown that there is a critical displacement from which the electrostatic force is no longer balanced by the restoring force and the piston falls down to the bottom electrode as presented in the right-hand part of Fig. 5(a). The static pull-in point displacement equals one third of the effective gap and the pull-in voltage is given by:

$$V_{PI} = \sqrt{\frac{8}{27} \frac{k g_{eff}^3}{\epsilon_0 A_G}}. \tag{9}$$

The down-state capacitance is defined by the dielectric layer thickness and equals:

$$C_{G\_D} = \frac{\epsilon_0 \epsilon_d A_G}{t_d}. \tag{10}$$

In this configuration, the high down-state to up-state capacitance ratio is achievable. However, there is a problem induced by a non-adiabatic pull-down motion. According to [10], the impact kinetic energy loss is one of the dominant loss mechanisms in a MEMS relay. The kinetic energy loss cannot be suppressed by the increasing ramping time, as after the pull-in point, we lose control under the motion of the piston. In order to avoid this issue, a solution with a controlled dynamic should be proposed.

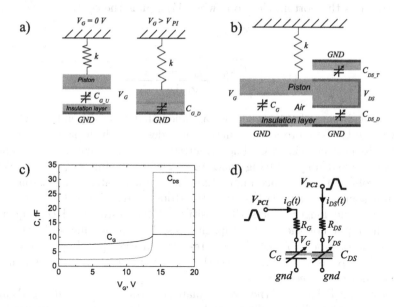

Fig. 5. (a) Electromechanical capacitance in up (left) and down (right) states. (b) Electrostatically-controlled variable capacitor C_{DS}. (c) C_G and C_{DS} capacitances according to V_G ($V_{DS} = 0$ V). (d) Test circuit.

As we discussed above, the static pull-in point displacement equals one third of the effective gap. We can thus avoid collapse if we add a stopper with a thickness greater than $2 g_{eff}/3$ to stop the mechanical motion before the pull-in. This solution allows us to reduce the impact energy loss and eliminate the uncontrolled dynamic caused by the voltage V_G.

4.2   Four-Terminal Parallel Plate Transducer with Stopper

Figure 5(b) shows a viable candidate for PCV implementation, where the gap between the electrodes can be modulated by the electrostatic force caused by the gate voltage, V_G, and the drain-source voltage, V_{DS}. The right part (input) is electrically isolated from the left which has the drain and source terminals (output). The output capacitance C_{DS} should be insensitive to V_{DS} when $V_G = 0$ V. In order to guarantee this, we add two couples of symmetrical electrodes, which form two capacitors C_{DS_T} and C_{DS_D}. The C_{DS} capacitance is the sum of the latter. When the input voltage V_G and the displacements are small, the electrostatic attractive force $F_{elDS}(z)$ in the output is almost balanced:

$$F_{elDS}(z) = \frac{\epsilon_0 A_{DS} V_{DS}^2}{2(g_0/3 + t_d/\epsilon_d - z)^2} - \frac{\epsilon_0 A_{DS} V_{DS}^2}{2(g_0/3 + t_d/\epsilon_d + z)^2}, \tag{11}$$

where A_{DS} is the symmetrical output electrode area of the C_{DS} capacitance and the initial output gap thickness equals $g_0/3$. For the selected gap value, the piston contacts the bottom electrode when V_G equals the contact voltage, V_{con} (12).

$$V_{con} = \sqrt{\frac{2k g_0 (2g_0/3 + t_d/\epsilon_d)^2}{3\epsilon_0 A_G}}. \tag{12}$$

In the beginning of this paper, we assumed that C_{DS} depends only on the input voltage V_G. The proposed structure provides us with the same behavior as with the Bennett clocking PC. The symmetric output capacitance C_{DS} allows pull-in to be avoided by applying non-zero V_{DS} when the input $V_G = 0$ V. When the input voltage V_G is ramped higher than the contact voltage, the piston comes into contact with the dielectric layer in the stopper area. After this contact, the value of V_{DS} no longer affects the position of the piston, and consequently, neither the input nor the output capacitances. The capacitances C_G and C_{DS} as a function of input voltage V_G are presented in Fig. 5(c) ($V_{DS} = 0$ V). The ratio $\frac{C_H}{C_L}$ for C_{DS} is about 9, whereas the variation of C_G capacitance is not as high and does not exceed 50%.

The dynamic behavior of the parallel plate transducer with an air-filled cavity is described by the following differential equation of motion:

$$m\ddot{z} = F_{elG}(z) + F_{elDS}(z) + F_{con}(z) - b\dot{z} - kz, \tag{13}$$

where we assume that the viscous damping coefficient b does not depend on the piston displacement. The limit of piston displacement due to the stopper is modelled by injecting an additional restoring force F_{con} as in work [11]. The adhesion force is neglected. The mechanical resonant frequency f and Q–factor of the system can be defined from (14) and (15).

$$f = \frac{1}{2\pi}\sqrt{\frac{k}{m}} \tag{14}$$

$$Q = \frac{\sqrt{mk}}{b} \tag{15}$$

4.3   Energy Conversion and Losses

In order to study the dynamic behavior of the 4-terminal variable capacitor, we performed transient electromechanical simulation of the circuit depicted in Fig. 5(d). However in this paper, only the case of maximal displacement and large capacitance variation is discussed ($V_G \geq V_{con}$). The equivalent parameters of the model are extracted from a fixed-fixed gold plate: length 103 µm, width 30 µm and thickness 0.5 µm, according to [11]. The residual stresses in the plate equal zero and only the linear component of stiffness is used in the model. The energy components in this system are:

$$E_{S1} = \int_0^{t_0} V_{PC1}(t)i_G(t)dt \qquad \text{Energy delivered by the first voltage source}$$

$$E_{S2} = \int_0^{t_0} V_{PC2}(t)i_{DS}(t)dt \qquad \text{Energy delivered by the second voltage source}$$

$$E_{C_G} = \frac{1}{2}C_G V_G^2 \qquad \text{Electrical energy stored in } C_G$$

$$E_{C_{DS}} = \frac{1}{2}C_{DS}V_{DS}^2 \qquad \text{Electrical energy stored in } C_{DS}$$

$$E_{R_G} = R_G \int_0^{t_0} i_G(t)^2 dt \qquad \text{Energy dissipated in the resistor } R_G$$

$$E_{R_{DS}} = R_{DS} \int_0^{t_0} i_{DS}(t)^2 dt \qquad \text{Energy dissipated in the resistor } R_{DS}$$

$$E_M = \frac{1}{2}kz^2 \qquad \text{Mechanical spring energy}$$

$$E_{KIN} = \frac{1}{2}mv^2 \qquad \text{Kinetic energy}$$

$$E_D = b\int_0^{t_0} v(t)^2 dt \qquad \text{Energy loss in damping}$$

$$\Delta E = E_{S1} - E_{C_G} - E_{R_G} - E_M - E_{KIN} - E_D \qquad \text{Energy balance}$$

where V_{PC1}, V_{PC2} are the output voltages of the two PC's, and i_G, and i_{DS} the currents through the resistors R_G and R_{DS}, respectively.

The smooth transition needed in any adiabatic logic family reduces the frequency. In CMOS-based digital circuits, logic states are encoded through two

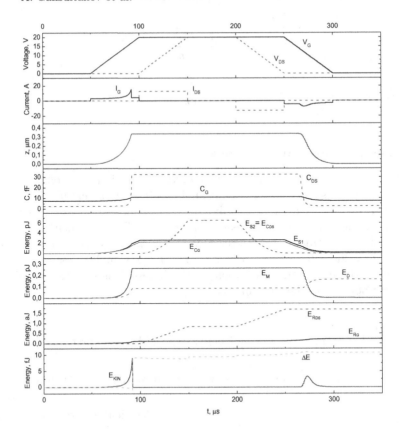

Fig. 6. Evolution of voltages applied to the four-terminal transducer model (first graph), currents (second graph), equivalent mass displacement (third graph), capacitances (fourth graph), energy components of electrical part (fifth graph), mechanical spring energy and damping loss (sixth graph), resistive losses (seventh graph), kinetic energy and energy balance (eighth graph) over time. We used the following parameters: $g_0 = 1$ μm, $t_d = 0.1$ μm, $\epsilon_d = 7.6$, $m = 1.19 \cdot 10^{-11}$ kg, $k = 4.72$ N/m, $b = 7.48 \cdot 10^{-6}$ Ns/m, $A_G = 8.53 \cdot 10^{-10}$ m^2, $A_{DS} = 0.47 \cdot 10^{-10}$ m^2, $V_{con} = 13.8$ V, $f = 100$ kHz, $Q = 0.5$, $T = 50$ μs, $R_G = R_{DS} = 1$ kΩ.

distinct voltage values, e.g. 0 and V_{DD}. Switching of a bit requires capacitance C to be charged or discharged. This represents the input capacitance of the following gate. In standard CMOS circuitry, switches are operated sharply over a time period $T \ll RC$, where R is the resistance in the charging part of the circuit. This leads to a power dissipation of about $\frac{1}{2}CV_0^2$ per operation [12]. In adiabatic computing, energy saving is achieved by operating the circuit in the $T \gg RC$ range. This allows the energy of the logic states to be recycled and reused, instead of conversion into heat [13]. In an electromechanical system such as CAL, the total dissipation is the sum of the losses in the electrical and mechanical domains [14]. To reduce power dissipation, the ramping time should be much more than both the electrical RC and mechanical $\propto 1/f$ time constants. The time constants of the model follow $1/f = 10\,\mu\text{s}$, so that $R_{DS}C_{DSmax} = 32.5$ ps. The time required for the variable capacitance to mechanically change up-state to down-state is significantly longer than the RC electrical constant. This means that mechanical motion is adiabatic in the electrical domain. However, a smooth transition is needed for the maximal time constant.

For the first simulation and model verification, we selected a Bennett clocking PC with $T = 5/f = 50\,\mu\text{s}$ and $V_{PC1max} = V_{PC2max} = 20$ V. The results are shown in Fig. 6. During the charging process of C_G, part of the electrical energy is converted into mechanical energy. Charging or discharging the C_{DS} capacitor does not lead to energy conversion as the capacitance remains constant. When discharging C_G, part of the mechanical spring energy stored in the system is recovered in the first voltage source. The difference between transferred and received energy is determined by damping, kinetic and resistive losses. However, mechanical loss dominates, and the resistive loss is 5 orders of magnitude lower than the mechanical one. The kinetic energy loss is only 6% of the damping loss for this particular case. The total dissipated energy during one cycle is 172 fJ. The ratio of the total dissipated energy to the energy delivered by the first voltage source is 0.067. Consequently, most of the energy provided is recovered. We also checked the difference between the energy provided by the voltage sources and all the other energy components (eighth graph of Fig. 6). The energy saving law is satisfied, i.e. the step in the ΔE graph is caused by kinetic energy loss during impact. This step is related to the work by the contact force F_{con} which limits the piston motion. This simulation therefore allows us to verify that the proposed model is energy consistent and can be used for further variable capacitance development.

In Fig. 7(a), we present the effect of ramping time T on the maximum energy components during one cycle. All other parameters are the same as in the previous calculation. The resistive loss is very small and is thus not given in Fig. 7. As discussed above, increasing the ramping time decreases the mechanical and total loss values. The latter decreases proportionally: $T^{-0.8}$. This demonstrates the absence of any non-adiabatic losses for the proposed design. However, the main drawback of this approach is the decrease in the operating frequency.

The results for the maximum energy components during one cycle in relation to Q–factor are shown in Fig. 7(b). The ramping time is fixed and equals $50\,\mu\text{s}$ $(5/f)$. The increase in Q–factor decreases the total mechanical loss value. For example the Q–factor increases from 0.5 to 10 which reduces the total loss from 172 fJ to 45 fJ per cycle. The loss reduction is monotonous for this case. Therefore, we can say that an increase in Q–factor allows a decrease in loss without dramatically decreasing the operating frequency. The maximal value of the Q–factor is limited by the idle phase between the ramping-down and ramping-up stages. This time should be sufficient to decay the vibration after input voltage decrease.

The developed electromechanical model of the variable MEMS capacitance has been successfully verified. In addition, the main loss mechanisms have been

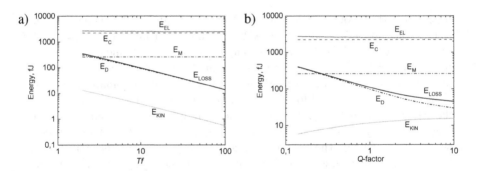

Fig. 7. Simulated maximal energy components: (a) according to ramping time ($Q = 0.5$); (b) according to Q–factor ($Tf = 5$).

established, and the adiabatic loss decreases also demonstrated for an electro-mechanical device with Bennett clocking actuation. The energy dissipated during one cycle is in the order hundreds of fF and still far from the energy dissipated by a nano-scale FET transistor which is in the order a fraction of fF. However, scalability is possible for the proposed electromechanical devices and with appropriate ramping time and Q–factor selection it could overcome this level and try to confirm or go lower than the Landauer limit. The proposed model will be used for further CAL circuit design and analysis, including reversible gate circuits.

5   Conclusion

The present work focused on the analysis and hardware implementation of CAL at the gate level. First, we demonstrated that basic logic functions can be implemented using a capacitive voltage divider with variable capacitors. It was then shown that the load capacitance of the next logic gates is a critical parameter in the design of CAL-based circuits. A possible design of a four-terminal variable capacitors has been proposed and discussed.

In order to analyze all loss mechanisms, an analytical compact model of the electrostatically-actuated variable capacitor has been developed. In electro-mechanical adiabatic systems, total loss is a sum of the losses in all electrical and mechanical domains, where mechanical loss dominates due to a relatively high mechanical time constant. To decrease these losses, the ramping time T and Q–factor should be appropriately chosen. The main drawback of an increase in ramping time is the decrease in operating frequency. The absence of non-adiabatic losses and leakages allows us to construct reversible gates with ultra-low power consumption.

The developed electromechanical model of the variable MEMS capacitance will be used for further CAL circuits design and analysis.

References

1. Landauer, R.: Irreversibility and heat generation in the computing process. IBM J. Res. Dev. **5**(3), 183–191 (1961)
2. Teichmann, P.: Adiabatic Logic: Future Trend and System Level Perspective. Springer Science in Advanced Microelectronics, vol. 34. Springer, Netherlands (2012)
3. Snider, G.L., Blair, E.P., Boechler, G.P., Thorpe, C.C., Bosler, N.W., Wohlwend, M.J., Whitney, J.M., Lent, C.S., Orlov, A.O.: Minimum energy for computation, theory vs. experiment. In: 11th IEEE International Conference on Nanotechnology, pp. 478–481 (2011)
4. Spencer, M., Chen, F., Wang, C.C., Nathanael, R., Fariborzi, H., Gupta, A., Kam, H., Pott, V., Jeon, J., Liu, T.-J.K., Markovic, D., Alon, E., Stojanovic, V.: Demonstration of integrated micro-electro-mechanical relay circuits for VLSI applications. IEEE J. Solid-State Circ. **46**(1), 308–320 (2011)
5. Houri, S., Billiot, G., Belleville, M., Valentian, A., Fanet, H.: Limits of CMOS technology and interest of NEMS relays for adiabatic logic applications. IEEE Trans. Circuits Syst. I Regul. Pap. **62**(6), 1546–1554 (2015)
6. Lee, J.O., Song, Y.-H., Kim, M.-W., Kang, M.-H., Oh, J.-S., Yang, H.-H., Yoon, J.-B.: A sub-1-volt nanoelectromechanical switching device. Nat. Nanotechnol. **8**(1), 36–40 (2013)
7. Pawashe, C., Lin, K., Kuhn, K.J.: Scaling limits of electrostatic nanorelays. IEEE Trans. Electron Devices **60**(9), 2936–2942 (2013)
8. Loh, O.Y., Espinosa, H.D.: Nanoelectromechanical contact switches. Nat. Nanotechnol. **7**(5), 283–295 (2012)
9. Pillonnet, G., Houri, S., Fanet, H.: Adiabatic capacitive logic: a paradigm for low-power logic. In: IEEE International Symposium of Circuits and Systems ISCAS, May 2017 (in press)
10. Rebeiz, G.M.: RF MEMS: Theory, Design, and Technology. Wiley, Hoboken (2004)
11. Van Caekenberghe, K.: Modeling RF MEMS devices. IEEE Microwave Mag. **13**(1), 83–110 (2012)
12. Paul, S., Schlaffer, A.M., Nossek, J.A.: Optimal charging of capacitors. IEEE Trans. Circuits Syst. I: Fundam. Theory Appl. **47**(7), 1009–1016 (2000)
13. Koller, J.G., Athas, W.C.: Adiabatic switching, low energy computing, and the physics of storing and erasing information. In: Proceedings of Physics of Computation Workshop, October 1992, pp. 267–270 (1992)
14. Jones, T.B., Nenadic, N.G.: Electromechanics and MEMS. Cambridge University Press, New York (2013)

Implementing Reversible Object-Oriented Language Features on Reversible Machines

Tue Haulund[(⊠)], Torben Ægidius Mogensen, and Robert Glück

DIKU, Department of Computer Science,
University of Copenhagen, Copenhagen, Denmark
qvr916@alumni.ku.dk, torbenm@di.ku.dk, glueck@acm.org

Abstract. We extend the reversible language Janus with support for class-based object-oriented programming, class inheritance and subtype-polymorphism. We describe how to implement these features on reversible hardware - with emphasis on the implementation of reversible dynamic dispatch using virtual method tables. Our translation is effective (i.e. garbage-free) and we demonstrate its practicality by implementation of a fully-featured compiler targeting the reversible assembly language PISA.

1 Introduction

In the present paper, we consider the techniques required for realizing reversible object-oriented language features on reversible machines. In particular, we identify effective (i.e. garbage-free) approaches to reversible dynamic dispatch using virtual method tables, in contrast to the compiler-generated dispatch methods suggested in [10] for the reversible OOP language Joule.

As a means of illustrating the proposed techniques, we extend the reversible language Janus [7,11,12] with support for object-oriented programming. A feature-complete, non-optimizing compiler has been implemented for this language, utilizing the methods presented in this paper.

Janus uses a stack-based memory model where local variables are lexically scoped and must be disposed of in the opposite order they were created. Our variant of Janus continues with this approach by also storing class instances directly on the program stack - which means that the language can be implemented without the use of a reversible memory heap. Nevertheless, the techniques we present in this paper are intended to be generally applicable and should carry over to other reversible languages with a more elaborate memory model.

A traditional Janus program consists of one or more procedure definitions. In place of procedures, we use *classes* as the basic building blocks of a program. Each class definition contains one or more class methods, represented by a parameterized list of program statements. A program statement may be either a reversible control flow primitive; a reversible variable update (or swap); an object block; a local integer block or a method invocation.

Even though the overall program structure is different, most components of the original Janus language remains: Reversible control flow structures, reversible

© Springer International Publishing AG 2017
I. Phillips and H. Rahaman (Eds.): RC 2017, LNCS 10301, pp. 66–73, 2017.
DOI: 10.1007/978-3-319-59936-6_5

variable updates, local variable blocks and expressions. We refer to [11,12] for a thorough description of Janus and its features. The translation schemes provided in this paper are intended to complement the Janus-to-PISA translation from [1] and are presented using the same notation. An in-depth presentation of our work on reversible object-oriented programming is available in [6], including a complete description and formal semantics of a reversible object-oriented language.

The following example program modelling shapes in two-dimensional space illustrates the overall structure of a program:

```
 1  class Shape
 2      int x, y
 3
 4      method translate(int dx, int dy) x += dx; y += dy
 5      method resize(int ds) skip  //Abstract method
 6
 7  class Circle inherits Shape
 8      int radius
 9
10      method resize(int ds) radius += ds
11
12      // Out ^= 1 if (px, py) is inside the circle
13      method contains(int px, int py, int out)
14          local int dx = (px - x) * (px - x)
15          local int dy = (py - y) * (py - y)
16          out ^= dx + dy < (radius * radius)
17          delocal dx = (px - x) * (px - x)
18          delocal dy = (py - y) * (py - y)
19
20  class Program
21      int result
22
23      method main()
24          construct Circle c
25          call c::translate(5, 5)
26          call c::resize(3)
27          call c::contains(2, 2, result)
28          uncall c::resize(3)
29          uncall c::translate(5, 5)
30          destruct c
```

2   Classes and Inheritance

As is the case for conventional (i.e. irreversible) OOP languages, each class defines a number of fields and methods, and may also specify a base class. If a class is derived from a base class, it inherits the data fields and class methods of that class. Inherited class methods may be overridden in the derived class, provided the type signature of the methods are identical. Collectively, the classes of a program form a hierarchy, and inheritance is used to establish a subtype relation over class instances.

Classes serve as an encapsulation mechanism; a class instance is a bundle of data and program code. Direct outside access to class data is disallowed, only class methods may access the class fields. All class fields are in scope within each class method and may be accessed indiscriminately. For the sake of simplicity, we do not support access modifiers, friend classes or other mechanisms for fine-grained control over data access. Such features are useful, but data access control can be implemented in the usual fashion (as compile-time restrictions), even when targeting reversible hardware.

3 Aliasing

A variable update statement from Janus is reversible only when the value of the right-hand side expression does not depend on the value of the memory cell being updated. In Janus, this can be verified by simple syntactic analysis, because the language is designed to make it impossible for two different identifiers within the same scope to refer to the same location in memory. Consequently, if the identifier on the left-hand side of an update does not occur in the right-hand side expression, the update is reversible.

In contrast to Janus, direct access to class fields from within a class method must be considered when judging the reversibility of a statement in a reversible OOP language. Specifically, two restrictions apply in order to avoid aliasing in our OOP variant of Janus: No single identifier may be passed to more than one parameter in a single method invocation and a class field may not be passed as an argument to a method of that same class. These restrictions place an added burden on the programmer and limit the usability of the language. In return, they allow for simple compile time detection of irreversible updates.

An alternative approach to the aliasing restriction is to insert run time checks around each variable update [10], which issues an error if an update is irreversible. However, this incurs a cost in execution time and in code size. With a static aliasing analysis, these costs can be minimized by omitting the run time checks wherever the compiler can guarantee that an update is reversible.

4 Translation

In the following sections we will provide translation schemes from our high-level OOP language to the reversible assembly language PISA. We refer to [5] for a complete list of PISA instructions. A complete formalization of the PISA language and the Pendulum machine was given in [3] and a translation from Janus to PISA was presented in [1]. PISA is also the target language of the R compiler [4,5].

In addition to the regular PISA instructions, we make use of the following 4 pseudoinstructions (where r_{sp} refers to the register holding the stack pointer sp):

$$\text{SUBI} \quad r \quad i \quad \overset{\text{def}}{=} \quad \text{ADDI} \quad r \quad -i$$

$$\text{PUSH} \quad r \quad \overset{\text{def}}{=} \quad \left[\text{EXCH} \quad r \quad r_{sp} \,, \quad \text{ADDI} \quad r_{sp} \quad 1 \right]$$

$$\text{POP} \quad r \quad \overset{\text{def}}{=} \quad \left[\text{SUBI} \quad r_{sp} \quad 1 \,, \quad \text{EXCH} \quad r \quad r_{sp} \right]$$

$$\text{CALL} \quad r \quad \overset{\text{def}}{=} \quad \left[\text{SWAPBR} \quad r, \quad \text{NEG} \quad r \right]$$

4.1   Objects and Memory

In a reversible language we cannot simply leave values in unused memory and then overwrite them later on when the memory is needed again - this would lead to a loss of information which compromises reversibility. As a result, we require unused memory to already be zero-cleared at the time of object instantiation, so the fields of each new object have a known initial value. To maintain the memory in this state, we must ensure that any memory marked as unused does not contain non-zero values. Consequently, all the state that has accumulated within an object must be zero-cleared before the object is deallocated.

Like local variables in Janus, we use lexical scoping for class instances which means they can be stored on the program stack rather than in a reversible memory-heap (which, on the other hand, would allow for staggered allocation/deallocation of objects). We use a symmetric **construct/destruct** block to define the lifetime of an object. Consider the following statement, where c is the name of a class, x is an identifier and s is a statement:

$$\textbf{construct } c\ x \quad s \quad \textbf{destruct } x$$

Before the sub-statement s is executed, an object of type c is instantiated. Initially, the fields of this new class instance are all zero, since the newly allocated object resides in zero-cleared memory. Within the statement s, the identifier x refers to the new object and the state of the object may be mutated through invocation of class methods. When the statement s has been executed, the state of the object must have been zero-cleared – otherwise the system cannot reversibly reclaim the memory occupied by the object. It is up to the programmer to maintain this invariant, otherwise the program stops with an error indication. Symmetric record construction/deconstruction was first suggested in [2,10].

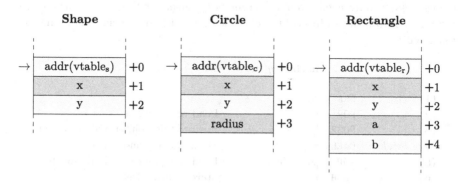

Fig. 1. Memory layout of 3 class instances

Figure 1 illustrates the memory layout of 3 objects based on the class hierarchy from the example program in Sect. 1. An object consists of a number of class fields and a pointer to the virtual method table which resides in a static memory segment before the program and the program stack. We can implement this object instantiation with the following series of PISA instructions:

$$\textbf{construct } c\ x \quad s \quad \textbf{destruct } x$$

(1)	XOR	r_x	r_{sp}	; Store address of new object x in r_x
(2)	XORI	r_v	$label_{vt}$	; Store address of vtable in r_v
(3)	EXCH	r_v	r_{sp}	; Push address of vtable onto stack
(4)	ADDI	r_{sp}	$size_c$	; Allocate space for new object
(5)	$\cdots\cdots$			; Code for statement s
(6)	SUBI	r_{sp}	$size_c$	; Deallocate space occupied by zero-cleared object
(7)	EXCH	r_v	r_{sp}	; Pop vtable address into r_v
(8)	XORI	r_v	$label_{vt}$	; Clear r_v
(9)	XOR	r_x	r_{sp}	; Clear r_x

Register r_{sp} contains the stack pointer while r_x and r_v are free registers. The immediate $label_{vt}$ represents the address of the virtual method table for class c while $size_c$ equals the size of an instance of class c.

4.2 Methods

The calling convention in [1] is a generalized version of the PISA calling convention from [5], modified to support recursion. Our translation uses a similar approach with added support for method parameters and pass-by-reference semantics.

To facilitate access to class fields from within a class method, each translated method is given an extra hidden parameter which contains the address of the object to which the method belongs at each invocation. When a method accesses a class field, it only needs to add the memory offset for that field to the object pointer to obtain the address of the class field. The PISA translation of a method q is given by:

$$\textbf{method } q(\textbf{int } x_1,\ \textbf{int } x_2) \quad q_{body}$$

(1)	q_{top} :	BRA	q_{bot}	
(2)		POP	r_{ro}	; Load return offset
(3)		PUSH	$[r_{x_2},\ r_{x_1},\ r_{this}]$	; Restore this-pointer and arguments
(4)	$label_q$:	CALL	r_{ro}	; Method entry and exit point
(5)		POP	$[r_{this},\ r_{x_1},\ r_{x_2}]$	; Load this-pointer and arguments
(6)		PUSH	r_{ro}	; Store return offset
(7)		$\cdots\cdots$		; Code for method body q_{body}
(8)	q_{bot} :	BRA	q_{top}	

The caller transfers control to instruction (4) after which the object-pointer and method arguments are popped off the stack, the return offset is stored and the body is executed. The method prologue works identically for both directions of execution which avoids the need for multiple translations of the same method to support reverse execution.

4.3 Dynamic Dispatch

A virtual method call involves three overall steps:

1. **Lookup:** Fetch the memory address of the method implementation using the virtual method table of the object.

2. **Jump:** Compute the memory offset relative to the address of the jump instruction, push the arguments to the program stack, jump to the method and pop the arguments from the program stack after the call returns.

3. **Cleanup:** Uncompute the memory offset to reobtain the absolute memory address, zero-clear registers by lookup in the virtual table.

The following series of instructions shows the PISA translation of a virtual method invocation:

call x::$q(x_1,\ x_2)$

(1)		EXCH	r_v	r_x	; Get address of vtable
(2)		ADDI	r_v	$offset_q$	; Lookup q in vtable
(3)		EXCH	r_t	r_v	; Get address of q
(4)		XOR	r_{tgt}	r_t	; Copy address of q
(5)		EXCH	r_t	r_v	; Place address back in vtable
(6)		SUBI	r_v	$offset_q$	; Restore vtable pointer
(7)		EXCH	r_v	r_x	; Restore object pointer
(8)		PUSH	$[r_{x_2},\ r_{x_1},\ r_x]$		; Push args and new'*this*' onto stack
(9)		SUBI	r_{tgt}	$label_{jmp}$	; Calculate jump offset
(10)	$label_{jmp}$:	CALL	r_{tgt}		; Jump to method
(11)		ADDI	r_{tgt}	$label_{jmp}$	; Restore absolute jump value
(12)		POP	$[r_x,\ r_{x_1},\ r_{x_2}]$		; Pop args and new'*this*' from stack
(13)		EXCH	r_v	r_x	; Get address of vtable
(14)		ADDI	r_v	$offset_q$	; Lookup q in vtable
(15)		EXCH	r_t	r_v	; Get address of q
(16)		XOR	r_{tgt}	r_t	; Clear address of q
(17)		EXCH	r_t	r_v	; Place address back in vtable
(18)		SUBI	r_v	$offset_q$	; Restore vtable pointer
(19)		EXCH	r_v	r_x	; Restore object pointer

Since the virtual table pointer is stored at offset 0, the address of the virtual table can be procured simply by dereferencing the pointer to the object. The lookup in the table involves adding a fixed offset to the virtual table address. The offset is determined by the compiler and corresponds to the entry in the virtual table for the method that is being invoked. Since memory access in PISA works by swapping out values, we use Bennett's method to create a copy of the address in a register before swapping it back into the virtual table. This ensures that the virtual table is returned to its original state before we jump to the method. The jump itself is accomplished dynamically, with the CALL pseudo-instruction.

All jump targets in PISA must be relative to the address of the jump instruction. Normally, absolute jump addresses are converted to relative jump offsets at load time but since the target address is not known until run time in this case, we must compute the relative offset manually. We do this by subtracting the address of the jump instruction from the absolute address of the method implementation, fetched from the virtual table. After the jump, we undo this computation to reobtain the absolute address which can then be XOR zero-cleared by looking up the same address again in the virtual table. In effect, we undo the entire lookup phase of the virtual call, thereby zero-clearing all the registers involved in the dispatch process.

The entire sequence of PISA instructions representing the virtual call is *palindromic* with respect to its own inversion. Consequently, the virtual call mechanism will behave the same regardless of the direction of execution. Virtual *uncalls* are implemented in the same manner as virtual calls, only the direction of execution is reversed before the jump to the method implementation:

$$\textbf{uncall } x\!::\!q(x_1,\ x_2)$$

(9)		SUBI	r_{tgt}	$label_{jmp}$	; Calculate jump offset
--	top_{jmp}	RBRA	bot_{jmp}		; Flip direction
(10)	$label_{jmp}$:	CALL	r_{tgt}		; Jump to method
--	bot_{jmp}	BRA	top_{jmp}		; Paired branch
(11)		ADDI	r_{tgt}	$label_{jmp}$	; Restore absolute jump value

5   Conclusion

We described an extension to the reversible language Janus which adds support for OOP, class inheritance and subtype-polymorphism. We also provided a translation from this language to the reversible assembly language PISA. We showed how the addition of basic OOP features does *not* interfere with the reversibility of the language.

We established how reversible dynamic dispatch can be implemented on a reversible machine, by means of virtual method tables. The feasibility of the proposed translation was demonstrated by implementation of a fully-fledged compiler. We believe this is important because it demonstrates that language features central to mainstream OOP languages such as C++ or Java can be made accessible to the field of reversible computing.

It is our hope that our reversible OOP language and the techniques employed in its translation can serve as a basis for further research into reversible object-oriented programming. In order to move away from stack allocated objects, which are simple to implement but cumbersome to work with, more work is needed on the topics of reversible memory heaps and reversible dynamic memory management. Some work has already been done on these topics with regards to reversible functional languages [2,8,9].

Acknowledgments. The authors would like to thank the European COST Action IC 1405 "Reversible Computation" for its valuable support and Ulrik Pagh Schultz for his insightful comments.

References

1. Axelsen, H.B.: Clean translation of an imperative reversible programming language. In: Knoop, J. (ed.) CC 2011. LNCS, vol. 6601, pp. 144–163. Springer, Heidelberg (2011). doi:10.1007/978-3-642-19861-8_9
2. Axelsen, H.B., Glück, R.: Reversible representation and manipulation of constructor terms in the heap. In: Dueck, G.W., Miller, D.M. (eds.) RC 2013. LNCS, vol. 7948, pp. 96–109. Springer, Heidelberg (2013). doi:10.1007/978-3-642-38986-3_9
3. Axelsen, H.B., Glück, R., Yokoyama, T.: Reversible machine code and its abstract processor architecture. In: Diekert, V., Volkov, M.V., Voronkov, A. (eds.) CSR 2007. LNCS, vol. 4649, pp. 56–69. Springer, Heidelberg (2007). doi:10.1007/978-3-540-74510-5_9
4. Frank, M.P.: The R programming language and compiler, MIT Reversible Computing Project Memo #M8 (1997)
5. Frank, M.P.: Reversibility for efficient computing. Ph.D. thesis, Massachusetts Institute of Technology (1999)
6. Haulund, T.: Design and Implementation of a Reversible Object-Oriented Programming Language. Master's thesis, University of Copenhagen, DIKU (2016)
7. Lutz, C.: Janus: a time-reversible language, Letter to R. Landauer (1986)
8. Mogensen, T.Æ.: Reference counting for reversible languages. In: Yamashita, S., Minato, S. (eds.) RC 2014. LNCS, vol. 8507, pp. 82–94. Springer, Cham (2014). doi:10.1007/978-3-319-08494-7_7
9. Mogensen, T.Æ.: Garbage collection for reversible functional languages. In: Krivine, J., Stefani, J.-B. (eds.) RC 2015. LNCS, vol. 9138, pp. 79–94. Springer, Cham (2015). doi:10.1007/978-3-319-20860-2_5
10. Schultz, U.P., Axelsen, H.B.: Elements of a reversible object-oriented language. In: Devitt, S., Lanese, I. (eds.) RC 2016. LNCS, vol. 9720, pp. 153–159. Springer, Cham (2016). doi:10.1007/978-3-319-40578-0_10
11. Yokoyama, T., Axelsen, H.B., Glück, R.: Principles of a reversible programming language. In: Computing Frontiers, pp. 43–54. ACM (2008)
12. Yokoyama, T., Glück, R.: A reversible programming language and its invertible self-interpreter. In: Partial Evaluation and Semantics-based Program Manipulation, pp. 144–153. ACM (2007)

Reversible Circuit Synthesis

Designing Parity Preserving Reversible Circuits

Goutam Paul[1(✉)], Anupam Chattopadhyay[2], and Chander Chandak[3]

[1] Cryptology and Security Research Unit (CSRU),
R.C. Bose Centre for Cryptology and Security,
Indian Statistical Institute, Kolkata 700 108, India
goutam.paul@isical.ac.in
[2] School of Computer Engineering,
Nanyang Technological University (NTU), Singapore, Singapore
anupam@ntu.edu.sg
[3] Liv Artificial Intelligence Pvt. Ltd., Bengaluru, India
chandar.chandak@gmail.com

Abstract. With the emergence of reversible circuits as an energy-efficient alternative of classical circuits, ensuring fault tolerance in such circuits becomes a very important problem. Parity-preserving reversible logic design is one viable approach towards fault detection. Interestingly, most of the existing designs are ad hoc, based on some pre-defined parity preserving reversible gates as building blocks. In the current work, we propose a systematic approach towards parity preserving reversible circuit design. We prove a few theoretical results and present two algorithms, one from reversible specification to parity preserving reversible specification and another from irreversible specification to parity preserving reversible specification. We derive an upper-bound for the number of garbage bits for our algorithm and perform its complexity analysis. We also evaluate the effectiveness of our approach by extensive experimental results and compare with the state-of-the-art practices. To our knowledge, this is the first work towards systematic design of parity preserving reversible circuit and more research is needed in this area to make this approach more scalable.

Keywords: Fault tolerance · Parity · Quantum computing · Reversible circuits

1 Introduction and Motivation

It is known that erasure of a single bit of information dissipates heat equivalent to $K_B T \ln 2$ [3,12], where $K_B = 1.38 \times 10^{-23}$ J/K is Boltzmann constant and T is the room temperature in Kelvin. This heat dissipation is in conformity with the laws of thermodynamics applied to any irreversible process. Using reversible logic implementation of Boolean functions, it is theoretically possible to make heat dissipation and hence power loss negligible. Though classical logic is not reversible, it is possible to represent classical Boolean functions using reversible logic [2]. On the other hand, any quantum computation is based on unitary

---

The original version of this chapter was revised: Table 2 was corrected. An erratum to this chapter can be found at 10.1007/978-3-319-59936-6_20

© Springer International Publishing AG 2017
I. Phillips and H. Rahaman (Eds.): RC 2017, LNCS 10301, pp. 77–89, 2017.
DOI: 10.1007/978-3-319-59936-6_6

evolution of quantum mechanical systems and is inherently reversible. However, with increasing demand on low power design, reversible logic finds application not only in quantum circuits, but also in designing conventional circuits for encoding/decoding etc [34].

Any physical device performing classical or quantum computation is subject to error due to noise in the environment or imperfections in the device. *Fault tolerant computing* can mitigate this. There are two broad approaches towards fault tolerance - one focuses on fault prevention and the other focuses on first fault detection and then fault correction. For fault detection, usage of redundant parity bits is one of the most popular approaches. For classical circuits, *bit flip* is the most common type of error. For quantum circuits, in addition to bit flip, there might be *phase flip* as well. In this short technical note, we focus on bit flip errors.

Most common method for detecting bit-flip errors in storage or transmission is by means of parity checking. Classically, most arithmetic and other processing functions do not preserve the parity. One has to use redundant circuitry to compute and check the parity. In general, making a reversible circuit fault-tolerant is much more difficult than classical circuit, since reversible logic allows no feedback or fan-out. The notion of parity-preserving arithmetic circuits goes back to [19]. Later, in [20], the concept of *parity preserving reversible circuits* was introduced. The idea is to design the reversible circuit in such a way that the parity between the input and the output bits are automatically conserved in absence of any error.

After [20], there has been a series of sporadic works in this area, such as designing adders [11], divider [4], multiplier [23], multiplexer [25], ALU [26] etc. The work [36] discusses the various steps required in the logic design of quantum circuits.

However, all of these designs are ad hoc, based on some pre-defined parity preserving reversible gates as building blocks. To the best of our knowledge, in this article, we for the first time propose a novel and systematic approach towards parity preserving reversible circuits design. We provide some related theoretical results and give two algorithms. The first algorithm converts a reversible specification to parity preserving reversible specification and the second one converts an irreversible specification directly to parity preserving reversible specification.

There are other approaches than parity preservation, for achieving fault-tolerance in reversible circuits, as described in [17] and in [18]. The advantage of parity-preserving circuit is that one need not do any extra operations in order to detect errors or faults; the fault detection becomes a by-product of the usual computation in the circuit. With this motivation, we focus on designing parity-preserving reversible circuits in this paper.

2   Reversible Logic Synthesis

An n-variable Boolean function is *reversible* if all its output patterns map uniquely to an input pattern and vice-versa. It can be expressed as an n-input, n-output bijection or alternatively, as a permutation over the truth value set $\{0, 1, \ldots 2^{n-1}\}$. The problem of reversible logic synthesis is to map such a reversible Boolean function on a reversible logic gate library.

The gates are characterized by their implementation cost in quantum technologies, which is dubbed as Quantum Cost (QC) [14, 16]. Reversible logic gates can also be represented as an unitary transformation, therefore serving as building blocks for quantum computers. Few prominent classical reversible logic gates are presented below.

- NOT gate: On input A, it produces $\overline{A}$ as output.
- CNOT gate: On input (A, B), it produces $(A, A \oplus B)$ as output.
- CCNOT gate: Also known as Toffoli gate. On input (A, B, C), it produces $(A, B, AB \oplus C)$ as output. This gate can be generalized with Tof_n gate, where first $n - 1$ variables are used as control lines. NOT and CNOT gates are denoted as Tof_1 and Tof_2 respectively.
- Peres gate: A sequence of $Tof_3(a, b, c)$, $Tof_2(a, b)$ or its inverse is known as Peres gate.
- Controlled Swap gate, also known as Fredkin gate. On input (A, B, C), it produces $(A, \overline{A}.B + A.C, \overline{A}.C + A.B)$ as output. This gate can be generalized with $Fred_n$ gate $(n > 1)$, where first $n - 2$ variables are used as control lines.

Multiple sets of reversible gates form an universal gate library for realizing classical Boolean functions such as, (i) NCT: NOT, CNOT, Toffoli. (ii) NCTSF: NOT, CNOT, Toffoli, SWAP, Fredkin. (iii) GT: Tof_n. (iv) GTGF: Tof_n and $Fred_n$. Of late, Clifford+T gate library is preferred for Quantum circuit construction due to the known constructions of Clifford group of operators and T gate for most promising error correcting codes, including surface code. In this work, we focus on the logical fault tolerance issue and focus on the classical reversible logic gates. Efficient Clifford+T realization of classical reversible logic gates form an important research problem.

Reversible logic synthesis begins from a given n-variable Boolean function, which can be irreversible. The first step is to convert it to a reversible Boolean function by adding distinguishing output bits, known as *garbage outputs*. When additional input Boolean variables are needed for constructing the output function, those are referred as *ancilla*. In this work, we focus on minimizing the number of garbage outputs. However, for a full generalized analysis, one should consider joint minimization of both the numbers of garbage outputs and the ancilla inputs.

Reversible logic synthesis methods can be broadly classified in four categories as following. A different and more detailed classification is presented in a recent survey of reversible logic synthesis methods [24].

- **Exact and Optimal methods:** These methods consider step-by-step exhaustive enumeration or formulating the logic synthesis as a SAT problem [7] or reachability problem [10]. Optimal implementations for all 4-variable Boolean functions [6] and for selected benchmarks up to 6-variable Boolean functions are known [9].

- **Transformation-based method** [13,35]: These methods use a weighted graph representation for performing the transformations, while [13] proceed row-wise in the Boolean truth-table.
- **Methods based on decision diagrams** [29,32]: In this approach, each node of the decision diagram is converted to an equivalent reversible circuit structure. These methods reported excellent scaling for large Boolean functions, low QC at the cost of high number of garbage bits.
- **ESOP-based methods:** For classical logic synthesis, the exclusive sum of products (ESOP) formulation is studied well for specific target technologies [15]. For reversible logic synthesis, the ESOP formulation [8] maps directly to the basic reversible logic gates and has led to significant research interest.

Among the above methods, methods based on Decision Diagrams and ESOP-based methods can synthesize an irreversible Boolean specification to reversible circuit by adding extra garbage lines. However, these methods do not guarantee the minimum garbage count. On the other hand, determination of minimum garbage count and their assignment is non-trivial, particularly for Boolean functions with large number of variables [33]. To the best of our knowledge, no automatic reversible logic synthesis tool supports automatic derivation of parity-preserving Boolean specification from an irreversible/reversible Boolean specification. Our flow proposed in the paper can be complemented with any reversible logic synthesis flows, which work on reversible Boolean specifications.

3   Theoretical Results

First we discuss how to convert a reversible Boolean specification (that does not necessarily consider parity preservation) into parity-preserving reversible specification. Before proceeding, we count the number of n-variable parity preserving reversible Boolean functions in Theorem 1.

Theorem 1. *Total number of n-variable parity preserving reversible Boolean functions is* $\left(2^{n-1}!\right)^2$.

Proof. In the truth table of an n-variable reversible Boolean function, there are 2^n input and output rows. Half of the 2^n input (or output) rows, i.e., total 2^{n-1} rows would have odd parity and the other half would have even parity. For the function to be parity-preserving, the odd-parity input rows must map to the odd-parity output rows. There are $2^{n-1}!$ such mappings. Corresponding to each of these, the even-parity input rows must map to the even-parity output rows and there are again $2^{n-1}!$ such mappings. Hence the result follows.

The method of constructing a parity-preserving reversible specification from any reversible specification is described in the proof of Theorem 2.

Theorem 2. *Given any n-variable reversible Boolean specification, it can be converted to a parity-preserving reversible Boolean specification with the introduction of at most one extra variable.*

Proof. If the function is already parity-preserving, we need not do anything. If not, then in the output column of the truth table, we can just put a 0 in the parity-matching rows and a 1 in the parity-mismatching rows. On the input side, the extra variable can be set to the constant 0. Hence the result follows.

3.1 Direct Method of Converting Irreversible Specification to Parity-Preserving Reversible Specification

Next, we discuss the case when we are given an irreversible Boolean specification. One simple approach can be a two-phase procedure: first, to use some standard approaches [33] for converting the irreversible specification to a reversible specification, and next, use the result of Theorem 2. However, the first phase in this approach may incur unnecessary extra garbage bits. To avoid this problem, we provide a direct method of converting a given irreversible specification to a parity-preserving reversible specification with theoretically bounded number of extra bits. The method is as follows.

Since the specification is irreversible, the output rows must contain duplicate bit-strings. Suppose there are n input variables and hence 2^n rows in the truth table. Suppose there are $k < 2^n$ distinct output bit-strings, with the counts $n_1, \ldots, n_k$, such that $\sum_{i=1}^{k} n_i = 2^n$. For each $i = 1, \ldots, k$, out of n_i rows with the same output bit-string, let $n_{i,p}$ be the number of rows where the input and the output parity is matching and so $n_i - n_{i,p}$ is the number of rows where the parity is not matching. To differentiate the matching rows we need at least $\lceil \log_2 n_{i,p} \rceil$ extra bits. Similarly, to differentiate the mismatching rows, we need at least $\lceil \log_2 (n - n_{i,p}) \rceil$ extra bits. Hence, for the rows corresponding to the bit-string category i, the number of extra bits needed is at most one more than the maximum of these two numbers. The one additional bit may be required to match the parity, in case the specification with the garbage bits is not already parity-preserving. Thus, the total number of extra bits needed is given by the maximum of the above quantity over all i's. Hence, with the above formulation, we have the following result.

Theorem 3. *The number of extra bits needed by the proposed algorithm to convert an irreversible specification to parity-preserving reversible specification is at most*

$$\max_{i=1}^{k}\{\max\{\lceil \log_2 n_{i,p} \rceil, \lceil \log_2 (n - n_{i,p}) \rceil\}\} + 1.$$

Note that the expression before 1 is the number of garbage lines needed to convert the irreversible specification to reversible specification which has been explained in the following subsection.

3.2 Algorithm and Its Complexity Analysis

We present the algorithm for converting an irreversible specification to parity-preserving reversible specification in Algorithm 1. Suppose $x_1, \ldots, x_k$ are k integers $\in \{0, \ldots, 2^n - 1\}$ corresponding to the distinct output bit-strings. Note that according to our notation, x_i appears n_i times. We will keep two arrays $match$ and $mismatch$ as follows. In the algorithm, $match[x_i]$ will contain $n_{i,m}$ and $mismatch[x_i]$ will contain $n - n_{i,m}$. The array $count[i]$, for $0, \ldots, 2^n - 1$, is filled from top to bottom order, corresponding to each output row as follows: $count[i]$ contains how many times the i-th output row has appeared so far starting from the top row in both the cases when the parity is preserved and when it is not preserved.

ALGORITHM 1. Irreversible to Parity Preserving Reversible Specification

---

    Input: n, An integer array $out[0 \ldots 2^n - 1]$, containing the decimal equivalent of the output rows of an n-variable Boolean function.

    Output: Parity preserving reversible specification.

1 $max = 0$;

2 **for** $i = 0$ *to* $2^n - 1$ **do**

3 | $match[i] = 0$, $mismatch[i] = 0$, $count[i] = 0$;

    end

4 **for** $row \leftarrow 0$ **to** $2^n - 1$ **do**

5 | **if** *parity matches* **then**

6 | | $match[out[row]]$++;

7 | | $count[row] = match[out[row]]$;

8 | | **if** $max < match[out[row]]$ **then**

9 | | | $max = match[out[row]]$;

    | **end**

    | **end**

10 | **else**

11 | | $mismatch[out[row]]$++;

12 | | $count[row] = mismatch[out[row]]$;

13 | | **if** $max < mismatch[out[row]]$ **then**

14 | | | $max = mismatch[out[row]]$;

    | **end**

    | **end**

    end

15 $g = \log_2 max + 1$;

16 Add g columns to the Boolean output specification;

17 **for** $row \leftarrow 0$ **to** $2^n - 1$ **do**

18 | $k = count[row]$;

19 | Append binary value of k in the $g - 1$ bits;

20 | Use the last bit, if necessary, to match parity;

    end

Now we present the complexity of our algorithm in Theorem 4.

Theorem 4. *For an n-input m-output Boolean specification, the running time of Algorithm 1 is $O((n + m)2^n)$.*

Proof. The maximum number of input or output rows in the Boolean specification is 2^n. Let there be $k < 2^n$ distinct output bit-strings with the counts $n_1, \ldots, n_k$, such that $\sum_{i=1}^{k} n_i = 2^n$. For each row we have to compute the number of 1's in the input and output bit-strings for computing the parity. The algorithmic complexity for this traversal is $O((n + m)2^n)$, which accounts for Steps 2 to 14. After this computation, we have one more iteration over the output rows through Step 17 to 20, the running time of which is dominated by $O((n + m)2^n)$. Hence the result follows.

4   Experimental Results

The proposed algorithm has been implemented and tested on several benchmark circuits, using C++ on an Intel(R) Core(TM) i5-3570 CPU (Quad-core) with 3.40 GHz clock and 6 MB cache, having Linux version 2.6.32-358.6.2.el6.x86_64 as the OS, and gcc version 4.4.7 as the compiler. First, we compared our automatically generated parity-preserving reversible circuits with manually created parity-preserving reversible circuits reported by others. Our comparison metric is the number of additional garbage lines required for preserving parity. Quantum cost and Gate Count for different specifications can vary considerably. In the paper we have given an example of rd53 circuit. For this circuit we can have a total of $(10! \times 10! \times 5! \times 5! = 1.8962193e + 17)$ different possible parity preserved specifications. Even Table 2 in the paper with Full Adder Boolean specification has $(3! \times 3! = 36)$ different possible reversible specifications.

4.1   Comparison with State-of-the-Art

We apply the proposed algorithm on Half Adder and Full Adder as two test cases. The transformation of irreversible Boolean specification to a reversible one is depicted in Tables 1 and 2 respectively, with the required number of constant input and garbage lines. The ancilla inputs and garbage outputs are referred as A_i and G_i respectively. The reversible specification thus obtained can be used to implement the reversible circuit using the well-known reversible logic synthesis methods for garbage-free synthesis [13].

We do not compare the gate count and quantum cost incurred in realizing the circuit as the proposed algorithm does not aim to optimize those parameters. Our aim was to minimize the number of garbage lines. For the parity preserved half adder circuit obtained from the proposed algorithm, the gate count and quantum cost required for the realization of the circuit are 8 and 28 respectively. The approach followed for the construction of the circuit is similar to the transformation based synthesis as proposed in [13]. The circuit is shown in Fig. 1.

Table 1. Half Adder Boolean specification

| Irreversible specification | | Reversible specification | | | | | |
Input	Output	Input	A_1	A_2	Output	G_1	G_2
00	00	00	0	0	00	0	0
01	10	01	0	0	10	0	0
10	10	10	0	0	10	1	1
11	01	11	0	0	01	0	1

Table 2. Full Adder Boolean specification

| Irreversible specification | | Reversible specification | | | | | | |
Input	Output	Input	A_1	A_2	Output	G_1	G_2	G_3
000	00	000	0	0	00	0	0	0
001	10	001	0	0	10	0	0	0
010	10	010	0	0	10	0	1	1
011	01	011	0	0	01	0	0	1
100	10	100	0	0	10	1	0	1
101	01	101	0	0	01	0	1	0
110	01	110	0	0	01	1	0	0
111	11	111	0	0	11	0	0	1

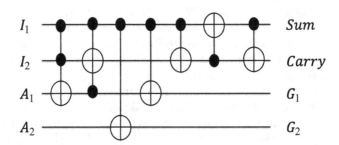

Fig. 1. Realization for the parity preserved half adder circuit as per Table 1

In terms of the ancilla and garbage count, we obtain exactly the same number for both the Half Adder and Full Adder circuits as obtained manually in [1, 27].

It is also worthwhile to compare with the online testability approaches proposed in [17, 18]. There, an additional parity line and modulo-redundancy is added corresponding to every reversible gate after the circuit is synthesized. Naturally, this leads to a significant design overhead, which can be up to 300% in terms of gate count [18]. Even with such an overhead, there are fault scenarios that cannot be covered. In contrast, our proposition only requires $2N$ additional CNOT gates, where N is the number of inputs in the parity-preserved reversible circuit. The CNOT gates are targeted towards one additional parity line, similar to the *Preamble* and *Postamble* blocks suggested in [18].

A limitation of our approach is that it assumes a rather simplistic bit-flip model arising from classical reversible logic circuits. In the context of, say, Quantum technologies, the fault models are different [22] and requires a deeper analysis. For example, it is indeed possible to interpret a Single Missing Gate Fault (SMGF) or Single Missing Control Fault (SMCF) as a bit-flip, though, it is not guaranteed that a parity-preserving reversible circuit can lead to a 100% detection of all possible missing faults. For that, the propagation of an individual bit-flip and the masking effects of the subsequent gates need to be taken into account. Moreover, the correlation between parity violation and the two kinds of missing faults is circuit specific. Clearly, it is an interesting open problem to identify the minimum performance overhead to guarantee complete fault coverage with a solution lying between gate-wise redundancy advocated earlier [18] and circuit-level parity-preservation proposed here.

4.2   Tests for Boolean Functions with Large Variable Count

We also tried the algorithm for several Boolean functions with large number of variables, for which obtaining a parity-preserving Boolean specification manually would be hard.

As an example, our algorithm converts the irreversible specification *rd53* [13] into reversible one as enlisted in Table 3. A summary of all the functions we tried is presented in Table 4. In this table, the *tar* functions are from Tarannikov's paper [31]. From [31, Eq. 2], we use the parameter c as 001 to construct an 8-variable, 2-resilient function then we get tar82_2_001.pla. Similarly tar93_110.pla and tar93_101.pla are 9 variable 3-resilient functions with the c vector as 110 and 101 respectively. The functions like $rdNK$ is presented in several benchmarks on reversible logic synthesis [16]. The input weight function $rdNK$ has N inputs and $K = \lfloor logN \rfloor + 1$ outputs. Its output is the binary encoding of the number of ones in its input. The other functions are obtained from RevKit benchmark [28].

Table 3. Reversible Boolean specification for rd53 function

Input	A_1	A_2	A_3	Output	G_1	G_2	G_3	G_4	G_5
00000	0	0	0	000	0	0	0	0	0
00001	0	0	0	001	0	0	0	0	0
00010	0	0	0	001	0	0	0	1	1
00011	0	0	0	010	0	0	0	0	1
00100	0	0	0	001	0	0	1	0	1
00101	0	0	0	010	0	0	0	1	0
00110	0	0	0	010	0	0	1	0	0
00111	0	0	0	011	0	0	0	0	1
01000	0	0	0	001	0	0	1	1	0
01001	0	0	0	010	0	0	1	1	1
01010	0	0	0	010	0	1	0	0	0
01011	0	0	0	011	0	0	0	1	0
01100	0	0	0	010	0	1	0	1	1
01101	0	0	0	011	0	0	1	0	0
01110	0	0	0	011	0	0	1	1	1
01111	0	0	0	100	0	0	0	0	1
10000	0	0	0	001	0	1	0	0	1
10001	0	0	0	010	0	1	1	0	1
10010	0	0	0	010	0	1	1	1	0
10011	0	0	0	011	0	1	0	0	0
10100	0	0	0	010	1	0	0	0	0
10101	0	0	0	011	0	1	0	1	1
10110	0	0	0	011	0	1	1	0	1
10111	0	0	0	100	0	0	0	1	0
11000	0	0	0	010	1	0	0	1	1
11001	0	0	0	011	0	1	1	1	0
11010	0	0	0	011	1	0	0	0	0
11011	0	0	0	100	0	0	1	0	0
11100	0	0	0	011	1	0	0	1	1
11101	0	0	0	100	0	0	1	1	1
11110	0	0	0	100	0	1	0	0	0
11111	0	0	0	101	0	0	0	0	1

Table 4. Summary of results for exemplary Boolean functions with large no. of variables

Function	Input count	Output count	Garbage count	Ancilla count	Runtime (ms)
tar82_2_001.pla	8	1	8	1	0.66
tar93_110.pla	9	1	8	0	1.89
tar93_101.pla	9	1	8	0	1.63
rd53	5	3	5	3	0.18
rd73	7	3	7	3	0.35
rd84	8	4	8	4	0.64
rd20_5	20	5	19	4	34.70
rd10_4	10	4	9	3	23.17
0410184_85.pla	14	14	1	1	14.17
cycle10_2_61.pla	12	12	1	1	3.39
ham15_30.pla	15	15	1	1	30.15
ham7_29.pla	7	7	1	1	0.20
ham8_64.pla	8	8	1	1	0.31
life_175.pla	9	1	9	1	0.45
squar5.pla	5	8	1	4	6.77
urf4_89.pla	11	11	1	1	1.76
urf6.pla	15	15	1	1	29.21
plus63mod8192.pla	13	13	1	1	6.76

5   Conclusion and Future Work

We propose the first systematic algorithm to convert any irreversible specification into a parity-preserving reversible specification. In existing works such as in [11,27], a new specific gate is introduced to realize one particular parity-preserving circuit. However, these gates may not be useful to realize other circuits. Our method is fully automated and general and can work on any given circuit. The relevant code for the Algorithm 1 has been shared at [5].

In the current work, we have focused on bit-flip error only. However, the fault coverage for different logical fault models [22] arising in the context of Quantum circuit implementation requires further work, which we plan to undertake. Another interesting future work could be to tackle the complexity of the input representation.

One limitation of our work is that it uses truth-table specification and hence is not scalable for large variables. An interesting future work could be exploring the possibility of direct synthesis of parity-preserving circuits based on more compact representations, such as BDDs or other hierarchical reversible logic synthesis [30]. Such an approach may be more efficient for functions of larger number of variables and hence more scalable. Moreover, as pointed out in a recent work [21], even if a reversible circuit is parity preserving, it has to be checked against a particular fault model. As part of our future work, we also plan to inject faults at different gates and estimate the fault coverage of our circuits against different fault models.

References

1. Azad Khan, M.H.: Design of full-adder with reversible gates. In: International Conference on Computer and Information Technology, pp. 515–519 (2002)
2. Bennett, C.H.: Logical reversibility of computation. IBM J. Res. Dev. **17**, 525–532 (1973)
3. Bérut, A., Arakelyan, A., Petrosyan, A., Ciliberto, S., Dillenschneider, R., Lutz, E.: Experimental verification of Landauer's principle linking information and thermodynamics. Nature **483**, 187–189 (2012)
4. Dastan, F., Haghparast, M.: A novel nanometric fault tolerant reversible divider. Int. J. Phys. Sci. **6**(24), 5671–5681 (2011)
5. https://github.com/cchandak/parity_preserving_rev_ckt
6. Golubitsky, O., Falconer, S.M., Maslov, D.: Synthesis of the optimal 4-bit reversible circuits. In: Proceedings of DAC, pp. 653–656 (2010)
7. Grosse, D., Wille, R., Dueck, G.W., Drechsler, R.: Exact multiple-control toffoli network synthesis with SAT techniques. IEEE TCAD **28**(5), 703–715 (2009)
8. Gupta, P., Agrawal, A., Jha, N.K.: An algorithm for synthesis of reversible logic circuits. IEEE TCAD **25**(11), 2317–2330 (2006)
9. Grosse, D., Wille, R., Dueck, G.W., Drechsler, R.: Exact multiple-control tooli network synthesis With SAT techniques. IEEE TCAD **28**(5), 703–715 (2009). doi:10.1109/TCAD.2009.2017215
10. Hung, W.N.N., Xiaoyu, S., Guowu, Y., Jin, Y., Perkowski, M.: Optimal synthesis of multiple output boolean functions using a set of quantum gates by symbolic reachability analysis. IEEE TCAD **25**(9), 1652–1663 (2006)
11. Islam, M.S., Rahman, M.M., Begum, Z., Hafiz, A., Al Mahmud, A.: Synthesis of fault tolerant reversible logic circuits. In: Proceedings of IEEE Circuits and Systems International Conference on Testing and Diagnosis, pp. 1–4 (2009)
12. Landauer, R.: Irreversibility and heat generation in the computing process. IBM J. Res. Dev. **5**, 183–191 (1961)
13. Miller, D.M., Maslov, D., Dueck, G.W.: A transformation based algorithm for reversible logic synthesis. In: Proceedings of DAC, pp. 318–323 (2003)
14. Miller, D.M., Wille, R., Sasanian, Z.: Elementary quantum gate realizations for multiple-control toffoli gates. In: Proceedings of International Symposium on Multiple-Valued Logic, pp. 288–293 (2011)
15. Mishchenko, A., Perkowski, M., Fast heuristic minimization of exclusive-sums-of-products. In: Proceedings of the Reed-Muller Workshop, pp. 242–250 (2001)
16. Maslov, D.: Reversible Benchmarks. http://webhome.cs.uvic.ca/~dmaslov, Accessed Jun 2013
17. Nayeem, N.M., Rice, J.E.: Online testable approaches in reversible logic. J. Electron. Test. **29**(6), 763–778 (2013)
18. Nashiry, M.A., Bhaskar, G.G., Rice, J.E.: Online testing for three fault models in reversible circuits. In: Proceedings of ISMVL, pp. 8–13 (2011). doi:10.1109/ISMVL.2015.36
19. Parhami, B.: Parity-preserving transformations in computer arithmetic. In: Proceeding of SPIE, vol. 4791, pp. 403–411 (2002)

20. Parhami, B.: Fault-tolerant reversible circuits. In: Proceeding of 40th Asilomar Conference Signals, Systems, and Computers, Pacific Grove, CA, pp. 1726–1729, October 2006

21. Przigoda, N., Dueck, G.W., Wille, R., Drechsler, R.: Fault detection in parity preserving reversible circuits. In: Proceeding of IEEE 46th International Symposium on Multiple-Valued Logic (ISMVL), Sapporo, Japan, pp. 44–49, 18–20 May 2016

22. Polian, I., Fiehn, T., Becker, B., Hayes, J.P.: A family of logical fault models for reversible circuits. In: Proceedings of Asian Test Symposium, pp. 422–427 (2011)

23. Qi, X., Chen, F., Zuo, K., Guo, L., Luo, Y., Hu, M.: Design of fast fault tolerant reversible signed multiplier. Int. J. Phys. Sci. **7**(17), 2506–2514 (2012)

24. Saeedi, M., Markov, I.L.: Synthesis and optimization of reversible circuits - a survey. In: CoRR abs/1110.2574, http://arxiv.org/abs/1110.2574 (2011)

25. Saligram, R., Hegde, S.S., Kulkarni, S.A., Bhagyalakshmi, H.R., Venkatesha, M.K.: Design of fault tolerant reversible multiplexer based multi-boolean function generator using parity preserving gates. Int. J. Comput. Appl. **66**(19), 20–24 (2013)

26. Saligram, R., Hegde, S.S., Kulkarni, S.A., Bhagyalakshmi, H.R., Venkatesha, M.K.: Design of parity preserving logic based fault tolerant reversible arithmetic logic unit. In: CoRR abs/1307.3690, http://arxiv.org/abs/1307.3690 (2013)

27. Syal, N., Sinha, H.P., Sheenu: Comparison of different type parity preserving reversible gates and simple reversible gates. In: International Journal of Research and Innovation in Computer Engineering, vol. 1, issue 1 (2011)

28. Soeken, M., Frehse, S., Wille, R., Drechsler, R.: RevKit: a toolkit for reversible circuit design. In: Proceedings of Workshop on Reversible Computation, pp. 64–76 (2011)

29. Soeken, M., Wille, R., Hilken, C., Przigoda, N., Drechsler, R.: Synthesis of reversible circuits with minimal lines for large functions. In: Proceedings of ASP-DAC, pp. 85–92 (2012). doi:10.1109/ASPDAC.2012.6165069

30. Soeken, M., Chattopadhyay, A.: Unlocking efficiency and scalability of reversible logic synthesis using conventional logic synthesis. In: Proceedings of the 53rd Annual Design Automation Conference (DAC), Article no. 149, Austin, Texas, 05–09 June 2016

31. Tarannikov, Y.: New constructions of resilient boolean functions with maximal nonlinearity. In: Matsui, M. (ed.) FSE 2001. LNCS, vol. 2355, pp. 66–77. Springer, Heidelberg (2002). doi:10.1007/3-540-45473-X_6

32. Wille, R., Drechsler, R.: BDD-based synthesis of reversible logic for large functions. In: Proceedings of DAC, pp. 270–275 (2009)

33. Wille, R., Keszöcze, O., Drechsler, R.: Determining the minimal number of lines for large reversible circuits. In: Proceedings of DATE, pp. 1–4 (2011)

34. Wille, R., Drechsler, R., Osewold, C., Garcia-Ortiz, A.: Automatic design of low-power encoders using reversible circuit synthesis. In: Proceedings of DATE, pp. 1036–1041 (2012). doi:10.1109/DATE.2012.6176648

35. Zheng, Y., Huang, C.: A novel toffoli network synthesis algorithm for reversible logic. In: Proceedings of ASP-DAC, pp. 739–744 (2009)

36. Wille, R., Chattopadhyay, A., Drechsler, R.: From reversible logic to quantum circuits: logic design for an emerging technology. In: Proceedings of International Conference on Embedded Computer Systems: Architectures, Modeling and Simulation (SAMOS), pp. 268–274 (2016)

REVS: A Tool for Space-Optimized Reversible Circuit Synthesis

Alex Parent[1,2], Martin Roetteler[2(✉)], and Krysta M. Svore[2]

[1] Institute for Quantum Computing, University of Waterloo,
200 University Avenue West, Waterloo, ON, Canada
alexparent@gmail.com
[2] Quantum Architectures and Computation Group,
Microsoft Research, One Microsoft Way, Redmond, WA 98052, USA
{martinro,ksvore}@microsoft.com

Abstract. Computing classical functions is at the core of many quantum algorithms. Conceptually any classical, irreversible function can be carried out by a Toffoli network in a reversible way. However, the Bennett method to obtain such a network in a "clean" form, i.e., a form that can be used in quantum algorithms, is highly space-inefficient. We present REVS, a tool that allows to trade time against space, leading to circuits that have a significantly smaller memory footprint when compared to the Bennett method. Our method is based on an analysis of the data dependency graph underlying a given classical program. We report the findings from running the tool against several benchmarks circuits to highlight the potential space-time tradeoffs that REVS can realize.

1 Introduction

The ability to compute classical functions is at the core of many interesting quantum algorithms, including Shor's algorithm for factoring, Grover's algorithm for unstructured search, and the HHL algorithm for inverting linear systems of equations. While conceptually any classical, irreversible function can be carried out by a reversible Toffoli network, the standard way to obtain such a network is highly space-inefficient: the so-called Bennett method leads to a number of qubits that is proportional to the circuit size of the given classical, irreversible function [3].

We show that it is possible to trade time against space in reversible circuit synthesis, leading to circuits that have a significantly smaller memory footprint than the ones generated by the Bennett method. To this end, we implemented a tool for space-optimized reversible synthesis. We applied our tool to a suite of challenge problems that include a subset of several classical circuits benchmarks such as the ISCAS and MCNC benchmarks, as well as reversible benchmarks such as the Maslov benchmarks and the RevLib benchmarks. We show that it is typically possible to reduce the total number of required ancillas by a factor of $4X$ at a moderate increase of the total number of gates by less than $3X$.

© Springer International Publishing AG 2017
I. Phillips and H. Rahaman (Eds.): RC 2017, LNCS 10301, pp. 90–101, 2017.
DOI: 10.1007/978-3-319-59936-6_7

Prior work. Several tools were developed for synthesizing reversible circuits, ranging from low-level tools [13,15,24,26,30–32], over various optimizations [24], to high-level programming languages and compilers [9–11,22,23,29,33,36]. See also [25] for a survey. We are interested in methods that optimize space, i.e., methods that synthesize target functions while using as few ancillas as possible.

The implied trade-off is between circuit size, as measured by the total number of Toffoli gates, and circuit width, as measured by the total number of qubits. Methods to obtain such trade-offs have been studied in the literature before, notably in the theoretical computer science community where space-time trade-offs based on trading qubits (lines) for gates [7,27,34,35] and tradeoffs based on Bennett's pebble game have been known for quite some time [4–6,12]. Our work implements a compiler that optimizes for space, trading it for a possibly a slightly larger gate count and possibly for a longer compilation time.

Our contribution. We improve the space-efficiency of Toffoli networks by analyzing the data flow dependencies of the given input program or truth table. This allows to clean some of the required ancilla bits much earlier than possible with the Bennett method. Another key component that allowed us to improve the memory footprint while keeping the circuit size of the resulting networks relatively small, is the combination of known techniques for Boolean Exclusive Sum-Of-Products (ESOP) [17,18] minimization with our dependency-graph based methods for early cleanup.

Specifically, we considered the RevLib benchmarks [1] and the Maslov benchmarks [14]. Our main result is that for some of the benchmarks we can improve the total number of qubits needed. This typically comes at an increase of the overall gate count, however, for some of the benchmarks our method achieves an improvement in terms of number of qubits *and* total number of Toffoli gates.

Generally, the methods described in this paper aim at large circuits, i.e., they are *scalable*: our reversible synthesis method starts from high-level descriptions in a functional programming language.

2   Reversible Circuits

Reversible functions are Boolean functions $f : \{0,1\}^n \rightarrow \{0,1\}^n$ that can be inverted on all outputs, i.e., the functions that correspond to permutations of a set of cardinality 2^n. As with classical circuits, reversible functions can be constructed from universal gate sets: for instance, it is known that the Toffoli gate which maps $(x,y,z) \mapsto (x,y,z \oplus xy)$, together with the controlled-NOT gate (CNOT) which maps $(x,y) \mapsto (x,x \oplus y)$ and the NOT gate which maps $x \mapsto x \oplus 1$, is universal for reversible computation. The group generated by all NOT, CNOT, and Toffoli gates on $n \geq 4$ bits is isomorphic to the alternating group A_{2^n} of even permutations which is a group of order $(2^n)!/2$. Hence, any given target function, when considered as a permutation π can be implemented over this gate set at the expense of at most 1 additional qubit since $\mathbf{1} \otimes \pi = \mathrm{diag}(\pi,\pi)$ is even.

Most classical functions $f : \{0,1\}^n \to \{0,1\}^m$ are not invertible. To make a classical function reversible a permutation π on a larger space has to be constructed that implements f on a subset of size 2^n of the inputs. These extra bits are commonly denoted *ancilla* bits and are used as *scratch space*, i.e., temporary bits which store intermediate results of a computation. A very important difference to classical computing is that scratch bits cannot just be overwritten when they are no longer needed: any ancilla that is used as scratch space during a reversible computation must be returned to the initial value—which is commonly assumed to be the value 0—computationally.

Moreover, if this return to a "clean" value is not achieved, the function cannot be safely used inside a quantum computer as its use might lead to unwanted entanglement of the computational registers with the ancilla qubits. This in turn can destroy desired interferences crucial for quantum algorithms [20]. If a Toffoli network computes a target function in a way that leaves garbage bits that are unclean, then one can turn this into a clean network using Bennett's method, however, this leads to a 2X increase in circuit size and additional qubits to store the output.

The number of Toffoli gates used in the implementation of a given permutation is the basic measure for the circuit *size* that we use in this paper. Counting Toffolis only is justified from the theory of fault-tolerant quantum computing [20] since the Toffoli gate (and the T gate) has a substantial cost, whereas the cost of so-called Clifford gates, such as CNOT and NOT, can usually be neglected. Another related metric is the overall depth of the circuit, measured usually in the form of T-gate-depth. Implementations of the Toffoli gate over the Clifford+T gate set are known [20]. The other basic parameter in our design space is circuit *width*, measured as the maximum number of qubits needed during any point, i.e., the maximum number of input qubits, output qubits, and ancilla qubits.

Generally, our goal is to trade time for space, i.e., to achieve a reduction in the total number of qubits required. In turn, we are willing to pay a price in terms of a slight increase in the total number of Toffoli gates and in terms of compilation time. Our trade-off is justified by the limited number of qubits available in experimental quantum devices.

3 Dependency Analysis

Analyzing the dependencies between the instructions in a basic function, between functions, and between larger units of code is a fundamental topic in compiler design [2,19]. Typically, dependency analysis consists of finding codes units and to identify them with nodes in a directed acyclic graph (DAG). The directed edges in the graph are the dependencies between the basic units, i.e., anything that might constrain the execution order, for instance control dependencies that arise from the control flow in the program, or branchings that happen conditional on the value of a variable or the causal dependencies that arise from one unit having to wait for the output of another unit before the computation can proceed.

```
let xor4 (a:bool array) (b:bool array) =
    let c = Array.zeroCreate 4
    for i in 0 .. 3 do
        c.[i] <- a.[i] <> b.[i]
    c
let and4 (a:bool array) (b:bool array) =
    let d = Array.zeroCreate 4
    for i in 0 .. 3 do
        d.[i] <- a.[i] && b.[i]
    d
let mutable a = Array.zeroCreate 4
a <- xor4 a b
and4 a c
```

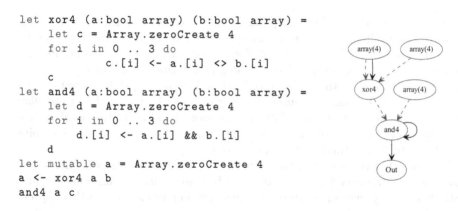

(a) F# snippet   (b) Corresponding MDD

Fig. 1. (a) Simple F# code example of a function that uses arrays and in place operations. (b) Corresponding mutable data dependency (MDD) graph with data dependency arrows (dashed) and mutation arrows (bold).

3.1   Mutable Data Dependency Graphs (MDDs)

We used the .NET language F# to implement a compiler for a language that can express classical, irreversible functions and turn them into reversible networks. The language itself is also a subset of F# which has the advantage that all programs expressed in the language also have an abstract interpretation as executable programs that can be run on the .NET common language run-time (CLR). This helps with testing of the reversible circuits generated by our compiler as it is possible to (a) generate a Toffoli network from the source program and (b) get a trace from the execution on a classical computer and then to compare (a) and (b).

The compilation itself follows some steps that are common for domain-specific approaches. As our language is embedded into F#, we can first invoke the F# compiler to generate an abstract syntax tree (AST) for the input program. Using so-called active patterns [28] we turn the AST into an internal representation that represents the dependency graph of the program. The nodes of this graph capture the control flow and data dependencies between expressions, but also identify which blocks can be computed by in-place operations and which blocks have to be computed by out-of-place operations. Because of this latter feature is related to which elements of the dependency graph are mutable and which are not, we call this data structure the Mutable Data Dependency graph or MDD.

Which parts of the code can be computed by an in-place operation is inferred by which variables are labeled in F# as mutable together with the external knowledge about whether for an expression involving these variables an in-place implementation is actually known. An example for the latter is the addition operation for which we can choose either an in-place implementation $(a, b) \mapsto (a, a + b)$ or an out-of-place implementation $(a, b, 0) \mapsto (a, b, a + b)$.

The nodes of the MDD correspond to inputs, computations, initialized and cleaned-up bits. Inputs nodes can correspond to individual variables but also to entire arrays which are also represented as a single node and treated atomically. Computation nodes correspond to any expression that occurs in the program and that manipulates the data. Initialized and cleaned-up bits correspond to bits that are part of the computation and which can be used either as ancillas or to hold the actual final output of the computation. Initialization implies that those qubits are in the logical state 0 and the cleaned-up state means these bits are known to be returned back in the state 0.

The directed edges in a MDD come in two flavors: data dependencies and mutations. Data dependencies are denoted by dashed arrows and represent any data dependency that one expression might have in relation to any other expression. Mutations are denoted by bold arrows and represent parts of the program that are changed during the computation. By tracking the flow of the mutations one can then ultimately determine the scheduling of the expressions onto reversible operations and re-use a pool of available ancillas. This helps to reduce the space requirements of the computation, in some cases even drastically so.

First, a number of arrays are used to store data in a way that allows for easy access and indexing. Note that in F# the type `array` is inherited from the .NET array type and by definition is a mutable type. This information is used when the MDD for the program is constructed as our compiler knows that in principle the values in the array can be updated and overwritten. Whether this can actually be leveraged when compiling a reversible circuit will of course depend on other factors as well, namely whether the parts of the data that is invoked in assignments (denoted by $<-$) is used at a later stage in the program, in which case the data might have to be recomputed.

When resolving the AST of a function, each node will either be another function or an input variable. If the node is a function, we recursively compute the AST for all of the function inputs adding the results to the graph. Upon doing so, we use the index numbers of these results as the inputs for the operation and then add the operation to the graph. If the node is a variable, the algorithm looks up its name in a map of currently defined variables and returns an index to its node. The type of the operation determines which arrows will be solid input arrows and which will be data dependencies, i.e., controls. An example is shown in Fig. 1.

3.2   Eager Cleanup Strategy

From Bennett's work on reversible Turing machines it follows that any function can be implemented by a suitable reversible circuit [3]: if an n-bit function $x \mapsto f(x)$ can be implemented with K gates over $\{\text{NOT}, \text{AND}\}$, then the reversible function $(x, y) \mapsto (x, y \oplus f(x))$ can be implemented with at most $2K + n$ gates over the Toffoli gate set. The basic idea behind Bennett's method is to replace all AND gates with Toffoli gates, then perform the computation, copy out the result, and undo the computation. One potential disadvantage of Bennett's method is the large number of ancillas it requires as the required memory scales proportional

---

Algorithm 1. EAGER Performs eager cleanup of an MDD.

Require: An MDD G in reverse topological order, subroutines LastDependentNode, ModificationPath, InputNodes.

1: $i \leftarrow 0$
2: **for each** node **in** G **do**
3:     **if** modificationArrows node $= \emptyset$ **then**
4:         dIndex $\leftarrow$ LastDependentNode of node in G
5:         path $\leftarrow$ ModificationPath of node in G
6:         input $\leftarrow$ InputNodes of path in G
7:         **if** None (modificationArrows input) $\geq$ dIndex **then**
8:             cleanUp $\leftarrow$ (Reverse path) $++$ cleanNode
9:         **end if**
10:     **else**
11:         cleanUp $\leftarrow$ uncleanNode
12:         $G \leftarrow$ Insert cleanUp Into G After dIndex
13:     **end if**
14: **end for**
15: **return** G

---

to the circuit *size* of the initial, irreversible function f. Nevertheless, Bennett's method is useful to clean up garbage qubits in some situations where our improved synthesis method, which we call the "eager cleanup" strategy, does not succeed. The basic idea behind eager cleanup is to process the MDD in inverse topological order and try to clean up qubits that are no longer needed as early as possible. To do this, when we find a node A which does not have an outgoing modification arrow we first find the node furthest along in topological order which depends on it B. We then consider all inputs in the modification path of A. If any of the inputs have outgoing arrows modification arrows pointing levels previous to B we may not clean the bit eagerly as its inputs are no longer available. If the inputs do not have modification arrows pointing at levels previous to B we can immediately clean it up by reversing all operations along its modification path. In many cases, the eager cleanup strategy leads to lower number of qubits used compared to Bennett's original method [3]. A pseudo-code implementation of the eager cleanup strategy is shown in Algorithm 1.

4 Boolean Expression Generation

REVS handles higher-level, irreversible programs using cleanup strategies such as Bennett's method or the eager cleanup strategy mentioned in the previous section. This is particularly useful if the irreversible program has control flow such as loops, branchings, and subroutine calls. If a piece of the given code corresponds to a Boolean expression directly, then synthesis is handled differently: in these cases truth-table based techniques such as the ones described in [15] could be applied, however, in the current implementation we follow a simple flow that takes the Boolean function, either given in BLIF or PLA format, transforms

---

Algorithm 2. ESOP-FACTOR Find and factor common ESOP expressions.

Require: Boolean expression *exprs* as list of (*input, output*) pairs, integer *sizeParam* to specify maximum group size.

1: outputGroups ← group *exprs* with identical output
2: factorGroups ← Divide each group in outputGroups into groups of size *sizeParam* or less
3: **for each** group in factorGroups **do**
4:     xorExpr ← expression formed by XORing all input expressions in group together
5:     factoredExpr ← use multi-level optimization techniques to factor xorExpr
6:     circuit ← apply boolean expression generation algorithm to factoredExpr
7: **end for**
8: **return** circuit

---

it into exclusive-sum-of-product (ESOP) format using Exorcism [18], and then further process it using strategies that again allow tradeoffs between circuit size and number of qubits used. We briefly sketch these methods next and show the application to some benchmarks used in reversible synthesis.

4.1 Boolean Function Synthesis Benchmarks

The Berkeley Logic Interchange Format (BLIF) and the Programmable Logic Array format (PLA) allow logic level circuit description of a classical operation. Both formats allow the specification of hierarchical logical circuits, based on a simple text input form. Circuits can have combinational components, which typically are given by a collection of truth tables using separate lines for each input/output combinations, where "don't cares" are allowed. Circuits are also allowed to have sequential components such as latches.

BLIF underlies many circuit benchmarks that have been used primarily by the Circuit and Systems community in the 80s and 90s. These benchmarks include the ISCAS'85, ISCAS'89, MCNC'91, LGSynth'91 and LGSynth'92 collections [16]. We identified all examples from the union of these benchmarks that *only* use combinational circuit elements. For those Boolean functions in principle a reversible circuit can be computed. We obtained a set of 135 benchmark circuits which we used to test the performance of our Boolean generation subroutines. On these circuits we typically found that our tool REVS decreased the number of ancillas by a factor of $4x$ while increasing the number of gates only moderately.

PLA underlies benchmarks for reversible circuit synthesis that typically start as classical, irreversible functions expressed in this format. The two benchmarks we considered are the RevLib benchmarks [1] and the Maslov benchmarks [14]. We optimized the reversible circuits for space using the methods described in this paper and compared it to the best known circuits in the RevLib and Maslov databases. While generally, we get a tradeoff between space and time, in some cases we found circuits that are more efficient in terms of number of qubits *and* the total circuit size.

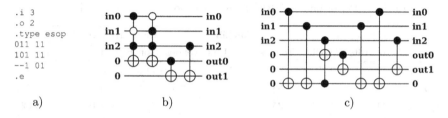

a)   b)   c)

Fig. 2. An example illustrating the synthesis based on factorization of output groups for ESOP files. Shown in (a) is a simple example of an ESOP file corresponding to the output functions $(f_0(x_0, x_1, x_2), f_1(x_0, x_1, x_2))$, where $f_0(x_0, x_1, x_2) = \overline{x_0}x_1x_2 \oplus x_0\overline{x_1}x_2$ and $f_1(x_0, x_1, x_2) = \overline{x_0}x_1x_2 \oplus x_0\overline{x_1}x_2 \oplus x_2$. Running REVS with parameter $p = 0$ treats each line in the ESOP file as a group. This turns each line into a multiply-controlled Toffoli gate as shown in (b). Running REVS with parameter $p = 1$ allows REVS to group up to 2 lines together, provided that the lines have identical outputs. In the example, the first two lines are grouped together which allows to factor the sum of the corresponding input product terms as $\overline{x_0}x_1x_2 \oplus x_0\overline{x_1}x_2 = (\overline{x_0}x_1 \oplus x_0\overline{x_1})x_2$. The factor $(\overline{x_0}x_1 \oplus x_0\overline{x_1})$ is then simplified to $x_0 \oplus x_1$ and computed into a new ancilla qubit which is then afterwards uncomputed. Overall, the T-gate complexity of the resulting circuit is small, however, the total number of qubits used has increased by 1. The circuits in (b) and (c) were rendered using QCViewer [21].

4.2   Optimizations for Boolean Circuits

In general, given a set of AND expressions that are combined using OR we want to find sets of mutually exclusive statements that minimize the use of AND. We consider each AND expression to be a vertex on a graph and add edges between vertices that are mutually exclusive. Now we cover this graph using the smallest possible number of cliques using an algorithm that solves the CLIQUE-COVER problem, which asks to partition the vertices of a graph into cliques. NP-completeness of CLIQUE-COVER for given upper bound k of allowed cliques is well-known, however, practical approximation algorithms exist [8].

After finding a cliques partition each set of mutually exclusive statements can be implemented by evaluating the AND statements and combining all of the values on a single ancilla using XOR for each clique. These results can then be combined using OR statements. We can pre-process the given file in such a way that the cliques will be grouped in the output. This yields a new file, however, the effect of the reordering is that instead of OR functions now the much cheaper XOR functions can be used.

We ran REVS against a suite of benchmarks from the RevLib database. In Table 1 we report on improvements over the best known circuits. Our tool improved so far only one instance of the Maslov database, namely the benchmark that consists of computing a Boolean function that computes the bits of the permanent of a given 3×3 binary matrix. Shown in Table 1 are the qubit and gate costs for the eager cleanup method and in comparison the corresponding cost with the best circuit from the database. The total number of qubits in the first data column is the number of ancillas from the second data column plus

Table 1. Performance of REVS on a selection of benchmark circuits.

Name	Our Method			RevLib		Comparison (rel.)		Time
	Tot. Bits	Ancillas	Toffolis	Tot. Bits	Toffolis	Tot. Bits	Toffolis	
4mod5	7	2	1	7	4	1.00	0.25	0.00s
5xp1	23	6	83	23	365	1.00	0.23	0.02s
6sym	11	4	35	14	16	0.79	2.19	0.02s
alu4	61	39	2821	33	10456	1.85	0.27	3.70s
apex5	228	23	3727	1025	1860	0.22	2.00	15.59s
bw	36	3	73	87	159	0.41	0.46	0.01s
con1	13	4	16	13	63	1.00	0.25	0.01s
decod24	6	0	1	6	4	1.00	0.25	0.00s
e64	193	63	4096	195	130	0.99	31.5	0.17s
ex1010	38	18	6581	29	31219	1.31	0.21	6.92s
f51m	52	30	1774	35	6207	1.49	0.29	1.97s
frg2	336	54	8950	1219	2186	0.28	4.09	1913.09s
hwb9	33	15	2915	170	394	0.19	7.40	3.13s
max46	20	10	195	17	689	1.18	0.28	0.20s
mini-alu	9	3	14	10	10	0.90	1.40	0.00s
pdc	102	46	3222	619	1105	0.16	2.91	85.16s
rd84	26	14	170	34	50	0.76	3.40	0.13s
seq	107	31	3310	1617	3343	0.07	0.99	1.21s
spla	95	33	3232	489	1054	0.19	3.07	75.11s
sqrt8	18	6	32	18	158	1.00	0.20	0.02s
squar5	16	3	36	17	155	0.94	0.23	0.01s
t481	19	2	26	20	68	0.95	0.38	0.01s

the number of inputs and outputs. Typically, a space improvement of around 4X can be observed at an increase of the number of gates by around 3X. For the benchmarks shown in bold, our tool found a circuit that is better in both, the number of bits and the total number of gates.

It should be noted also that all ancilla bits computed by our tool are returned clean whereas some of the circuits in [31] leave garbage behind which would lead to a further increase in the gate count and the number of ancillas. In case the gate counts in RevLib were given in terms of multiply controlled gates, we converted the gates into Toffoli gates using $2n-3$ Toffoli gates per n-fold controlled NOT. Among the examples we observed with large possible improvement in terms of space was frg2 where a space reduction of almost a factor 4 was achieved. This however came at a significant increase in compilation time for this specific example which was caused by a large number of same output values which led to a large number of possible groupings. In our reference implementation all possible groupings were explored and the minimum picked which lead to the outlier in compilation cost. Using a greedy strategy for the groupings, a reduction of this compilation time is possible. The compilation time are measured with respect to an Intel i7-3667 @ 2 GHz 8 GB RAM processor running on a standard laptop.

We implemented the procedure that first performs the offline conversion of the given circuit to an equivalent circuit by performing the clique-cover-based XOR maximization. Then this circuit is converted directly into an MDD before cleanup and in doing so, our compiler finds the optimized grouping that replaces OR terms with XOR terms. As the next stage in the pre-processing, we then use the Exorcism-4 tool [18] to perform Exclusive Sum-Of-Product (ESOP) minimization. Afterward, we use factoring techniques from multi-level circuit optimization and minimize the size of the out expressions. A pseudo-code implementation of this factoring technique is given as Algorithm 2.

An example of how our Boolean expression generation allows to trade circuit size (and compilation time) for the total number of qubits used is shown in Fig. 2. Finally, since the processed PLA file is an xor sum on the outputs, MDD based cleanup can be done after each boolean expression to minimize the number of bits use.

5   Conclusions

We developed a tool that automates the translation of classical, irreversible programs into reversible programs. Contrary to previous approaches of reversible programming languages such as the reversible languages R or Janus [23], our language does not constrain the programmer. Also, in contrast to previous approaches for implementing Bennett-style strategies such as Quipper [9] our approach is more space efficient. We employ heuristic strategies which seek to identify parts of the program that lead to mutation which then can be implemented via in-place operations.

In order to manage the arising data dependencies, we introduced MDD graphs which capture data dependencies as well as data mutation in one graph. We prove that our eager cleanup strategy is correct, provided the mutation paths that occur in the MDD have no inter-path dependency. In case such dependencies arise, we clean up the paths using the standard Bennett strategy, which allows us to compile any program that can be expressed in our language into a Toffoli network.

We found examples where our dependency-graph based method for eager cleanup is better than Bennett's original method, even when Bennett's method is implemented by cleaning up at function boundaries. Using an example benchmark suite compiled from the classical circuits and systems community as well as known reversible benchmarks, we show that the method can be applied for medium to large scale problems.

References

1. Revlib - an online resource for reversible functions and circuits. http://www.revlib.org/
2. Aho, A.V., Lam, M.S., Sethi, R., Ullman, J.D.: Compilers: Principles, Techniques, and Tools. Addison Wesley, London (2007)
3. Bennett, C.H.: Logical reversibility of computation. IBM J. Res. Dev. **17**, 525–532 (1973)
4. Bennett, C.H.: Time/space trade-offs for reversible computation. SIAM J. Comput. **18**, 766–776 (1989)
5. Buhrman, H., Tromp, J., Vitányi, P.: Time and space bounds for reversible simulation. In: Orejas, F., Spirakis, P.G., Leeuwen, J. (eds.) ICALP 2001. LNCS, vol. 2076, pp. 1017–1027. Springer, Heidelberg (2001). doi:10.1007/3-540-48224-5_82
6. Pebble games and complexity. Ph.D. thesis, Electrical Engineering and Computer Science, UC Berkeley, Technical report: EECS-2013-145 (2013)
7. Chattopadhyay, A., Pal, N., Majumder, S.: Ancilla-quantum cost trade-off during reversible logic synthesis using exclusive sum-of-products (2014). arxiv:1405.6073
8. Goldschmidt, O., Hochbaum, D.S., Hurkens, C.A.J., Yu, G.: Approximation algorithms for the k-clique covering problem. SIAM J. Disc. Math. **9**(3), 492–509 (1996)
9. Green, A., LeFanu Lumsdaine, P., Ross, N., Selinger, P., Valiron, B.: Quipper: a scalable quantum programming language. In: PLDI 2013 (2013)
10. Heckey, J., Patil, S., Javadi Abhari, A., Holmes, A., Kudrow, D., Brown, K.R., Franklin, D., Chong, F.T., Martonosi, M.: Compiler management of communication and parallelism for quantum computation. In: ASPLOS 2015, pp. 445–456. ACM (2015)
11. JavadiAbhari, A., Patil, S., Kudrow, D., Heckey, J., Lvov, A., Chong, F.T., Martonosi, M.: ScaffCC: scalable compilation and analysis of quantum programs. Parallel Comput. **45**, 2–17 (2015)
12. Lange, K.J., McKenzie, P., Tapp, A.: Reversible space equals deterministic space. J. Comput. Syst. Sci. **60**(2), 354–367 (2000)
13. Lin, C.-C., Jha, N.K.: RMDDS: Reed-Muller decision diagram synthesis of reversible logic circuits. ACM J. Emerg. Technol. Comput. Syst. **10**(2), 14 (2014)
14. Maslov, D.: Reversible logic synthesis benchmarks page. http://webhome.cs.uvic.ca/~dmaslov/
15. Maslov, D., Miller, D.M., Dueck, G.W.: Techniques for the synthesis of reversible Toffoli networks. ACM Trans. Des. Autom. Electron. Syst. **12**(4), 42 (2007)
16. Minkovich, K.: BLIF benchmark suite. http://cadlab.cs.ucla.edu/~kirill/
17. Mishchenko, A., Brayton, R., Chatterjee, S.: Boolean factoring and decomposition of logic networks. In: Proceedings of the IEEE/ACM International Conference on Computer-Aided Design, pp. 38–44. IEEE Press (2008)
18. Mishchenko, A., Perkowski, M.: Fast heuristic minimization of exclusive sum-of-products, 2001. Exorcism is available as part of the ABC software. https://people.eecs.berkeley.edu/~alanmi/
19. Muchnick, S.S.: Compiler Design and Implementation. Morgan Kaufmann, San Francisco (1997)
20. Nielsen, M.A., Chuang, I.L.: Quantum Computation and Quantum Information. Cambridge University Press, Cambridge (2000)
21. Parent, A., Parker, J., Burns, M., Maslov, D.: Quantum Circuit Viewer. Poster presentation at TQC 2013, University of Guelph, Canada. Software (2013). https://github.com/aparent/QCViewer, http://qcirc.iqc.uwaterloo.ca/

22. Parent, A., Roetteler, M., Svore, K.M.: Reversible circuit compilation with space constraints (2015). arXiv:1510.00377
23. Perumalla, K.S.: Introduction to Reversible Computing. CRC Press, Boca Raton (2014)
24. Saeedi, M., Markov, I.L.: Constant-optimized quantum circuits for modular multiplication and exponentiation. Quantum Information and Computation **12**(5&6), 361–394 (2012)
25. Saeedi, M., Markov, I.L.: Synthesis and optimization of reversible circuits - a survey. ACM Comput. Surv. **45**(2), 21 (2013)
26. Shafaei, A., Saeedi, M., Pedram, M.: Reversible logic synthesis of k-input, m-output lookup tables. In: DATE 2013, pp. 1235–1240 (2013)
27. Soeken, M., Robert Wille, R., Hilken, Ch., Przigoda, N., Drechsler, R.: Synthesis of reversible circuits with minimal lines for large functions. In: Proceedings of ASP-DAC 2012 (2012)
28. Syme, D., Granicz, A., Cisternino, A.: Expert F# 3.0. Apress Publishing, New York (2012)
29. Thomsen, M.K.: A functional language for describing reversible logic. In: Forum on Specification and Design Languages, pp. 135–142. IEEE (2012)
30. Viamontes, G.F., Markov, I.L., Hayes, J.P.: Quantum Circuit Simulation. Springer, Heidelberg (2009)
31. Wille, R., Drechsler, R.: BDD-based synthesis of reversible logic for large functions. In: Proceedings of DAC 2009, pp. 270–275 (2009)
32. Wille, R., Drechsler, R.: Towards a Design Flow for Reversible Logic. Springer, Dodrecht (2010)
33. Wille, R., Offermann, S., Drechsler, R.: SyReC: a programming language for synthesis of reversible circuits. In: Specification Design Languages (FDL), pp. 1–6 (2010)
34. Wille, R., Soeken, M., Drechsler, R.: Reducing the number of lines in reversible circuits. In: Proceedings of DAC 2010, pp. 647–652 (2010)
35. Wille, R., Soeken, M., Miller, D.M., Drechsler, R.: Trading off circuit lines and gate costs in the synthesis of reversible logic. Integration **47**(2), 284–294 (2014)
36. Yokoyama, T., Glück, R.: A reversible programming language and its invertible self-interpreter. In: PEPM 2007, pp. 144–153 (2007)

Towards VHDL-Based Design
of Reversible Circuits
Work in Progress Report

Zaid Al-Wardi[1,2(✉)], Robert Wille[3,4], and Rolf Drechsler[1,4]

[1] Institute of Computer Science, University of Bremen, 28359 Bremen, Germany
{alwardi,drechsle}@informatik.uni-bremen.de
[2] Collage of Engineering, Al-Mustansiriya University, Baghdad, Iraq
[3] Institute for Integrated Circuits, Johannes Kepler University Linz, Linz, Austria
robert.wille@jku.at
[4] Cyber-Physical Systems, DFKI GmbH, 28359 Bremen, Germany

Abstract. *Hardware Description Languages* (HDL) facilitate the design of complex circuits and allow for scalable synthesis. While rather established for conventional circuits, HDLs for reversible circuits are in their infancy and usually require a deep understanding of the reversible computing concepts. This motivates the question whether reversible circuits can also efficiently be designed with conventional HDLs, such as VHDL. This work discusses this question. By this, it provides the basis towards a design flow that requires no or only little knowledge of the reversible computation paradigm which could ease the acceptance of this non-conventional computation paradigm amongst designers and stakeholders.

1 Introduction

The majority of reversible circuit design and synthesis methodologies are derived from functional descriptions provided in terms of truth tables, two-level descriptions, decision diagrams, or similar (Boolean) function representations (see e.g. surveys provided in [1,2]). These approaches are limited by their restricted scalability and are not competitive to the state-of-the-art design flows available for conventional circuits.

Hardware Description Languages (HDL) address scalable design of digital circuits [3]. In fact, the design of conventional circuitry heavily relies on established HDLs such as VHDL or Verilog. For reversible circuit design, a clear trend towards higher levels of abstractions can be seen [4,5]. The proposed approaches employ the reversible computation paradigm with its characteristics as well as restrictions and, hence, rely on dedicated concepts such as reversible assignments, reversible control logic, etc. Since, historically, design focused on circuits following the conventional computing paradigm, those concepts are usually rather unfamiliar amongst HDL-designers.

This motivates the question whether reversible circuits can also efficiently be designed with conventional HDLs such as VHDL or Verilog. Obviously, this

© Springer International Publishing AG 2017
I. Phillips and H. Rahaman (Eds.): RC 2017, LNCS 10301, pp. 102–108, 2017.
DOI: 10.1007/978-3-319-59936-6_8

```
1    entity test is
2        port (a,b: in bit; f: out bit);
3    end entity test;
4
5    architecture dataflow of example is
6        signal w: bit;
7    begin
8  S1:     f <=    a and w;
9  S2:     w <=    not b;
10   end architecture dataflow;
```

Fig. 1. Simple VHDL program

would break with many concepts and may lead to drawbacks such as the need to embed non-reversible HDL description means into reversible circuitry (causing overhead e.g. in terms of additional circuit lines).

In this work, we address this issue and choose the widely used hardware description language VHDL as an example of a conventional HDL. We discuss its suitability to synthesize reversible circuits. The findings from the resulting observations provide the basis towards a design flow that requires no or only little knowledge of the reversible computation paradigm. At the same time, it pinpoints to the weaknesses and open issues to be addressed in order to make VHDL-based design indeed a more accessible alternative to the existing design solutions for reversible circuits. Possible directions how to address these weaknesses are discussed in this work.

2   Realizing VHDL Signals

VHDL signal types can directly be mapped to signals of the reversible circuits. More precisely, a VHDL signal is mapped to a reversible circuit line[1].

In Fig. 1 we can see a VHDL code that declares different types of signals, which are mapped to lines with different specifications as follows:

1. **Input ports a,b:** These lines carry input values to the circuit and remain unchanged within a circuit.
2. **Output port f:** This has a constant '0' input, then an expression is assigned to this signal (line) by a statement within the architecture body.
3. **Internal signal w:** This line represent an internal wire. It is similar to output ports in that it is initially constant '0' and assigned in the same way as well. The difference between outputs and wires is that wires facilitate computing other signal(s) and then are considered garbage outputs.
4. **Implicit lines:** These lines are similar to internal signals in that they have constant '0' inputs and constitute garbage outputs, but are not explicitly

---

[1] For simplicity, in the following a line refers to an N-line bundle representing an N-bit signal (accordingly, a single line in figures represent an N-bit circuit line-bundle).

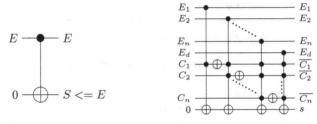

a. Simple assignment   b. Conditional signal assignement

Fig. 2. Realization of signal assignment

declared within the code. Such lines are mandatory to compute non-reversible operations, e.g. to compute the expression (a and w) in Fig. 1, line (8).

3   Realizing VHDL Statements

With the signals defined and initially realized in the circuit, the realizations of the respective operations in terms of reversible gates can be conducted. To this end, all statements in the VHDL code are traversed and synthesized. A statement is considered as a sub-system that performs some action to realize the desired operation.

3.1   Signal Assignment

A statement, in its simplest form, is usually composed of an expression which is evaluated and whose result is afterwards assigned to a circuit signal (i.e. a statement usually has the form S <= E;), with E being the expression and S being the signal to which the result is assigned). The realization of the underlying expressions is covered afterwards in the following section. Realizing signal assignment (a non-reversible operation) is possible when the target signal is known to be a constant '0' [6]. This assignment is realized using Toffoli gates, as shown in Fig. 2a.

Conditional signal assignment statements appear in the following form:
(S <= E1 **when** C1 **else** E2 **when** C2 ... **else** En **when** Cn **else** Ed;).

This assignment requires a case distinction to decide which expression is to be assigned to the target signal. Figure 2b shows a possible realization for this.

3.2   Components

Components are entities instantiated within the architecture of another entity. Each instance places a sub-circuit definition within the main circuit. Figure 3 shows a VHDL code that declares a component, then instantiates it twice within the architecture body.

This structural style of describing systems is preferred for synthesis purposes. Component sub-circuits should be determined first, and this sub-circuit definition is to be placed in the main circuit for each instant. The only change is the mapping of component lines into the main circuit lines; therefore a `port map` is associated with each instance to serve as a look-up table for this mapping, as shown in Fig. 4.

```
1    entity main is
2        port(   x,y,z: in bit; result: out bit);
3    end entity main;
4
5    architecture structural of main is
6        component test is
7            port(a,b: in bit; f: out bit);
8        end component test;
9        signal temp: bit;
10   begin
11 L1:    test port map (a => x,  b => y,  f => temp);
12 L2:    test port map (a => temp, b => z,  f => result);
13   end architecture structural;
```

Fig. 3. Structural VHDL architecture with declared and instantiated components

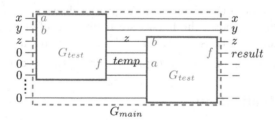

Fig. 4. Using component circuits to synthesize the VHDL code from Fig. 3

4   Realizing Expressions

Up to this point, the discussion assumes that expressions are values that are, somehow, available on certain circuit lines like any other signal. This skips a core issue, namely how to realize expressions. VHDL provides a set of operations to be used in expressions. These operations are not necessarily reversible. An additional line with constant inputs is applied to make a non-reversible function reversible [7] (leading to the implicit lines as discussed in Sect. 2). This is exactly how the reversible HDL SyReC tackles this problem [4]. Hence, realizing an expression E which is combined with N operators will implicitly add N constant lines to the circuit. This is considered a serious drawback [8].

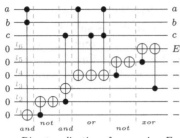

a. Direct realization of expression E

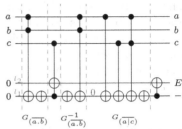

b. Line-aware realization of expression E

Fig. 5. Circuits realizing expression E from Example 1

Line-awareness when realizing HDL expressions can tangibly increase the overall efficiency of this approach [9]. The reduction can be started by reconsidering the necessity of adding lines in some special cases, such as with not, xor, + and −. These operators are reversible, hence, can be computed with no additional line. Further reduction in lines may be obtained by reverse computing (re-computing) intermediate values and reusing these lines for further computations [9]. To reverse a computation, just repeat it in the reverse order of gates.

Example 1. Consider the Boolean expression E $(\overline{a.b}.c \oplus \overline{a|c})$, which has the following form in VHDL: (**not**(a **and** b) **and** c **xor not**(a **or** c)) . The value of E is computed based on six Boolean operations. Hence, six constant input lines are required to compute this expression. Figure 5a shows a reversible circuit to compute E. Figure 5b shows the line-aware realization of the same expression using only two constant lines, in which $G^{-1}_{\overline{(a.b)}}$ re-computes line l_1. This line is used once more to compute the sub-expression (**not** (a **or** c)), using $G_{\overline{(a|c)}}$.

5   Overall Realization

Using the realization schemes described above for signals, statements, and expressions, an overall realization can be obtained for a given VHDL code. To this end, the respectively obtained sub-circuits need to be accordingly connected. In conventional hardware, it does not matter which statement is synthesized first, the resulting hardware will be exactly the same because of statements' concurrency [3]. The reversible computation scheme, on the other hand, is processing signals in a cascade fashion. Consequently, signals are successively computed. A simple algorithm, based on signal dependence, can be applied to determine the correct order in which statements are to be synthesized. Hence, the order in which statements are synthesized may differ from the order in which they appear in the code. Figure 6a shows such an example. The figure shows the correct realization of the VHDL code from Fig. 1, where statement S2 is synthesized before S1 to resolve the issue of signal dependence.

The two statements S1 and S2 from Fig. 1 have expressions on their right hand sides. A constant '0' line is needed, in this example, to compute each expression.

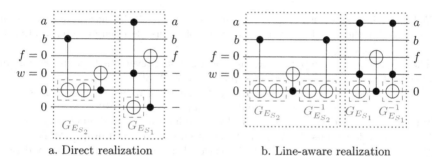

a. Direct realization   b. Line-aware realization

Fig. 6. Circuits realization of VHDL code from Fig. 1

As a result, two implicit lines are added to realize the circuit (see Fig. 6a). For complex codes, implicit lines keep accumulating throughout the code – resulting in large numbers of circuit lines. A line-aware realization on the overall module level may also re-compute lines to realize garbage-free statements [4]. This allows statements to reuse implicit lines. In Fig. 6b, the implicit line used for statement S2 is re-computed and then reused for S1. This arrangement realizes the circuit with only one implicit line – compared to the two lines needed in the circuit shown in Fig. 6a.

6   Conclusions

In this work, we discussed how to realize VHDL code as reversible circuits. To this end, we considered the realization of the corresponding signal declarations, statements, as well as expressions. Based on that, two different schemes for the overall realization of the desired circuit have been proposed – with a particular focus on the number of eventually resulting circuit lines. With these contributions, we provide an initial basis towards a VHDL-based reversible circuit design flow that requires no or only little knowledge of the reversible computation paradigm. For future work, it is planed to consider more data-types with associated operators, as well as covering more statements and settings.

Acknowledgments. This work has partially been supported by the European Union through the COST Action IC1405.

References

1. Drechsler, R., Wille, R.: From truth tables to programming languages: progress in the design of reversible circuits. In: International Symposium on Multi-valued Logic, pp. 78–85 (2011)
2. Saeedi, M., Markov, I.L.: Synthesis and optimization of reversible circuits - a survey. ACM Comput. Surv. (2011)
3. Ashenden, P.J.: The Designers Guide to VHDL, 3rd edn. Elsevier (2008)

4. Wille, R., Schönborn, E., Soeken, M., Drechsler, R.: SyReC: a hardware description language for the specification and synthesis of reversible circuits. Integr. VLSI J. **53**, 39–53 (2016)
5. Thomsen, M.K.: A functional language for describing reversible logic. In: Forum on Specification and Design Languages, pp. 135–142 (2012)
6. Wille, R., Soeken, M., Drechsler, R.: Reducing the number of lines in reversible circuits. In: Design Automation Conference, pp. 647–652 (2010)
7. Wille, R., Keszöcze, O., Drechsler, R.: Determining the minimal number of lines for large reversible circuits. In: Design, Automation and Test in Europe (2011)
8. Wille, R., Soeken, M., Miller, D.M., Drechsler, R.: Trading off circuit lines and gate costs in the synthesis of reversible logic. Integr. VLSI J. **47**(2), 284–294 (2014)
9. Al-Wardi, Z., Wille, R., Drechsler, R.: Towards line-aware realizations of expressions for HDL-based synthesis of reversible circuits. In: Krivine, J., Stefani, J.-B. (eds.) RC 2015. LNCS, vol. 9138, pp. 233–247. Springer, Cham (2015). doi:10.1007/978-3-319-20860-2_15

Reversible Circuit Optimization

Optimizing the Reversible Circuits Using Complementary Control Line Transformation

Sai Phaneendra Parlapalli$^{(\boxtimes)}$, Chetan Vudadha, and M.B. Srinivas

Department of Electrical Engineering, Birla Institute of Technology and Science
(BITS) - Pilani, Hyderabad Campus, Hyderabad, India
`phani.parlapalli@gmail.com`

Abstract. In this paper, a transformation method is presented which converts complementary control lines of a reversible gate pair to equal/similar control lines. A set of optimization rules is discussed that take advantage of the increased equal control lines to reduce the cost. A greedy optimization algorithm, which uses the proposed transformation method and the optimization rules, is presented. Results for a large set of benchmarks confirm that the proposed algorithm performs better when compared with other Exclusive-OR Sum-Of-Product (ESOP) based methods available in the literature.

1 Introduction

Research on reversible logic is motivated by its applications in emerging technologies like quantum computing [14] and optical computing [4] as well as the need for ultra low power design [3,10,20]. Traditional synthesis methods cannot be directly applied to realize a reversible logic circuit because fan-out and feedback are not allowed in this logic. Such constraints inspired researchers to develop synthesis methods that target reversible logic exclusively. These methods may be classified broadly as exact methods and heuristic methods [16,19]. Exact methods generate reversible circuits optimized in terms of circuit cost. However, they can be applied only to functions with very small number of variables (upto 6) [19]. On the other hand, heuristic methods have been used to synthesize functions with a large number of variables. However, circuits obtained by these methods have been found to be sub-optimal in terms of cost. This led to the development of post-synthesis optimization methods like template based optimization [11], rule based optimization [1,7], factor based decomposition [6,12] etc., to further reduce the circuit cost.

Post-synthesis optimization methods have been applied either on gates having only positive control lines [11] or on gates having both positive and negative control lines [1,7]. In both these cases, the structures of gates having equal control lines have been decomposed into simpler structures, thereby resulting in the reduction of the circuit cost [7,12]. However, if gates have unequal control lines i.e., if positive control connection and negative control connection appear on the same line, they are left untouched. In this paper, a transformation algorithm,

© Springer International Publishing AG 2017
I. Phillips and H. Rahaman (Eds.): RC 2017, LNCS 10301, pp. 111–126, 2017.
DOI: 10.1007/978-3-319-59936-6_9

which works on a pair of gates by transforming unequal control lines to equivalent equal control lines, is presented. Further, a set of existing rules and a new rule are discussed, which can be applied on the circuit post transformation, to reduce the cost. Finally, using this algorithm and a set of rules, a greedy optimization algorithm is implemented and applied on a set of benchmark reversible circuits. The resulting circuits show an average cost improvement of 45% when compared with the initial benchmark circuits.

Rest of the paper is organized as follows: Sect. 2 gives background on reversible logic circuits. The proposed transformation algorithm and rules for a gate pair as well as the greedy optimization method for a gate netlist are presented in Sect. 3. Simulation results and comparison with existing methods are given in Sect. 4 and conclusions are drawn in Sect. 5.

2   Background

2.1   Reversible Logic Circuits

A logic function f is called *reversible logic function* if there is a one-to-one mapping between inputs and outputs and is bijective. A reversible logic circuit for a function can be realized by cascading reversible gates like NOT, CNOT, Toffoli and multi-control Toffoli (MCT) gates [18]. The standard representation of basic reversible gates and a cascade of these gates to form a reversible circuit are shown in Fig. 1. An MCT gate is represented as $MCT(C;t)$ where C is a set of control lines and t is the target line. When all the positive (negative) control lines of the gate, represented as $\bullet (\circ)$, are set to '1' ('0'), a MCT gate inverts the target line, represented as $\oplus$.

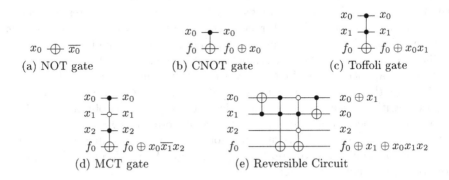

(a) NOT gate   (b) CNOT gate   (c) Toffoli gate

(d) MCT gate   (e) Reversible Circuit

Fig. 1. Reversible gates and reversible circuit

2.2   Quantum Cost of a Reversible Logic Circuit

The Quantum Cost (QC) of a reversible gate is the number of primitive quantum gates required to implement the gate functionality. The primitive gates of quantum library followed in this paper are NOT, CNOT, controlled V and controlled V+ gates. The QC of a reversible gate is calculated using the cost function given in RevKit tool [17]. The cost of a reversible circuit is the sum of the cost of individual reversible gates in the circuit.

3   Proposed Optimization Approach

In this section, an algorithm to transform unequal control lines to equal control lines for a pair of gates is explained. Next, a set of rules are applied on the transformed gate netlist. Finally, a greedy optimization method is presented which uses the transformation algorithm and the rules to optimize a gate netlist.

3.1   Motivation

As explained earlier, post-synthesis optimization methods have been used to improve the sub-optimal circuits generated by the existing synthesis methods. One such optimization method has been discussed in [7], where a set of gates has been transformed to simpler gates by applying certain rules. For example, consider two gates shown in Fig. 2(a). These two gates, which differ by one control line, can be merged into a single gate and the simplified gate netlist is shown in Fig. 2(b). However, this rule can be applied only if the other control lines of the gate pair are equal but not when they are different as shown in Fig. 2(c). In order to address this issue, an algorithm is presented in this paper to convert unequal control lines to equal control lines.

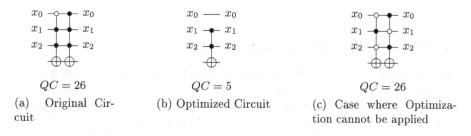

(a)   Original Circuit   (b) Optimized Circuit   (c) Case where Optimization cannot be applied

Fig. 2. Example case for optimization method presented in [7]

3.2   Basic Idea

In a gate pair, if a control line has positive control connection on one gate and negative control connection on the other, then that line is termed as *complementary control line (CCL)*. For example, the control line x_0 for the gates in Fig. 2(c) has negative control connection on the first gate and positive control connection on the second. This control line is termed as CCL for that gate pair. The basic idea in this paper is to convert such CCLs of a gate pair to equal control lines by adding CNOT gates to the circuit. This is illustrated with Example 1 given below.

Example 1. Consider the gate pair shown in Fig. 3(a). This gate pair has three CCLs (x_0, x_1, x_2). The gate g_1, represented by $(\overline{x_0}x_1\overline{x_2}) \oplus f_0$ can be written as $(\overline{x_0}(x_0 \oplus x_1)\overline{x_2}) \oplus f_0$. Similarly, the gate g_2, represented by $(x_0\overline{x_1}x_2) \oplus f_0$, can be written as $(x_0(x_0 \oplus x_1)x_2) \oplus f_0$. The term $(x_0 \oplus x_1)$ is now the common factor among the two gates. For realization of this common factor, CNOT gates are added to the gate pair g_1 and g_2 as shown in Fig. 3(b). As a result, the CCL x_1 has transformed to an equal control line.

It has to be noted however that, in a gate pair with k CCLs, at most $k - 1$ CCLs can be transformed to equal control lines. The remaining CCL cannot be transformed because it has to be used as a control line for the CNOT gates that are added. After the transformation, different rules can be applied on the transformed gate pairs to reduce their cost.

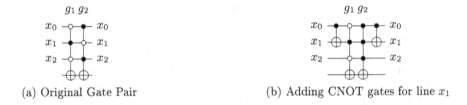

(a) Original Gate Pair   (b) Adding CNOT gates for line x_1

Fig. 3. Illustration of Example 1

3.3   The Gate Transformation Algorithm

The method for converting CCLs to equal control lines for a given pair of gates is presented in Algorithm 1. This algorithm takes two gates G_i and G_j as inputs and returns a gate netlist G_t as output. The set of CCLs (represented as *ccl*), if any, in the given gate pair are extracted using the function *ExtractComplementLines*. From *ccl*, a line is randomly selected as the *baseline* using the function *random* and is subsequently removed from *ccl*. Now, for each line l_i in *ccl*, a CNOT gate with the *baseline* as control line and l_i as the target line is added to an intermediate gate netlist called *CG*. The function *value* determines whether the control connection of a line in a gate is positive or negative control. The line l_i in gates G_i and G_j is set to negative control if it has the same control connection as the *baseline*, else is set to positive control. This updates the initial gate pair G_i and G_j. Finally, the output gate netlist G_t is generated by cascading the *CG* before and after the updated gate pair G_i and G_j. The proposed gate transformation algorithm is illustrated in Example 2.

Algorithm 1. Gate Transformation Algorithm for a Pair of Gates

1: **Input:** Gates G_i, G_j
2: **Output:** Gate Netlist G_t
3: **begin**
4: $ccl = ExtractComplementLines(G_i, G_j)$
5: **if** $ccl = \phi$ **then exit**
6: $baseline = random(ccl)$
7: $ccl = ccl - \{baseline\}$
8: $CG = \phi$
9: **for each** $l_i \in ccl$ **do**
10:     $append(CNOT(baseline, l_i), CG)$
11:     **if** $value(G_i, baseline) == value(G_i, l_i)$ **then**
12:         $G_i(l_i) = G_j(l_i) = NegativeControl$
13:     **else**
14:         $G_i(l_i) = G_j(l_i) = PositiveControl$
15:     **end if**
16: **end for**
17: $G_t = append(CG, G_i, G_j, CG)$
18: **return** G_t
19: **end**

Example 2. Consider two gates g_i and g_j shown in Fig. 4(a), given as inputs to Algorithm 1. First, the function $ExtractComplementLines$ extracts the lines x_0, x_1, x_2 as CCLs for the gate pair and assigns them to the set ccl ($ccl = \{x_0, x_1, x_2\}$). Next, assuming that the *random* function selects the line x_0 as the *baseline* from ccl, it is removed from ccl and is updated to $\{x_1, x_2\}$.

In the first iteration, line x_1 from the set ccl is selected as line l_i. A CNOT gate with x_0 (the *baseline*) as control line and x_1 (line l_i) as target line is added to the gate netlist CG. Since the function *value* returns the control connections of x_0 and x_1 in gate g_i as negative and positive control respectively, the line x_1 in gates g_i and g_j is updated to positive control. At the end of the first iteration, status of the gate netlist CG and that of gates g_i and g_j are shown in Fig. 4(b).

The algorithm then proceeds to update the gate netlist CG and the gate pair g_i, g_j for the remaining lines in the ccl. Figure 4(c) shows the status after the second iteration. Finally, the gate netlist CG is added before and after the updated gates g_i and g_j to form the output gate netlist G_t as shown in Fig. 4(d).

3.4   Rule Based Optimization on Transformed Gate Netlist

In this sub-section, two existing rules and a newly proposed one are presented which can be used to optimize the transformed gate netlist. The existing rules used have been presented in [7] and are briefly explained as follows:

1. *Merging Rule:* A pair of gates can be merged into a single gate if they have the same target lines, one CCL and any remaining control lines that are equal.

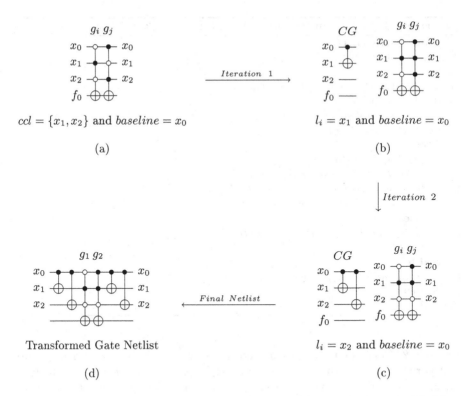

Fig. 4. Illustration of gate transformation algorithm (a) Initial gate pair (b) After iteration 1 (c) After iteration 2 (d) Final transformed gate netlist

This rule is represented as Eq. 1 given below:

$$MCT(C \cup \{x_i\}; x_t) \circ MCT(C \cup \{\overline{x_i}\}; x_t) = MCT(C; x_t) \tag{1}$$

where C is a set of equal control lines.

2. *Replacement Rule:* A pair of gates can be replaced with two gates if they have the same target lines, one CCL, a control line with control connection only on one gate and any remaining control lines that are equal.

This rule is represented as Eq. 2 given below:

$$MCT(C \cup \{x_i, x_j\}; x_t) \circ MCT(C \cup \{\overline{x_i}\}; x_t) =$$
$$MCT(C \cup \{x_i, \overline{x_j}\}; x_t) \circ MCT(C; x_t) \tag{2}$$

where C is a set of equal control lines.

These rules can be used on a pair of gates if it has only one CCL but not more. However, the proposed transformation algorithm enables the usage of above rules on a gate pair that has one or more than one CCL. This is because the algorithm can reduce any number of CCLs in a gate pair to one CCL as described in

Sect. 3.3. The procedure is illustrated with Examples 3 and 4 for merging and replacement rules, respectively.

Example 3. Consider a pair of gates shown in Fig. 5(a). These gates cannot be optimized using merging rule as they have more than one CCL. After the application of the proposed algorithm however, the resulting gate netlist has only one CCL as shown in Fig. 5(b). The gates g_1 and g_2 in the resulting netlist have the same target line, one CCL and two equal control lines. Thus, g_1 and g_2 can be merged into a single gate g_m using the merging rule. The final gate netlist is shown in Fig. 5(c) where it can be seen that the cost of the gate netlist has reduced from 26 to 9.

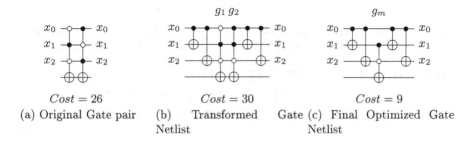

Fig. 5. Illustration of Example 3

Example 4. Consider a pair of gates shown in Fig. 6(a). These gates cannot be optimized using the replacement rule because they have more than one CCL. After the algorithm is applied however, the resulting gate netlist has only one CCL as shown in Fig. 6(b). The gates g_1 and g_2 in the resulting netlist have the same target line, one CCL, the line x_4 with control connection only on gate g_1 and three equal control lines. Thus, g_1 and g_2 can be replaced with two other gates g_3 and g_4. The final gate netlist is shown in Fig. 6(c) where it can be seen that the cost of the gate netlist has reduced from 90 to 72.

While the above examples illustrate the existing rules, a new decomposition rule, which uses equal control lines in a given gate pair, is proposed in this work. Before describing this rule, a definition for *unused line* is presented below:

Definition 1. *(Unused line): If a line in a gate netlist is neither a control line nor a target line then it is termed as unused line.*

Decomposition Rule: Consider a pair of gates g_1 and g_2 with same target line x_t, K equal control lines, C CCLs and $P(Q)$ lines that have control connection

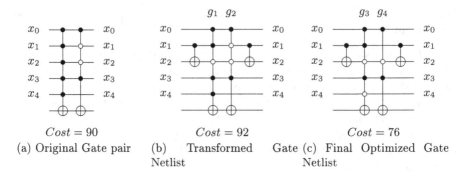

$Cost = 90$

(a) Original Gate pair

$Cost = 92$

(b)   Transformed   Gate
Netlist

$Cost = 76$

(c) Final Optimized Gate
Netlist

Fig. 6. Illustration of Example 4

in $g_1(g_2)$ but not in $g_2(g_1)$. If an unused line x_u is available, then the gate pair can be decomposed into a network of smaller gates using the following equation:

$$MCT(K \cup C \cup P; x_t) \circ MCT(K \cup C \cup Q; x_t) =$$
$$MCT(C \cup P; x_u) \circ MCT(C \cup Q; x_u) \circ MCT(K \cup \{x_u\}; x_t) \circ$$
$$MCT(C \cup P; x_u) \circ MCT(C \cup Q; x_u) \circ MCT(K \cup \{x_u\}; x_t)$$
$$(3)$$

This decomposition rule is illustrated with the help of the following example:

Example 5. Consider the gate pair g_1 and g_2 shown in Fig. 7(a). These gates have the same target line, three equal control lines, one CCL. Line x_4 has control connection only in g_1 while line x_5 has control connection only in g_2. As can be observed, line x_6 is unused line for this gate pair. Using the decomposition rule given by Eq. 3, these gates can be decomposed into a network of smaller gates. The resulting decomposed gate netlist is shown in Fig. 7(b).

Usage of this rule results in an optimized netlist only if the number of equal control lines is more than unequal control lines in the gate pair. Therefore, increasing the number of equal control lines increases the possibility of obtaining reduced gate netlist. The proposed transformation method enables the usage of the decomposition rule by increasing the number of equal control lines. Example 6 illustrates the usage of the decomposition rule after applying the transformation method for a pair of gates.

Example 6. Consider two gates g_1 and g_2 shown in Fig. 8(a). The decomposition rule cannot be applied on this gate pair because there are no equal control lines. Applying the gate transformation algorithm to transform CCLs to equal control lines results in the gate netlist shown in Fig. 8(b). Since the gates g_a and g_b have three equal control lines, the decomposition rule can be applied. The final decomposed gate netlist is shown in Fig. 8(c) where it can be seen that the cost has reduced from 104 to 78.

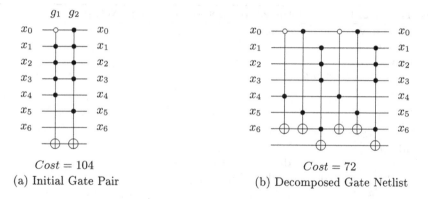

Cost = 104

(a) Initial Gate Pair

Cost = 72

(b) Decomposed Gate Netlist

Fig. 7. Illustration of proposed decomposition rule

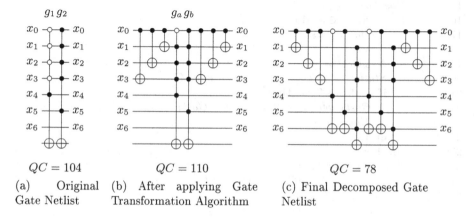

$QC = 104$

(a)   Original
Gate Netlist

$QC = 110$

(b)   After   applying   Gate
Transformation Algorithm

$QC = 78$

(c)   Final Decomposed Gate
Netlist

Fig. 8. Illustration of Example 6

In the next sub-section a greedy optimization algorithm, that utilizes the reduction rules presented above to reduce the cost of the given gate netlist, is presented.

3.5   Greedy Optimization

In the greedy optimization algorithm given in Algorithm 2, a reversible gate netlist G is given as input and a gate netlist G' is returned. Initially, the gate netlist G is traversed and the gates with equal control lines but different target lines are merged using the function $target\_merging$ [21]. This avoids regeneration of the same gate for different target lines. Since the reduction rules presented in Sect. 3.4 can be applied only on the gates with equal target lines, a set of segments consisting of gates with equal target lines is generated and assigned to *Segment*.

Algorithm 2. Greedy Optimization Method for a Gate Netlist

1: **Input:** Reversible Gate Netlist G
2: **Output:** Modified Gate Netlist G'
3: **begin**
4:   $GN = target\_merging(G)$
5:   $Segment = \phi$
6:   $G' = \phi$
7: **for each** $g \in GN$ **do**
8:     $insert(Segment[target(g)], g)$
9: **end for**
10: **for each** $sg \in Segment$ **do**
11:     **while** sg is not empty **do**
12:         $flag = false$
13:         $G_i = select\_gate(sg)$
14:         $RemoveGate(sg, G_i)$
15:         $CostTable(G_i) = \phi$
16:         **for each** $G_j \in sg$ **do**
17:             $Status = False$
18:             $G_t = \phi$
19:             $NewCost = \infty$
20:             $Status, G_t, NewCost = translate(G_i, G_j)$
21:             **if** $Status$ is $True$ **then**
22:                 $CostTable(G_i) = \{G_j, G_t, NewCost\}$
23:                 $flag = True$
24:             **end if**
25:         **end for**
26:         **if** $flag$ is $True$ **then**
27:             $G_p, G_{new} = LeastCost(CostTable(G_i))$
28:             $Append(G', G_{new})$
29:             $RemoveGate(sg, G_p)$
30:         **else**
31:             $Append(G', G_i)$
32:         **end if**
33:     **end while**
34: **end for**
35: **return** G'
36: **end**

For a sg in $Segment$, each gate G_i is paired with every other gate G_j and is given to the $translate$ function. This function takes a gate pair and checks for the possibility of reduction using the transformation algorithm and the rules presented in Sect. 3.4. If a possibility exists for a reduction of that pair, the function returns $Status$ as $True$, the reduced gate netlist as G_t and its cost as $NewCost$. Also, the gate netlist G_t and its cost $NewCost$ are added to the $CostTable(G_i)$ and the $flag$ is set to $True$.

After G_i is paired with every other gate G_j in sg, the status of $flag$ is checked. If the $flag$ is $False$, it indicates that there is no reduction possible for the gate

G_i when paired with any other gate in that segment and the gate G_i is added to the output gate netlist G'. If it is $True$ then the function $LeastCost$ scans the $CostTable(G_i)$ and returns a gate G_p that results in maximum possible reduction when paired with G_i. This function also returns G_{new} which is the reduced gate netlist for the gate pair G_i and G_p. Finally, the gate netlist G_{new} is added to the output gate netlist G' and the gate G_p is subsequently removed from the segment sg. This process is repeated for each sg in the $Segment$.

4   Simulation Results

The greedy optimization method has been applied on different benchmark reversible circuits to evaluate its efficiency in terms of cost. The reversible gate netlist obtained from Exclusive-OR Sum of Product (ESOP) based synthesis method presented in [9] is given as the input for the optimization method.

The quantum cost for different benchmark circuits after applying the optimization method is shown in Table 1. The first column gives the benchmark name while the second and third columns provide the cost of input gate netlist and the gate netlist obtained after target merging (line no 4 of Algorithm 2), respectively. The fourth column gives the cost of the final gate netlist obtained after applying the optimization algorithm. The fifth and sixth columns give the percentage improvement over the initial gate netlist and the gate netlist obtained after target merging, respectively. It is seen from the Table 1 that in the best case, there is a considerable reduction of quantum cost of up to 84%. An average cost improvement of about 45% is observed over all the benchmarks considered in the table.

A comparison of costs obtained from the optimization method with different ESOP based methods [2,5,8,13,15] is presented in Table 2. The first column gives the name of the benchmark circuit while the columns 2–6 indicate the quantum cost of respective benchmark circuits realized with existing ESOP based methods [2,5,8,13,15]. Column 7 provides the quantum cost to realize that benchmark using the proposed optimization method. Column 8 shows the percentage improvement of quantum cost achieved compared to the existing methods that give the best reduction for that benchmark.

It can be seen from the table that there is an improvement of up to 48% in quantum cost. For arithmetic benchmark circuits like *frg2*, *in0*, *max46*, etc., and large benchmark circuits like *misex3*, *table3*, etc., there is a reduction in the quantum cost. However, for some benchmarks like *add6, bw, z4* etc., the optimization method results in higher quantum cost when compared to the existing ones [2,5,13]. This is because of limited availability of a required gate pair that can be transformed using the algorithm and the rules presented earlier.

Table 1. Comparison with original gate netlist

Benchmark	Cost of input gate netlist	Cost after merge	Cost of proposed method	% Impr w.r.t. proposed method	
				Original	After merge
5xp1	1264	809	773	**38.84**	**4.45**
9sym	10937	10937	3055	**72.07**	**72.07**
add6	6679	5157	3848	**42.39**	**25.38**
alu1	205	205	205	0.00	0.00
alu2	4623	4306	3090	**33.16**	**28.24**
alu3	2432	1976	1828	**24.84**	**7.49**
alu4	43635	36913	25007	**42.69**	**32.25**
apex4	252939	39818	39806	**84.26**	**0.03**
apex5	49161	31891	27960	**43.13**	**12.33**
apla	3806	1713	1601	**57.93**	**6.54**
bw	4464	820	820	**81.63**	**0.00**
C17	77	77	77	0.00	0.00
clip	7445	3842	1837	**75.33**	**52.19**
cm150a	803	803	785	**2.24**	**2.24**
con1	150	150	150	0.00	0.00
cordic	343959	172199	64504	**81.25**	**62.54**
cu	1191	747	747	**37.28**	**0.00**
dc2	1957	1097	1017	**48.03**	**7.29**
decod	2001	460	460	**77.01**	**0.00**
dist	7489	3723	2739	**63.43**	**26.43**
e64	26129	23751	23751	**9.10**	**0.00**
ex1010	178709	54154	52822	**70.44**	**2.46**
ex2	146	146	140	**4.11**	**4.11**
ex3	76	76	59	**22.37**	**22.37**
f2	262	118	83	**68.32**	**29.66**
f51m	30300	26533	19374	**36.06**	**26.98**
frg2	186500	103876	97001	**47.99**	**6.62**
in0	20639	7623	7501	**63.66**	**1.60**
majority	133	133	110	**17.29**	**17.29**
max46	4524	4524	2876	**36.43**	**36.43**
misex1	935	358	358	**61.71**	**0.00**
misex3	106810	46381	40771	**61.83**	**12.10**
misex3c	104924	46977	41886	**60.08**	**10.84**
mlp4	3878	2511	2129	**45.10**	**15.21**
mux	800	800	768	**4.00**	**4.00**
pm1	494	188	188	**61.94**	**0.00**

(*continued*)

Table 1. (*continued*)

Benchmark	Cost of input gate netlist	Cost after merge	Cost of proposed method	% Impr w.r.t. proposed method	
				Original	After merge
radd	721	659	483	**33.01**	**26.71**
rd84	2520	2334	1751	**30.52**	**24.98**
root	3618	1829	1548	**57.21**	**15.36**
sao2	7702	3688	3324	**56.84**	**9.87**
spla	94371	30518	26862	**71.54**	**11.98**
sqn	2096	1348	791	**62.26**	**41.32**
sqr6	989	609	549	**44.49**	**9.85**
sqrt8	583	477	312	**46.48**	**34.59**
squar5	365	234	231	**36.71**	**1.28**
t481	229	229	205	**10.48**	**10.48**
table3	79348	17662	16863	**78.75**	**4.52**
urf3	146687	53963	50761	**65.40**	**5.93**
z4	517	494	352	**31.91**	**28.74**

Table 2. Comparison with ESOP based methods

Benchmark	[15]	[13]	[8]	[2]	[5]	Proposed Method	% Impr
5xp1	1349	786	865	–	807	773	**1.65**
add6	6362	–	5084	2683	–	3848	**−43.42**
alu2	5215	–	4476	–	3679	3090	**16.01**
alu3	2653	–	–	–	1919	1828	**4.74**
alu4	48778	41127	43850	–	38635	25007	**35.27**
apex4	256857	35840	50680	51284	–	39806	**−11.07**
apex5	–	33830	–	–	33803	27960	**17.29**
apla	4051	1683	–	–	1709	1601	**4.87**
bw	–	637	–	2233	790	820	**−28.73**
C17	97	–	–	–	–	77	**20.61**
clip	6616	3824	4484	–	3218	1837	**42.91**
cm150a	844	–	–	–	–	785	**6.99**
con1	207	162	–	–	–	150	**7.41**
cordic	349522	187620	–	–	111955	64504	**42.38**
cu	1332	781	–	–	780	747	**4.23**
dc2	1956	1084	–	–	1099	1017	**6.18**
decod	1924	399	–	976	–	460	**−15.29**

(*continued*)

Table 2. (*continued*)

Benchmark	[15]	[13]	[8]	[2]	[5]	Proposed Method	% Impr
dist	7414	3700	–	–	–	2739	**25.97**
e64	–	–	–	–	24345	23751	**2.44**
ex1010	183726	52788	–	77293	–	52822	−0.06
ex2	153	–	–	118	–	140	−18.64
ex3	97	–	–	73	–	59	**19.18**
f2	274	112	–	116	–	83	**25.89**
f51m	34244	28382	–	–	25119	19374	**22.87**
frg2	–	112008	–	–	114239	97001	**13.40**
in0	22196	7949	–	–	–	7501	**5.64**
majority	147	–	–	106	–	110	−3.77
max46	4432	–	–	3239	–	2876	**11.21**
misex1	1017	332	466	–	352	358	−7.83
misex3	122557	49076	67206	–	54132	40771	**16.92**
misex3c	118578	49720	85330	52600	–	41886	**15.76**
mlp4	3827	2496	–	–	–	2129	**14.70**
mux	826	–	–	784	–	768	**2.04**
pm1	582	–	–	290	–	188	**35.17**
radd	798	–	–	349	–	483	−38.40
rd84	2598	–	2062	–	1965	1751	**10.89**
root	3486	1811	–	–	1583	1548	**2.21**
sao2	7893	3767	5147	–	–	3324	**11.76**
spla	–	–	49419	–	45478	26862	**40.93**
sqn	2170	–	–	1183	–	791	**33.14**
sqr6	1090	583	–	–	–	549	**5.83**
sqrt8	584	–	461	–	–	312	**32.32**
squar5	476	–	251	–	–	231	**7.97**
t481	237	–	237	–	–	205	**13.50**
table3	86173	–	35807	–	32286	16863	**47.77**
urf3	–	53157	–	56766	–	50761	**4.51**
z4	674	489	–	260	–	352	−35.38

5   Conclusion

In this paper, an algorithm to transform complementary control lines of a gate pair to equal control lines has been presented. It is shown that this algorithm enables the usage of a set of rules by converting CCLs to equal control lines. A greedy optimization technique which uses the transformation algorithm and the rules to optimize the given gate netlist has also been presented and discussed. Simulation results show that there is a significant reduction in the quantum cost of benchmark circuits with a maximum of 84% and an average of 45% when compared to the original gate netlist. Further, a comparison of the proposed optimization method with the existing ESOP based methods shows an improvement in quantum cost of up to 48%.

Acknowledgements. This work was supported in part by Council of Scientific & Industrial Research (CSIR) grant (ref.-09/1026(0007)/2012-EMR-I).

References

1. Arabzadeh, M., Saeedi, M., Zamani, M.S.: Rule-based optimization of reversible circuits. In: Proceedings of the 2010 Asia and South Pacific Design Automation Conference, pp. 849–854. IEEE Press (2010)
2. Bandyopadhyay, C., Rahaman, H., Drechsler, R.: Improved cube list based cube pairing approach for synthesis of ESOP based reversible logic. In: Gavrilova, M.L., Tan, C.J.K., Thapliyal, H., Ranganathan, N. (eds.) Transactions on Computational Science XXIV. LNCS, vol. 8911, pp. 129–146. Springer, Heidelberg (2014). doi:10.1007/978-3-662-45711-5_8
3. Bennett, C.H.: Logical reversibility of computation. IBM J. Res. Dev. **17**(6), 525–532 (1973)
4. Cuykendall, R., Andersen, D.R.: Reversible optical computing circuits. Opt. Lett. **12**(7), 542–544 (1987)
5. Datta, K., Gokhale, A., Sengupta, I., Rahaman, H.: An ESOP-based reversible circuit synthesis flow using simulated annealing. In: Chaki, R., Saeed, K., Choudhury, S., Chaki, N. (eds.) Applied Computation and Security Systems. AISC, vol. 305, pp. 131–144. Springer, New Delhi (2015). doi:10.1007/978-81-322-1988-0_8
6. Datta, K., Rathi, G., Sengupta, I., Rahaman, H.: An improved reversible circuit synthesis approach using clustering of ESOP cubes. ACM J. Emerg. Technol. Comput. Syst. (JETC) **11**(2), 15 (2014)
7. Datta, K., Sengupta, I., Rahaman, H.: A post-synthesis optimization technique for reversible circuits exploiting negative control lines. IEEE Trans. Comput. **64**(4), 1208–1214 (2015)
8. Drechsler, R., Finder, A., Wille, R.: Improving ESOP-based synthesis of reversible logic using evolutionary algorithms. In: Di Chio, C., et al. (eds.) EvoApplications 2011. LNCS, vol. 6625, pp. 151–161. Springer, Heidelberg (2011). doi:10.1007/978-3-642-20520-0_16
9. Fazel, K., Thornton, M., Rice, J.: ESOP-based Toffoli gate cascade generation. In: IEEE Pacific Rim Conference on Communications, Computers and Signal Processing, pp. 206–209 (2007)
10. Landauer, R.: Irreversibility and heat generation in the computing process. IBM J. Res. Dev. **5**(3), 183–191 (1961). http://dx.doi.org/10.1147/rd.53.0183
11. Maslov, D., Dueck, G.W., Miller, D.M.: Techniques for the synthesis of reversible Toffoli networks. ACM Trans. Des. Autom. Electron. Syst. **12**(4) (2007). http://doi.acm.org/10.1145/1278349.1278355
12. Miller, D.M., Wille, R., Drechsler, R.: Reducing reversible circuit cost by adding lines. In: 40th IEEE International Symposium on Multiple-Valued Logic (ISMVL), pp. 217–222. IEEE (2010)

13. Nayeem, N.M., Rice, J.E.: A shared-cube approach to ESOP-based synthesis of reversible logic. Facta Univ. Ser. Electron. Energ. **24**(3), 385–402 (2011)
14. Nielsen, M.A., Chuang, I.L.: Quantum Computation and Quantum Information. Cambridge University Press, Cambridge (2010)
15. Rice, J., Fazel, K., Thornton, M., Kent, K.: Toffoli gate cascade generation using ESOP minimization and QMDD-based swapping. In: Proceedings of the Reed-Muller Workshop (RM 2009), pp. 63–72 (2009)
16. Saeedi, M., Markov, I.L.: Synthesis and optimization of reversible circuits - a survey. ACM Comput. Surv. (CSUR) **45**(2), 21 (2013)
17. Soeken, M., Frehse, S., Wille, R., Drechsler, R.: RevKit: a toolkit for reversible circuit design. Mult. Valued Log. Soft Comput. **18**(1), 55–65 (2012)
18. Toffoli, T.: Reversible computing. In: Bakker, J., Leeuwen, J. (eds.) ICALP 1980. LNCS, vol. 85, pp. 632–644. Springer, Heidelberg (1980). doi:10.1007/3-540-10003-2_104
19. Wille, R., Drechsler, R.: Towards a Design Flow for Reversible Logic. Springer, Dordrecht (2010)
20. Wille, R., Drechsler, R., Osewold, C., Garcia-Ortiz, A.: Automatic design of low-power encoders using reversible circuit synthesis. In: Proceedings of the Conference on Design, Automation and Test in Europe (DATE 2012), pp. 1036–1041. EDA Consortium, San Jose (2012). http://dl.acm.org/citation.cfm?id=2492708.2492966
21. Wille, R., Soeken, M., Otterstedt, C., Drechsler, R.: Improving the mapping of reversible circuits to quantum circuits using multiple target lines. In: 18th Asia and South Pacific Design Automation Conference (ASP-DAC), pp. 145–150. IEEE (2013)

An ESOP Based Cube Decomposition Technique for Reversible Circuits

Sai Phaneendra Parlapalli$^{(\boxtimes)}$, Chetan Vudadha, and M.B. Srinivas

Department of Electrical Engineering, Birla Institute of Technology and Science
(BITS) - Pilani, Hyderabad Campus, Hyderabad, India
phani.parlapalli@gmail.com

Abstract. Reversible logic finds applications in emerging technologies such as quantum computing, optical computing, etc. This has motivated research into development of synthesis and optimization algorithms for reversible circuits. In this paper, a set of rules is presented for the decomposition of a pair of multi-control Toffoli gates (MCT) to reduce the quantum cost of reversible circuits. These rules find pairs of MCT gates, which when decomposed to a network of smaller gates, result in reduced quantum cost. This technique is used in conjunction with an Exclusive-OR Sum-Of-Product (ESOP) based reversible circuit synthesis algorithm to check its efficiency. Results indicate that there is a reduction in quantum cost of several benchmark circuits when compared to the known ESOP based synthesis algorithms.

1 Introduction

Motivated by the applications of reversible logic in emerging technologies, many algorithms and methodologies have been developed during the past decade to synthesize and optimize reversible logic circuits. A survey on different synthesis and optimization techniques has been presented in [12,18]. These include exact/optimal methods, heuristics methods, etc. The exact/optimal methods generate optimal circuits in terms of cost but are applicable only to functions with very small number of variables, whereas, heuristic methods can synthesize large functions (typically 30 or less variables [18]) but generate sub-optimal circuits. To handle a larger number of variables, high-level function descriptions like Binary Decision Diagram (BDD) [6,17], Exclusive-OR Sum Of Product (ESOP) [4,5,9] have been proposed for the synthesis of reversible logic circuits. While these methods are scalable for a much higher number of variables, the synthesized circuits are far from optimal.

The present work focuses on synthesis of reversible logic circuits using ESOP based technique. A decomposition algorithm is presented which decomposes pairs of ESOP product terms into smaller product terms while eliminating the redundant terms for the same functionality. This results in the reduction of the size of the reversible gate which has a direct impact in the reduction of quantum cost of the final synthesized circuit.

© Springer International Publishing AG 2017
I. Phillips and H. Rahaman (Eds.): RC 2017, LNCS 10301, pp. 127–140, 2017.
DOI: 10.1007/978-3-319-59936-6_10

The rest of the article is organized as follows: Sect. 2 discusses the basic concepts of reversible circuits and their ESOP representation. A review of existing ESOP based synthesis techniques and related work is presented in Sect. 3 while the proposed decomposition algorithm is presented in Sect. 4. Finally experimental results and comparison with existing techniques are discussed in Sect. 5, and conclusions are drawn in Sect. 6.

2   Background

2.1   Reversible Circuits

A reversible Boolean function is a multi-input, multi-output Boolean function which has an equal number of inputs and outputs. It has a one-to-one mapping between inputs and outputs and is bijective. A cascade of reversible gates realizes a reversible circuit for a given function. Among several reversible gates that exist in literature, the most basic gates are *NOT*, *CNOT* and *Toffoli* gates [15]. A Toffoli gate inverts the target line, represented as $\oplus$ in Fig. 1, when all *positive* control lines, represented as •, are equal to '1'. Similarly, a *negative* control in Toffoli gate, represented as ∘, indicates the control line is active when it is equal to '0'. A n-bit multi control Toffoli (MCT) gate is a generalized Toffoli gate with $n-1$ control lines and is represented as $MCT(C; t)$, where C is the set of control lines and t is the target line. The standard gate representation of these reversible gates is shown in Fig. 1.

In this paper, *quantum cost (QC)*, which is the equivalent cost of reversible gate in quantum technology, is taken as a cost metric to evaluate the cost of reversible circuits. The quantum cost for Toffoli gate and MCT gates are calculated using the cost function given in RevKit tool [14]. If a gate has all *negative* control lines, then the cost of the gate is incremented by one [7]. The cost of a circuit is the sum of the cost of individual reversible gates in the circuit.

(a) Toffoli

(b) Multi-Control Toffoli (MCT)

Fig. 1. Basic reversible gates

Decomposition of an MCT Gate. Any MCT gate can be decomposed into a network of smaller gates. A fundamental decomposition method is presented in Lemma 7.3 of [2] by which any MCT gate of size m (where $m \geqslant 5$) can be decomposed into a network of two gates, each of size p and two gates of size $m - p + 1$ each, given at least one empty line (line which is not a control or target line for an MCT gate) is present in the circuit. For example, the decomposition of a MCT gate, $G = MCT(x_0, x_1, x_2, x_3, x_4; f_0)$, of size 5 into a network of four gates of size 3 (i.e., $p = 3$) is shown in Fig. 2. In this paper, gates in the network that are realized on an empty line are termed as *secondary gates* (represented as *sg* in Fig. 2) and the gates that are realized on the actual target line, i.e., f_0 are termed as *primary gates* (represented as *pg* in Fig. 2). Assuming symbol 'o' denotes composition (cascading of the gates/circuits), the decomposition network of gate G can be written in terms of '*sg*' and '*pg*' as:

$$G = sg \circ pg \circ sg \circ pg$$

Fig. 2. Decomposition of MCT gate into network of four smaller gates

2.2   Exclusive-OR Sum-Of-Products (ESOP)

A traditional Sum-of-Product (SOP) is a method of representing a function using AND-OR expression, i.e., OR of several product terms. Likewise, an Exclusive-or sum-of-products (ESOP) is a type of representation in AND-EXOR expression [8], i.e., exclusive-OR of several product terms. The individual product terms in an ESOP expression are called as *cubes* and the variables in its *positive* or *negative* polarity form are called as *literals*. For example, consider a function in SOP form as $f = x_0 \overline{x_1} + x_0 x_2$, the ESOP equivalent form of the same is $f = x_0 \overline{x_1} \oplus x_0 x_1 x_2$. Further, $x_0 \overline{x_1}$, $x_0 x_1 x_2$ are termed as *cubes* and variables x_0, x_1, $\overline{x_1}$, x_2 are termed as *literals*. In general the cubes are represented as a vector of inputs, i.e., for n variables where $x_0, x_1, \ldots, x_{n-1}$ are inputs and $x_i \in \{0, 1, -\}$, the cube C_i is represented as cube $C_i = <x_0 x_1 \ldots x_{n-1}>$. The '$-$' in a cube indicates that the variable at that position has not appeared in the cube and is termed as a '*don't care*' literal.

In this paper, ESOP functions are represented as a list of cubes called *cube lists*. As an example, consider two functions $f_1 = x_0 \overline{x_1} \oplus x_0 x_1 x_2$ and $f_2 = \overline{x_0} \oplus x_0 x_1 x_2$, where x_0, x_1 and x_2 are input variables and f_1 and f_2 are outputs. The cube list along with the cube outputs and representation of cubes for the functions f_1 and f_2 are shown in Fig. 3.

	x_0 x_1 x_2 f_1 f_2
$C_1(x_0\overline{x_1})$	1 0 − 1 0
$C_2(x_0x_1x_2)$	1 1 1 1 1
$C_3(\overline{x_0})$	0 − − 0 1

(a)

C_i	$< x_0x_1x_2 >$
C_1	$< 10- >$
C_2	$< 111 >$
C_3	$< 0 - - >$

(b)

Fig. 3. (a) *Cube list* and (b) representation of cubes for functions $f_1 = x_0\overline{x_1} \oplus x_0x_1x_2$ and $f_2 = \overline{x_0} \oplus x_0x_1x_2$

3   Related Work

The ESOP based synthesis approach for reversible circuits has been introduced in [5]. In this approach, the cubes corresponding to every output variable are mapped to a MCT gate. Later, different techniques have been presented to reduce the quantum cost of these circuits. A template matching approach has been presented in [10] by which different templates are applied on a cascade of MCT gates to reduce the quantum cost. A synthesis approach was presented in [13] which uses positive and negative control gates to eliminate the usage of NOT gates for negative literals in the cubes. Further, a set of transformation rules is defined to transfer the targets on outputs to some input lines which helps in reducing number of lines in the circuit. An ordering based technique has been presented in [11] to reorder the ESOP cubes such that the number of NOT gates is reduced. In addition to this a set of transformation rules have also been presented to improve the quantum cost of the circuit. Based on these transformation rules, a simulated annealing based approach has been developed in [3] to reduce the quantum cost of circuit. In order to reduce the number of CNOT gates used for sharing MCT gates among their outputs, a shared cube synthesis approach has been presented in [9] which finds multiple outputs that have the largest number of common cubes. These common cubes are first mapped on to respective MCT gates and then CNOT gates are added to share the common cubes between the outputs. All these techniques use EXORCISM-4 tool [8] to generate a cube list. EXORCISM-4 is a general tool that generates Ex-OR cube list from truth tables or SOP expressions. There are techniques [1,4] which use custom algorithms to generate cube lists targeting only reversible circuits.

In this paper, a decomposition technique for a pair of cubes is proposed to improve the quantum cost of a reversible circuit. This technique selects a pair of cubes from the cube list and decomposes them into smaller cubes without any change in the functionality.

4   Proposed Cube Decomposition Technique

4.1   General Idea

The synthesis algorithms/methods of reversible circuits typically generate sub-optimal circuits and thus optimization methods are applied to reduce circuit's quantum cost. Among the optimization methods, one of the methods is decomposing the MCT gates in the circuit into a network of smaller gates and removal of redundant gates, if any. In general, this decomposition is applied independently on individual gates and thus generation of maximum number of redundant gates may not happen. Rather than applying decomposition on individual gates, if the decomposition is applied on a pair of gates with a systematic approach, the chances of generation of redundant gates are higher. For example, consider a pair of gates shown in Fig. 4(a) and two different types of decomposition for the same are shown in Figs. 4(b) and (c). The first decomposition is applied independently on individual gates and the second decomposition is applied pairwise generating identical primary gates. The dotted box in Fig. 4(c) contains primary gates that are equal and thus redundant, and hence which can be removed from the circuit thereby reducing the quantum cost of pairwise decomposition circuit.

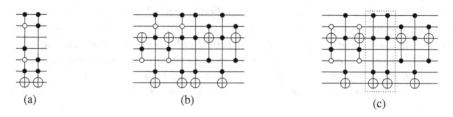

(a)   (b)   (c)

Fig. 4. (a) Initial circuit *(QC = 78)* (b) Individual gate decomposition *(QC = 98)* (c) Pairwise decomposition *(QC = 62)*

The following lemma proves different conditions by which redundant gates can be generated when decomposing a pair of gates.

Lemma 1. *Consider two MCT gates G_1 and G_2. If the primary (or secondary) gates of two decomposed MCT gates, G_1 and G_2, are identical or if one of the primary (or secondary) gates of $G_1(G_2)$ is identical to other gate $G_2(G_1)$, then redundant gates can be generated which can be removed from the circuit.*

Proof. Consider two MCT gates G_1 and G_2 and the decomposed network of these gates in terms of their primary and secondary gates are represented as:

$$G_1 = sg_1 \circ pg_1 \circ sg_1 \circ pg_1 \ \& \ G_2 = sg_2 \circ pg_2 \circ sg_2 \circ pg_2$$

where pg_1, pg_2 represents primary gates and sg_1, sg_2 represents secondary gates for gate G_1 and G_2 respectively. The general circuit realization for the cascade of gates G_1 and G_2 is given as:

$$G_1 \circ G_2 = G_1 \circ G_2^{-1} \quad [\because \text{MCT gates are self-inverse}]$$
$$= sg_1 \circ pg_1 \circ sg_1 \circ pg_1 \circ pg_2 \circ sg_2 \circ pg_2 \circ sg_2 \tag{1}$$

If the primary gates of two MCT gates are equal, then $pg_1 \circ pg_2 = \varnothing$. Thus, primary gates are redundant and can be removed from the circuit. Then the Eq. (1) reduces to:

$$G_1 \circ G_2 = sg_1 \circ pg_1 \circ sg_1 \circ sg_2 \circ pg_2 \circ sg_2 \tag{2}$$

Similarly, if the primary gates of one of the gates is equal to the other undecomposed gate, then $pg_1 \circ G_2 = \varnothing$. Thus, the cascade of gate G_1 and G_2 can be reduced to:

$$\begin{aligned} G_1 \circ G_2 &= sg_1 \circ pg_1 \circ sg_1 \circ pg_1 \circ G_2 \\ &= sg_1 \circ pg_1 \circ sg_1 \end{aligned} \tag{3}$$

$\square$

Thus, from the above discussion, a systematic decomposition of these MCT gates into a network of smaller gates can result in the reduction of cost of circuit implementation. This can be directly applied in ESOP based synthesis because of its advantage that the cubes can be directly realized using MCT gates. Thus, the decomposition problem in terms of ESOP cubes can be formulated as:

Given a pair of cubes C_1 and C_2, the generation of secondary gates, sg_1, sg_2, and primary gates, pg_1, pg_2, for the pair of cubes such that the primary gates are equal or one of the primary gates is equal to other cube's MCT gate realization.

The MCT gate realization of a cube C is represented as $G(C)$. In the next subsection, the generation of these primary and secondary gates for a given pair of cubes is explained.

4.2   Generation of Primary and Secondary Gates

In order to generate the primary and secondary gates for a given pair of cubes, the input variables of these cubes are assigned to three different groups i.e., *equal, unequal* and *target*. The variables of a cube that are equal to the other cube (with same literal value) are assigned to Equal group (E). The variables of a cube that are not equal with the other cube are assigned to Unequal group (U) and the variables that are not present in the cube, i.e., having don't care term as values are assigned to Target group (T). The representation for these three groups is given as follows.

$$E_a = E_b = \{x_i : a_i = b_i \neq \text{'} - \text{'}\}$$

$$U_a = \{x_i : a_i \neq b_i, a_i \neq \text{'} - \text{'}\} \ \& \ U_b = \{x_i : b_i \neq a_i, b_i \neq \text{'} - \text{'}\}$$

$$T_a = \{x_i : a_i = \text{'} - \text{'}\} \ \& \ T_b = \{x_i : b_i = \text{'} - \text{'}\}$$

where, a_i and b_i indicate the value of variable x_i in cube C_a, C_b respectively and the suffix a, b of a group indicates the group belongs to cube C_a, C_b respectively. As an example, consider two cubes, $C_a = <10-101>$ and $C_b = <11--11>$.

The *equal*, *unequal* and *target* for the cube pair are given as: $E_a = E_b = \{x_0, x_5\}$, $U_a = \{x_1, x_3, x_4\}$ & $U_b = \{x_1, x_4\}$ and $T_a = \{x_2\}$ & $T_b = \{x_2, x_3\}$. The variables in the target group of a cube can be taken as empty lines, which are the target lines for the generation of secondary gate. Considering empty line is represented as x_t and actual target line for an MCT gate is represented as t, the primary and secondary gates in terms of *equal* and *unequal* groups are given as:

$$pg = MCT(E, x_t; t) \ \& \ sg = MCT(U; x_t)$$

From the above expressions, E, U and t are known variables and the only unknown variable that needs to be derived is x_t. Depending on the availability of x_t in the target groups of a pair of cubes, there are different cases in the generation of primary and secondary gates. These cases are discussed in the following subsections.

Case 1. If $T_a \cap T_b \neq \phi$, then one of the variables (denoted as x_t) from set $T_a \cap T_b$ can be chosen as the target line for the generation of secondary gates for a pair of cubes. Since, the target line of secondary gate is also a control line for primary gate, x_t is added to the list of control lines for the primary gates. Thus, the final primary and secondary gates representations are:

$$sg_1 = MCT(U_a; x_t) \ , \ sg_2 = MCT(U_b; x_t)$$

$$pg_1 = pg_2 = MCT(E_a, x_t; t)$$

As an example, consider two cubes, $C_a = <10-101>$ and $C_b = <11--11>$ and the *equal*, *unequal* and *target* groups are given as:$E_a = E_b = \{x_0, x_5\}, U_a = \{x_1, x_3, x_4\}$ & $U_b = \{x_1, x_4\}, T_a = \{x_2\}$ & $T_b = \{x_2, x_3\}$. There exist a common variable x_2 in both target groups T_a and T_b which acts as target line in the generation of secondary gates. Thus, the primary and secondary gates for the cube C_a and C_b are $sg_1 = MCT(x_1, x_3, x_4; x_2) \ , \ sg_2 = MCT(x_1, x_4; x_2), pg_1 = pg_2 = MCT(x_0, x_5, x_2; f_0)$. From Lemma 1, if the primary gates of both the cubes are equal then the cascade of cubes can be given as $G(C_a) \circ G(C_b) = sg_1 \circ pg_1 \circ sg_1 \circ sg_2 \circ pg_2 \circ sg_2$. The final circuit implementation for the cascade of cube C_a and C_b is shown in Fig. 5.

(a) Circuit before Cube Decomposition

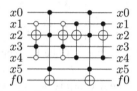

(b) Circuit after Cube Decomposition

Fig. 5. Cube decomposition for a pair of cube with same empty line as target line

Case 2. The previous approach can be used only if there exists a variable in both the target groups of cube pair. In this subsection, another approach is presented if there is no common variable present in both target groups, i.e., $T_a \cap T_b = \phi$. Here, two variables, x_{ta} and x_{tb}, are chosen one from each target groups T_a and T_b respectively. These variables act as empty lines in the generation of secondary gates for their respective cubes. Further, these variables act as control lines for primary gates for cube C_a and C_b and thus the primary gates can be represented as

$$pg_1 = MCT(E_a, x_{ta}; t) \ \& \ pg_2 = MCT(E_b, x_{tb}; t)$$

From the above equations, the primary gates for cube pair are not equal. In order to make them equal, the variable x_{tb} is added to the primary gate of cube C_a and variable x_{ta} is added to the primary gate of cube C_b. As x_{tb} is also a variable in unequal group of cube C_a, but covered in primary gates this variable can be removed in the generation of secondary gate for cube C_a. Similarly with variable x_{ta} for cube C_b. Thus the final gate realization of primary and secondary gates is:

$$pg_1 = pg_2 = MCT(E_a, x_{ta}, x_{tb}; t)$$

$$sg_1 = MCT(U_a - \{x_{tb}\}; x_{ta}) \ \& \ sg_2 = MCT(U_b - \{x_{ta}\}; x_{tb})$$

As an example, consider two cubes, $C_a = <10 - 101>$ and $C_b = <1 - 1011>$ and the *equal*, *unequal* and *target* groups are given as: $E_a = E_b = \{x_0, x_5\}$, $U_a = \{x_1, x_3, x_4\}$ & $U_b = \{x_2, x_3, x_4\}$ and $T_a = \{x_2\}$ & $T_b = \{x_1\}$. There is no common variable that exists in both the target groups. Thus, x_2 is selected for the generation of secondary gate for cube C_a and x_1 for cube C_b. Thus the primary and secondary gates for the cube C_a and C_b are $sg_1 = MCT(x_3, x_4; x_2), sg_2 = MCT(x_3, x_4; x_1), pg_1 = pg_2 = MCT(x_0, x_5, x_1, x_2; f_0)$. From Lemma 1, if the primary gates of both the cubes are equal then the cascade of cubes can be given as $G(C_a) \circ G(C_b) = sg_1 \circ pg_1 \circ sg_1 \circ sg_2 \circ pg_2 \circ sg_2$. The final circuit implementation for the cascade of cube C_a and C_b is shown in Fig. 6.

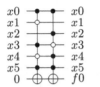

(a) Circuit before Cube Decomposition

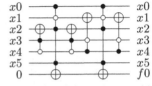

(b) Circuit after Cube Decomposition

Fig. 6. Cube decomposition for a pair of cube with different empty line as target line

Case 3. As discussed earlier, for a cascade of two MCT gates if one of the MCT gate's primary gate is equal to other MCT gate then the cost of circuit realization can be reduced. For a pair of cubes, this condition is satisfied when one of the cube's unequal group has only one variable and the same variable is present in the target group of other cube. The cube which has only one variable (denoted as x_t) in unequal group is not decomposed and the other cube is decomposed with the same variable as target line for its secondary gate. The primary and secondary gates of decomposed cube can be expressed as: $sg1 = MCT(U_a; x_t)$, $pg1 = MCT(E_a, x_t; t)$.

For example, consider two cubes, $C_a = \;<110-1>$ and $C_b = \;<1--11>$. The *equal, unequal* and *target* groups for cube pair are: $E_a = E_b = \{x_0, x_4\}$, $U_a = \{x_1, x_2\}$ & $U_b = \{x_3\}$, $T_a = \{x_3\}$ & $T_b = \{x_1, x_2\}$. The unequal group of cube C_b has only one variable, x_3, which is also present in the target group of cube C_a. This variable acts as a target line for cube C_a, while cube C_b is not decomposed. The secondary and primary gate for cube C_a is expressed as $sg1 = MCT(x_1, x_2; x_3)$, $pg1 = MCT(x_0, x_4, x_3; f_0)$. The MCT gate implementation of cube C_b is $G(C_b) = MCT(x_0, x_3, x_4; t)$. According to Lemma 1, if the primary gate of one MCT gate is equal to other MCT gate then the cascade of gates can be given as $G_1 \circ G_2 = sg_1 \circ pg_1 \circ sg_1$. The final circuit implementation for the cascade of cubes C_a and C_b is shown in Fig. 7.

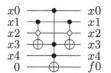

| (a) Before Cube Decomposition | (b) After Cube Decomposition |

Fig. 7. Only one cube is decomposed in the pair of cube

4.3   Algorithm for Cube Decomposition

In this section, the algorithm for cube decomposition technique is presented. The input to the algorithm is *cube_list*, which has a list of cubes and output is reversible gate net-list *GateNetlist*. In the algorithm, initially a cube C_i from the given *cube_list* is extracted. This cube is checked with the other cubes in the *cube_list* for any possible decomposition using the function *CheckingDecomposition()*. This function returns true if the pair of cubes can be decomposed with any one of the proposed decomposition technique else it returns false.

If the return value is false, then the gate realization of cube C_i is added to the *GateNetlist*. If the return value is true, the corresponding cost of the decomposed circuit is calculated using function *DecompCost()*. After all the cubes in the *cube_list* are checked for the decomposition condition, the cube which has the least decomposed circuit cost is termed as *BestCube* and the cost is $BestCost$ for cube C_i. If the $BestCost$ is less than the cost of MCT realization of cube C_i plus the cost of $BestCube$, then the $MCTList()$ function returns the decomposed network of smaller cubes using the proposed decomposition techniques. The decomposed circuit, generated for the cubes C_i and $BestCube$, is appended to the $GateNetlist$. If the $BestCost$ is greater than the cost of MCT realization of cube C_i plus the cost of $BestCube$, then the gate realization of cube C_i is added to the $GateNetlist$. The pseudo code of this algorithm is given below:

Algorithm 1. Cube Decomposition Algorithm

1: **Input:** $cube\_list$
2: **Output:** Reversible $GateNetlist$
3: **begin**
4: **while** $cube\_list$ is not empty **do**
5:     $flag = false$
6:     $C_i = pop(cube\_list)$
7:     $BestCost = \infty$
8:     **for each** cube $C_j \in cube\_list$ **do**
9:         **if** $CheckDecomposition(C_i, C_j)$ is $true$ **then**
10:             $Cost_{deco} = DecompCost(C_i, C_j)$
11:             $InitCost = MCTCost(C_i) + MCTCost(C_j)$
12:             **if** $min\{BestCost, InitCost\} > Cost_{deco}$ **then**
13:                 $flag = true$
14:                 $BestCost = Cost_{deco}$
15:                 $BestCube = C_j$
16:                 $BestDeco = MCTList(C_i, C_j)$
17:             **end if**
18:         **end if**
19:     **end for**
20:     **if** $flag$ is $true$ **then**
21:         $AddToArray(GateNetlist, BestDeco)$
22:         $DeleteCube(cube\_list, BestCube)$
23:     **else**
24:         $AddToArray(GateNetlist, GenerateMCT(C_i))$
25:     **end if**
26: **end while**
27: **return** $GateNetlist$
28: **end**

---

5   Simulation Results and Comparisons

The proposed algorithm has been used to implement various reversible benchmark circuits available in RevLib [16] and compared with existing ESOP based reversible circuit synthesis techniques such as [1, 3, 4, 9, 10]. The cubes list can be generated either by EXORCISM-4 tool or other cube list generation techniques [1, 4]. To evaluate the proposed approach, quantum cost reduction obtained by existing cube transformation techniques that use EXORCISM-4 tool are considered.

Table 1 compares the quantum cost of related and existing ESOP based synthesis techniques with the proposed one. The first column indicates the benchmark name in alphabetical order. Columns 2–6 indicate the quantum cost of existing ESOP based synthesis techniques for the corresponding benchmarks. The techniques presented in columns 2–4 use EXORCISM-4 tool to generate cube list whereas techniques presented in columns 5 and 6 use their own methods to generate the cube lists. Column 7 indicates the quantum cost of the corresponding benchmark using the proposed technique. The final column shows the percentage improvement of quantum cost achieved compared to the existing techniques that give the best reduction for that benchmark.

Table 1. Comparison with existing approaches

Benchmark	[10]	[9]	[3]	[4]	[1]	Proposed approach	% Impr
5xp1	1349	786	807	865	–	759	**3.44**
9sym	5781	10943	3406	16487	1895	2222	−17.26
add6	6362	–	–	5084	2683	3629	−35.26
alu1	243	–	–	–	156	156	**0.00**
alu2	5215	–	3679	4476	–	3458	**6.01**
alu3	2653	–	1919	–	–	1828	**4.74**
alu4	48778	41127	38635	43850	–	31220	**19.19**
apex4	256857	35840	–	50680	51284	37018	−3.29
apex5	–	33830	33803	–	–	29842	**11.72**
apla	4051	1683	1709	–	–	1601	**4.87**
bw	–	637	790	–	2233	649	−1.88
C17	97	–	–	–	–	78	**19.59**
clip	6616	3824	3218	4484	–	2889	**10.22**
cm150a	844	–	–	–	–	785	**6.99**
con1	207	162	–	–	–	150	**7.41**
cordic	349522	187620	111955	–	–	91935	**17.88**
cu	1332	781	780	–	–	747	**4.23**
dc2	1956	1084	1099	–	–	1019	**6.00**
decod	1924	399	–	–	976	436	−9.27
dist	7414	3700	–	–	–	3367	**9.00**
e64	–	–	24345	–	–	23751	**2.44**
ex1010	183726	52788	–	–	77293	52467	**0.61**

(*continued*)

Table 1. (*continued*)

Benchmark	[10]	[9]	[3]	[4]	[1]	Proposed approach	% Impr
ex2	153	–	–	–	118	140	−18.64
ex3	97	–	–	–	73	59	**19.18**
f2	274	112	–	–	116	107	**4.46**
f51m	34244	28382	25119	–	–	22042	**12.25**
frg2	–	112008	114239	–	–	97183	**13.24**
in0	22196	7949	–	–	–	7501	**5.64**
majority	147	–	–	–	106	106	**0.00**
max46	4432	–	–	–	3239	2875	**11.24**
misex1	1017	332	352	466	–	338	−1.81
misex3	122557	49076	54132	67206	–	42098	**14.22**
misex3c	118578	49720	–	85330	52600	42868	**13.78**
mlp4	3827	2496	–	–	–	2303	**7.73**
mux	826	–	–	–	784	768	**2.04**
pm1	582	–	–	–	290	188	**35.17**
radd	798	–	–	–	349	316	**9.46**
rd84	2598	–	1965	2062	–	1687	**14.15**
root	3486	1811	1583	–	–	1533	**3.16**
sao2	7893	3767	–	5147	–	3244	**13.88**
spla	–	–	45478	49419	–	28220	**37.95**
sqn	2170	–	–	–	1183	1222	−3.30
sqr6	1090	583	–	–	–	597	−2.40
sqrt8	584	–	–	461	–	314	**31.89**
squar5	476	–	–	251	–	231	**7.97**
t481	237	–	–	237	–	205	**13.50**
table3	86173	–	32286	35807	–	17454	**45.94**
urf3	–	53157	–	–	56766	51622	**2.89**
z4	674	489	–	–	260	388	−49.23

For the 49 benchmarks considered, the quantum cost has reduced for 39 benchmarks using the proposed cube decomposition technique when compared to existing ones. Benchmarks like *misex3*, *rd84*, *cordic*, *alu4*, *spla*, *table3* have improved by more than 14% when compared to existing synthesis techniques. Further, the proposed algorithm consumes a very less synthesis time with a maximum of 5 s for *frg2* benchmark when implemented in Python programming language on a workstation with Intel E3-1220 processor with 8 GB of primary memory running Windows 7.

6   Conclusion

Reversible logic is known for its applications in emerging technologies such as quantum computing, optical computing, etc. In this paper, an ESOP based cube decomposition algorithm has been proposed to reduce the quantum cost of reversible circuits. Using this algorithm, a pair of cubes is decomposed into a network of smaller gates while eliminating redundant gates. The algorithm has been implemented to synthesize different benchmark circuits and the results indicate that there is a reduction in quantum cost for a majority of benchmarks.

Acknowledgements. This work was supported in part by Council of Scientific & Industrial Research (CSIR) grant (ref.-09/1026(0007)/2012-EMR-I).

References

1. Bandyopadhyay, C., Rahaman, H., Drechsler, R.: Improved cube list based cube pairing approach for synthesis of ESOP based reversible logic. In: Gavrilova, M.L., Tan, C.J.K., Thapliyal, H., Ranganathan, N. (eds.) Transactions on Computational Science XXIV. LNCS, vol. 8911, pp. 129–146. Springer, Heidelberg (2014). doi:10.1007/978-3-662-45711-5_8
2. Barenco, A., Bennett, C.H., Cleve, R., DiVincenzo, D.P., Margolus, N., Shor, P., Sleator, T., Smolin, J.A., Weinfurter, H.: Elementary gates for quantum computation. Phys. Rev. A **52**(5), 3457 (1995)
3. Datta, K., Gokhale, A., Sengupta, I., Rahaman, H.: An ESOP-based reversible circuit synthesis flow using simulated annealing. In: Chaki, R., Saeed, K., Choudhury, S., Chaki, N. (eds.) Applied Computation and Security Systems. AISC, vol. 305, pp. 131–144. Springer, New Delhi (2015). doi:10.1007/978-81-322-1988-0_8
4. Drechsler, R., Finder, A., Wille, R.: Improving ESOP-based synthesis of reversible logic using evolutionary algorithms. In: Di Chio, C., et al. (eds.) EvoApplications 2011. LNCS, vol. 6625, pp. 151–161. Springer, Heidelberg (2011). doi:10.1007/978-3-642-20520-0_16
5. Fazel, K., Thornton, M., Rice, J.: ESOP-based Toffoli gate cascade generation. In: IEEE Pacific Rim Conference on Communications, Computers and Signal Processing, pp. 206–209 (2007)
6. Lin, C.C., Jha, N.K.: RMDDS: Reed-Muller decision diagram synthesis of reversible logic circuits. J. Emerg. Technol. Comput. Syst. **10**(2), 14:1–14:25 (2014). http://doi.acm.org/10.1145/2564923
7. Miller, D.M., Sasanian, Z.: Recent developments on mapping reversible circuits to quantum gate libraries. In: International Symposium on Electronic System Design (ISED), pp. 17–22. IEEE (2012)
8. Mishchenko, A., Perkowski, M.: Fast heuristic minimization of exclusive-sums-of-products. In: Proceedings of the 5th Reed-Muller Workshop, pp. 242–250 (2001)
9. Nayeem, N.M., Rice, J.E.: A shared-cube approach to ESOP-based synthesis of reversible logic. Facta Univ. Ser. Electron. Energ. **24**(3), 385–402 (2011)
10. Rice, J., Fazel, K., Thornton, M., Kent, K.: Toffoli gate cascade generation using ESOP minimization and QMDD-based swapping. In: Proceedings of the Reed-Muller Workshop (RM 2009), pp. 63–72 (2009)

11. Rice, J., Nayeem, N.: Ordering techniques for ESOP-based Toffoli cascade generation. In: IEEE Pacific Rim Conference on Communications, Computers and Signal Processing (PacRim), pp. 274–279. IEEE (2011)
12. Saeedi, M., Markov, I.L.: Synthesis and optimization of reversible circuits - a survey. ACM Comput. Surv. (CSUR) **45**(2), 21 (2013)
13. Sanaee, Y., Dueck, G.W.: ESOP-based Toffoli network generation with transformations. In: 40th IEEE International Symposium on Multiple-Valued Logic (ISMVL), pp. 276–281. IEEE (2010)
14. Soeken, M., Frehse, S., Wille, R., Drechsler, R.: RevKit: a toolkit for reversible circuit design. Mult. Valued Log. Soft Comput. **18**(1), 55–65 (2012)
15. Toffoli, T.: Reversible computing. In: Bakker, J., Leeuwen, J. (eds.) ICALP 1980. LNCS, vol. 85, pp. 632–644. Springer, Heidelberg (1980). doi:10.1007/3-540-10003-2_104
16. Wille, R., Grosse, D., Teuber, L., Dueck, G., Drechsler, R.: RevLib: an online resource for reversible functions and reversible circuits. In: 38th International Symposium on Multiple Valued Logic. ISMVL 2008. pp. 220–225, May 2008
17. Wille, R., Drechsler, R.: BDD-based synthesis of reversible logic for large functions. In: Proceedings of the 46th Annual Design Automation Conference, pp. 270–275. ACM (2009)
18. Wille, R., Drechsler, R.: Towards a Design Flow for Reversible Logic. Springer, Dordrecht (2010)

Controlled and Uncontrolled SWAP Gates in Reversible Logic Synthesis

Md Asif Nashiry[1]([✉]), Mozammel H.A. Khan[2], and Jacqueline E. Rice[1]

[1] Department of Mathematics and Computer Science,
University of Lethbridge, Lethbridge, AB T1K 3M4, Canada
{asif.nashiry,j.rice}@uleth.ca
[2] Department of Computer Science and Engineering,
East West University, Aftabnagar, Dhaka 1212, Bangladesh
mhakhan@ewubd.edu

Abstract. This paper presents a quantum-level realization and synthesis approach using SWAP and Fredkin (SF) gates. Our quantum realization of negative-controlled Fredkin gate requires five 2-qubit elementary quantum gates, the same as that required for realizing a positive-controlled Fredkin gate. We also propose and evaluate the performance of a synthesis approach using SF gates for realizing conservative reversible functions. Our result shows that circuit realization for conservative function using SF gates is more efficient than Toffoli gates. We achieve up to 87% improvement in gate count and quantum cost for (4×4) conservative reversible functions.

Keywords: Reversible logic · SWAP gate · Fredkin gate · Toffoli gates · Mixed polarity gates · Quantum gates · Logic synthesis · Conservative functions

1 Introduction

A logic gate is a reversible gate if the output function of the gate is bijective [1]. The two most widely used reversible logic gate families are NOT-CNOT-Toffoli (NCT) and SWAP-Fredkin (SF). A SWAP gate is a (2×2) reversible logic gate which interchanges the input bits at the output. Fredkin and Toffoli proposed a reversible controlled swap gate (also called Fredkin gate) in [2]. This gate is a positive-controlled gate i.e. it swaps the two target inputs when the control input is 1. The authors showed that it is a universal gate and thus any reversible circuit can be synthesized using only Fredkin gates. One example of this is in [4], where Bruce et al. proposed a design for a full-adder using five positive-controlled Fredkin gates.

Smolin and DiVincenzo presented an implementation of the positive-controlled Fredkin gate using five 2-qubit elementary quantum gates in [3]. We propose a realization of the negative-controlled Fredkin gate, that like the positive-controlled Fredkin gate, requires five 2-qubit elementary quantum gates.

© Springer International Publishing AG 2017
I. Phillips and H. Rahaman (Eds.): RC 2017, LNCS 10301, pp. 141–147, 2017.
DOI: 10.1007/978-3-319-59936-6_11

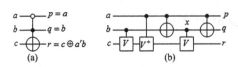

(a)

(b)

Fig. 1. (a) Toffoli gate with top negative control and bottom positive control and (b) its realization.

Table 1. Behaviour of the circuit shown in Fig. 1(b).

Control		Target	Output
a	b	c	r
0	0	c	c
0	1	c	c'
1	0	c	c
1	1	c	c

We also propose a transformation based synthesis algorithm using SF gates for realizing conservative reversible functions. A conservative reversible function has the same number of 1s in both the input and output vectors of the function.

2   Realization of Negative-Controlled Fredkin Gate

To realize our proposed negative-controlled Fredkin gate we use a Toffoli gate with top negative control and bottom positive control as an intermediate gate. Realization of a Toffoli gate with top positive control and bottom negative control is presented in [5]. This realization requires five 2-qubit elementary quantum gates. We follow this technique and present a realization of a Toffoli gate with top negative control and bottom positive control in Fig. 1(b), also requiring five 2-qubit elementary quantum gates. The symbol and realization of a negative-controlled Fredkin gate are shown in Fig. 2. The two target inputs are only swapped at the target outputs when the control input $a = 0$ (Table 1).   If the

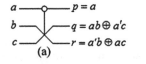
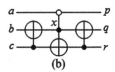

(a)

(b)

Fig. 2. (a) Negative-controlled Fredkin gate and (b) its realization with two Feynman gates and one Toffoli gate with top negative control and bottom positive control.

Toffoli gate shown in Fig. 2(b) is decomposed using the realization illustrated in Fig. 1(b), and the last two Feyman gates are rearranged using the equivalence shown in Fig. 3, the result is the circuit in Fig. 4. The operation of the two gates in a dashed box can be expressed using 4×4 unitary matrices. As these two gates are in cascade, their final operation will be another 4×4 unitary matrix. Therefore, the two gates in practice work as one 2-qubit quantum gate. Thus, the realization of the negative-controlled Fredkin gate requires five 2-qubit elementary quantum gates. A similar argument is used in [3].

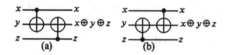

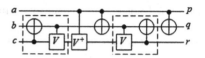

Fig. 3. Circuits of (a) and (b) are equivalent.

Fig. 4. Realization of a negative-controlled Fredkin gate.

3   SF Based Synthesis Approach

The basic working principle of the transformation based synthesis algorithm is to apply reversible operations to a reversible function in order to generate an identity function. The first such algorithm was proposed by Miller et al. [6]. The authors applied gates from the NCT gate library. In the basic algorithm the reversible logic operations are applied to the output of the function's truth table. The following is the basis of transformation based logic synthesis approach.

Table 2. Truth table of a (3×3) reversible function.

	Input			Output			
	a_i	b_i	c_i	a_o	b_o	c_o	
(0)	0	0	0	0	0	0	(0)
(1)	0	0	1	1	0	0	(4)
(2)	0	1	0	0	0	1	(1)
(3)	0	1	1	0	1	1	(3)
(4)	1	0	0	0	1	0	(2)
(5)	1	0	1	1	0	1	(5)
(6)	1	1	0	1	1	0	(6)
(7)	1	1	1	1	1	1	(7)

Step 0: If $f(0) = 0$, no transformation is required; go to step 1. If $f(0) \neq 0$, apply a (1×1) Toffoli gate (NOT gate) in order to achieve $f(0) = 0$.

Step 1: For $1 \leqslant i < 2^m - 1$: If $f(i) = i$, no transformation is required and proceed to next i. If $f(i) \neq i$, apply the smallest $(k \times k)$ Toffoli gate, $k = 2$ to n in order to make $f^i(i) = i$.

The choice of gate during each step of transformation is crucial in order to maintain convergence. The gate chosen in each step of transformation must not change the order of bits of the previous steps. Consider the (3×3) reversible function $f = \sum(0, 4, 1, 3, 2, 5, 6, 7)$ in Table 2. The circuit which is generated by following the basic transformation algorithm is presented in Fig. 5.

The basic premise of SF-based transformation synthesis is the same as that presented in [6]; however instead of using logic gates from the NCT gate family

Table 3. Transformation stages of the function in Table 2 using SF based transformation.

Output			Step 0 (i)			Step 1 (ii)			Step 2 (iii)			Step 3 (iv)			Step 4 (v)		
a	b	c	a^0	b^0	c^0	a^1	b^1	c^1	a^2	b^2	c^2	a^3	b^3	c^3	a^4	b^4	c^4
0	0	0	0	0	0	0	0	0	0	0	0	0	0	0	0	0	0
1	0	0	1	0	0	0	0	1	0	0	1	0	0	1	0	0	1
0	0	1	0	0	1	1	0	0	0	1	0	0	1	0	0	1	0
0	1	1	0	1	1	1	1	0	1	1	0	0	1	1	0	1	1
0	1	0	0	1	0	0	1	0	1	0	0	1	0	0	1	0	0
1	0	1	1	0	1	1	0	1	0	1	1	1	1	0	1	0	1
1	1	0	1	1	0	0	1	1	1	0	1	1	0	1	1	1	0
1	1	1	1	1	1	1	1	1	1	1	1	1	1	1	1	1	1
			—			S(a,c)			S(a,b)			F(b;a,c)			F(a;b,c)		

we use only SWAP and Fredkin gates. We use the same function from Table 2 to demonstrate the SF-based transformation synthesis. We also use the simple one direction transformation for this example. Table 3 shows the transformation stages. The resulting circuit realization of the function from Table 2 is displayed in Fig. 6.

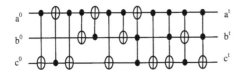

Fig. 5. Basic transformation synthesis for the function in Table 2.

Fig. 6. SF based synthesis for the function in Table 2.

4 Comparison of NCT and SF Based Synthesis Approaches

It is important to observe that the function in Table 2 is a conservative function and Figs. 5 and 6 show two circuit designs for this function. In Fig. 6, we have a gate count of 4 as compared to a gate count of 12 for the circuit in Fig. 5. The quantum cost of the implementation in Fig. 6 is $(2 \times 3) + (2 \times 5) = 16$, where the quantum cost for the circuit realization in Fig. 5 is 28. The percentages of decrease in gate count and quantum cost are 67% and 43% respectively, which is a very significant improvement.

In order to compare the SF based transformation approach with NCT based transformation from a wider perspective, we have generated all possible (3 × 3) conservative reversible functions. We have realized all 36-(3 × 3) conservative functions using both algorithms. The highest percentage of reduction in gate count is 67% for more than half of the (3 × 3) conservative reversible functions. The ability of changing two bits at a time gives SF gates an advantage over the NCT gate family for realizing conservative reversible circuits.

SF based synthesis also performs better than NCT based synthesis when comparing quantum cost. Among the 36 functions, we have achieved lower QC for almost 70% of the functions. For the remaining functions, the QC is the same for both approaches. There is not a single instance where the NCT based synthesis performs better than our proposed approach. The highest percentage of decrease in quantum cost is 70% and the average percentage of reduction of quantum cost is 29%.

As mentioned above, the proposed transformation algorithm using the SF gate family follows the greedy approach. We have designed our algorithm in this way in order to offer a fair comparison, since the basic transformation based synthesis algorithm which is proposed in [6] also follows the greedy approach. At every step of transformation, the algorithm selects a gate which costs less in terms of quantum cost. For example, if we observe column (ii) of Table 3, we need to transform 100 into 010. There are two choices for this mapping. We could use either a SWAP gate S(a,b) or a negative controlled Fredkin gate, $F'(a, b; c)$. The proposed SF gate based transformation selects a SWAP gate, S(a,b) because a SWAP gate has lower quantum cost than a Fredkin gate. However, if we use a $F'(a, b; c)$ at this stage, we get a circuit which is presented in Fig. 7. The use of $F'(a, b; c)$ gate reduces the quantum cost from 16 to 13 as we compared with the circuit in Fig. 6. Moreover, one less gate is needed in this circuit realization. The circuit in Fig. 8 is even more simplified design for the reversible function from Table 2. Figure 8 shows that the gate count is 2 and the quantum cost is 10. Now if we compare the gate count and quantum cost of Fig. 8 with that of the NCT gate based basic transformation synthesis (Fig. 5), the gate count has been reduced from 12 to 2, a 6 times reduction. The quantum cost has been reduced from 28 to 10, which is an improvement of almost a factor of 3. We have also generated all possible 414720 conservative (4 × 4) reversible function. However unlike the case of (3 × 3) functions, there are some circuit realizations where the gate count and quantum cost increase when using SF

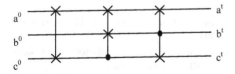

Fig. 7. Another circuit realization for the function from Table 2.

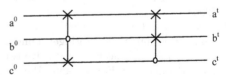

Fig. 8. More efficient circuit realization for the function from Table 2.

gate based transformation synthesis. Among all the (4×4) conservative reversible functions, the quantum cost increases for 27213 (6.5%) functions and the gate count increases for 2 functions. The highest percentage of reduction in gate count by using our proposed synthesis algorithm is 87% and the reduction in gate count, on average, is 61%. We achieve the highest percentage of reduction of quantum cost is 87%. The average percentage of decrease of quantum cost over all 414720 functions is 35%.

5   Conclusion

The contribution of this work is twofold. First, we present a unique realization of a negative-controlled Fredkin gate using five 2-qubit elementary quantum gates. Secondly, we propose a transformation based synthesis algorithm using SF gates for the realization of conservative reversible functions. After applying our approach to all possible (3×3) and (4×4) conservative functions we see that the synthesis of conservative reversible functions using SF gates is more efficient than using NCT gates. For (3×3) functions we show reductions in GC and QC of 67% and 70% respectively, while for (4×4) functions we achieve even higher reductions of 87% in both GC and QC. We also show that the percentage of reduction in GC and QC can be further improved by choosing gates intelligently instead of by following a greedy approach. Finally, this paper shows the usefulness of a negative control Fredkin gate in circuit realization.

The outcome of this work indicates that the synthesis process in reversible logic could be more efficient if we knew the class of a reversible function in advance. Therefore, classifying reversible functions and using the benefits of SF-gates in circuit realization for different classes of functions will be an important area of further research.

Acknowledgment. The second author was involved in this work at the University of Lethbridge, Lethbridge, AB, Canada while on sabbatical from East West University, Dhaka, Bangladesh. The first and third author carried out this work with the support of NSERC.

References

1. Shende, V.V., Prasad, A.K., Markov, I.L., Hayes, J.P.: Synthesis of reversible logic circuits. IEEE Trans. Comput. Aided Des. Integr. Circuits Syst. **22**(6), 710–722 (2003)
2. Fredkin, E., Toffoli, T.: Conservative logic. In: Andrew, A. (ed.) Collision-Based Computing, pp. 47–81. Springer, London (2002)
3. Smolin, J.A., DiVincenzo, D.P.: Five two-bit quantum gates are sufficient to implement the quantum Fredkin gate. Phys. Rev. A **53**(4), 2855 (1996)

4. Bruce, J.W., Thornton, M.A., Shivakumaraiah, L., Kokate, P.S., Li, X.: Efficient adder circuits based on a conservative reversible logic gate. In: Proceedings of IEEE Computer Society Annual Symposium on VLSI 2002, pp. 83–88 (2002)
5. Maslov, D., Miller, D.M.: Comparison of the cost metrics for reversible and quantum logic synthesis. arXiv preprint quant-ph/0511008 (2005)
6. Miller, D.M., Maslov, D., Dueck, G.W.: A transformation based algorithm for reversible logic synthesis, in Proceedings on Design Automation Conference, pp. 318–323. IEEE (2003)

Testing and Fault Tolerance

A Method to Reduce Resources
for Quantum Error Correction

Ritajit Majumdar[1(✉)], Saikat Basu[2], and Susmita Sur-Kolay[2]

[1] B.P. Poddar Institute of Management and Technology,
Maulana Abul Kalam Azad University of Technology, Kolkata, India
majumdar.ritajit@gmail.com
[2] Advanced Computing and Microelectronics Unit,
Indian Statistical Institute, Kolkata, India

Abstract. In a quantum logic circuit, the minimum number of qubits required in a quantum error-correcting code (QECC) to correct a single error was shown by Laflamme to be five. Due to the presence of multi-control gates in the circuit block for a 5-qubit QECC, this block cannot be readily implemented with present day technology. Further, the fault-tolerant decomposition of the QECC circuit block requires a large number of quantum logic gates (resources). In this paper, we (i) propose a smaller 5-qubit error detection circuit which can also correct a single error in 2 of the 5 qubits, and (ii) establish how to use a 3-qubit error correction circuit to correct the single errors when detected in the other 3 qubits. This approach to quantum error-correction circuit design, functionally equivalent to a 5-qubit QECC, yields a significant reduction in the number of quantum logic gates. For a given quantum logic circuit, we also provide a scheme to decide the locations where these error detection and error correction blocks are to be placed in attaining reduction in gate requirement compared to the case where the original 5-qubit QECC block is used. A comparative study of the resource requirement for the benchmark circuits shows that the proposed method outperforms even Shor and Steane codes in terms of resources. Thus, our proposed method provides quantum error correction with minimum qubit requirement and reduced resource requirement on the average.

1 Introduction

The evolution of a quantum state is mathematically represented by a unitary transformation. Quantum computing is reversible since any unitary matrix U has an inverse which is equal to its complex conjugate ($U^\dagger$). However, the state of interest, which is referred to as the system, may be coupled with some other quantum state, which is referred to as the environment. When this composite system undergoes some unitary evolution, the evolution of the constituent states may not be unitary. This incorporates error in the quantum system. An error is nothing but an operator. It is best represented when the state of the system is denoted by the density matrix notation [1,2] as $\rho = \sum_i p_i |\psi_i\rangle\langle\psi_i|$ where p_i is the

© Springer International Publishing AG 2017
I. Phillips and H. Rahaman (Eds.): RC 2017, LNCS 10301, pp. 151–161, 2017.
DOI: 10.1007/978-3-319-59936-6_12

probability that the system is in the state $|\psi_i\rangle$. For a pure state $|\psi\rangle$, the density matrix is simply $|\psi\rangle\langle\psi|$. If an error E occurs on the state ρ with probability p, then the evolution of the state is denoted as

$$E(\rho) = (1 - p)\rho + p.E\rho E^\dagger \tag{1}$$

A quantum error correcting code $\mathcal{R}$ is a mapping such that the composition of $\mathcal{R}$ with E gives back the original quantum state, i.e.,

$$(\mathcal{R} \circ E)(\rho)(E^\dagger \circ \mathcal{R}^\dagger) = \rho \tag{2}$$

An error in a quantum system can also be modelled as a quantum channel. Some quantum error models include Amplitude damping channel, Phase damping channel and Pauli channel [1,2]. In this paper, we have considered the Pauli channel as the error model. The Pauli matrices $\mathbb{I}$, X, Z and Y form the basis for 2×2 dimensional operator space [1]. Hence a code which can correct the Pauli errors can also correct any linear combination of them, i.e., all errors in the 2×2 space. If the error probability is p and the probability of each of X, Z and Y errors is considered to be equal ($\mathbb{I}$ implies no error and hence is not considered), then the evolution of the quantum system is given as

$$E(\rho) = (1 - p)\rho + \frac{p}{3}(X\rho X^\dagger + Z\rho Z^\dagger + Y\rho Y^\dagger) \tag{3}$$

2   Resource Requirement for 5-Qubit QECC

A quantum operation may be realized by one or more quantum gates forming a network of gates or a circuit. Given a quantum system for performing certain operations, a quantum circuit has to be obtained with minimum number of gates, which are also termed as resources. The depth of the circuit and the number of operations to be executed are also important factors in designing a quantum circuit. Additionally, such a circuit requires quantum error correcting code (QECC) for error-free operations. But the QECC also requires a circuit block to be designed appropriately.

Several QECCs have been proposed in the literature to correct a single error in a qubit [3–6]. Gottesman has provided a group theoretic model of errors in a quantum system. His stabilizer formulation provides an operator-level mechanism for correcting quantum errors [7]. It has been shown by Laflamme et al. [5] that in order to correct a single error in a qubit, the information of the qubit must be distributed into at least 5 qubits. An important aspect of this code by Laflamme is that the encoding and the decoding circuits are identical. Furthermore, it is extremely difficult to maintain the superposition of a qubit. Hence, the 5-qubit code provides a better option for error correction than the other codes [3,4,6].

The encoding and decoding circuits of the 5-qubit code, proposed by Laflamme [5], has a number of multi-control gates, which cannot be implemented readily in modern day technologies. Due to the presence of these multi-control operations, the fault-tolerant decomposition requires a large number of gates. Also these gates can be noisy, and incorporate errors in the circuit. Moreover, the error correction requires a significant amount of time due to more gate operations and thus hinders the speed of the computation. FTQLS [8] provides the fault-tolerant decomposition of any quantum circuit in different technologies viz. Ion Trap (IT), Quantum Dot (QD), Linear Photonics (LP), Non-linear Photonics (NP), Neutral Atom (NA) and Superconductor (SC). In Table 1, we compare the number of gate operations and the number of cycles per operation for Shor, Steane and Laflamme codes for each of the six available technologies, as obtained from FTQLS. It is evident from Table 1 that while the qubit requirement of Laflamme code is low, the gate count is significantly larger than for the other two codes.

Table 1. Comparison of gate count and number of cycles of both encoding and correction circuits for QECCs of Shor, Steane and Laflamme respectively

QECC	Technology	Qubits	Ancilla	Total number of qubits	Gate count	Cycles
Shor	IT	9	8	$9 + 8 = 17$	105	24
Steane		7	6	$7 + 6 = 13$	85	30
Laflamme		5	-	5	1641	1432
Shor	QD	9	8	$9 + 8 = 17$	133	116
Steane		7	6	$7 + 6 = 13$	127	191
Laflamme		5	-	5	3353	19602
Shor	LP	9	8	$9 + 8 = 17$	56	164
Steane		7	6	$7 + 6 = 13$	55	172
Laflamme		5	-	5	1751	2310
Shor	NP	9	8	$9 + 8 = 17$	56	196
Steane		7	6	$7 + 6 = 13$	55	206
Laflamme		5	-	5	2437	2566
Shor	NA	9	8	$9 + 8 = 17$	87	22
Steane		7	6	$7 + 6 = 13$	95	29
Laflamme		5	-	5	1892	1657
Shor	SC	9	8	$9 + 8 = 17$	84	196
Steane		7	6	$7 + 6 = 13$	85	242
Laflamme		5	-	5	2604	9070

In order to overcome these shortcomings, we have proposed a smaller 5 qubit circuit for error detection which can also correct errors in 2 of the 5 qubits. Given a quantum circuit, one can insert this detection circuit block at certain points in the given circuit so that if an error is likely to be detected, only then the correction circuit block is also placed. We have computed the time interval for placing this error detection block to obtain reduction in resources. We have also shown the percentage savings in the resource requirement for different benchmark circuits using this proposed technique.

Shor and Steane codes require more qubits for error correction than the code by Laflamme (refer Table 1). However, the resource requirement of the former two is much less than for the 5 qubit code. Hence once can argue that these two codes be used rather than the proposed technique which requires both detection and correction steps in the worst case. However, we show that in average case, our proposed technique requires less resources than the Shor and Steane codes too. Hence, this technique is superior both in terms of qubits as well as resources.

The paper has been organised as follows. In Sect. 2 we propose a new quantum circuit for error detection and compute the time interval for placing this block in a quantum circuit. Section 3 shows the use of the error detection circuit along with a 3 qubit error correction circuit to replace the error correction circuit of the 5 qubit code. We also show the percentage savings provided by this method. In Sect. 4, we show the percentage savings in different benchmark circuits. We conclude in Sect. 5.

3   5-Qubit Quantum Error Detection Circuit

In classical computing, error may cause the bit to flip from 0 to 1 or vice versa. However, in quantum computing, a qubit can incur bit flip or phase flip errors, or both [9]. Thus quantum error correction has two requirements: detection of the type of error and detecting the location of the error. While the former operation is possible using 4 qubits only [10], at least 5 qubits are necessary for both operations [5]. A code which is capable of detecting only the type of error is called a quantum error detection code, while a quantum error correction code can both detect the type and its location. Qubit is an essential resource which must be minimized in quantum computation. This is because it is difficult to preserve the superposition nature of a qubit. Any modification of the original superposition results in loss of information [1]. So using 5-qubit code is preferable for error correction since it requires the minimum number of qubits. However, Table 1 shows that this code has significantly large resource requirement.

In this paper, our proposal is to place a quantum error detection block at certain points in the circuit. If error is likely to be detected, only then the correction block is also placed there. However, the 4-qubit error detection code is not applicable here because encoding the information of a single qubit into 4 qubits only will not allow to correct errors when necessary. The qubit should be encoded using the 5-qubit code by Laflamme to allow error correction whenever necessary.

We propose a 5-qubit error detection block as shown in Fig. 1. This block can act on the 5-qubit system which has been encoded using Laflamme code. In Fig. 1, $|q_0\rangle$ up to $|q_4\rangle$ are the data qubits and the last four are ancilla qubits. $|q_5\rangle, |q_6\rangle$ check for bit error while $|q_7\rangle, |q_8\rangle$ check for phase errors. This block checks whether the first four and the last four qubits are in the same state. If they are not, then an error is detected. Instead of the error correcting block in [5],

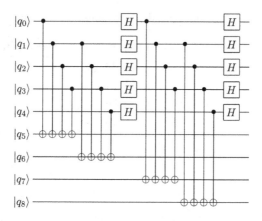

Fig. 1. Proposed 5-qubit error detection block

we place the detection block of Fig. 1 after certain time interval. The correction block is placed at the location where an error is likely to be detected.

A salient question arises here: at which locations should the error detection and the error correction blocks be placed in a given quantum circuit? We provide a bound on the time interval that can be allowed between two error detection blocks, in terms of the probability of error. This time interval may vary with the technology used, since the probability of error at a quantum gate or of decoherence (memory error) differs with the technology for implementing it. Furthermore, if the error detection block is placed at intervals greater than this bound, then the larger error correction block is mandated and hence resource reduction cannot be achieved.

Let p be the error probability per nanosecond (ns), D and C be the gate count of the 5-qubit detection circuit and the 5-qubit correction circuit respectively. We consider that we check for errors at interval of n ns. The probability of no errors occurring after n ns is $(1-p)^n$, and hence the error probability is $(1-(1-p)^n)$. When a single error occurs, then the resource requirement is $(D+C)$ since both error detection as well as correction block must be placed. It is only D when there is no error. So the resource requirement for each time error correction is performed, is

$$(1-p)^n.D + (1-(1-p)^n).(D+C) \tag{4}$$

If this technique is not used, then after each time interval only the correction block is placed, i.e., the resource requirement is C each time. For our proposed method to be advantageous, the resource requirement of this method should be at most C, i.e.,

$$(1-p)^n.D + (1-(1-p)^n).(D+C) \leq C \tag{5}$$

A simple calculation gives us the following inequality

Table 2. Gate counts D and C for error detection and correction in various technologies

Technology	# Gates for error correction (C)	# Gates for error detection (D)	$\frac{D}{C}$
IT	843	36	0.043
SC	1301	34	0.026
LP	874	26	0.03
NP	1217	26	0.021
NA	900	34	0.038
QD	1518	52	0.034

$$(1-p)^n \geq \frac{D}{C} \tag{6}$$

We have used FTQLS [8] to obtain the fault-tolerant version of the error correction block [5] and the error detection block (Fig. 1). The ratio of D to C is provided in Table 2. Note here that in Table 1, we reported the total gate count for both encoding and correction blocks. However, since the encoding block remains same in both cases, in Table 2 we have the gate count of the error correction block of the Laflamme code only to compare with the proposed error detection block.

In [11], the authors have addressed error tracing in quantum circuits. They have placed error correction blocks only when the error probability exceeds a predefined threshold. This technique has allowed them to reduce the required number of error correction blocks significantly compared to the ideal case. Similarly, we propose that error correction can be performed after certain time gap of n ns. For different values of p, the inequality of (6) enables us to the find the maximum permissible value of n for obtaining a circuit with very low probability of error. In Table 3, we give the estimated error probability in different technologies as obtained from [12].

Table 3. Probability of worst gate and memory error in different technologies [12]

Technology	Probability of gate error	Memory error (per ns)
QD	9.89×10^{-1}	3.47×10^{-2}
NA	8.12×10^{-3}	0.00
LP	1.01×10^{-1}	9.80×10^{-4}
NLP	5.20×10^{-3}	9.80×10^{-5}
SC	1.00×10^{-5}	1.00×10^{-5}
IT	3.19×10^{-9}	2.52×10^{-12}

In Table 4, we show the values of n for different values of p in the technologies considered. We have varied p from 10^{-8} to 10^{-1}. However, certain error

Table 4. Time interval $n(ns)$ of error detection with error probability p ranging from 10^{-5}/ns to 10^{-1}/ns) for different technologies

Technology	$p = 10^{-8}$	$p = 10^{-7}$	$p = 10^{-6}$	$p = 10^{-5}$	$p = 10^{-4}$	$p = 10^{-3}$	$p = 10^{-2}$	$p = 10^{-1}$
IT	84397007	8439701	843970	84397	8440	844	84	9
SC	×	×	3649657	364965	36495	3648	364	35
LP	×	×	×	350655	35064	3505	349	34
NP	×	×	3863231	386322	38631	3862	385	37
NA	×	32701690	3270168	327016	32701	3269	326	32
QD	×	×	×	×	×	3380	337	33

probabilities are too low for some of the technologies; for example $p = 10^{-9}$ for QD (see Table 3) is not feasible. Such entries in Table 4 are denoted by a '×'.

Thus Table 4 provides an upper bound of the time interval between placing two error detection blocks in a quantum circuit for a particular technology.

4   Savings in Resources by Our Proposed Method

We consider the proposed quantum error detection circuit of Fig. 1 once more. After the quantum error detection block is placed, one needs to check the syndromes in the 4 ancilla qubits, of which first two indicate bit error and last two indicate phase error. We consider only the bit flip error syndrome for the time being. If the syndrome is 00, it indicates that the circuit is free of bit error. If the syndrome is 10, it indicates that the last four qubits are in the same state, but the 1st four qubits are not. This is possible only if error has occurred in the 1st qubit. Similarly, if 01 is the syndrome, then it is possible to determine that the 5th qubit has error. However, if the syndrome is 11, then it is not possible to determine which of the remaining 3 qubit is erroneous. The similar is true for syndromes for phase flip errors too. Thus when there is any error on the 1st or last qubit, this error detection block can both identify the error type and its position; hence can correct it.

If error is in one of the other 3 qubits, then this proposed error detection circuit can detect it, but cannot determine its position uniquely. So we need to place the error correction block. However, when the error syndrome is 11, we are sure that the error is not in the first or last data qubit. Hence it is not necessary to place the 5-qubit error correcting block to correct errors in one of 3 qubits. Rather, we place a 3-qubit error correction block as shown in Fig. 2.

We now consider the worst case scenario, where an error has been detected by the error detection block of Fig. 1 but this block cannot correct it. So we need to place the 3-qubit error correcting block of Fig. 2. In this scenario our proposed technique requires the maximum resource (5-qubit error detection + 3-qubit error correction). In Table 5, we show the percentage savings that the worst case scenario of our proposed technique gives over the ideal situation of placing a 5-qubit error correction block. From the table we see that for all technologies, our proposed technique provides an average reduction of 94.70% with respect to [5].

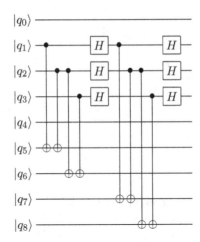

Fig. 2. 3-qubit error correcting block

Table 5. Percentage savings by using the proposed technique over the 5-qubit QECC

Technology	Ideal 5-qubit EC	Detection block	3-qubit EC	Total	Savings (%)
IT	843	36	28	64	92.4
SC	1301	34	22	56	95.7
LP	874	26	14	40	95.4
NP	1217	26	14	40	96.7
NA	900	34	22	56	93.8
QD	1518	52	36	88	94.2
Average savings (%) with respect to [5]					94.70

5   Resource Savings Analysis

In Table 5, we have shown the percentage savings compared to Laflamme code for worst case scenario. However, it is not expected that each time both the detection and correction block need to be placed. At a location where the probability of error is almost zero, placing the detection block alone is sufficient. In this section, we provide an analysis of the resource requirement.

In [11], the authors have introduced the mechanism of error tracing for linear and concatenated Bacon-Shor [6], Steane [4] and Knill C_4 code [13]. 5-qubit error correction code was not used for error tracing purpose. Here, we use a similar approach for different error thresholds and compute the percentage savings in resources. Using the technique of [11], we propose placing the error correction and detection block after some predefined threshold. Let the error threshold be p_{th}. So, we place both the detection and correction block only when the error

Table 6. Comparative study of savings in different benchmark circuits

Circuit Name	PMD	Threshold	# QECC in [11]	Resource in [11]			Our resource	Savings (%) with respect to Steane Code
				9 qubit	7 qubit	5 qubit		
2 qubit Grover's Search	IT	0.001	0	0	0	0	0	-
		0.01	0	0	0	0	0	-
		0.1	0	0	0	0	0	-
	SC	0.001	0	0	0	0	0	-
		0.01	0	0	0	0	0	-
		0.1	0	0	0	0	0	-
	LP	0.001	20	840	760	17480	521	31.45
		0.01	20	840	760	17480	523	31.18
		0.1	20	840	760	17480	548	27.89
	NP	0.001	21	882	798	25557	547	31.45
		0.01	9	378	342	10953	236	30.99
		0.1	0	0	0	0	0	-
	NA	0.001	21	1218	1050	18900	715	31.90
		0.01	10	580	500	9000	343	31.40
		0.1	1	58	50	900	37	26.00
	QD	0.001	33	3036	2277	50094	1718	24.55
		0.01	33	3036	2277	50094	1728	24.11
		0.1	33	3036	2277	50094	1835	19.41
4 qubit Reversible Adder	IT	0.001	0	0	0	0	0	-
		0.01	0	0	0	0	0	-
		0.1	0	0	0	0	0	-
	SC	0.001	2	116	100	2602	69	31.00
		0.01	0	0	0	0	0	-
		0.1	0	0	0	0	0	-
	LP	0.001	104	4368	3952	90896	2706	31.55
		0.01	104	4368	3952	90896	2719	31.20
		0.1	104	4368	3952	90896	2850	27.90
	NP	0.001	104	4368	3952	126568	2706	31.55
		0.01	51	2142	1938	62067	1334	31.16
		0.1	7	294	266	8519	192	27.82
	NA	0.001	127	7366	6350	114300	4321	31.95
		0.01	57	3306	2850	51300	1950	31.58
		0.1	19	1102	950	17100	688	27.58
	QD	0.001	189	17388	13041	286902	9835	24.59
		0.01	189	17388	13041	286902	9897	24.10
		0.1	189	17388	13041	286902	10509	19.42
4 qubit quantum Fourier Transform Circuit	IT	0.001	0	0	0	0	0	-
		0.01	0	0	0	0	0	-
		0.1	0	0	0	0	0	-
	SC	0.001	5	290	250	4215	171	31.6
		0.01	0	0	0	0	0	-
		0.1	0	0	0	0	0	-
	LP	0.001	233	9786	8854	203642	6062	31.54
		0.01	233	9786	8854	203642	6091	31.20
		0.1	233	9786	8854	203642	6385	27.88
	NP	0.001	233	9786	8854	283561	6062	31.54
		0.01	117	4914	4446	142389	3059	31.20
		0.1	15	630	570	18255	411	27.89
	NA	0.001	237	13746	11850	213300	8064	31.95
		0.01	117	6786	5850	105300	4004	31.56
		0.1	18	1044	900	16200	652	27.56
	QD	0.001	558	51336	38502	847044	29037	24.58
		0.01	558	51336	38502	847044	29217	24.11
		0.1	558	51336	38502	847044	31025	19.42
3 qubit Bernstein Vazirani search circuit	IT	0.001	0	0	0	0	0	-
		0.01	0	0	0	0	0	-
		0.1	0	0	0	0	0	-
	SC	0.001	0	0	0	0	0	-
		0.01	0	0	0	0	0	-
		0.1	0	0	0	0	0	-
	LP	0.001	21	882	798	18354	547	31.45
		0.01	21	882	798	18354	549	31.20
		0.1	21	882	798	18354	576	27.81
	NP	0.001	21	882	798	25557	547	31.45
		0.01	9	378	342	10953	236	30.99
		0.1	0	0	0	0	0	-
	NA	0.001	19	1102	950	17100	647	31.90
		0.01	8	464	400	7200	274	31.50
		0.1	1	58	50	900	37	26.00
	QD	0.001	23	2116	1587	34914	1197	24.58
		0.01	23	2116	1587	34914	1205	24.07
		0.1	23	2116	1587	34914	1279	19.40
Average savings (%) with respect to Steane Code								28.34

probability $p = p_{th}$. From Eq. 4, the expected resource requirement for placing the detection and/or correction block each time is

$$(1 - p_{th})D + (1 - (1 - p_{th}))(D + C) = D + p_{th}C.$$

This equation gives the expected resource requirement when the error detection and/or correction block(s) are placed. In Table 6, we show the expected percentage savings in resource for different benchmark quantum circuits. In addition to comparing our technique with the ideal situation of placing the 5-qubit error correcting code, we also compare our proposed technique with Shor and Steane codes.

It can be observed from Table 6 that Steane code has the minimum resource requirement of the three codes (Shor, Steane and Laflamme). The percentage savings shown in this table is with respect to Steane code only, since it has the minimum resource requirement. Our proposed technique shows an average resource reduction of 28.34% over Steane code [4].

Another observation from the benchmark table is that with the increase in probability threshold, the percentage savings decreases, i.e., the resource requirement of our proposed technique increases. This is natural because if when the error threshold is increased, the probability of error occurring increases. Hence, it is more likely to detect errors for higher threshold. So the probability that both detection and correction block needs to be placed increases with the increase in error threshold. Hence the resource requirement of the proposed technique also increases, resulting in a decrease in the percentage savings.

The resulting values from the benchmark circuits (Table 6) clearly show that our proposed technique has minimal resource requirement and minimum qubit requirement and hence is superior to all the three error correcting codes considered (Shor, Steane, Laflamme).

6   Conclusion

In this paper we have proposed a technique to replace the 5 qubit error correction code. Though this code requires the minimum number of qubits, its resource requirement is extremely high since it contains a few multi-control gates. These gates cannot be directly implemented in a fault-tolerant manner, and the fault-tolerant decomposition requires a large number of gates. Our proposed technique uses two steps: error detection, and if error is likely to be detected, then error correction. The total qubit requirement does not increase in this technique. One can still perform error correction with 5 qubits only. However, in the original 5 qubit code [5], no ancilla qubits are required for error correction. But our proposed technique requires 4 ancilla qubits. Nevertheless, these qubits are all initialized to $|0\rangle$ and the superposition property of these qubits are not necessary for the proposed mechanism. Hence effectively they behave like reversible bits and can be reused more than once.

We have shown the percentage savings that the technique proposed here provides. Furthermore, we have used our technique on some benchmark circuits too and have shown the savings in gate count. Hence, this method provides a way for performing error correction using the minimum number of qubits and also reduces the gate count significantly. A future prospect will be to find the minimum resource requirement for quantum error correction and to check where our proposed technique stands compared to it.

References

1. Nielsen, M.A., Chuang, I.L.: Quantum Computation and Quantum Information. Cambridge University Press, Cambridge (2010)
2. Wilde, M.M.: Quantum Information Theory. Cambridge University Press, New York (2013)
3. Shor, P.W.: Scheme for reducing decoherence in quantum computer memory. Phys. Rev. A **52**, R2493–R2496 (1995)
4. Steane, A.M.: Error correcting codes in quantum theory. Phys. Rev. Lett. **77**, 793–797 (1996)
5. Laflamme, R., Miquel, C., Paz, J.P., Zurek, W.H.: Perfect quantum error correcting code. Phys. Rev. Lett. **77**, 198–201 (1996)
6. Bacon, D.: Operator quantum error-correcting subsystems for self-correcting quantum memories. Phys. Rev. A **73**, 012340 (2006)
7. Gottesman, D.: Stabilizer codes and quantum error correction. arXiv preprint arXiv:quant-ph/9705052 (1997)
8. Lin, C.C., Chakrabarti, A., Jha, N.K.: FTQLS: fault-tolerant quantum logic synthesis. IEEE Trans. Very Large Scale Integr. VLSI Syst. **22**(6), 1350–1363 (2014)
9. Gottesman, D.: An introduction to quantum error correction and fault-tolerant quantum computation. Quantum Inform. Sci. Contrib. Math. **68**, 13–60 (2009)
10. Grassl, M., Beth, T., Pellizzari, T.: Codes for the quantum erasure channel. Phys. Rev. A **56**, 33–38 (1997)
11. Majumdar, R., Basu, S., Mukhopadhyay, P., Sur-Kolay, S.: Error tracing in linear and concatenated quantum circuits. arXiv preprint arXiv:1612.08044 (2016)
12. Suchara, M., Faruque, A., Lai, C.Y., Paz, G., Chong, F., Kubiatowicz, J.D.: Estimating the resources for quantum computation with the QuRE toolbox. Technical report, DTIC Document (2013)
13. Knill, E.: Quantum computing with realistically noisy devices. Nature **434**(7029), 39–44 (2005)

Test Pattern Generation Effort Evaluation
of Reversible Circuits

Abhoy Kole[1], Robert Wille[2], Kamalika Datta[3], and Indranil Sengupta[4(✉)]

[1] B.P. Poddar Institute of Management and Technology, Kolkata, India
abhoy.kole@gmail.com
[2] Johannes Kepler University Linz, Linz, Austria
robert.wille@jku.at
[3] National Institute of Technology Meghalaya, Shillong, India
kdatta@nitm.ac.in
[4] Indian Institute of Technology Kharagpur, Kharagpur, India
isg@iitkgp.ac.in

Abstract. The problem of synthesis and optimization of reversible and quantum circuits have drawn the attention of researchers for more than one decade. With physical technologies for realizing the quantum bits (qubits) being announced, the problem of testing such circuits is also becoming important. There have been several works for identifying fault models for reversible circuits, and test generation algorithms for the same. In this work, we aim to show that the problem of testing reversible circuits with respect to recent fault models (like missing gate, missing control, reduced control, etc.) is easy, and it is not really worth to spend time and effort for generating better test patterns. To establish this point, test generators using two extreme scenarios have been implemented: a naive test generator that is very fast but does not guarantee optimality and a SAT-based test generator that is slow but guarantees smallest test sets. Experiments have been carried out on reversible benchmark circuits, which establish the fact that the size of the test patterns does not drastically differ across the spectrum.

Keywords: Reversible circuit · ATPG · SAT · Optimization

1 Introduction

A circuit is said to be reversible if it provides a bijective mapping between the input and output lines, which implies that the number of input and output lines are equal. A reversible circuit is composed as a cascade of simple reversible gates, without any fanout or feedback connections. Reversible circuits have been studied extensively in the literature as an alternate computing paradigm with some potential for low power design (see e.g. [2,8] or, more recently, [3]) or quantum computation [11].

Particular for the latter domain, how to implement corresponding circuits has intensely been considered. To this end, various methods for synthesis and

© Springer International Publishing AG 2017
I. Phillips and H. Rahaman (Eds.): RC 2017, LNCS 10301, pp. 162–175, 2017.
DOI: 10.1007/978-3-319-59936-6_13

optimization have been proposed (see e.g. [4,14]). For their physical realization, various quantum gates and methods of decomposing reversible circuits to circuits composed of the corresponding gate library have been reported. Here, particular the NCV library [9] or more recently the Clifford+T [1] library received attention. In this regard, it has to be considered that, in a quantum circuit, information is represented in terms of qubits, which can not only be in the states 0 and 1, but also any superposition of them. Reversible circuits however provide a good basis for this, since every quantum gate operation is also reversible in nature.

With various technologies beginning to emerge that are able to implement and manipulate qubits, researchers have also been looking at the various fault effects and models that such circuits can be subjected to. In conventional gate level circuits, where each gate is physically implemented and a signal moves from one gate to the next, wire-level fault models like stuck-at or bridging faults have become popular. In contrast, a quantum circuits consists of a set of qubits whose interactions are controlled by applying a sequence of control pulses; in other words, the same set of qubits perform the gate operations sequentially. Therefore, wire-level fault models are not relevant to quantum circuits, and newer fault models like missing-gate or missing-control have been proposed.

There have been several reported works that target the testing of faults in reversible circuits – and, by this, conduct *Automatic Test Pattern Generation* (ATPG). Initial works [12] used the stuck-at fault models for reversible circuits; however, subsequent works relied on more realistic fault models addressing physical realization constraints [5]. The various test pattern generation methods that have been reported can be broadly categorized as: (a) branch-and-bound methods [5], (b) methods based on *Integer Linear Programming* (ILP) [13], SAT-based and PBO-based methods [17–19], etc. In addition, there has been several works on *design for testability* (DFT), where by adding some extra gates or controls, the faults can be tested using very few test patterns [10].

Most of these methods suffer from scalability problems as they often aim to find the best possible, i.e. smallest possible, solution and rely on tools like ILP, SAT, or PBO solvers that do not scale well with problem size. In this work, we are questioning whether these efforts are really worth it. In fact, it is evident that the problem of testing reversible circuits is much simpler as compared to that for conventional circuits – since the problems of controllability and observability are naturally solved by the bijective mappings for every gate operation. Because of this, it is rather easy to implement an ATPG tool that would run very fast and, at the same time, still would generate the desired set of test patterns which is of moderate size.

Motivated by that, the main objectives of the proposed work is as follows:

(a) Evaluate test generation methods from an effort-quality tradeoff point of view. Specifically, how naive ATPG algorithms perform as compared to the optimum ATPG approaches.
(b) Establish the fact that it does not make much sense to spend time and effort in minimizing the number of test patterns in reversible circuits. Because of its inherent properties, such circuits in any case do not require too many patterns for testing.

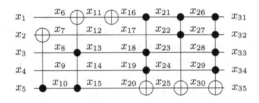

Fig. 1. Example reversible circuit

The rest of the paper is organized as follows. Section 1 provides a brief literature survey covering reversible circuits and gates, the fault models, and the notable test generation works reported in the literature. Section 2 provides the details for our proposed evaluation, where we discuss a naive test generation approach that is fast but non-optimal, and a SAT-based approach that is slow but optimal. Results of the experimental evaluation will be presented and discussed in Sect. 3. Finally, Sect. 4 summarizes the work with concluding remarks and some directions for future work.

In this section, we briefly review the basics of reversible circuits, the fault models, and the test generation approaches that have been proposed for reversible circuits.

1.1 Reversible Circuits and Gates

In our work, we only consider reversible circuits that are composed of multiple-control Toffoli (MCT) gates, also known as k-CNOT gates. A k-CNOT gate has $k + 1$ inputs and outputs, with k control connections $(c_1, c_2, \ldots, c_k)$ and one target line t. The logic value of the target line t gets inverted only when all the lines with control connections are at logic 1, while the logic values of all the other lines remain unchanged. In other words, the new value of t becomes $t_{new} = (c_1.c_2 \cdots c_k) \oplus t$.

Figure 1 shows a reversible circuit with 6 gates, comprising of one 0-CNOT gate, one 1-CNOT gate, two 2-CNOT gate, one 3-CNOT gate and one 4-CNOT gate.

Since the state of the target line of a k-CNOT gate is computed using the XOR operation, it is clear that every gate is reversible; if the output vector is applied to the output of the gate, we get back the previous input. When we generate test vectors to detect faults in the gates, this property results in the following unique characteristics.

(a) For any state vector S_i applied to the input of any gate g_i, it will map to a unique state vector in the primary outputs (PO). Any bit change(s) in S_i will result in a different unique state vector in PO. This is due to the bijective property of reversible circuits.
(b) For any state vector S_i applied to the input of any gate g_i, it is always possible to get a unique state vector at the primary inputs (PI). This can be

achieved by back-tracing from gate g_i, and evaluating every gate encountered in the reverse direction.

These characteristics help to solve the controllability and observability problems during testing of reversible circuits, which is known to be one of the biggest obstacles in the testing of conventional circuits.

1.2   Reversible Circuit Fault Models

It is known that reversible gates can be decomposed into quantum gates using some quantum gate library (e.g. NCV). It has been mentioned in [11] that quantum gates can be implemented using various nanotechnologies. Some of these approaches use the quantum states of sub-atomic particles (like spin-up and spin-down) to represent the qubits. The qubit states are modified by applying very short-width electromagnetic pulses to implement the quantum gate functions. In trapped-ion technology, for instance, individual atoms can represent the qubits. The atomic states are altered by applying precise laser pulses of specified frequency and duration. A sequence of such pulses has to be applied in time to execute the gates that comprise a reversible or quantum circuit.

In some earlier works, classical stuck-at or bridging fault models at the reversible circuit level was considered. However, because of the dynamic nature of evaluation of the quantum gates by application of pulses, the applicability of such wire-oriented classical fault models is doubtful. As discussed in [5], a suitable fault model in the quantum domain should largely be technology independent, and based on errors with regards to the application of evaluation pulses. The following fault scenarios can result.

(a) *Missing Gate Fault*, where due to absence of a pulse, a gate might not evaluate at all.

(b) *Repeated Gate Fault*, where due to multiple pulses being generated instead of just one, a gate might be evaluated multiple (say, k) times. Since the effect of two identical gate operations cancel each other, when k is even, this also reduces to the *Missing Gate Fault*. And when k is odd, the fault is undetectable.

(c) *Missing Control Fault* (also known as *Partial Missing Gate Fault*) where a gate gets evaluated even when some subset of the control lines is active, because of partially misaligned or mistuned gate pulses.

(d) *Additional Control Fault*, where some control connection gets added in addition to the already existing connections.

Earlier works have considered single missing gate fault (SMGF), and single missing control fault (SMCF/1-PMGF) for test generation and analysis. However, SMCF can be generalized to *Partial Missing Gate Fault (PMGF)*, where multiple missing control faults within a gate can also occur. Inclusion of one additional control line leads to single additional control fault (SACF). Besides that, the considerations conducted in this work can similarity be applied to any other fault model for reversible circuits (even those which are about to be proposed in the future).

1.3   Existing ATPG Solutions for Reversible Circuits

Various works on *Automatic Test Pattern Generation* (ATPG) for reversible circuits have been reported in the literature. The problem of test set generation and
reduction of test set has been addressed using ILP in [12,13]. Exact approaches
that generate smallest test set has also been considered previously in [18,19].
The authors in [6,7] proposed approaches to derive test sets for detecting multiple missing-gate faults in reversible circuits. Besides exact approaches (using
SAT and PBO), a simulation based approach has also been considered in [17].

2   Proposed Work

In the present paper, we aim to evaluate how the effort in generating tests for
reversible circuits correlate with the quality of test vectors generated. For the
purpose of evaluation, we have considered two extremes of the spectrum with
respect to test generation in a reversible circuit:

(a) A naive approach that directly generates a test for an undetected fault that
    is expected to require larger number of test vectors.
(b) An exact (minimal) approach that would generate the smallest possible test
    set.

In the following subsections, we evaluate and compare the number of test vectors
for these two extreme scenarios.

2.1   Naive Test Pattern Generation

Consider a reversible circuit consisting of p gates $\{G_1, G_2, \ldots, g_p\}$. For every
gate G_i, $i = 1$ to p, we do the following:

(i)   Generate the fault list F consisting of all faults according to a given fault
      model.
(ii) Generate a set of vectors $\{V_i\}$ at the input of gate G_i that can detect all
      faults $f \in F$ in G_i.
(iii) Repeat the following steps for all vectors $v \in \{V_i\}$:
      (a) Back propagate v to obtain the corresponding input test vector, say T.
          Since every gate is reversible, for a given v, T will be unique.
      (b) Carry out fault simulation with test vector T to determine the faults in
          F that get detected.
      (c) Remove the detected faults from F (*fault dropping*).
(iv) Continue with Step i. The process terminates as soon as the fault list F
      becomes empty.

To detect an SMCF in G_i, all control lines (except the missing one) have
to be assigned to 1, while the missing control line has to be assigned to 0. The
assignment of the remaining lines can be chosen arbitrarily. Similarly, to detect
an SMGF in G_i, all control lines have to be assigned to 1, while the remaining

lines can be arbitrarily assigned. Again, to detect single additional control fault (SACF) in G_i, all control lines except the additional one have to be assigned to 1, and the additional line has to be assigned to 0. The assignment of the remaining lines can be arbitrarily chosen.

Three alternate methods for filling up the remaining lines (i.e. the don't care bits) have been studied:

(a) *0-filling*: where a don't care line is set to logic value 0.
(b) *1-filling*: where a don't care line is set to logic value 1.
(c) *Random filling*: where a don't care line is randomly set to 0 or 1.

The naive test generation approach with the three alternatives for don't care filling have been studied for the SMGF and SMCF models. The overall runtime of this naive approach is $\mathcal{O}(n^2)$ (For a reversible circuit with n gate, the number of generated test vectors encompassing all fault models is Cn, where C is a constant, and back propagation and fault dropping for each test vector on average is $\frac{n}{2} + n$.).

2.2   Exact (Minimal) Test Pattern Generation

In this subsection we discuss an approach that uses Boolean satisfiability to generate minimum test patterns for detecting faults in a reversible circuit. To this end, we utilize a SAT formulation which is similar to the one proposed in [18]. We state below the SAT formulation for SMGF and for SMCF. We also discuss the SAT formulation of the combined SMGF+SMCF model and the PMGF model which have not been considered earlier. By this we show that this solution (and, hence, the considerations conducted here) can be applied to ATPG of reversible circuits in general and does not rely on a particular fault model.

(a) **SMGF**: The SAT based formulation for detecting the presence of SMGF in a circuit C is:

$$\bigwedge_{i=1}^{n} I_i \wedge \bigwedge_{g_k \in C} \left(\bigvee_{i=1}^{n} f_i(g_k) \right) \tag{1}$$

where for the k-th $C^m NOT$ gate, g_k $(T(\{x_1^i, x_2^i, \ldots, x_m^i\}; x_{m+1}^i))$ from i-th circuit instance $f_i(g_k) = x_1^i \wedge x_2^i \wedge \cdots \wedge x_m^i$ for all missing gate, $g_k \in C$.

(b) **SMCF**: The SAT based formulation for detecting the presence of SMCF in a circuit C is:

$$\bigwedge_{i=1}^{n} I_i \wedge \bigwedge_{g_k \in C} \left(\bigvee_{i=1}^{n} f_i'(g_k) \right) \tag{2}$$

where for the k-th $C^m NOT$ gate, g_k $(T(\{x_1^i, x_2^i, \ldots, x_m^i\}; x_{m+1}^i))$ from i-th circuit instance $f_i'(g_k) = x_1^i \wedge x_2^i \wedge \cdots \wedge \overline{x_j^i} \wedge \cdots \wedge x_m^i$ for all missing control line, $x_j^i \in \{x_1^i, x_2^i, \ldots, x_m^i\}$.

(c) **SMGF+SMCF**: We can also combine the SMGF and SMCF fault models in a single unified formulation. The SAT formulation for the combined fault model for a given circuit C is:

$$\overbrace{\bigwedge_{i=1}^{n} I_i \wedge \bigwedge_{g_k \in C} \left(\bigvee_{i=1}^{n} f_i(g_k) \right)}^{SMGF} \wedge \overbrace{\bigwedge_{g_k \in C} \left(\bigvee_{i=1}^{n} f_i'(g_k) \right)}^{SMCF} \qquad (3)$$

where for the k-th $C^m NOT$ gate, g_k $(T(\{x_1^i, x_2^i, \ldots, x_m^i\}; x_{m+1}^i))$ from i-th circuit instance $f_i(g_k) = x_1^i \wedge x_2^i \wedge \cdots \wedge x_j^i \wedge \cdots \wedge x_m^i$ for all missing gate, $g_k \in C$ and $f_i'(g_k) = x_1^i \wedge x_2^i \wedge \cdots \wedge \overline{x_j^i} \wedge \cdots \wedge x_m^i$ for all missing control line, $x_j^i \in \{x_1^i, x_2^i, dots, x_m^i\}$.

(d) **PMGF**: The PMGF fault model is a superset of the SMCF fault model. The SAT based formulation for detecting PMGFs in a circuit C is:

$$\bigwedge_{i=1}^{n} I_i \wedge \bigwedge_{g_k \in C} \left(\bigvee_{i=1}^{n} f_i^1(g_k) \right) \wedge \ldots \left(\bigvee_{i=1}^{n} f_i^n(g_k) \right) \qquad (4)$$

where for the k-th $C^m NOT$ gate, g_k $(T(\{x_1^i, x_2^i, \ldots, x_m^i\}; x_{m+1}^i))$ from i-th circuit instance

$$f_i^1(g_k) = x_1^i \wedge \cdots \wedge \overline{x_j^i} \wedge \cdots \wedge x_m^i,$$
$$f_i^2(g_k) = x_1^i \wedge \cdots \wedge \overline{x_j^i} \wedge \cdots \wedge \overline{x_k^i} \wedge \cdots \wedge x_m^i,$$
$$\ldots = \ldots,$$
$$f_i^n(g_k) = \overline{x_1^i} \wedge \overline{x_2^i} \wedge \cdots \wedge \overline{x_m^i}.$$

Here the term $f_i^1(g_k)$ is identical to the term $f_i'(g_k)$ of SMCF.

(e) **SMGF+PMGF**: We can also combine the SMGF and PMGF fault models in a single unified formulation. The SAT formulation for the combined fault model for a given circuit C is:

$$\overbrace{\bigwedge_{i=1}^{n} I_i \wedge \bigwedge_{g_k \in C} \left(\bigvee_{i=1}^{n} f_i(g_k) \right)}^{SMGF} \wedge \overbrace{\bigwedge_{g_k \in C} \left(\bigvee_{i=1}^{n} f_i^1(g_k) \right) \wedge \ldots \left(\bigvee_{i=1}^{n} f_i^n(g_k) \right)}^{PMGF} \qquad (5)$$

where for the k-th $C^m NOT$ gate, g_k $(T(\{x_1^i, x_2^i, \ldots, x_m^i\}; x_{m+1}^i))$ from i-th circuit instance

$$f_i(g_k) = x_1^i \wedge x_2^i \wedge \cdots \wedge x_j^i \wedge \cdots \wedge x_m^i,$$
$$f_i^1(g_k) = x_1^i \wedge x_2^i \wedge \cdots \wedge \overline{x_j^i} \wedge \cdots \wedge x_m^i,$$
$$f_i^2(g_k) = x_1^i \wedge \cdots \wedge \overline{x_j^i} \wedge \cdots \wedge \overline{x_k^i} \wedge \cdots \wedge x_m^i,$$
$$\ldots = \ldots,$$
$$f_i^n(g_k) = \overline{x_1^i} \wedge \overline{x_2^i} \wedge \cdots \wedge \overline{x_m^i}.$$

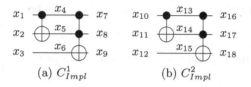

(a) C^1_{Impl} (b) C^2_{Impl}

Fig. 2. An example circuit with multiple instances

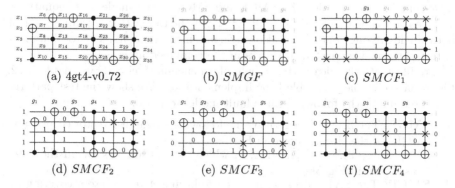

(a) 4gt4-v0_72   (b) $SMGF$ (c) $SMCF_1$

(d) $SMCF_2$ (e) $SMCF_3$ (f) $SMCF_4$

Fig. 3. Detecting $SMGF$ and $SMCF$ faults for (a) the benchmark 4gt4-v0_72 with variables assigned before and after each gate operation, (b) input pattern detects all possible SMGFs that may produce affected output and (c)–(f) undesired output and corresponding specific SMCFs detected by different input patterns

The basic idea behind the generation of minimal test sets for reversible circuit using SAT based approach is illustrated with the help of an example illustrated in Fig. 2. If the number of test vectors required is t, then we need to have t instances of the circuit with all the lines distinctly labeled. The figure shows two instances C^1_{Impl} and C^2_{Impl} for $t = 2$.

For the instance C^1_{Impl} (see Fig. 2a) the equations representing the circuit behavior are formed as:

$$I_1 = (x_4 = x_1) \wedge (x_5 = x_2 \oplus x_1) \wedge (x_6 = x_3) \wedge (x_7 = x_4)$$
$$\wedge (x_8 = x_5) \wedge (x_9 = x_6 \oplus x_4 x_5)$$

Similarly, for the instance C^2_{Impl} shown in Fig. 2b, the equations are formed as:

$$I_2 = (x_{13} = x_{10}) \wedge (x_{14} = x_{11} \oplus x_{10}) \wedge (x_{15} = x_{12})$$
$$\wedge (x_{16} = x_{13}) \wedge (x_{17} = x_{14}) \wedge (x_{18} = x_{15} \oplus x_{13} x_{14})$$

The SAT formulation for SMCF as per Eq. (2) will be

$$I_1 \wedge I_2 \wedge (\overline{x_1} \vee \overline{x_{10}}) \wedge (\overline{x_4} x_5 \vee \overline{x_{13}} x_{14}) \wedge (x_4 \overline{x_5} \vee x_{13} \overline{x_{14}})$$

The SAT formulation for SMGF as per Eq. (1) will be

$$I_1 \wedge I_2 \wedge (x_1 \vee x_{10}) \wedge (x_4 x_5 \vee x_{13} x_{14})$$

Given these formula as inputs, a SAT solver will provide a set of test vectors as output.

2.3   Test Generation for Several Fault Models Using SAT Solver

If we combine the equations for SMCF and SMGF into a single set of equations, and feed the same to a SAT solver, we shall get the test patterns required to test both single missing-control and also single missing-gate faults. The total number of test patterns is expected to be less in the combined approach.

We illustrate the idea with the help of a benchmark circuit, viz. 4gt4-v0_72. Figure 3a shows the reversible logic implementation. We show the test patterns generated under the following three fault model scenario.

(a) **SMGF**: The SAT solver returns the following single test vector covering all SMGFs of the circuit shown in Fig. 3a:
   (i) $[x_1, x_2, x_3, x_4, x_5] = [1, 0, 1, 1, 1]$, which detects SMGFs for all the gates as shown in Fig. 3b.
(b) **SMCF**: The SAT solver returns the following 4 test vectors covering all SMCFs of the circuit shown in Fig. 3a:
   (i) $[x_1, x_2, x_3, x_4, x_5] = [1, 1, 1, 1, 0]$, which detects SMCFs for the gates g_1, g_2, g_4, g_5 and g_6 as shown in Fig. 3c.
   (ii) $[x_1, x_2, x_3, x_4, x_5] = [1, 1, 1, 1, 1]$, which detects SMCFs for the gates g_5 and g_6 as shown in Fig. 3d.
   (iii) $[x_1, x_2, x_3, x_4, x_5] = [1, 0, 1, 0, 1]$, which detects SMCFs for the gates g_4 and g_6 as shown in Fig. 3e.
   (iv) $[x_1, x_2, x_3, x_4, x_5] = [0, 0, 0, 1, 1]$, which detects SMCFs for the gates g_2, g_4 and g_6 as shown in Fig. 3f.
(c) **Combined (SMGF+SMCF)**: For the combined formulation, the SAT solver returns the following 5 test vectors covering all SMGFs and SMCFs of the circuit shown in Fig. 3a:
   (i) $[x_1, x_2, x_3, x_4, x_5] = [1, 1, 1, 1, 1]$, which detects SMCFs for the gates g_5 and g_6, and SMGFs for the gates g_1, g_2, g_3 and g_4 as shown in Fig. 3d.
   (ii) $[x_1, x_2, x_3, x_4, x_5] = [0, 0, 0, 1, 1]$, which detects SMCFs for the gates g_2, g_4 and g_6, and SMGFs for the gates g_1, g_3 and g_5 as shown in Fig. 3f.
   (iii) $[x_1, x_2, x_3, x_4, x_5] = [1, 0, 1, 1, 1]$, which detects SMGFs for the gates g_1, g_2, g_3, g_4, g_5 and g_6 as shown in Fig. 3b.
   (iv) $[x_1, x_2, x_3, x_4, x_5] = [1, 1, 1, 1, 0]$, which detects SMCFs for the gates g_1, g_2, g_4, g_5 and g_6 as shown in Fig. 3c.
   (v) $[x_1, x_2, x_3, x_4, x_5] = [1, 0, 1, 0, 1]$, which detects SMCFs for the gates g_4 and g_6, and SMGFs for the gates g_1, g_2, g_3 and g_5 as shown in Fig. 3e.
(d) **PMGF**: The SAT solver returns 15 test vectors covering all PMGFs of the circuit shown in Fig. 3a.
(e) **Combined (SMGF+PMGF)**: For the combined formulation, the SAT solver returns 16 test vectors covering all SMGFs and PMGFs of the circuit shown in Fig. 3a.

3   Experimental Evaluation

Experiments have been carried out on reversible benchmark circuits available in [16]. The naive test generator (with fault simulator) have been implemented in C and run on a core-i3 machine with 4GB RAM, running Ubuntu v16.04. The test generators using SAT solvers have been implemented on the RevKit [15] platform, using C++ and Python, and run on the same core-i3 machine.

Using these implementations, we conducted the evaluations motivated in Sect. 1. Tables 1 and 2 provide a summary of some of the obtained numbers. More precisely, Table 1 shows the results of the SAT-based ATPG implementation with combined fault models and also the naive ATPG implementation. Results for 0-filling, 1-filling and random filling (best out of 5 runs) are also shown. Table 2 show the results for larger benchmark circuits using the naive ATPG tool with 0-filling, 1-filling and random-filling. Since those benchmarks cannot be handled by the SAT-based exact approach (due to run-time limitations), no corresponding numbers for this solutions are provided here.

Based on these numbers (as well as further case studies for which we cannot present all numbers due to page limitations), the following conclusions can be drawn:

Table 1. Combined fault model and comparison with naive approach

Benchmarks				SAT based ATPG						Naive ATPG (SMGF+SMCF)			
Circuit	d	n	c	Separate		SMGF+SMCF		SMGF+PMGF		0-fill	1-fill	r-fill	T
				F_{tot}	P_{tot}	P	T	P	T	P	P	P	
4gt4-v0_78	13	5	1	31	8	6	0.01	16	0.04	9	7	7	0.00
4gt12-v0_86	14	5	1	34	6	5	0.01	16	0.05	10	7	8	0.00
decod24-enable_32	14	9	6	31	3	3	0.01	4	0.01	6	5	3	0.00
mod5d1_16	15	8	3	34	3	3	0.01	4	0.01	9	7	5	0.00
4_49_16	16	4	0	40	8	5	0.01	8	0.02	8	5	7	0.00
miller_5	16	8	5	40	5	5	0.02	6	0.02	8	7	7	0.00
3_17_6	17	7	4	37	4	3	0.02	4	0.01	7	5	6	0.00
mini-alu_84	20	10	6	47	3	3	0.03	4	0.01	9	6	8	0.00
rd53_131	28	7	2	52	15	10	0.04	16	0.08	14	13	14	0.00
rd84_142	28	15	7	77	7	5	0.09	5	0.04	29	10	9	0.00
sym6_63	29	14	8	72	5	5	0.05	6	0.04	17	11	9	0.00
4_49_7	42	15	11	103	5	5	0.06	6	0.06	14	11	8	0.00
ham15_108	70	15	0	195	17	11	0.17	16	0.36	12	12	11	0.00
hwb5_13	88	28	23	219	5	5	0.30	6	0.20	29	17	10	0.00
ham15_109	109	15	0	235	11	7	0.23	16	0.39	15	10	9	0.00
ham15_107	132	15	0	484	20	16	78.59	–	–	37	24	23	0.04
hwb6_14	159	46	40	400	6	5	0.51	6	0.57	51	30	13	0.06
ex5p	647	206	198	1551	–	–	–			172	117	17	3.55

d: number of gates, n: number of lines, c: number of constant lines
F_{tot}: total number of faults, T: Time in seconds
P_{tot}: total number of test patterns (when run separately)
P: number of test patterns, r: random filling

Table 2. ATPG test patterns for larger benchmarks

Benchmarks				Faults		ATPG			
Circuit	d	n	c	F_1	F_2	0-fill	1-fill	r-fill	Time (s)
9symml_195	129	10	1	474	129	222	193	194	0.2
add6_196	229	19	7	853	229	210	174	141	0.68
alu2_199	157	16	6	567	157	211	198	202	0.33
alu4_201	1063	22	8	5535	1063	1735	1549	1573	120.77
bw_291	307	87	82	432	307	49	37	13	0.26
clip_206	174	14	5	653	174	175	163	160	0.34
dist_223	185	13	5	727	185	155	144	147	0.32
e64-bdd_295	387	195	130	454	387	135	129	14	0.9
f51m_233	663	22	8	3296	663	1252	1091	1127	33.67
frg1_234	212	31	3	1343	212	928	447	697	2.78
ham15_298	153	45	30	157	153	33	26	8	0.04
hwb7_302	281	73	66	426	281	76	40	14	0.27
hwb7_62	331	7	7	582	331	66	52	47	0.29
hwb8_116	749	8	8	1317	749	126	85	77	2.62
hwb8_303	449	112	104	686	449	126	53	14	1.05
hwb9_123	1959	9	9	3596	1959	275	168	150	38.59
hwb9_304	699	170	161	1068	699	184	73	17	3.55
in0_235	338	26	11	2107	338	423	406	408	3.37
in2_236	405	29	10	2475	405	506	454	451	5.26
life_238	107	10	1	387	107	138	136	129	0.1
max46_240	107	10	1	371	107	189	172	171	0.13
mlp4_245	131	16	8	480	131	138	92	95	0.15
plus127mod8192_162	910	13	13	5704	910	1072	105	311	27.61
plus63mod8192_164	492	13	13	3064	492	765	121	286	6.65
rd84_253	111	12	4	315	111	116	116	107	0.09
sym10_262	194	11	1	818	194	307	290	313	0.71
sym9_148	210	10	1	756	210	210	10	29	0.17
sym9_193	129	10	1	474	129	222	193	195	0.21
table3_264	1012	28	14	8002	1012	978	912	946	53.52
tial_265	1041	22	8	5517	1041	1767	1625	1614	119.85
urf1_150	1517	9	9	6077	1517	259	149	148	20.56
urf1_151	1487	9	9	5878	1487	256	149	144	19.68

d: number of gates, n: number of lines, c: number of constant lines
F_1: number of SMCFs, F_2: number of SMGFs

- Exact test pattern generation using the SAT-based exact approach is time-consuming and not scalable. While small circuits can indeed be handled in some seconds, no results can be obtained for circuits composed of some dozens of circuit lines and hundreds of gates. This is not very surprising considering the exponential complexity of guaranteeing minimal test sets.
- Despite the efforts spent on guaranteeing minimality, determining the minimal test set often yields only moderate improvements compared to the naive approach. In fact, the size of the test sets obtained by the naive approach is often only a few patterns bigger than the test sets obtained by the SAT-based minimal approach.

These evaluations confirm that, from an effort-quality tradeoff point of view, there is no real need to spent much effort into the optimization of test pattern generation for reversible circuits. In fact, naive solutions as sketched in this work already yield results which are close to the optimum. In contrast, further improving them towards minimality often comes with an increase in the run-time and a substantially reduced scalability so that it is often not worthwhile to spent these efforts (for a relatively small gain).

4   Conclusion

In this paper we have carried out an evaluation of the various alternate test generation techniques for reversible circuits, and how it impacts the quality of the test. To observe the entire spectrum of variability, we have implemented test generators touching the two extremes. Firstly, a naive test generator has been implemented that is very fast and uses a greedy approach to generate test patterns. Secondly, a SAT based test generator has been implemented that generates the smallest test set but requires large run times. The variation in the number of test patterns, in spite of a very large variation in run times, is not significantly large. This summarizes the main finding of the work, namely, test generation for reversible circuit is easy and naive solutions are often sufficient. Vice versa, it is not worthwhile to spent much efforts on the development of more sophisticated solutions since the possible gain will be moderate.

Although SAT-based exact approach produces smaller number of test patterns compared to naive approach as shown in Fig. 4a, it takes longer duration even for circuits with small number of gates, as shown in Fig. 4b. Here the comparison is made for the benchmarks with upto 109 gates reported in Table 1. Figure 4c shows 0-filling produces larger number of test patterns than 1-filling and r-filling as presented for larger benchmarks in Table 2.

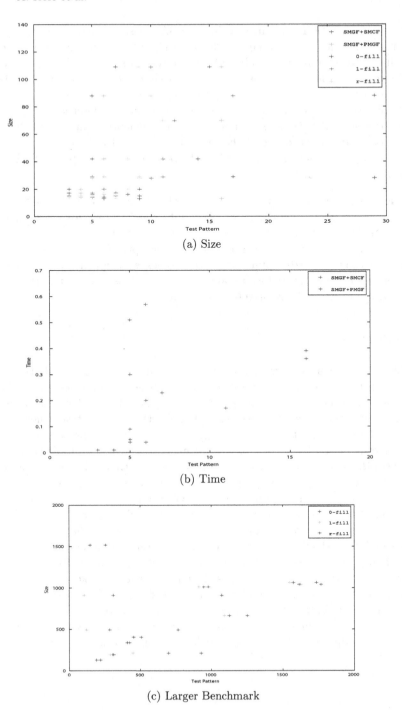

(a) Size

(b) Time

(c) Larger Benchmark

Fig. 4. Evaluation of approaches (a) comparison of number of test patterns generated using SAT-based and naive approaches for smaller size benchmarks from Table 1, (b) time taken by various SAT-based approaches and corresponding test pattern generated for small size benchmark from Table 1 compared to naive approach and (c) number of test patterns generated by different naive approaches for the benchmarks from Table 2

References

1. Amy, M., Maslov, D., Mosca, M., Roetteler, M.: A meet-in-the-middle algorithm for fast synthesis of depth-optimal quantum circuits. IEEE Trans. CAD **32**(6), 818–830 (2013)
2. Bennett, C.H.: Logical reversibility of computation. IBM J. Res. Dev. **17**(6), 525–532 (1973)
3. Berut, A., Arakelyan, A., Petrosyan, A., Ciliberto, S., Dillenschneider, R., Lutz, E.: Experimental verification of Landauer's principle linking information and thermodynamics. Nature **483**, 187–189 (2012)
4. Drechsler, R., Wille, R.: From truth tables to programming languages: progress in the design of reversible circuits. In: International Symposium on Multi-valued Logic (2011)
5. Hayes, J.P., Polian, I., Becker, B.: Testing for missing-gate faults in reversible circuits. In: Asian Test Symposium, pp. 100–105 (2004)
6. Kole, D.K., Rahaman, H., Das, D.K., Bhattacharya, B.B.: Derivation of automatic test set for detection of missing gate faults in reversible circuits. In: International Symposium on Electronic System Design (ISED), pp. 200–205, December 2011
7. Kole, D.K., Rahaman, H., Das, D.K., Bhattacharya, B.B.: Derivation of test set for detecting multiple missing-gate faults in reversible circuits. Comput. Electr. Eng. **39**(2), 225–236 (2013)
8. Landauer, R.: Irreversibility and heat generation in computing process. IBM J. Res. Dev. **5**(3), 183–191 (1961)
9. Miller, D.M., Wille, R., Sasanian, Z.: Elementary quantum gate realizations for multiple-control Toffolli gates. In: International Symposium on Multi-valued Logic (2011)
10. Mondal, J., Das, D.K., Kole, D.K., Rahaman, H.: A design for testability technique for quantum reversible circuits. In: East-West Design & Test Symposium (EWDTS 2013) (2012)
11. Nielsen, M., Chuang, I.: Quantum Computation and Quantum Information. Cambridge University Press, New York (2000)
12. Patel, K.N., Hayes, J.P., Markov, I.L.: Fault testing for reversible circuits. IEEE Trans. CAD **23**(8), 1220–1230 (2004)
13. Polian, F., T., Becker, B., Hayes, J.P.: A family of logical fault models for reversible circuits. In: Asian Test Symposium, pp. 422–427 (2004)
14. Saeedi, M., Markov, I.L.: Synthesis and optimization of reversible circuits - a survey. ACM Comput. Surv. **45**(2), 21:1–21:34 (2013)
15. Soeken, M., Frehse, S., Wille, R., Drechsler, R.: RevKit: an open source toolkit for the design of reversible circuits. In: Vos, A., Wille, R. (eds.) RC 2011. LNCS, vol. 7165, pp. 64–76. Springer, Heidelberg (2012). doi:10.1007/978-3-642-29517-1_6
16. Wille, R., Grosse, D., Teuber, L., Dueck, G.W., Drechsler, R.: Revlib: an online resource for reversible functions and reversible circuits. In: International Symposium on Multi-valued Logic, pp. 220–225, May 2008
17. Wille, R., Zhang, H., Drechsler, R.: ATPG for reversible circuits using simulation, Boolean satisfiability, and pseudo Boolean optimization. In: IEEE Annual Symposium on VLSI, pp. 120–125, July 2011
18. Zhang, H., Frehse, S., Wille, R., Drechsler, R.: Determining minimal testsets for reversible circuits using Boolean satisfiability. In: AFRICON, pp. 1–6 (2011)
19. Zhang, H., Wille, R., Drechsler, R.: SAT-based ATPG for reversible circuits. In: International Design and Test Workshop, pp. 149–154, December 2010

Automatic Test Pattern Generation for Multiple Missing Gate Faults in Reversible Circuits
Work in Progress Report

Anmol Prakash Surhonne[1,2]([✉]), Anupam Chattopadhyay[1], and Robert Wille[3]

[1] Nanyang Technological University, Singapore, Singapore
anmolpra001@e.ntu.edu.sg, anupam@ntu.edu.sg
[2] Technical University of Munich, Munich, Germany
[3] Institute for Integrated Circuits,
Johannes Kepler University Linz, Linz, Austria
robert.wille@jku.at

Abstract. Logical reversibility is the basis for emerging technologies like quantum computing, may be used for certain aspects of low-power design, and has been proven beneficial for the design of encoding/decoding devices. Testing of circuits has been a major concern to verify the integrity of the implementation of the circuit. In this paper, we propose the main ideas of an ATPG method for detecting two missing gate faults. To that effect, we propose a systematic flow using *Binary Decision Diagrams* (BDDs). Initial experimental results demonstrate the efficacy of the proposed algorithms in terms of scalability and coverage of all testable faults.

1 Introduction

Reversible circuits represent an emerging technology based on a computation paradigm which significantly differs from conventional circuits. In fact, they allow bijective operations only, i.e., n-input n-output functions that map each possible input vector to a unique output vector. Reversible computation enables several promising applications and, indeed, surpasses conventional computation paradigms in many domains including but not limited to quantum computation (see, e.g., [1]), certain aspects of low-power design (as experimentally observed, e.g., in [2]), encoding and decoding devices (see, e.g., [3,4]), or verification (see, e.g., [5]).

Accordingly, also the consideration of the design of reversible circuits received significant interest. In comparison to conventional circuit design, new concepts and paradigms have to be considered here. For example, fanout and feedback are not directly allowed. This affects the design of reversible circuits and requires alternative solutions. To this end, several design approaches have been introduced. An overview of that is, e.g., provided in [6,7].

In parallel, how to physically build reversible and quantum circuits is being investigated and led to first promising results (see, e.g., [8,9]). With this, also

© Springer International Publishing AG 2017
I. Phillips and H. Rahaman (Eds.): RC 2017, LNCS 10301, pp. 176–182, 2017.
DOI: 10.1007/978-3-319-59936-6_14

the question of how to prevent and detect faults in the physical realization became relevant. In particular for quantum computation, this is a crucial issue: Quantum systems are much more fault-prone than conventional circuits, since the phenomenon of quantum de-coherence forces the qubit states to decay – resulting in a loss of quantum information which, eventually, causes faults. Faults also do originate from the fact that quantum computations are conducted by a stepwise application of gates on qubits.

As a result, researchers studied different fault models and the respective methods for *Automatic Test Pattern Generation* (ATPG). In that regard, one of the earliest works on different fault models for quantum circuits is [10], which proposed these models based on the implementation principles of quantum circuits using trapped ion technology [1]. The types of fault model included, for example, the *single missing gate fault* (SMGF), the *partial missing gate fault* (PMGF), and the multiple missing gate fault (MMGF). However, mainly ATPG methods for single faults have been proposed thus far (see e.g. [11–13]).

2 Background

To keep the remainder of this work self-contained, this section briefly reviews the basics of reversible circuits as well as ATPG and the fault models considered for this kind of circuits.

2.1 Reversible Circuits

Reversible circuits are digital circuits with the same number of input signals and output signals. Furthermore, reversible circuits realize bijections, i.e. each input assignment maps to a unique output assignment. Accordingly, computations can not only be performed from the inputs to the outputs but also in the other direction. Reversible circuits are composed as cascades of reversible gates. The *Toffoli gate* [14] is widely used in the literature and also considered in this paper.

Definition 1. *Given a set of variables or signals $X = \{x_1, x_2, \ldots, x_n\}$, a Toffoli gate $G(C, t)$ is a tuple of a possibly empty set $C \subset X$ of control lines and a single target line $t \in X \setminus C$. The Toffoli gate inverts the value on the target line if all values on the control lines are set to 1 or if $C = \emptyset$. All remaining values are passed through unaltered. In the following, Toffoli gates are also denoted as* Multiple Controlled Toffoli *(MCT)* gates.

2.2 Test of Reversible Circuits

As in conventional circuits, *Automatic Test Pattern Generation* (ATPG) methods for reversible circuits aim at determining a set of stimulus patterns (denoted as *testset*) in order to detect faults in a circuit with respect to an underlying fault model. A single missing gate fault is defined as follows.

Definition 2. *Let $G(C, t)$ be a gate of a reversible circuit. Then, a Single Missing Gate Fault (SMGF) appears if instead of G no gate is executed (i.e. G completely disappears). The method to detect SMGF is widely studied and can be referred in previous works.*

Definition 3. *Let $\mathcal{G}$ be a set of k gates from a reversible circuit. Then, a Multiple Missing Gate Fault (MMGF) appears if instead of $\mathcal{G}$ no gates are executed (i.e. all gates $\mathcal{G}$ completely disappear in G).*

In the following, we consider MMGFs with two missing gates. However, the methods described below can easily be extended for an arbitrary number of faulty gates. From here on forward, MMGF is referred to as missing of two gates. In order to detect MMGFs, the respective gates have to be activated so that the faulty behaviour can be observed at the outputs of the circuit. However, in case of multiple faults, the absence of one gate within the circuit may cause the deactivation of another gate in the circuit – leading to masking effects. Besides that, the absence of two gates may lead to no change in the outputs – leading to an undetectable fault. Because of that, the dependencies of two gates considered as one MMGF have to be analyzed in order to generate a test pattern.

Definition 4. *Two gates G_x and G_y $(x < y)$ are said to be dependent if the target line of G_x is involved in the activation of the SMGF of G_y. More precisely, a Toffoli gate G_y is dependent from gate G_x, if the target line of G_y is the control line of G_x or if G_y is dependent on another gate G_z which is dependent from G_x.*

3   ATPG for MMGF Detection

This section describes the proposed approach for ATPG of MMGFs. The goal is to obtain a test set that covers all possible faults with a minimum number of test patterns. The proposed solution has four phases. First, test patterns for SMGFs, i.e. for the single faults, are obtained and compactly stored in a BDD. Based on that, the dependencies already discussed in the previous section are analyzed. The results from these two steps (i.e. the patterns for all SMGFs as well as the information about the dependencies of the gates in the currently considered circuit) are then utilized in order to obtain MMGF test sets. Finally, a covering algorithm is applied to minimize the obtained test set – yielding a minimal result covering all MMGFs.

3.1   Test Generation for SMGFs

In order to obtain all desired test patterns, it is assumed that only one gate is faulty at a time in this step. Also, the faults are detected at the primary outputs of the circuits and no distinction is made between different types of lines like output, garbage etc. Constant inputs of the circuit are assumed to be variable for the purpose of testing. For a circuit with n lines and N gates, there are N SMGFs, and the test patterns are obtained by activating the considered gate.

Overall, this yields 2^{n-k} possible test patterns that can be obtained for testing a SMGF. In order to compactly store them, *Binary Decision Diagrams* (BDDs, [15]) are applied.

3.2 Dependency Analysis

The next step is to analyse the dependencies between all combinations of two faulty gates as discussed in Sect. 2.2. The following pseudo-code describes how the dependencies between the gates are obtained.

Algorithm 1. Dependency Analysis

N : Number of gates of the circuit.
G_x : Gate numbered x.
$Table[N]$: Table storing the dependencies of the N gates.
for $i = 0$; $i < N$; $i + +$ **do**
    for $j = 0$; $j < i$; $j + +$ **do**
        if $targetLine(G_j) = controlLine(G_i)$ **then**
            Insert G_j to $Table[i]$.
            Insert all the gates G_j is dependent from to $Table[i]$.
        end if
    end for
end for

3.3 MMGF Test Generation

Using the test patterns for SMGFs as well as information about the dependencies of all combinations of two faulty gates, now the respective test patterns for MMGFs with two faulty gates can be obtained. More precisely, without loss of generality, consider two gates G_x and G_y as well as their test patterns for corresponding SMGFs (denoted as $S(G_x)$ and $S(G_y)$). If these two gates are independent to each other, we determine two test patterns (denoted as $M(G_y, G_x)_1$ and $M(G_y, G_x)_2$): one test pattern to activate the gate G_x and not G_y and another to activate G_y. More precisely:

$$M(G_y, G_x)_1 = S(G_y) \qquad M(G_y, G_x)_2 = (S(G_x) \cap \overline{S(G_y)})$$

If the two gates are dependent on each other, we determine two other tests patterns: one test pattern to activate the gate G_x and not G_y and vice versa. More precisely:

$$M(G_y, G_x)_1 = (S(G_y) \cap \overline{S(G_x)}) \qquad M(G_y, G_x)_2 = (S(G_x) \cap \overline{S(G_y)})$$

Besides that, masking may occur leading to untestable faults (as discussed in Sect. 2.2). A fault is untestable using this method if

$$M(G_y, G_x)_i = \{\emptyset\} \text{ where } i = \{1, 2\}$$

Using this as basis, the respective determinations can efficiently be conducted on the BDD. More precisely, the BDD containing the SMGF test patterns are manipulated for all the MMGF yielding a BDD with n inputs and $2 * {}^{N}C_2$ outputs.

3.4   Minimal Test Set Determination

Once all the test patterns for the individual MMGFs are obtained, it is tried to derive the minimal testset covering all the faults. To that effect, two different techniques are proposed.

First, row and column reduction of a covering table [16] is implemented following a greedy scheme. *Second*, a covering algorithm is implemented using the BDDs to determine a minimum cover of the stored patterns. For a circuit with n lines, the covering BDD has 2^n inputs and 1 output. Having that, the minimum test set is equivalently represented by the minimum-weighted path from the output of the BDD to the 1-terminal of the BDD, where the *then* arc has a weight of 1 and the *else* arc has a weight of 0.

4   Experimental Results

The ideas proposed above have prototypically been implemented on a Ubuntu Linux system running on a Intel(R) Core(TM) $i7 - 3630QM$ CPU $64bit@2.4Ghz$ and $6GB$ of RAM. For the first two steps, i.e. determining the SMGF testset and the dependency analysis, Revkit [17] has been applied. For the remaining steps, the BDD package $CUDD$ [18] was employed. All experiments were conducted on benchmark circuits obtained from Revlib [19]. Table 1 presents the obtained experimental results. The results show that the algorithm performed well for larger circuits covering a large number of faults. We obtained 100% fault coverage for circuits like $rd73\_140$ and $rd84\_142$, whereas the worst performance was for the circuit $ex3\_229$ with a coverage of 28.6. This was due to a large number of NOT gates, and hence the performance could be improved by DFT techniques. For the circuits $rd32 - v0\_66$ and $root\_255$, the SMGF and MMGF test patterns are identical. This is because all the dependent faults of these circuits are untestable. Considering the two covering methods, i.e. the greedy heuristic vs. the BDD-based approach, clearly shows the difference in runtime – especially for large circuits, where the BDD-based covering could not be completed after a long time. This was expected as the BDD-based approach obtains an exact, i.e. minimal cover, while the heuristic solution only approximates that. Besides that, it can be observed that the test set size determined by the greedy heuristic is, for most cases, the same as the minimal size obtained by the BDD-based approach. That is, the quality of the heuristic is rather good and often yields test sets which are close to the optimum. It should also be noted that the untestable faults are due to the function of the algorithm, and other methods can be used to detect these faults, which will be considered in the future work where we try to increase the coverage to 100%.

Table 1. Experimental results

SMGF							MMGF						
Circuit	N	n	Type	TP	TP_G	TP_{BDD}	TF	D	U	%D	%U	T_G	T_{BDD}
cm82a_208	22	8	MCT	4	9	8	231	21	107	9.1	46.3	0.08s	6s
ex3_229	7	6	MCT	2	3	3	21	4	15	19	71.4	0.01s	0.01s
graycode6_47	5	6	MCT	1	4	3	10	0	0	0	0	0.01s	0.04s
ham3_102	5	3	MCT	2	4	4	10	6	1	60	10	0.01s	0.01s
hwb4_52	11	4	MCT	2	6	6	55	41	3	74.5	5.5	0.01s	0.04s
hwb5_55	24	5	MCT	3	12	11	276	192	78	69.6	28.3	0.03s	0.1s
majority_239	8	6	MCT	3	4	4	28	6	18	21.4	64.3	0.01s	0.01s
mini-alu_167	6	4	MCT	3	5	5	15	15	1	100	6.7	0.01s	0.02s
mod10_171	10	4	MCT	3	6	6	45	29	20	64.4	44.4	0.01s	0.03s
mod5adder_128	15	6	MCT	2	8	7	105	59	66	56.2	62.9	0.02s	0.12s
mod5d1_63	7	5	MCT	1	4	4	21	4	2	19	9.5	0.01s	0.02s
mod8-10_177	14	5	MCT	2	6	6	91	53	41	58.2	45.1	0.01s	0.03s
rd32-v0_66	4	4	MCT	2	2	2	6	2	2	33.3	33.3	0.01s	0.03s
rd53_137	16	7	MCT	2	9	8	120	44	36	36.7	30	0.05s	0.07s
sym6_145	36	7	MCT	1	6	6	630	0	180	0	28.6	0.1s	0.13s
xor5_254	7	6	MCT	1	3	3	21	2	10	9.5	47.6	0.01s	0.06s
ham7_105	21	7	MCT	3	9	5	210	35	14	16.7	6.7	0.05s	–
hwb5_53	55	5	MCT	4	21	21	1485	1396	98	94	6.6	0.02s	0.15s
hwb6_56	126	6	MCT	8	43	43	7875	7614	328	96.7	4.2	1.7s	1.9s
3_17_13	6	3	MCT	2	4	4	15	12	7	80	46.7	0.01s	0.01s
root_255	99	13	MCT	14	14	–	4851	660	660	13.6	13.6	16s	–
rd73_140	20	10	MCT	3	6	–	190	72	0	37.9	0	1s	–
rd84_142	28	15	MCT	3	8	–	378	125	0	33.1	0	90s	–
adr4_197	55	13	MCT	6	13	–	1485	65	525	4.4	35.4	38s	–
ham15_108	70	15	MCT	8	26	–	2415	1474	154	61	6.4	100s	–
hwb7_59	289	7	MCT	14	71	–	41616	40735	742	97.9	1.8	48s	–
hwb7_60	166	7	MCT	8	32	–	13695	13683	71	99.9	0.5	7s	–
0410184_169	46	14	MCT	1	9	–	1035	315	274	30.4	26.5	8s	–

N - Number of gates   n - Number of lines.
TP - Number of test patters covering all SMGF.
TP_G - Number of test patterns covering all MMGF using greedy method.
TP_{BDD} - Number of test patterns covering all MMGF using BDD based covering algorithm.
TF - Total Number of MMGF faults.   D - Number of dependencies.
U - Number of untestable faults.
T_G Time taken for obtaining test patterns using greedy method.
T_BDD Time taken for obtaining test patterns using BDD based covering algorithm.
%D - Percentage of dependencies = $(D/TF) * 100$
%U - Percentage of untestable faults = $(U/TF) * 100$

Acknowledgement. This work has partially been supported by the EU COST Action IC1405.

References

1. Nielsen, M., Chuang, I.: Quantum Computation and Quantum Information. Cambridge University Press, New York (2000)
2. Berut, A., Arakelyan, A., Petrosyan, A., Ciliberto, S., Dillenschneider, R., Lutz, E.: Experimental verification of landauer's principle linking information and thermodynamics. Nature **483**, 187–189 (2012)
3. Wille, R., Drechsler, R., Osewold, C., Garcia-Ortiz, A.: Automatic design of low-power encoders using reversible circuit synthesis. In: Design, Automation and Test in Europe, pp. 1036–1041 (2012)
4. Zulehner, A., Wille, R.: Taking one-to-one mappings for granted: advanced logic design of encoder circuits. In: Design, Automation & Test in Europe (2017)
5. Amarú, L., Gaillardon, P.-E., Wille, R., De Micheli, G.: Exploiting inherent characteristics of reversible circuits for faster combinational equivalence checking. In: Proceedings of the Conference on Design, Automation & Test in Europe. EDA Consortium, pp. 175–180 (2016)
6. Drechsler, R., Wille, R.: From truth tables to programming languages: progress in the design of reversible circuits. In: International Symposium on Multi-Valued Logic, pp. 78–85 (2011)
7. Saeedi, M., Markov, I.L.: Synthesis and optimization of reversible circuits - a survey. ACM Comput. Surv. **45**(2), 21:1–21:34 (2011)
8. Vandersypen, L.M.K., Steffen, M., Breyta, G., Yannoni, C.S., Sherwood, M.H., Chuang, I.L.: Experimental realization of Shor's quantum factoring algorithm using nuclear magnetic resonance. Nature **414**, 883 (2001)
9. Desoete, B., Vos, A.D.: A reversible carry-look-ahead adder using control gates. INTEGRATION VLSI J. **33**(1–2), 89–104 (2002)
10. Polian, I., Fiehn, T., Becker, B., Hayes, J.P.: A family of logical fault models for reversible circuits. In: Asian Test Symposium, pp. 422–427 (2005)
11. Patel, K.N., Hayes, J.P., Markov, I.L.: Fault testing for reversible circuits. In: Asian Test Symposium, pp. 410–416 (2003)
12. Hayes, J.P., Polian, I., Becker, B.: Testing for missing-gate-faults in reversible circuits. In: Asian Test Symposium, pp. 100–105 (2004)
13. Wille, R., Zhang, H., Drechsler, R.: ATPG for reversible circuits using simulation, Boolean satisfiability, and pseudo Boolean optimization. In: IEEE Computer Society Annual Symposium on VLSI, pp. 120–125 (2011)
14. Toffoli, T.: Reversible computing. In: Bakker, J., Leeuwen, J. (eds.) ICALP 1980. LNCS, vol. 85, pp. 632–644. Springer, Heidelberg (1980). doi:10.1007/3-540-10003-2_104
15. Bryant, R.E.: Graph-based algorithms for Boolean function manipulation. IEEE Trans. Comput. **35**(8), 677–691 (1986)
16. Bushnell, M., Agrawal, V.: Essentials of Electronic Testing for Digital, Memory and Mixed-Signal VLSI Circuits, vol. 17. Springer Science & Business Media, New York (2004)
17. Soeken, M., Frehse, S., Wille, R., Drechsler, R.: RevKit: an open source toolkit for the design of reversible circuits. In: Vos, A., Wille, R. (eds.) RC 2011. LNCS, vol. 7165, pp. 64–76. Springer, Heidelberg (2012). doi:10.1007/978-3-642-29517-1_6
18. Somenzi, F.: Cudd: Cu decision diagram package release 2.4. 2 (2009)
19. Wille, R., Große, D., Teuber, L., Dueck, G.W., Drechsler, R.: Revlib: An online resource for reversible functions and reversible circuits. In: International Symposium on Multi-Valued Logic, pp. 220–225 (2008)

Quantum Circuits

Exact Global Reordering for
Nearest Neighbor Quantum Circuits Using A*

Alwin Zulehner$^{(\boxtimes)}$, Stefan Gasser, and Robert Wille

Institute for Integrated Circuits, Johannes Kepler University Linz, Linz, Austria
{alwin.zulehner,stefan.gasser,robert.wille}@jku.at

Abstract. Since for certain realizations of quantum circuits only adjacent qubits may interact, qubits have to be frequently swapped – leading to a significant overhead. Therefore, optimizations such as exact global reordering have been proposed, where qubits are reordered such that the overall number of swaps is minimal. However, to guarantee minimality all $n!$ possible permutations of qubits have to be considered in the worst case – which becomes intractable for larger circuits. In this work, we tackle the complexity of exact global reordering using an A* search algorithm. The sophisticated heuristics for the search algorithm proposed in this paper allow for solving the problem in a much more scalable fashion. In fact, experimental evaluations show that the proposed approach is capable of determining the best order of the qubits for circuits with up to 25 qubits, whereas the recent state-of-the-art already reaches its limits with circuits composed of 10 qubits.

1 Introduction

Quantum computations employ an emerging technology where operations are performed on quantum bits (qubits) rather than conventional bits that can only represent two basis states. Exploiting quantum physical effects of qubits like superposition and entanglement allow to reduce the computational complexity of certain tasks significantly compared to conventional logic (cf. [1]). Well known examples are Shor's algorithm (cf. [2]) for integer factorization or Grover's algorithm for database search (cf. [3]). Such quantum computations are usually described using so-called quantum circuits, where qubits are represented as circuit lines. Operations on a subset of these qubits are described by quantum gates.

However, for many physical realizations, quantum circuits have to employ constraints on the interaction distance of qubits. More precisely, quantum gates can only be applied to adjacent qubits. To fulfill this requirement, SWAP operations (gates) that swap the values of two adjacent qubits are added to the quantum circuit – leading to a significant overhead. This overhead can be reduced by permuting the order of the qubits (circuit lines).

A broad variety of different approaches has been presented for this purpose – including solutions relying on templates [4], local and global reordering strategies [4], dedicated data-structures [5–8], or look-ahead schemes [9]. Also exact

© Springer International Publishing AG 2017
I. Phillips and H. Rahaman (Eds.): RC 2017, LNCS 10301, pp. 185–201, 2017.
DOI: 10.1007/978-3-319-59936-6_15

approaches, i.e. solutions guaranteeing the minimal number of SWAP gate insertions, have been proposed [10,11]. The work published in [11] provides a comprehensive overview of the state-of-the-art. All these approaches particularly focus
on how to properly reorder the qubits in the circuit so that the respective interaction distance (and, hence, the number of required SWAP gates) is reduced.

In this work, we focus on global reordering. Here, heuristic as well as exact
solutions have been proposed. Exact solutions are of particular interest as they
guarantee the minimal number of SWAP insertions. Guaranteeing minimality,
however, significantly increases the complexity of the considered problem. In
the worst case, all $n!$ possible permutations of qubits have to be considered –
an exponential complexity. We tackle this exponential complexity by using the
A^* search algorithm, i.e. a state-space search algorithm that traverses – guided
by dedicated heuristics – only parts of the exponential search space until an
optimal solution is determined. Experimental evaluations show that the proposed
approach is able to determine the optimal order of the qubits (circuit lines) for
quantum circuits composed of up to $n = 25$ qubits, whereas state-of-the-art
solutions for exact global reordering are currently limited to $n = 10$ qubits.

This paper is structured as follows. In Sect. 2, we review nearest neighbor
compliant quantum circuits. Based on that, we discuss the effect of globally
permuting the order of the circuit lines in Sect. 3. In Sect. 4, we propose two
approaches to determine the optimal order of the qubits using the A^* search
algorithm and discuss their differences. Finally, the proposed approaches are
experimentally evaluated in Sect. 5 while Sect. 6 concludes the paper.

2   Nearest Neighbor Compliant Quantum Circuits

In contrast to conventional computation, *quantum computation* [1] operates
on qubits instead of bits. A *qubit* is a two-state quantum system, with basis
states $|0\rangle \equiv \binom{1}{0}$ and $|1\rangle \equiv \binom{0}{1}$ (representing Boolean values 0 and 1, respec-
tively). Furthermore, a qubit can be in a superposition of these basis states, i.e.
$|x\rangle = \alpha |0\rangle + \beta |1\rangle$, where the complex amplitudes α and β satisfy $|\alpha|^2 + |\beta|^2 = 1$.
Note that the state of a qubit cannot directly be observed, because measurement
collapses the qubit into one of the two basis states $|0\rangle$ or $|1\rangle$. More precisely, the
qubit collapses to basis state $|0\rangle$ with probability $|\alpha|^2$ and to basis state $|1\rangle$ with
probability $|\beta|^2$.

This simply extends to quantum systems composed of n qubits. Such a system is in a superposition of its 2^n basis states. Operations on such systems are
performed through multiplication of appropriate $2^n \times 2^n$ unitary matrices.

A usual representation for quantum computations are *quantum circuits*. Here,
the respective qubits are denoted by solid *circuit lines*. Operations are represented by *quantum gates*. These operations may operate on a subset of the circuit lines only. Table 1 lists common 1-qubit quantum gates together with the
corresponding unitary matrices describing their operation. In order to perform
operations on more than one qubit, *controlled quantum gates* are applied. These
gates are composed of a *target line* $|t\rangle$ and a control line $|c\rangle$ and realize the
unitary operation represented by the matrix

Table 1. Quantum gates

Hadamard-Gate		Pauli-Y-Gate	
$-\boxed{\text{H}}-$	$\frac{1}{\sqrt{2}}\begin{pmatrix} 1 & 1 \\ 1 & -1 \end{pmatrix}$	$-\boxed{\text{Y}}-$	$\begin{pmatrix} 0 & -i \\ i & 0 \end{pmatrix}$
Pauli-X-Gate		Pauli-Z-Gate	
$-\boxed{\text{X}}-$	$\begin{pmatrix} 0 & 1 \\ 1 & 0 \end{pmatrix}$	$-\boxed{\text{Z}}-$	$\begin{pmatrix} 1 & 0 \\ 0 & -1 \end{pmatrix}$
V-Gate		S-Gate	
$-\boxed{\text{V}}-$	$\frac{1+i}{2}\begin{pmatrix} 1 & -i \\ -i & 1 \end{pmatrix}$	$-\boxed{\text{S}}-$	$\begin{pmatrix} 1 & 0 \\ 0 & e^{\frac{i\pi}{2}} \end{pmatrix}$
W-Gate		T-Gate	
$-\boxed{\text{W}}-$	$\frac{1}{2}\begin{pmatrix} 1+\sqrt{i} & 1-\sqrt{i} \\ 1-\sqrt{i} & 1+\sqrt{i} \end{pmatrix}$	$-\boxed{\text{T}}-$	$\begin{pmatrix} 1 & 0 \\ 0 & e^{\frac{i\pi}{4}} \end{pmatrix}$

$$M = \begin{pmatrix} 1 & 0 & 0 & 0 \\ 0 & 1 & 0 & 0 \\ 0 & 0 & & \\ 0 & 0 & & U \end{pmatrix},$$

where U denotes the operation applied to the target line. In the remainder of this work, we use the following formal notation:

Definition 1. *A quantum circuit is denoted by the cascade $G = g_1 g_2 \dots g_{|G|}$ of gates (in figures drawn from left to right), where $|G|$ denotes the total number of gates. The number of qubits and, thus, the number of circuit lines is denoted by n. The costs of a quantum circuit (also denoted as* quantum cost*) are defined by the number $|G|$ of gates.*

Example 1. Figure 1 shows a quantum circuit composed of $n = 2$ circuit lines and $|G| = 2$ gates. This circuit gets $|00\rangle$ as input and transforms the state of the underlying quantum system to $\frac{1}{\sqrt{2}} \cdot |00\rangle + \frac{1}{\sqrt{2}} \cdot |11\rangle$.

In the recent years, researchers proposed several physical realizations for quantum circuits. This led to a better understanding of their physical limitations and constraints, e.g. with respect to the interaction distance, decoherence time, or scaling (see e.g. [12–14]). Besides that, so-called *nearest neighbor constraints* have to be satisfied for many quantum circuit architectures. This particularly holds for technologies based on proposals for ion traps [15–17], nitrogen-vacancy centers in diamonds [18,19], quantum dots emitting linear cluster states linked

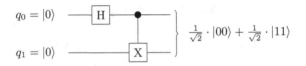

Fig. 1. Quantum circuit

by linear optics [20], laser manipulated quantum dots in a cavity [21], and super-conducting qubits [22,23]. Here, nearest neighbor constraints limit the interaction distance between gate qubits and require that computations are performed between adjacent, i.e. nearest neighbor, qubits only.

In order to formalize this restriction for electronic design automation, a corresponding metric representing the costs of a quantum circuit to become nearest neighbor compliant has been introduced in [4]. There, the authors defined the *Nearest Neighbor Cost* as follows:

Definition 2. *Assume a 2-qubit quantum gate $g(c,t)$ with a control at the line c and a target at line t, where c and t are numerical indices holding $0 \leq c, t < n$. Then, the* Nearest Neighbor Cost *(NNC) for g is calculated using the distance between the target and the control line. More precisely,*

$$NNC(g) = |c - t| - 1.$$

As a result, a single control gate g is termed nearest neighbor compliant *if $NNC(g) = 0$. 1-qubit gates are assumed to have NNC of 0. The resulting NNC for a quantum circuit is defined by the sum of the NNC of its gates, i.e.*

$$NNC(G) = \sum_{g \in G} NNC(g).$$

A quantum circuit G is termed nearest neighbor compliant *if $NNC(G) = 0$, i.e. if all quantum gates are 1-qubit gates or adjacent 2-qubit gates.*

Example 2. Consider the circuit G depicted in Fig. 2(a). Gates are denoted by $G = g_1 \ldots g_7$ from the left to the right. As can be seen, gates g_2, g_4, g_5, as well as g_6 are non-adjacent and have nearest neighbor costs of $NNC(g_2) = 2$, $NNC(g_4) = 1$, $NNC(g_5) = 1$, as well as $NNC(g_6) = 2$, respectively. Hence, the entire circuit has nearest neighbor costs of $NNC(G) = 6$.

A naive way to make an arbitrarily given quantum circuit nearest neighbor compliant is to modify it by additional SWAP gates.

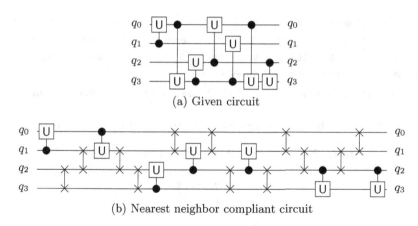

(a) Given circuit

(b) Nearest neighbor compliant circuit

Fig. 2. Establishing nearest neighbor compliance

Definition 3. *A SWAP gate is a quantum gate* $g(q_i, q_j)$ *including two qubits* q_i, q_j *and maps* $(q_0, \ldots, q_i, q_j, \ldots, q_{n-1})$ *to* $(q_0, \ldots, q_j, q_i, \ldots, q_{n-1})$. *That is, a SWAP gate realizes the exchange of two quantum values (in figures drawn using two connected × symbols).*

These SWAP gates allow for making all control lines and target lines adjacent and, by this, help to satisfy the nearest neighbor constraint. More precisely, a cascade of adjacent SWAP gates can be inserted in front of each gate g with non-adjacent circuit lines in order to shift the control line of g towards the target line, or vice versa, until they are adjacent. Afterwards, SWAP gates are inserted to restore the original order of circuit lines.

Example 3. Consider again the circuit depicted in Fig. 2(a). In order to make this circuit nearest neighbor compliant, SWAP gates in front and after all these gates are inserted as shown in Fig. 2(b).

3   Global Reordering for Nearest Neighbor Quantum Circuits

Global reordering became a suitable solution to reduce the cost of nearest neighbor compliant quantum circuits. Before adding SWAP gates to the circuit as reviewed in the previous section, the position of the qubits (circuit lines) is changed in order to reduce the number of required SWAP gates. An example illustrates the idea.

Example 4. Consider again the quantum circuit depicted in Fig. 2(a) and its nearest neighbor compliant version shown in Fig. 2(b). Permuting the order of qubits from $q_0 q_1 q_2 q_3$ to $q_2 q_0 q_3 q_1$ results in the circuit depicted in Fig. 3(a) – the nearest neighbor cost are reduced from 6 to 3. Hence, only 6 (instead of 12) SWAP gates are required to make the circuit nearest neighbor compliant (cf. Fig. 3(b)).

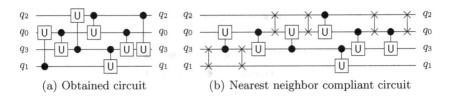

(a) Obtained circuit   (b) Nearest neighbor compliant circuit

Fig. 3. Global Reordering (applied to the circuit from Fig. 2(a))

Table 2. Adjacency matrix for the circuit in Fig. 2(a)

	q_0	q_1	q_2	q_3
q_0	–	1	1	2
q_1	–	–	0	1
q_2	–	–	–	2
q_3	–	–	–	–

As demonstrated by the example above, the positions of the qubits have a significant impact on the nearest neighbor cost of the resulting circuit (and, thus, on the number of required SWAP gates). To simplify the determination of the resulting nearest neighbor cost for a specific order of the qubits, the concept of an *adjacency matrix* of a quantum circuit can be used. The entries of this matrix indicate how often two qubits have to be adjacent, i.e. how many gates exist in the quantum circuit that operate exactly on these qubits. More formally:

Definition 4. *Consider a quantum circuit composed of n qubits. Then, the adjacency matrix of this circuit is an $n \times n$ dimensional matrix M where the entries $m_{i,j}$, $0 \leq i,j < n$ provide the number of gates with the target and the controlling qubit at the ith and j^{th} position, or vice versa (i.e. the number of gates with $g(i,j)$ or $g(j,i)$).*

Since we do not distinguish between target and controlling qubit of a gate, the adjacency matrix is symmetric with respect to the main diagonal. Furthermore, the main diagonal of the matrix is skipped as well, because a single qubit cannot be the target and the controlling qubit of the same gate.

Example 5. Consider again the circuit depicted in Fig. 2(a). The according adjacency matrix is given in Table 2. To improve readability, we set all entries $m_{i,j}$ for which $j \leq i$ to *don't care* (denoted by –), because they contain redundant information. For example, the entry $m_{0,3}$ has value 2 because the circuit contains exactly two gates (the second and the sixth) for which qubits q_0 and q_3 have to be adjacent.

The adjacency matrix M of a quantum circuit can be used to determine the nearest neighbor cost (and, hence, the number of required SWAP gates) of a quantum circuit. More precisely:

$$NNC(M) = \sum_{i=0}^{n} \sum_{j=i+1}^{n} m_{i,j} \cdot (j - i - 1)$$

Example 5 (continued). The nearest neighbor cost of the circuit shown in Fig. 2(a) is:

$$NNC(M) = m_{0,1} \cdot 0 + m_{0,2} \cdot 1 + m_{0,3} \cdot 2 + m_{1,2} \cdot 0 + m_{1,3} \cdot 1 + m_{2,3} \cdot 0 = 6.$$

Consequently, 12 SWAP gates are required to make the circuit nearest neighbor compliant.

Permuting the order of the qubits does not require to update the adjacency matrix. Instead, the resulting nearest neighbor cost when applying a permutation π to the order of the qubits is determined by

$$NNC(M, \pi) = \sum_{i=0}^{n} \sum_{j=i+1}^{n} m_{i,j} \cdot (|\pi(j) - \pi(i)| - 1).$$

Example 5 (continued). If we apply the permutation $\pi = (1, 3, 0, 2)$ to the qubits of the circuit shown in Fig. 2(a), the new resulting order is $q_2 q_0 q_3 q_1$ (cf. Fig. 3(a)). This changes the nearest neighbor cost to:

$$NNC(M, \pi) = m_{0,1} \cdot 1 + m_{0,2} \cdot 0 + m_{0,3} \cdot 0 + m_{1,2} \cdot 2 + m_{1,3} \cdot 0 + m_{2,3} \cdot 1 = 3.$$

Using the *adjacency matrix* of a quantum circuit allows for efficiently computing the nearest neighbor cost of the circuit with a permuted order of qubits. However, determining the best possible permutation, which requires the least number of SWAP gates is a computationally complex task. In the worst case, all $n!$ possible permutations have to be considered – an exponential complexity. Previous attempts tried to tackle this complexity by exploiting reasoning engines such as satisfiability solvers (see [10,11]). However, their applicability is still limited to rather small quantum circuits, i.e. circuits with not more than $n = 10$ qubits.

4 Global Reordering Using A*

In this section, we propose an alternative solution for global reordering in order to generate cost-efficient nearest neighbor compliant quantum circuits. To this end, we employ the power of the A* search algorithm. In the following, we review the basics of the A* algorithm and how global reordering can be translated into a search problem first. Based on that, we discuss two strategies for how to traverse the search space for the considered problem using A* search.

4.1 A* Algorithm

The A* algorithm is a state-space search algorithm. To this end, (sub-)solutions of the considered problem are represented by state nodes. Nodes that represent a solution are called *goal nodes* (multiple goal nodes may exist). The main idea is to determine the cheapest path (i.e. the path with the lowest cost) from the root node to a goal node. Since the search space is typically exponential, sophisticated mechanisms are employed in order to keep considering as few paths as possible.

All state-space search algorithms are similar in the way that they start with a root node (representing an initial partial solution) which is iteratively expanded towards the goal node (i.e. the desired complete solution). How to choose the node that shall be expanded next depends on the actual search algorithm. For A* search, we determine the cost of each leaf-node of the search state. Then, the node with the lowest cost is chosen to be expanded next. To this end, we determine the cost $f(x) = g(x) + h(x)$ of a node x. The first part ($g(x)$) describes the cost of the current sub-solution (i.e. the cost of the path from the root to x). The second part describes the remaining cost (i.e. the cost from x to a goal node), which is estimated by a heuristic function $h(x)$. Since the node with the lowest cost is expanded, some parts of the search space (those that lead to expensive solutions) are never expanded.

Example 6. Consider the tree shown in Fig. 4. This tree represents the part of the search space that has already been explored for a certain search problem. The nodes that are candidates to be expanded in the next iteration of the A* algorithm are highlighted in blue. For all these nodes, we determine the cost $f(x) = g(x) + h(x)$. This sum is composed by the cost of the path from the root to the node x (i.e. the sum of the cost annotated at the respective edges) and the estimated cost of the path from node x to a goal node (provided in red). Consider the node labeled E. This node has cost $f(E) = (40 + 60) + 200 = 300$. The other candidates labeled B, C, and F have cost $f(B) = 580$, $f(C) = 360$, and $f(F) = 320$, respectively. Since the node labeled E has the fewest expected cost, it is expanded next.

Obviously, the heuristic cost should be as accurate as possible, to expand as few nodes as possible. If $h(x)$ always provides the correct minimal remaining cost, only the nodes along the cheapest path from the root node to a goal node would be expanded. But since the minimal costs are usually not known (otherwise, the search problem would be trivial to solve), estimations are employed. However, to ensure an optimal solution, $h(x)$ has to be *admissible*, i.e. $h(x)$ must not overestimate the cost of the cheapest path from x to a goal node. This ensures that no goal node is expanded (which terminates the search algorithm) until all nodes that have the potential to lead to a cheaper solution are expanded.

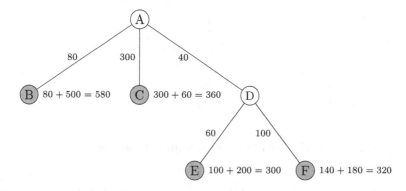

Fig. 4. A* search algorithm (Color figure online)

Example 6 (continued). Consider again the node labeled E. If $h(x)$ is admissible, the true cost of each path from this node to a goal node is greater than or equal to 200.

The general concept of the A* search algorithm as described above can easily be applied for exact global reordering of quantum circuits. In this case, the goal is to determine the permutation (the order) of the qubits, for which the fewest number of SWAPs gates are required in order to make the currently considered quantum circuit nearest neighbor compliant. Therefore, the nodes of the search space describe a (partial) permutation of the qubits. More precisely, a node with depth i (i.e. a node on with distance i to the root node) represents a partial permutation of i qubits. For simplicity, we label the nodes with the resulting order of the qubits instead of the partial permutation and neglect those qubits for which the permutation is not yet defined.

Example 7. Consider a quantum circuit composed of $n = 4$ qubits q_0, q_1, q_2, and q_3 as well as a partial permutation $\pi = (0, \Diamond, \Diamond, 1)$. This partial permutation maps qubit q_0 to the first position and qubit q_3 to the second position. The mapping for the other qubits is not defined and, hence, denoted by $\Diamond$ (also called *hole*). The resulting order of the qubits is then $q_0 q_3 \Diamond \Diamond$. For simpler graphical visualization, we label the node that represents π with $q_0 q_3$ – neglecting the qubits for which the position is not yet fixed.

A function $g(x)$ is needed to determine the cost of the path from the root to node x. Note that an edge in the tree describes a qubit that is added to the partial permutation. Consequently, the cost of the path from the root to node x can also be determined by the partial permutation that is represented by x. To this end, we determine the resulting nearest neighbor cost of the circuit. Since the permutation is only partially defined, we consider only those gates for which the position of the target and the controlling qubit is already fixed (i.e. these qubits have to occur in the partial permutation).

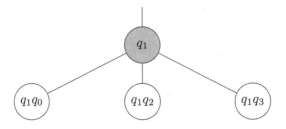

Fig. 5. Straightforward expansion strategy (Color figure online)

Example 8. Consider a node labeled $q_1 q_3 q_0$. The cost $g(x)$ of this node is determined by the nearest neighbor cost of all gates $g(c, t)$, for which $c, t \in \{0, 1, 3\}$. As discussed above, this cost can be determined from the adjacency matrix by $g(x) = m_{0,1} \cdot 1 + m_{0,3} \cdot 0 + m_{1,3} \cdot 0$.

Besides the representation of the (sub-) solutions and a cost function $g(x)$, we need two more things for exact global reordering for nearest neighbor quantum circuits using A*:

- An expansion strategy for the nodes, i.e. a strategy how another qubit shall be added to the partial permutation and
- an admissible heuristic function $h(x)$ to estimate the resulting cost from node x to a goal node that suits to the expansion strategy.

In the following sections, we propose two such expansion strategies and discuss their according heuristic function $h(x)$.

4.2   Straightforward Strategy

In this section, we discuss a straightforward expansion strategy for the nodes encountered during the A* algorithm and a corresponding admissible heuristic $h(x)$. To this end, we consider a quantum circuit composed of n qubits.

Consider a tree node with depth i. This node represents a partial permutation composed of i qubits. Hence, the position of i qubits is already fixed. To generate a permutation of $i + 1$ bits, we simply add one of the remaining qubits to the right of the already placed ones. Since $n - i$ such qubits exist, the expansion of the node yields $n - i$ successors. An example illustrates the idea.

Example 9. Consider a quantum circuit composed of $n = 4$ qubits q_0, q_1, q_2, and q_3, and assume that the node highlighted blue in Fig. 5 has to be expanded next. This node represents a partial permutation q_1. Since there are three qubits that are not contained in the partial permutation (q_0, q_2, and q_3), three successor nodes are generated. These nodes represent the partial permutations $q_1 q_0$, $q_1 q_2$, and $q_1 q_3$, respectively. The resulting nodes are illustrated in Fig. 5.

Based on this expansion strategy, we have to estimate the cost $h(x)$ of the path from node x to a goal node. Recall that a goal node represents a permutation of the qubits. Consequently, we estimate how much the nearest neighbor cost increase when appending the remaining qubits to the current order. To ensure admissibility of this heuristic, we consider each qubit individually. Appending a qubit q_j to the right of the current order changes the nearest neighbor cost by Δ_{q_j}. This increase is determined by the nearest neighbor cost of all gates for which q_j is the controlling or the target qubit. Furthermore, the other qubit involved in the gate has to be part of the current order. All these values Δ_{q_j} are then summed up to approximate the overall increase of the nearest neighbor cost $h(x)$. Obviously this leads to an under-approximation of the real cost, since not all remaining qubits can be appended at the same location and the nearest neighbor costs between the remaining qubits are not considered.

Example 9 (continued). Consider the node labeled $q_1 q_0$ in Fig. 5. Appending qubit q_2 to the right of the current order would increase the resulting cost by $\Delta_{q_2} = m_{1,2} \cdot 1 + m_{0,2} \cdot 0$. Analogously, appending qubit q_3 to the right would increase the resulting cost by $\Delta_{q_3} = m_{1,3} \cdot 1 + m_{0,3} \cdot 0$. Consequently, the overall cost increase is estimated by the sum $h(x) = \Delta_{q_2} + \Delta_{q_3} = m_{1,2} + m_{1,3}$.

4.3 Elaborated Strategy

While the solution introduced above employs a rather straightforward scheme, we additionally propose a more sophisticated approach for expansion and estimation – described in this section. Here, we allow qubits to be inserted not only to the right of the already placed ones, but at all possible positions within the partial permutation. To this end, we restrict that, within an expansion, only one qubit is considered (while in the straightforward scheme introduced above all remaining qubits are considered; albeit with a fixed position). More precisely, out of the remaining qubits we choose the one which occurs most often as target or controlling qubit (accelerating the search by focusing on qubits with many interactions within the circuit). An example illustrates the idea.

Example 10. Consider a quantum circuit composed of $n = 4$ qubits q_0, q_1, q_2, and q_3, and assume that the node highlighted blue in Fig. 6 has to be expanded next. This node represents a partial permutation $q_1 q_0$. Assume that qubit q_2 is considered next as this is the one of the remaining qubits which interacts most often in the considered circuit, i.e. occurs most often as target or controlling qubit. Since there are three possibilities where to insert qubit q_2, three successor nodes are generated. These nodes represent the partial permutations $q_2 q_1 q_0$, $q_1 q_2 q_0$, and $q_1 q_0 q_2$, respectively. The resulting nodes are illustrated in Fig. 6.

Since we have a different expansion strategy, another heuristic to approximate the remaining cost is required. In contrast to above, the position at which the remaining qubits are inserted is not fixed anymore. Therefore, we have to determine $\Delta_{q_j}^k$ for each position k at which a qubit q_j can be inserted. Then, Δ_{q_j} is the minimum of all these values (since the heuristic has to be admissible).

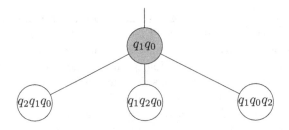

Fig. 6. Elaborated expansion strategy (Color figure online)

Finally, to estimate the overall cost increase when all remaining qubits q_j are inserted, we sum up all these values Δ_{q_j} to obtain $h(x)$.

Example 10 (continued). Consider again the node highlighted in blue in Fig. 6. The heuristic cost $h(x)$ of this node is determined as follows. For all remaining qubits (i.e. q_2 and q_3) we estimate the cost increase when adding the respective qubit to the permutation. Each remaining qubit can be inserted at three positions. Inserting the qubit q_2 at position zero (at the left of q_1) increases the nearest neighbor cost by $\Delta_{q_2}^0 = m_{0,2} \cdot 1$. Analogously, inserting the qubit at positions one and two yields $\Delta_{q_2}^1 = m_{0,1} \cdot 1$ and $\Delta_{q_2}^2 = m_{1,2} \cdot 1$, respectively. Then, the minimum $\Delta_{q_2} = \min\left(\Delta_{q_2}^0, \Delta_{q_2}^1, \Delta_{q_2}^2\right) = \min\left(m_{0,2}, m_{0,1}, m_{1,2}\right)$ of the three possibilities is determined. Analogously, $\Delta_{q_3} = \min\left(m_{0,3}, m_{0,1}, m_{1,3}\right)$ is determined. Finally, the sum of the minima is determined, i.e. $h(x) = \Delta_{q_2} + \Delta_{q_3}$.

4.4 Discussion

In this section, we compare the two expansion strategies proposed above. To this end, we analyze how many successor nodes are generated when expanding a node with depth i. For the straightforward strategy, such a node has $n - i$ successors, because each of the $n - i$ remaining literals can be appended to the right of the current order. In contrast, a node with depth i generates $i + 1$ successors when expanded using the elaborated strategy, because the qubit that is inserted is fixed and there are $i + 1$ possibilities where this qubit might be inserted.

Consider the case that the estimated cost of a node with depth i is larger than the minimum that can be achieved. This means that this node (and, therefore, also its child nodes) will never be expanded. In case we use the straightforward expansion strategy, we therefore prune $(n - i) \cdot (n - i - 1) \cdot \ldots \cdot 1 = (n - i)!$ possible solutions of the search tree. In contrast, if we apply the elaborated expansion strategy, we prune $(i+1) \cdot (i+2) \cdot \ldots \cdot n = n!/i!$ solutions. Consequently, eliminating a node with depth i prunes significantly more possible solutions if the elaborated expansion strategy is used. However, the heuristics to estimate the resulting cost is computationally more expensive for the elaborated expansion strategy. Since we have to determine the best position for each of the remaining qubits, $O(n^3)$ lookups in the adjacency matrix are required. In contrast, using the straightforward expansion strategy requires $O(n^2)$ such lookups.

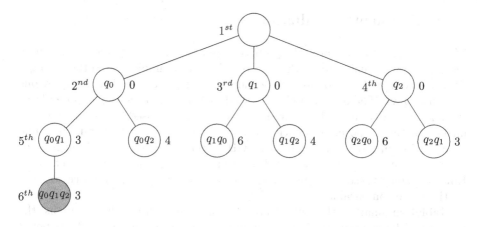

Fig. 7. Search tree of the straightforward expansion strategy

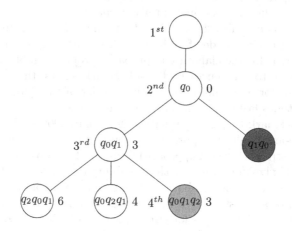

Fig. 8. Search tree of the elaborated expansion strategy

Example 11. Consider a quantum circuit with three circuit lines (denoted by q_0, q_1, and q_2), where the corresponding adjacency matrix has the entries $m_{0,1} = 4$, $m_{0,2} = 3$, and $m_{1,2} = 6$. Figures 7 and 8 show the resulting trees generated by the A* search algorithm using the naive expansion strategy and the elaborated expansion strategy, respectively. The black numbers attached to the nodes represent the corresponding cost $f(x)$. The red numbers indicate the iteration in which the nodes were expanded. Furthermore, the expanded goal node (i.e. the one that yields an optimal solution) is highlighted in blue. The node highlighted red in Fig. 8 can immediately be rejected by the search algorithm, because it is symmetric to the other node on this level. For the straightforward strategy, a total of six nodes had to be expanded until the optimal solution was determined. In contrast, using the elaborated strategy allows to determine the same solution by expanding only four nodes.

5   Experimental Evaluation

We experimentally evaluated the proposed approach and compared the obtained results to the current state-of-the-art. To this end, we implemented the A* algorithm as well as the proposed expansion strategies described in the previous section in Java. The quantum circuits used as benchmarks were composed from the ones available in RevLib [24] and those previously used in [11]. The experiments for the proposed approaches were conducted on a Java virtual machine with 6 GB of memory running on a 1.7 GHz Intel i5 processor. The runtimes for the current state-of-the-art were taken from the corresponding paper (cf. [11]). However, since these experiments were conducted on a similar processor, the runtimes are comparable.

Table 3 summarizes the obtained results. In the first three columns, we list the name of the benchmark, the number of qubits n, as well as the minimal number of SWAP gates required to make the quantum circuit nearest neighbor compliant. The fourth column lists the runtime of the current state-of-the-art approach [11]. The remaining columns list the runtime t, the number of created nodes, and the number of expanded nodes for the straightforward approach (proposed in Sect. 4.2) as well as for the elaborated approach (proposed in Sect. 4.3).

A comparison to the current state-of-the-art shows that the proposed approaches allow for determining the optimal order of the qubits in a runtime which is magnitudes faster that the current state-of-the-art. For example, one of the largest benchmark (*urf3_155*) requires more than 3000 CPU seconds using the state-of-the-art, while the approaches proposed here can solve this instance in few seconds (straightforward approach) or even a fraction of a second (elaborated approach) only. Moreover, also the scalability is significantly better: While, thus far, minimal results for global reordering were available for quantum circuits composed of at most $n = 10$ qubits, the solutions proposed in this work are capable of generating results for circuits with up to 25 qubits.

Besides that, the results also confirm the discussion from Sect. 4.4 on the differences between the two A* schemes. The straightforward approach runs into a time out of half an hour for some circuits with 14, 15, or 16 qubits. In contrast, the more elaborated expansion strategy can also determine a solution for these benchmarks in less than 100 s. A further analysis explains this: Using the elaborated strategy, fewer nodes are generated and also significantly fewer of them are further expanded. This is because eliminating a node close to the root node of the tree prunes a larger part of the search space. Even though this requires a computationally more complex heuristic function to estimate the cost of a node, it eventually pays off and yields significant speedups compared to the straightforward strategy.

Table 3. Experimental evaluation

Benchmark	n	SWAPs	s-o-t-a [11] t	Straightforward (Sect. 4.2)			Elaborated (Sect. 4.3)		
				t	Created	Expanded	t	Created	Expanded
decod24-v3_46	4	4	0.10	0.00	23	9	0.00	10	4
hwb4_52	4	18	0.10	0.00	33	14	0	10	4
rd32-v0_67	4	4	1.10	0.00	23	9	0.00	10	4
4gt11_84	5	2	0.10	0.00	43	13	0.00	15	5
4gt13-v1_93	5	8	0.10	0.00	54	17	0.00	15	5
4mod5-v1_23	5	30	0.10	0.00	118	43	0.00	15	5
aj-e11_165	5	52	0.10	0.00	89	31	0.00	15	5
hwb5_55	5	120	0.10	0.00	112	40	0.00	19	6
QFT5	5	20	0.10	0.00	206	87	0.00	23	7
hwb6_58	6	290	0.10	0.01	743	271	0.00	79	18
mod8-10_177	6	156	0.10	0.01	419	128	0.00	44	11
ham7_104	7	140	1.90	0.01	1407	391	0.02	151	30
rd53_135	7	136	1.80	0.01	1539	412	0.00	41	10
QFT8	8	112	20.00	0.32	69281	28962	0.05	2966	439
urf2_152	8	71280	22.00	0.04	19170	5604	0.00	845	136
QFT9	9	168	236.5	3.30	623530	260651	0.30	23127	2959
urf1_149	9	179832	241.30	0.21	84588	21384	0.05	5896	786
urf5_158	9	176284	247.00	0.44	137694	38582	0.03	3648	522
QFT10	10	240	2936.8	45.73	6235301	2606502	1.13	204568	23119
rd73_140	10	150	1579.4	0.08	49171	9064	0.02	3834	535
Shor3	10	4802	1846.2	0.19	103385	21548	0.00	1496	215
sym9_148	10	10984	2415.12	0.34	138043	28921	0.00	474	77
sys6-v0_144	10	114	1586.40	0.07	40315	7340	0.02	1990	290
urf3_155	10	453368	3023.60	1.55	445123	102912	0.03	7526	975
cycle10_2_110	12	4104	TO	25.34	5649298	1045869	0.30	34018	4011
Shor4	12	13588	TO	7.84	3095113	618714	0.13	12496	1493
plus63mod4096_163	13	113104	TO	481.68	39226031	6834319	0.44	36283	4246
0410184_169	14	48	TO	0.02	15935	1598	0.00	613	88
plus127mod8192_162	14	279520	TO	TO	-	-	2.03	162532	17469
plus63mod8192_164	14	149708	TO	TO	-	-	1.75	138771	15455
Shor5	14	34680	TO	TO	-	-	1.77	172154	16703
ham15_108	15	1340	TO	TO	-	-	1.11	78458	7910
rd84_142	15	284	TO	552.84	47396532	6167835	1.09	75770	8577
urf6_160	15	241208	TO	TO	-	-	92.89	5593552	517840
cnt3-5_180	16	340	TO	937.23	156966895	18710815	8.23	496214	50119
Shor6	16	76318	TO	TO	-	-	47.39	3310774	263822
add8_172	25	90	TO	499.31	48043975	3007062	60.13	990050	70269

6   Conclusions

In this work we have considered the problem of exact global reordering to minimize the number of SWAP gates required to make a quantum circuit nearest neighbor compliant. Using the A* algorithm to determine the optimal permutation of the order of the qubits allows for significant improvements compared to the state-of-the-art. While current approaches are able to determine a solution for circuits with up to 10 qubits, the approach proposed in this paper is able to determine an exact solution for circuits composed of up to 25 qubits.

Acknowledgements. This work has partially been supported by the European Union through the COST Action IC1405.

References

1. Nielsen, M., Chuang, I.: Quantum Computation and Quantum Information. Cambridge University Press, New York (2000)
2. Shor, P.W.: Polynomial-time algorithms for prime factorization and discrete logarithms on a quantum computer. SIAM J. Comput. **26**(5), 1484–1509 (1997)
3. Grover, L.K.: A fast quantum mechanical algorithm for database search. In: Symposium on the Theory of Computing, pp. 212–219 (1996)
4. Saeedi, M., Wille, R., Drechsler, R.: Synthesis of quantum circuits for linear nearest neighbor architectures. Quantum Inform. Process. **10**(3), 355–377 (2011)
5. Khan, M.H.: Cost reduction in nearest neighbour based synthesis of quantum Boolean circuits. Eng. Lett. **16**(1), 1–5 (2008)
6. Hirata, Y., Nakanishi, M., Yamashita, S., Nakashima, Y.: An efficient method to convert arbitrary quantum circuits to ones on a linear nearest neighbor architecture. In: Conference on Quantum, Nano and Micro Technologies, pp. 26–33 (2009)
7. Shafaei, A., Saeedi, M., Pedram, M.: Optimization of quantum circuits for interaction distance in linear nearest neighbor architectures. In: Design Automation Conference, pp. 41–46 (2013)
8. Wille, R., Quetschlich, N., Inoue, Y., Yasuda, N., Minato, S.: Using πDDs for nearest neighbor optimization of quantum circuits. In: Devitt, S., Lanese, I. (eds.) RC 2016. LNCS, vol. 9720, pp. 181–196. Springer, Cham (2016). doi:10.1007/978-3-319-40578-0_14
9. Wille, R., Keszocze, O., Walter, M., Rohrs, P., Chattopadhyay, A., Drechsler, R.: Look-ahead schemes for nearest neighbor optimization of 1d and 2d quantum circuits. In: ASP Design Automation Conference, pp. 292–297 (2016)
10. Wille, R., Lye, A., Drechsler, R.: Optimal SWAP gate insertion for nearest neighbor quantum circuits. In: ASP Design Automation Conference, pp. 489–494 (2014)
11. Wille, R., Lye, A., Drechsler, R.: Exact reordering of circuit lines for nearest neighbor quantum architectures. IEEE Trans. CAD **33**(12), 1818–1831 (2014)
12. Fowler, A.G., Devitt, S.J., Hollenberg, L.C.L.: Implementation of Shor's algorithm on a linear nearest neighbour qubit array. Quantum Inform. Comput. **4**, 237–245 (2004)
13. Meter, R.V., Oskin, M.: Architectural implications of quantum computing technologies. J. Emerg. Technol. Comput. Syst. **2**(1), 31–63 (2006)
14. Ross, M., Oskin, M.: Quantum computing. Commun. ACM **51**(7), 12–13 (2008)
15. Amini, J.M., Uys, H., Wesenberg, J.H., Seidelin, S., Britton, J., Bollinger, J.J., Leibfried, D., Ospelkaus, C., VanDevender, A.P., Wineland, D.J.: Toward scalable ion traps for quantum information processing. New J. Phys. **12**(3), 033031 (2010)
16. Kumph, M., Brownnutt, M., Blatt, R.: Two-dimensional arrays of radio-frequency ion traps with addressable interactions. New J. Phys. **13**(7), 073043 (2011)
17. Nickerson, N.H., Li, Y., Benjamin, S.C.: Topological quantum computing with a very noisy network and local error rates approaching one percent. Nat. Commun. **4**, 1756 (2013)
18. Devitt, S.J., Fowler, A.G., Stephens, A.M., Greentree, A.D., Hollenberg, L.C.L., Munro, W.J., Nemoto, K.: Architectural design for a topological cluster state quantum computer. New J. Phys. **11**(8), 083032 (2009)

19. Yao, N.Y., Gong, Z.X., Laumann, C.R., Bennett, S.D., Duan, L.M., Lukin, M.D., Jiang, L., Gorshkov, A.V.: Quantum logic between remote quantum registers. Phys. Rev. A **87**, 022306 (2013)
20. Herrera-Martí, D.A., Fowler, A.G., Jennings, D., Rudolph, T.: Photonic implementation for the topological cluster-state quantum computer. Phys. Rev. A **82**, 032332 (2010)
21. Jones, N.C., Van Meter, R., Fowler, A.G., McMahon, P.L., Kim, J., Ladd, T.D., Yamamoto, Y.: Layered architecture for quantum computing. Phys. Rev. X **2**, 031007 (2012)
22. Ohliger, M., Eisert, J.: Efficient measurement-based quantum computing with continuous-variable systems. Phys. Rev. A **85**, 062318 (2012)
23. DiVincenzo, D.P., Solgun, F.: Multi-qubit parity measurement in circuit quantum electrodynamics. New J. Phys. **15**(7), 075001 (2013)
24. Wille, R., Große, D., Teuber, L., Dueck, G.W., Drechsler, R.: RevLib: an online resource for reversible functions and reversible circuits. In: International Symposium on Multi-Valued Logic, pp. 220–225 (2008). RevLib is available at http://www.revlib.org

Improved Decomposition of Multiple-Control Ternary Toffoli Gates Using Muthukrishnan-Stroud Quantum Gates

P. Mercy Nesa Rani[1], Abhoy Kole[2], Kamalika Datta[1], and Indranil Sengupta[3(✉)]

[1] National Institute of Technology Meghalaya, Shillong, India
{mercyranip,kdatta}@nitm.ac.in
[2] B. P. Poddar Institute of Management and Technology, Kolkata, India
abhoy.kole@gmail.com
[3] Indian Institute of Technology Kharagpur, Kharagpur, India
isg@iitkgp.ac.in

Abstract. In conventional binary reversible circuit synthesis, reversible gates are decomposed into quantum gates using some standard quantum gate library. In recent years there has been increased attention in synthesis using ternary reversible gates since it leads to a reduction in the number of lines. However, very few works exist that address the problem of decomposing ternary reversible gates based on some ternary quantum gate library. Most of these works use Muthukrishnan-Stroud (M-S) gates for decomposition of ternary Toffoli gate, and they use a naive approach that requires an exponential (in number of control lines) number of M-S gates. Also the number of ancilla lines required is $(c - 1)$, where c is the number of control lines. The present paper proposes a method for decomposing ternary Toffoli gates to M-S gates that requires less number of ancilla lines, and also requires a number of M-S gates that is linear in c. A template-based post-decomposition optimization step has also been used to further reduce the number of M-S gates required. Decomposition results for up to 16 control lines have been presented.

1 Introduction

Energy dissipation is one of the most important issues in present-day fabrication technology. In general, conventional logic operations result in loss of information and hence some mandatory energy dissipation [7]. Also Bennett [2] showed that circuits with zero energy dissipation have to be reversible. This has motivated researchers to explore reversible logic as an alternative to conventional logic in circuit design.

A more compact and efficient information encoding can be obtained in an m-valued quantum system (where $m > 2$), as compared to binary quantum system. In a ternary quantum system ($m = 3$), a quantum digit is referred to as *qutrit*. In such a system, up to 63% reduction in the number of required lines (qutrits as compared to qubits in conventional quantum system) can be achieved [6]. In

I. Phillips and H. Rahaman (Eds.): RC 2017, LNCS 10301, pp. 202–213, 2017.
DOI: 10.1007/978-3-319-59936-6_16

general, ternary logic results in reduction in the number of lines as well as number of gates while realizing quantum circuits. A qutrit has three basis states denoted as $|0\rangle$, $|1\rangle$ and $|2\rangle$. The state of a qutrit can be represented either by one of the basis states, or by their linear superposition as: $|\varphi\rangle = \phi|0\rangle + \omega|1\rangle + \xi|1\rangle$, where ϕ, ω and ξ are complex numbers representing the probability amplitudes of the basis states. The condition required for normalization is $|\phi|^2 + |\omega|^2 + |\xi|^2 = 1$.

Ternary reversible logic functions can be synthesized using ternary reversible logic gates. The ternary reversible gates can be further decomposed into ternary elementary quantum gates. The number of such elementary gates can be used to define the quantum cost for the realization, where each of the elementary gates is assumed to be of unit cost. The ternary elementary gates used by researchers are *Muthukrishnan-Stroud (M-S) Gate* and *Ternary Shift Gate*. There exists very few works on ternary reversible gate decomposition into ternary elementary gates [4]. In this paper, we have proposed a decomposition scheme for ternary Toffoli gates of arbitrary sizes in terms of M-S gates using a set of ancilla lines fed by constant inputs $|0\rangle$, $|1\rangle$ or $|2\rangle$. A post-decomposition optimization step reduces the number of M-S gates to a number that is linear in the number of control lines. Earlier, authors in [14] have proposed a similar approach with linear increase in number of gates to realize the operation of an arbitrary size Toffoli gate without using any ancilla line.

The rest of the paper is organized as follows. Section 2 introduces a brief background of ternary reversible and elementary gates, and a brief literature survey of logic syntheses using such gates. Section 3 explains the proposed approach for decomposing ternary Toffoli gates of arbitrary size to a netlist of elementary M-S gates, and a template optimization process that is used to reduce the quantum cost of the netlist. Section 4 presents decomposition results for ternary Toffoli gates with up to 16 control lines, followed by concluding remarks in Sect. 5.

2 Background

In this section, we briefly present the important ternary reversible gates that have been proposed by researchers in synthesis, and also some of the elementary ternary gates that form the target for the proposed decomposition approach. Finally we briefly review some of the existing works in reversible logic synthesis using ternary gates.

2.1 Ternary Reversible Gates

For synthesis of arbitrary logic functions using ternary reversible logic, ternary reversible gates are used. The various ternary reversible gates used in the literature are ternary Toffoli gate, ternary Feynman or controlled-NOT gate, and ternary NOT gate.

(a) **Ternary Toffoli Gate** [8,15]: This gate triggers when its two control lines I_1 and I_2 are both in state $|1\rangle$ or $|2\rangle$ (i.e. $I_1 = I_2$). This causes the target line I_3 to change as $I_3 \oplus_3 1$. Figure 1(a) shows the schematic diagram of a ternary Toffoli gate which is activated when both the control lines are at $|2\rangle$.

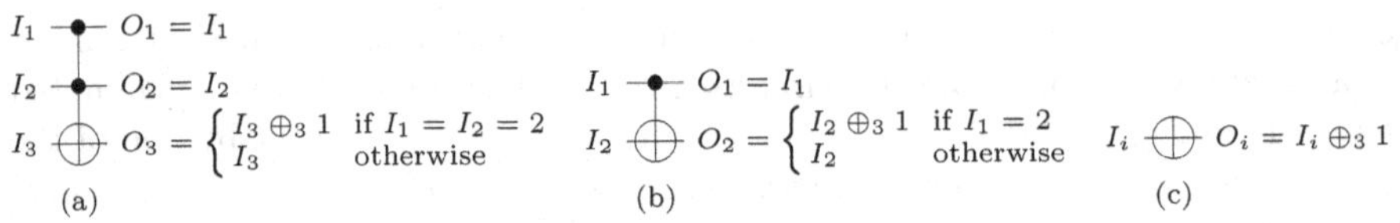

$I_1 \bullet O_1 = I_1$

$I_2 \bullet O_2 = I_2$

$I_3 \oplus O_3 = \begin{cases} I_3 \oplus_3 1 & \text{if } I_1 = I_2 = 2 \\ I_3 & \text{otherwise} \end{cases}$

(a)

$I_1 \bullet O_1 = I_1$

$I_2 \oplus O_2 = \begin{cases} I_2 \oplus_3 1 & \text{if } I_1 = 2 \\ I_2 & \text{otherwise} \end{cases}$

(b)

$I_i \oplus O_i = I_i \oplus_3 1$

(c)

Fig. 1. (a) Ternary Toffoli gate, (b) Ternary Feynman gate, (c) Ternary NOT gate

(b) **Ternary Feynman Gate** [4]: This gate triggers when the control line I_1 is at $|2\rangle$, and the target line I_2 changes as $I_2 \oplus_3 1$. Figure 1(b) shows the the schematic representation of a ternary Feynman gate.

(c) **Ternary NOT Gate** [16]: This gate changes the value on the target line I_1 as $I_1 \oplus_3 1$, Fig. 1(c) shows the schematic representation of a ternary NOT gate.

2.2   Ternary Elementary Gates

Elementary gates are the basic building blocks for realizing ternary reversible logic circuits. The cost of an elementary gate is assumed to be unity. The ternary elementary gates that have been used by researchers are *Ternary Shift Gate* [5] and *Muthukrishnan-Stroud (M-S) Gate* [13].

(a) **Ternary Shift Gates** [5]: Six ternary reversible shift operations are possible corresponding to the possible permutations of the values $0, 1$ and 2, which are realized using ternary shift gates (1×1). One of these corresponds to the identity permutation, I (Buffer). A ternary shift gate represents the Z-transformation, which can be realized using five unitary permutative matrices $Z(+1), Z(+2), Z(02), Z(12)$ and $Z(01)$. For example, for the input logic state $[0\ 1\ 2]$, the operations of the shift gates are defined as:

$$Z(I) = [0\ 1\ 2] \qquad Z(01) = [1\ 0\ 2]$$
$$Z(+1) = [1\ 2\ 0] \qquad Z(02) = [2\ 1\ 0]$$
$$Z(+2) = [2\ 0\ 1] \qquad Z(12) = [0\ 2\ 1]$$

(b) **Muthukrishnan-Stroud (M-S) Gate** [13]: It is a 2-qutrit ternary gate as shown in Fig. 2. It has controlling input I_1 that controls the output O_2, which is the Z-transformation of controlled input I_2 whenever $I_1 = |2\rangle$, where $Z \in \{+1, +2, 12, 01, 02\}$. M-S gates can be realized using ion-trap technology [3].

2.3   Existing Works in Ternary Reversible Logic Synthesis

The main motivation behind using ternary reversible logic for realizing logic functions is the fact that the amount of information per digit is high in ternary

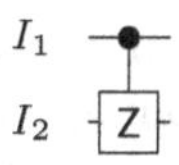

$$I_1 \quad\text{—•—}\quad O_1 = I_1$$

$$I_2 \quad \boxed{Z} \quad O2 = \begin{cases} Z \text{ transform of } I_2 & \text{if } I_1 = 2 \\ I_2 & \text{otherwise} \end{cases}$$

Fig. 2. M-S Gate

logic as compared to binary logic. This is expected to lead to more compact realizations requiring less number of quantum bits. Various ternary reversible logic synthesis approaches that have been reported in the literature can be grouped into four categories: (a) Group Theory based synthesis, (b) Ternary Galois Field Sum of Products (TGFSOP) based synthesis, (c) Ternary Decision Diagram (TDD) based synthesis, and (d) Soft Computing based synthesis.

In [11], Miller et al. presented a synthesis method for multi-valued reversible logic using heuristic algorithm. This method takes a reversible function F and transforms it to the identity mapping by finding a sequence of multi-valued logic gates. The merit of this approach is that it is faster for smaller circuits; however, it does not scale to larger functions. In [1], Basu et al. presented a synthesis method where a ternary function is first expressed in terms of the minterms. Two algorithms are proposed to simplify the minterms, which are then expressed in terms of projection operations L_i and J_i that can be directly mapped to M-S gates. Results for ternary benchmarks are provided that show a 31% improvement in cost as compared to previous works.

Khan et al. [5] proposed sixteen Ternary Galois Field Expansions (TGFE) and three different types of Ternary Decision Diagrams (TDD) to realize ternary benchmarks. As future works, the authors have suggested formulation of efficient heuristics for reducing the number of $SWAP$ and $Shift$ gates, and creation of a ternary benchmark library. Lukac et al. [9] proposed an evolutionary approach using genetic algorithm for quantum and reversible logic synthesis targeting to ternary logic system.

3   Proposed Decomposition Approach Using M-S Gates

In this section we present an approach for decomposing ternary Toffoli gates of arbitrary size into M-S gates. The following subsection discusses the realization of 3-input ternary Toffoli gates using M-S gates. The next subsection proposes some recursive formulations to decompose ternary multiple-control Toffoli gates into M-S gates, and also presents the overall algorithm for decomposition.

3.1   3-Input Ternary Toffoli Gate

Here we consider the decomposition of a ternary Toffoli gate using M-S gates. A ternary Toffoli gate $T_Z(\{c_1, c_2\}; t)$ has two control lines c_1 and c_2, a target line t, and realizes the Z-transformation corresponding to some ternary Shift operation. In the decomposition, the number of M-S gates required will be:

(a) 5, when a constant $|0\rangle$ ancilla line is used in the decomposition (see Fig. 3(b));
(b) 5, when a constant $|1\rangle$ ancilla line is used in the decomposition (see Fig. 3(c));
(c) 7, when a constant $|2\rangle$ ancilla line is used in the decomposition (see Fig. 3(d));

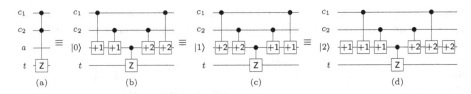

Fig. 3. Decomposition of ternary Toffoli gate. (a) A ternary Toffoli gate, (b) decomposition using constant $|0\rangle$, (c) decomposition using constant $|1\rangle$, (d) decomposition using constant $|2\rangle$

For different states of ancilla line a, the decomposition of $T_Z(C;t)$, with control lines $C = \{c_1, c_2\}$, can be expressed as follows:

Case 1: $a = |0\rangle$

$$T_Z^0(C;t) = M_1(c_1; a)M_1(c_2; a)M_Z(a; t)M_2(c_2; a)M_2(c_1; a) \tag{1}$$

Case 2: $a = |1\rangle$

$$T_Z^1(C;t) = M_2(c_1; a)M_2(c_2; a)M_Z(a; t)M_1(c_2; a)M_1(c_1; a) \tag{2}$$
$$= T_Z^0(C;t)^{-R}$$

where $-R$ in the superscript indicates *reverse*, i.e. the sequence of gates in the reverse order.

Case 3: $a = |2\rangle$

$$T_Z^2(C;t) = M_1(\emptyset; a)T_Z^0(C;t)M_2(\emptyset; a) \tag{3}$$

OR

$$T_Z^2(C;t) = M_2(\emptyset; a)T_Z^1(C;t)M_1(\emptyset; a) \tag{4}$$

In the following section, we refer to these ancilla lines as Type-$|0\rangle$, Type-$|1\rangle$, and Type-$|2\rangle$ ancilla lines respectively.

3.2   Ternary Multiple-Control Toffoli (TMCT) Gate

Decomposition of ternary multiple control Toffoli (TMCT) gate $T_Z(C;t)$ of size $n\ (> 3)$ can be accomplished in various ways depending on the number of ancilla lines available. We first present some theoretical results of decomposition, which form the foundation of the proposed approach.

Lemma 1. *The operation of a TMCT gate $T_Z(C;t)$ of size n $(n \geqslant 3)$ can be realized using $2^n - 3$ M-S gates and $n-2$ ancilla lines of type $|0\rangle$ when decomposed using following recursive structure:*

$$T_Z^0(C;t) = M_1(c_i;a)T_1^0(C';a)M_Z(a;t)T_2^0(C';a)M_2(c_i;a) \tag{5}$$

where $C' = C - \{c_i\}$ and ancilla a is assumed to be of type $|0\rangle$.

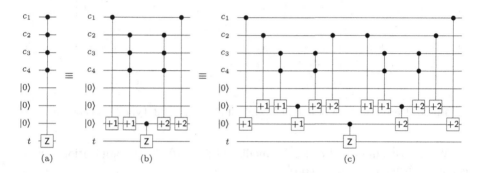

Fig. 4. Decomposition of a TMCT gate of size 5 using 3 Type-$|0\rangle$ ancilla lines

Proof. At each step of decomposition of a TMCT gate of size n, the structure represented by Eq. (5) yields a pair of TMCT gates of size $n - 1$ and 3 M-S gates. The process continues to level $n - 3$ until all gates are of size 3 (i.e. can be replaced by the structure Eq. (1)) or less. This results in 2^{n-3} size-3 ternary Toffoli gates and $(2^{n-3} - 1) \times 3$ M-S gates which in turn generates a cascade of $2^n - 3$ M-S gates. Figure 4 shows one such decomposition of a TMCT gate of size 5 that yields a circuit consisting of 29 M-S gates.

It is also possible to carry out the decomposition using smaller number of ancilla lines as stated in the following lemma.

Lemma 2. *The operation of a TMCT gate $T_Z(C;t)$ of size $n+1$ $(n > 3)$ can be realized using the following recursive structure when m $(\lceil \log_2 n \rceil \leqslant m \leqslant n - 2)$ ancilla lines of type $|0\rangle$ are available:*

$$T_Z^0(C;t) = T_1^0(C';a)T_1^0(C'';a)M_Z(a;t)T_2^0(C'';a)T_2^0(C';a) \tag{6}$$

where $C = C' \cup C''$, $C' \cap C'' = \emptyset$ and ancilla a is assumed to be of type $|0\rangle$.

Proof. Figure 5 shows the decomposition of a TMCT gate of size 8 using 3 ancillas lines of type $|0\rangle$. Initially, the set of control lines is partitioned into two disjoint subsets to realize the gate operation using the cascade shown in Fig. 5b. Each of these TMCT gates can be further decomposed reusing the same ancilla line. For example, Fig. 5c shows the realization of TMCT gate pair surrounded by dashed rectangle in Fig. 5b. An identical replacement can be made for the remaining TMCT gate pair with respective target operations.

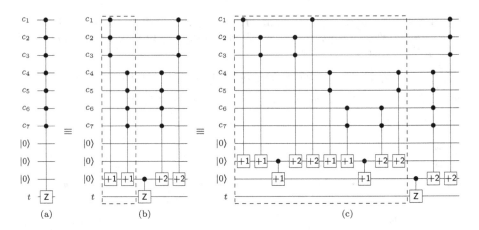

Fig. 5. Decomposition of a TMCT gate of size 8 using 3 Type-$|0\rangle$ ancilla lines

With least number of constant ancillas of type $|0\rangle$ the decomposition can be carried out using following corollary.

Corollary 1. *The realization of a TMCT gate $T_Z(C;t)$ of size $n+1$ ($n > 2$ and is an exact power of 2) requires $\frac{1}{3} \times (4^{\log_2 n+1} - 1)$ M-S gates when implemented using $\log_2 n$ ancillas of type $|0\rangle$.*

Proof. At each step of decomposition using ancilla a_i ($i = 1, 2, \dots$) of type $|0\rangle$, the structure of Eq. (6) generates a cascade consisting of 4 TMCT gates with exactly $\frac{n}{2}$ control lines and 1 M-S gate realizing the target operation, as shown in Fig. 6. At depth $\log_2 n - 1$ the structure results in a circuit consisting of $4^{\log_2 n-1}$ ternary Toffoli gates of size 3 and $\frac{1}{3} \times (4^{\log_2 n-1} - 1)$ M-S gates.

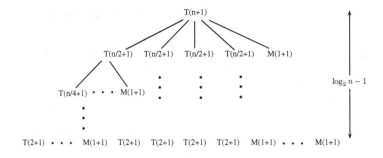

Fig. 6. Decomposition of a TMCT gate of size $n + 1$ using $\log_2 n$ constant ancilla of type $|0\rangle$

Considering all the above scenarios that require change in decomposition structure and also yields circuit with different M-S gate count, the following decomposition algorithm is formulated.

Algorithm 1.   *M-S mapping of a ternary Toffoli gate $T_z(C;t)$ of arbitrary size*

Input: a) Toffoli gate $T_z(C;t)$
          b) Ancilla lines $A = \{a_1, a_2, \ldots, a_n\}$
Output: An M-S gate implementation of $T_z(C;t)$ gate
begin
   if $(|C| > 1)$
      begin
        if $(|C| == 2)$ $//C = \{c_1, c_2\}$
          $ckt = M_1(c_1; a_1) \cup M_1(c_2; a_1) \cup M_z(a_1; t) \cup M_2(c_2; a_1) \cup M_2(c_1; a_1)$;
        else
          begin
            $len\_C' = 1$; $//$Default size
            if $(|A| = \lceil \log_2 |C| \rceil)$
              $len\_C' = \frac{|C|}{2}$;
            Split C into C' and C'' such that $(C' \cup C'' = C)$ &
              $(C' \cap C'' = \emptyset)$ & $(len\_C' = |C'|)$;
            $a = A[1]$;
            $A' = A[2 \ldots n]$;
            if $(|C'| = 1)$
              begin
                $ckt_1 = M_1(C'; a)$;
                $ckt_4 = M_2(C'; a)$;
              end
            else
              begin
                $ckt_1 = map(T_1(C'; a), A')$;
                $ckt_4 = map(T_2(C'; a), A')$;
              end
            endif
            if $(|C''| = 1)$
              begin
                $ckt_2 = M_1(C''; a)$;
                $ckt_3 = M_2(C''; a)$;
              end
            else
              begin
                $ckt_2 = map(T_1(C''; a), A')$;
                $ckt_3 = map(T_2(C''; a), A')$;
              end
            endif
            $ckt = ckt_1 \cup ckt_2 \cup M_z(a; t) \cup ckt_3 \cup ckt_4$;
          end
      endif
    return ckt;
end

4   Template Optimization and Results

In the previous section we have presented a scheme for decomposing a TMCT gate $T_Z(C;t)$ of size n $(n > 3)$ using m ancilla lines of type $|0\rangle$. The decomposition algorithm is not optimal and results in a netlist with lots of redundant gates, as shown in Fig. 7. Also the number of M-S gates required is dependent on the number of ancilla lines available during decomposition. For a TMCT gate of size $n+1$, the number of M-S gates is almost linear when decomposed using $\lceil \log_2 n \rceil$ ancilla lines, and it becomes exponential when $n - 1$ ancilla lines are used.

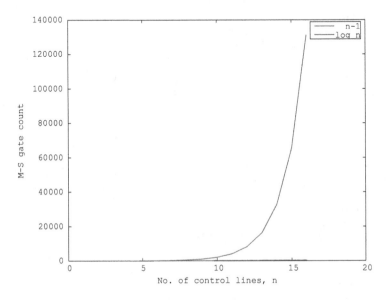

Fig. 7. Comparison of M-S gates requirement to realize the operation of a TMCT gate of size $n + 1$ using $\lceil \log_2 n \rceil$ and $n - 1$ constant ancillas of $|0\rangle$ type

In this section, we present a simple post-decomposition optimization scheme using which the number of M-S gates can be further reduced. For this purpose, we use the following identity templates:

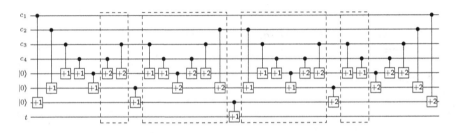

Fig. 8. M-S gate realization of a TMCT gate of size 5 using 3 type $|0\rangle$ ancilla lines

$$I = M_1(c;t)M_2(c;t) \tag{7}$$
$$= M_2(c;t)M_1(c;t) \tag{8}$$

where I is the identity operation, and the M-S gate pairs operate on the same control and target qutrits c and t respectively. The template based optimization using technique similar to the one used in [10,12]. The optimized M-S netlist for a TMCT gate $T(C;t)$ with up to 16 control lines, decomposed using m ancillas ($\lceil \log_2 |C| \rceil \leqslant m < |C| - 1$), is presented in Table 1. After optimization the

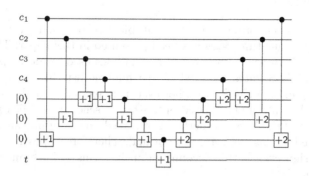

Fig. 9. Optimized M-S gate realization of a TMCT gate of size 5 using 3 type $|0\rangle$ ancilla lines

Table 1. Number of M-S gates required in realizing TMCT gates for upto 16 control lines

$|C|$	Number of ancilla lines of type $|0\rangle$														
	1	2	3	4	5	6	7	8	9	10	11	12	13	14	15
2	5														
3		9													
4		17	13												
5			21	17											
6			29	25	21										
7			37	33	29	25									
8			53	41	37	33	29								
9				49	45	41	37	33							
10				65	53	49	45	41	37						
11				73	69	57	53	49	45	41					
12				89	77	73	61	57	53	49	45				
13				97	93	81	77	65	61	57	53	49			
14				113	101	97	85	81	69	65	61	57	53		
15				129	117	105	101	89	85	73	69	65	61	57	
16				161	133	121	109	105	93	89	77	73	69	65	61

number of M-S gate count becomes linear, and maximum reduction is observed when $n - 2$ ancilla lines are used. The realization of a TMCT gate of size n using $n - 2$ constant ancilla lines yields a netlist of $4n - 7$ M-S gates. Figure 8 shows one such decomposition of a TMCT gate of size 5 using the recursive structure of Eq. (5). All the M-S gates surrounded by dashed rectangle are redundant and simplification using above templates result in a cascade of M-S gates similar to the one shown in Fig. 9.

5   Conclusion

A recursive approach for decomposing multiple-control ternary Toffoli gates into elementary M-S quantum gates has been presented in this paper. The approach uses a tradeoff between the number of ancilla lines used for decomposition, and the number of M-S gates required in the final netlist. Reuse of ancilla lines increases the number of M-S gates, however, it reduces the number of additional circuit lines. Also a template based optimization scheme has been presented to reduce the cost of the M-S gate netlist. Both the decomposition and optimization steps presented in this work are not optimal. Therefore, a possible future work can be to design even better decomposition in terms of both ancilla lines and M-S gate count.

References

1. Basu, S., Mandal, S.B., Chakrabarti, A., Sur-Kolay, S.: An efficient synthesis method for ternary reversible logic. In: International Symposium on Circuits and Systems (ISCAS), pp. 2306–2309 (2016)
2. Bennett, C.: Logical reversibility of computation. J. IBM Res. Dev. **17**(6), 525–532 (1973)
3. Cirac, J.I., Zoller, P.: Quantum computations with cold trapped ions. Phys. Rev. Lett. **74**, 4091–4094 (1995)
4. Khan, M.H.A.: Design of reversible/quantum ternary multiplexer and demultiplexer. In: Engineering Letters, pp. 174–178 (2006)
5. Khan, M.H.A., Perkowski, M.A., Khan, M.R., Kerntopf, P.: Ternary GFSOP minimization using Kronecker decision diagrams and their synthesis with quantum cascades. J. Multi Valued Logic Soft Comput. **11**, 567–602 (2005)
6. Khan, M.H.A.: GFSOP-based ternary quantum logic synthesis. In: Proceedings of the SPIE 7797, Optics and Photonics for Information Processing IV, pp. 1–15 (2010)
7. Landauer, R.: Irreversibility and heat generation in the computing process. J. IBM Res. Dev. **5**, 183–191 (1961)
8. Li, X., Yang, G., Zheng, D.: Logic synthesis of ternary quantum circuits with minimal qutrits. J. Comput. **8**(3), 1941–1946 (2013)
9. Lucac, M., Perkowski, M.A., Goi, H., Pivtoraiko, M., Yu, C.H., Chung, K., Jeech, H., Kim, B.G., Kim, Y.D.: Evolutionary approach to quantum and reversible circuits synthesis, artificial intelligence in logic design. Artif. Intell. Rev. **20**(3), 361–417 (2003)

10. Maslov, D., Dueck, G., Miller, D., Negrevergne, C.: Quantum circuit simplification and level compaction. IEEE Trans. Comput. Aided Des. Integr. Circuits Syst. **27**(3), 436–444 (2008)
11. Miller, D.M., Dueck, G., Maslov, D.: A synthesis method for MVL reversible logic. In: 34th International Symposium on Multiple-Valued Logic (ISMVL), pp. 74–80 (2004)
12. Miller, D., Sasanian, Z.: Lowering the quantum gate cost of reversible circuits. In: Proceedings of the International Midwest Symposium on Circuits and Systems, pp. 260–263 (2010)
13. Muthukrishnan, A., Stroud Jr., C.R.: Multivalued logic gates for quantum computation. Phys. Rev. A **62**(5), 052309/1-8 (2000)
14. Sasanian, Z., Wille, R., Miller, D.M.: Realizing reversible circuits using a new class of quantum gates. In: Proceedings of the Design Automation Conference, pp. 36–41 (2012)
15. Yang, G., Song, X., Perkowski, M., Wu, J.: Realizing ternary quantum switching networks without ancilla bits. J. Phys. A: Math. Gen. **38**, 1–10 (2005)
16. Yang, G., Xie, F., Song, X., Perkowski, M.: Universality of 2-qudit ternary reversible gates. J. Phys. A: Math. Gen. **39**, 7763–7773 (2006)

Efficient Construction of QMDDs for Irreversible, Reversible, and Quantum Functions

Philipp Niemann[1(✉)], Alwin Zulehner[2], Robert Wille[1,2], and Rolf Drechsler[1,3]

[1] Cyber-Physical Systems, DFKI GmbH, Bremen, Germany
Philipp.Niemann@dfki.de
[2] Institute for Integrated Circuits, Johannes Kepler University, Linz, Austria
{alwin.zulehner,robert.wille}@jku.at
[3] Department of Computer Science, University of Bremen, Bremen, Germany
drechsle@informatik.uni-bremen.de

Abstract. In reversible as well as quantum computation, unitary matrices (so-called *transformation matrices*) are employed to comprehensively describe the respectively considered functionality. Due to the exponential growth of these matrices, dedicated and efficient means for their representation and manipulation are essential in order to deal with this complexity and handle reversible/quantum systems of considerable size. To this end, *Quantum Multiple-Valued Decision Diagrams* (QMDDs) have shown to provide a compact representation of those matrices and have proven their effectiveness in many areas of reversible and quantum logic design such as embedding, synthesis, or equivalence checking. However, the desired functionality is usually not provided in terms of QMDDs, but relies on alternative representations such as Boolean Algebra, circuit netlists, or quantum algorithms. In order to apply QMDD-based design approaches, the corresponding QMDD has to be constructed first—a gap in many of these approaches. In this paper, we show how QMDD representations can efficiently be obtained for Boolean functions, both reversible and irreversible ones, as well as general quantum functionality.

1 Introduction

Reversible and quantum computation are alternative computational paradigms that have received significant attention in the past decades. In contrast to conventional computation, reversible computations are information loss-less such that the inputs of a computation can always be recovered from the outputs. The absence of information loss helps (at least theoretically) to avoid energy dissipation during computations and is used for certain aspects in low-power design.[1] Moreover, superconducting quantum interference devices [14], nanoelectromechanical systems [5,6], adiabatic circuits [1], and many further technologies utilize this compu-

---

[1] Initial experiments verifying the underlying link between information loss and thermodynamics have been reported in [2].

© Springer International Publishing AG 2017
I. Phillips and H. Rahaman (Eds.): RC 2017, LNCS 10301, pp. 214–231, 2017.
DOI: 10.1007/978-3-319-59936-6_17

tation paradigm. Reversibility of the respective operations is also an inherent characteristic of quantum computation [9]. The considered quantum systems are composed of *qubits* which, analogously to conventional bits, can represent a (Boolean) 0 or 1, but also superpositions of the two. This allows for solving many practically relevant problems (e.g. factorization [15] or database search [4]) exponentially faster than in classical computation. In both, reversible as well as quantum computation, unitary matrices (so-called *transformation matrices*) are employed to comprehensively describe the respectively considered functionality. *Quantum Multiple-Valued Decision Diagrams* (QMDDs, [13]) provide a compact, graphical representation of these matrices and allow for applying matrix operations like addition and multiplication directly on the data-structure. To this end, QMDDs have shown their effectiveness with respect to various critical tasks of reversible and quantum logic design. For example:

- Embedding: Due to the inherent reversibility of quantum and reversible logic, irreversible objective functions have to be embedded into reversible ones. For this purpose, a certain number of additional inputs (ancillary inputs) and outputs (garbage outputs) needs to be added and corresponding functionality is to be assigned in order to obtain reversibility. While it has been shown to be coNP-hard to determine an appropriate/minimal number of additional in- and outputs [17], the probably even larger problem is how to assign the additional mappings. QMDDs have been shown to be very efficient in this regard [20].
- Synthesis: Once a reversible function description is available, the synthesis problem of quantum and reversible logic is to determine an equivalent circuit representation in terms of a quantum or reversible gate library (e.g. Toffoli gates, the NCV library, or the Clifford+T library). QMDDs have successfully been employed for synthesis purposes in the past – particularly in order to realize larger reversible and quantum functionality with a minimum number of circuit lines and qubits, respectively (see e.g. [11,16]).
- Equivalence Checking: Frequently, designers are facing different functional descriptions, e.g. before and after a technology-mapping, employing different gate libraries, unoptimized and optimized versions, etc. In these cases, it is often helpful to prove whether different descriptions indeed realize the same functionality. Since QMDDs are canonic, they are very suited to conduct corresponding equivalence checks (see e.g. [12]).

However, in most cases the desired functionality is originally not provided in terms of QMDDs, but using alternative representations such as Boolean Algebra, circuit netlists, or quantum algorithms. In order to apply the corresponding approaches, the QMDD representing the considered functionality has to be constructed first. So far, it has not been considered in the literature yet how to do that efficiently.

In fact, for the Boolean domain, there is a large body of research on the construction of various description means for Boolean functions, e.g. Boolean algebra, circuit descriptions, or graphical representations. However, the resulting representations are far from the function matrix description that is required

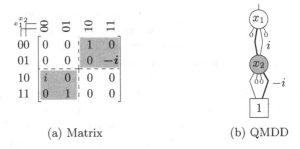

(a) Matrix   (b) QMDD

Fig. 1. Matrix and QMDD representation of a 2-qubit quantum operation.

to build the corresponding QMDD. In fact, most compact representations (algebraic or graphical) require an evaluation/traversal for each primary output in order to determine a particular input-output-mapping, i.e. a single entry of the function matrix. In the quantum domain, the desired functionality is usually given in terms of quantum algorithms or quantum circuits which are composed of modules or gates that realize a computational step (e.g. modular exponentiation) or quantum operations (e.g. rotations, controlled operations), respectively. The overall transformation matrix is computed by multiplying the matrices of the individual modules/gates, but those need to be constructed somehow first.

In this paper, we close these gaps and present detailed approaches for an efficient construction of QMDDs for Boolean as well as general quantum functionality. The paper is organized as follows: In Sect. 2, we provide a brief review of QMDDs. Afterwards, in Sects. 3 and 4, we present detailed approaches for an efficient construction of QMDDs for Boolean and quantum functionality, respectively. The results of a feasibility study to confirm the applicability of the proposed methodologies are provided in Sect. 5 before the paper is concluded in Sect. 6.

2   Quantum Multiple-Valued Decision Diagrams

In the following, we briefly introduce basic concepts and ideas of *Quantum Multiple-Valued Decision Diagrams* (QMDDs). For a more thorough introduction, we refer to [13]. QMDDs have been introduced as a data-structure for the efficient representation and manipulation of unitary, complex-valued matrices that are frequently considered in reversible and quantum computation.

Example 1. Figure 1a shows a transformation matrix of a 2-qubit quantum operation. Columns and rows (representing the inputs and outputs of the operation, respectively) are indexed by the same set of variables $\{x_1, x_2\}$.

The main idea of QMDDs is a recursive partitioning of the (square) transformation matrices and the use of edge weights to represent various complex-valued matrix entries. More precisely, a matrix of dimension $2^n \times 2^n$ is partitioned into four sub-matrices of dimension $2^{n-1} \times 2^{n-1}$ as follows:

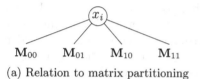

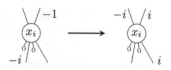

(a) Relation to matrix partitioning   (b) Normalization of weights

Fig. 2. QMDD vertices

$$M = \begin{bmatrix} M_{00} & M_{01} \\ M_{10} & M_{11} \end{bmatrix}$$

This partitioning is relative to the most significant row and column variable.

Example 2. Consider again the matrix shown in Fig. 1a. This matrix is partitioned with respect to variable x_1. The sub-matrices are identified by subscripts giving the row (output) and column (input) value for that variable identifying the position of the sub-matrix within the matrix. Using this partition, a matrix can be represented as a graph with vertices as shown in Fig. 2a. The vertex is labeled by the variable associated with the partition and has directional edges pointing to vertices corresponding to the sub-matrices. More precisely, the first, second, third, and fourth outgoing edge of the vertex (from left to right) points to a vertex representing M_{00}, M_{01}, M_{10}, and M_{11}, respectively.

The partitioning process can recursively be applied to each of the sub-matrices and to each of the subsequent levels of sub-matrices until one reaches the terminal case where each sub-matrix is a single value. The result is that the initial matrix is represented by a directed, acyclic graph (DAG)—the QMDD. By traversing the tree, one can access the successively partitioned sub-matrices of the original matrix down to the individual elements.

Example 3. Figure 1b shows the QMDD for the transformation matrix from Fig. 1a. Here, the single *root vertex* (labeled x_1) represents the whole matrix and has four outgoing edges to vertices representing the top-left, top-right, bottom-left, and bottom-right sub-matrix (from left to right). This decomposition is repeated at each partitioning level until the terminal vertex (representing a single matrix entry) is reached. To obtain the value of a particular matrix entry, one has to follow the corresponding path from the root vertex at the top to the terminal vertex while multiplying all edge weights on this path. For example, the matrix entry $-i$ from the top-right sub-matrix of Fig. 1a (highlighted bold) can be determined as the product of the weights on the highlighted path of the QMDD in Fig. 1b. For simplicity, we omit edge weights equal to 1 and indicate edges with a weight of 0 by stubs.

The performed decompositions unveil redundancies in the description for which representations can be shared—eventually yielding a rather compact representation of the matrix. More precisely, the edge weights in a QMDD are normalized in order to extract common multipliers and represent sub-matrices that only differ by a scalar factor by a shared vertex.

Example 4. The top-right and bottom-left sub-matrices of the matrix in Fig. 1a (highlighted in gray) differ by a scalar factor only (namely, i) and, thus, can be represented by a single, shared QMDD vertex as shown in Fig. 1b. In order to obtain shared vertices when constructing the QMDD, the following normalization scheme is performed: for each non-terminal vertex the weights of all outgoing edges are divided by the weight of the first non-zero edge. In other words, a vertex is normalized if, and only if, the first non-zero edge has weight 1. The extracted factor is then propagated to all incoming edges as shown in Fig. 2b.

Fortunately, the simple normalization scheme from Example 4 is sufficient to obtain the maximum shared vertex compression. No improvement is possible with more sophisticated normalization schemes [10]. However, by applying different variable orders, the QMDD size can often be reduced significantly. If, in contrast, a particular variable order is fixed, QMDDs are indeed canonical representations. This means that for a given matrix the corresponding QMDD representation is unique (for a fixed normalization scheme). Moreover, efficient algorithms have been presented for applying operations like matrix addition or multiplication directly on the QMDD data-structure.

Overall, QMDDs allow for applying matrix-based approaches in reversible and quantum logic design directly on this compact data-structure and, thus, make them applicable to systems of considerable size. However, the desired functionality needs to be on hand in terms of its QMDD representation first. As QMDDs are usually not the original description means, in the following we present a methodology for deriving QMDD representations from commonly used function representations for Boolean as well as quantum functionality.

3   Constructing QMDDs for Boolean Functionality

In this section, we describe how to obtain a QMDD representation for multi-output Boolean functions—both, irreversible and reversible ones.

3.1   General Idea and Methodology

A multi-output Boolean function $f: \mathbb{B}^n \rightarrow \mathbb{B}^m$ is commonly given in terms of descriptions of its *primary outputs* $f_1, \ldots, f_m$ (also termed *component functions*). These single-output Boolean functions $\mathbb{B}^n \rightarrow \mathbb{B}$ are commonly described in terms of Boolean Algebra, i.e. as *Sums of Products* (SOP), *Products of Sums* (POS), or the like. In the following, we focus on SOP representations, but any other description means can be treated similarly.

Matrices, however, as required for the construction of corresponding QMDDs, are usually not employed to describe these functions—with one exception: reversible Boolean functions can be interpreted as permutations of the set $\mathbb{B}^n$ and are frequently represented as *permutation matrices*. In these $2^n \times 2^n$ matrices $\mathbf{P}_f = [p_{i,j}]_{2^n \times 2^n}$, each column (row) denotes a possible input (output) pattern.

(a) Truth-table

x_1	x_2	f_1	f_2
0	0	0	0
0	1	0	1
1	0	0	1
1	1	1	0

(b) Function matrix

$x_1 x_2$

Inputs

	00	01	10	11
00	1	0	0	0
01	0	1	1	0
10	0	0	0	1
11	0	0	0	0

Outputs · f_1/y_1 · f_2/y_2

(c) Char. function

x_1	x_2	y_1	y_2	χ_f
0	0	0	0	1
0	0	0	1	0
0	0	1	0	0
0	0	1	1	0
0	1	0	0	0
0	1	0	1	1
⋮	⋮	⋮	⋮	⋮
1	1	1	1	0

Fig. 3. Representations of a half adder.

Moreover, $p_{i,j} = 1$ if, and only if, f maps the input pattern corresponding to column j to the output pattern corresponding to row i. Otherwise $p_{i,j} = 0$.

In order to have a baseline for the QMDD construction, these matrices can be generalized in a straightforward fashion to functions with different numbers of inputs and outputs. In fact, the *function matrix* of a Boolean function $f \colon \mathbb{B}^n \to \mathbb{B}^m$ needs to have the dimension $2^m \times 2^n$ in order to allow for the same correspondence of input (output) patterns and columns (rows).

Example 5. A *half adder* can be described by the multi-output Boolean function $f \colon \mathbb{B}^2 \to \mathbb{B}^2$ with component functions $f_1(x_1, x_2) = x_1 \wedge x_2$ (*carry*) and $f_2(x_1, x_2) = x_1 \oplus x_2 = x_1\overline{x_2} \vee \overline{x_1}x_2$ (*sum*). The corresponding truth-table and function matrix representations are shown in Figs. 3a and b, respectively. Each line of the truth-table is represented by a single 1 entry in the function matrix. For instance, the third line stating that $(1, 0)$ is mapped to $(0, 1)$ is represented by the 1 in the third column (10), second row (01).

In order to bridge the gap between the initial representation (which is essentially a more compact representation of the truth-table of f) and the targeted QMDD representation (which is essentially a more compact representation of the function matrix of f), the main idea is to employ the so-called *characteristic function* χ_f of f. This is a Boolean function $\mathbb{B}^n \times \mathbb{B}^m \to \mathbb{B}$ with n inputs labeled $x = x_1, \ldots, x_n$ and m inputs labeled $y = y_1, \ldots, y_m$, where $\chi_f(x, y) = 1$ if, and only if, $f(x) = y$. In other words, χ_f evaluates to true if, and only if, the backmost m inputs represent the correct output pattern that is generated when applying f to the input pattern specified by the first n inputs. Thus, the entries of the function matrix can be interpreted as the outcomes of χ_f.

Example 6. The characteristic function of the half adder from Example 5 is shown in Fig. 3c in terms of its truth-table. Each line corresponds to one entry of the function matrix. More precisely, writing all columns of the function matrix on top of each other would yield the χ_f column of the truth-table.

As it is infeasible to construct and store the whole function matrix at once due to its exponential complexity, we rather employ compact, graphical representations of Boolean functions (especially of the characteristic functions) from which the desired QMDD representation can then be derived directly without explicitly considering the function matrix. To this end, we make use of *Binary Decision Diagrams* (BDDs, [3]). These are similar to QMDDs, but each non-terminal vertex has only two instead of four outgoing edges (termed *high* and *low edge*) and represents a (single-output) Boolean function rather than a matrix. More precisely, the function f_v of a vertex v labeled by x_i is recursively defined as

$$f_v = \left(x_i \wedge f_{high(v)}\right) \vee \left(\overline{x_i} \wedge f_{low(v)}\right),$$

where $f_{high(v)}$ and $f_{low(v)}$ denote the functions represented by the high and low child, respectively. This equation has a strong analogy to the *Shannon decomposition* of f (wrt. a primary input x_i) which is given as

$$f = \left(x_i \wedge f_{x_i=1}\right) \vee \left(\overline{x_i} \wedge f_{x_i=0}\right).$$

Here, $f_{x_i=1}$ and $f_{x_i=0}$ are the so-called *co-factors* of f which are obtained by setting the primary input x_i to 1 and 0, respectively. The analogy between the two equations, on the one hand, justifies the claim that the BDD vertices represent the Shannon decomposition of f with respect to its primary inputs and, on the other hand, yields a blueprint for how to construct the BDD representation of a given function. Alternatively, as logical operations like AND, OR, etc. can be conducted directly and efficiently on BDDs, the BDD representation of an SOP can also be constructed by first building the BDDs for the individual products and then using the BDD equivalent of the logical OR operation to "sum up" the products.[2]

Example 7. The BDDs for the component functions of the half adder reviewed in Examples 5 and 6 are shown on the left-hand side of Fig. 4.

Overall, there is a well-developed methodology for constructing the BDD representation of the component functions of f. These BDDs have then to be composed in a second step to obtain the BDD of the characteristic function χ_f. Since the outcomes of χ_f essentially describe the entries of the desired function matrix, the resulting BDD can eventually be transformed to a QMDD. In the following, these steps are described in more detail.

3.2   Generating the BDD of the Characteristic Function

In order to derive the BDD representing the characteristic function χ_f of a multi-output function $f \colon \mathbb{B}^n \to \mathbb{B}^m$, we first introduce new variables y_i for the primary outputs of f (referred to as *output variables* in the following). While the original (input) variables are used to encode the column index of the function

---

[2] Actually, there is a large body of research on how to derive BDD representations from various other, algebraic or netlist-based, representations of Boolean functions.

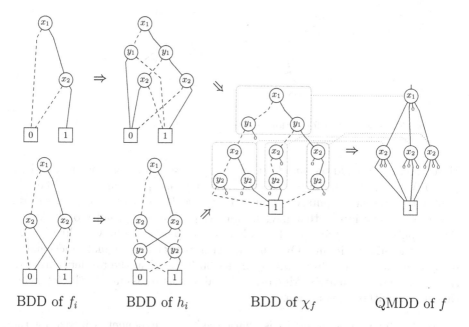

BDD of f_i BDD of h_i BDD of χ_f QMDD of f

Fig. 4. Construction of the QMDD for the half adder.

matrix, the output variables encode rows. Then, we construct the characteristic function for each output. More precisely, we construct the helper functions h_i given by

$$h_i(x_1, \ldots, x_n, y_i) = f_i(x_1, \ldots, x_n) \odot y_i,$$

where $\odot$ denotes the XNOR-operation. This logical operation—and, thus, the entire function h_i—evaluates to true if, and only if, both operands are equal, i.e. $f_i(x_1, \ldots, x_n) = y_i$. Consequently, the h_i-function can be interpreted as characteristic functions of the primary outputs of f.

Afterwards, the BDD of χ_f can be constructed by AND-ing the BDDs representing the h_i-functions as the following calculation shows:

$$h_1 \wedge h_2 \wedge \ldots \wedge h_m = 1$$
$$\Leftrightarrow \forall i \in \{1, \ldots, n\} : h_i = 1$$
$$\Leftrightarrow \forall i \in \{1, \ldots, n\}, (x_1, \ldots, x_n, y_1, \ldots, y_m) \in \mathbb{B}^{n+m} : f_i(x_1, \ldots, x_n) = y_i$$
$$\Leftrightarrow f(x_1, \ldots, x_n) = (y_1, \ldots, y_m)$$
$$\Leftrightarrow \chi_f(x_1, \ldots, x_n, y_1, \ldots, y_m) = 1$$

Remark 1. If $n > m$, i.e. if f has more primary inputs than outputs, we pad the function with zeros in order to obtain a Boolean function with the same number of inputs and outputs, such that the resulting function matrix is square.

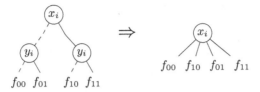

Fig. 5. General transformation rule from characteristic BDDs to QMDDs.

More precisely, we add $n - m$ additional constant outputs/component functions $f_j \equiv 0$. While these can, in principle, be added at any position, we add them in front of the original outputs/component functions. If, in contrast, $m > n$, we add $m - n$ additional inputs that have no impact on the functionality of f. Again, these inputs can, in principle, be added at any position, but we add them in front of the original inputs. Overall, this ensures that the original functionality is represented by the sub-matrix of dimension $2^m \times 2^n$ in the top-left corner of the square function matrix. Moreover, this allows us to assume in the following that $n = m$ without restriction.

As the BDD representing χ_f is guaranteed to be exponential in size for the variable order $x_1 \succ \ldots \succ x_n \succ y_1 \succ \ldots \succ y_m$ (at least for reversible functions), we enforce an interleaved variable order $x_1 \succ y_1 \succ x_2 \succ y_2 \succ \ldots \succ x_n \succ y_n$ when constructing the BDD for χ_f.

Example 8. Consider again the half adder example. The BDDs representing the helper functions $h_1 = f_1 \odot y_1$ and $h_2 = f_2 \odot y_2$ are computed using the BDD equivalent of the logical XNOR operation and are shown in Fig. 4 (next to the BDDs representing f_1 and f_2). By AND-ing these BDDs, we obtain the BDD representing χ_f which is shown in the center of Fig. 4. In this BDD, all edges pointing to the zero-terminal are indicated by stubs for the sake of a better readability and to emphasize the similarity to the targeted QMDD.

3.3   Transforming the BDD into a QMDD

With a BDD in interleaved variable order representing χ_f, the matrix partitioning employed by QMDDs is already laid out implicitly. In fact, corresponding bits of the column and row indices are represented by different, but adjacent variables (x_i and y_i), while QMDDs combine these in a single variable. Consequently, the BDD of χ_f can be transformed into the QMDD for f using the general transformation rule shown in Fig. 5. However, there are two special cases that have to be treated separately:

– If an input variable x_i is skipped (more precisely: a vertex labeled by y_i is the child of a vertex not labeled by x_i), this implies the x_i vertex would be redundant, i.e. high and low edge point to the same vertex. This case can easily be handled by setting $f_{00} = f_{10} = f_0$ or $f_{01} = f_{11} = f_1$, respectively,

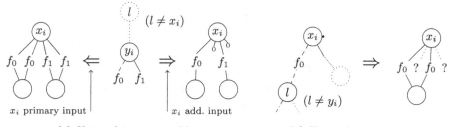

(a) Skipped input variables   (b) Skipped output variables

Fig. 6. Handling skipped variables.

as illustrated on the left-hand side of Fig. 6a. If, however, x_i is not an original input of the function, but has been introduced later in order obtain the same number of in- and outputs, we set $f_{10} = f_{11} = 0$ instead to ensure that the original functionality occurs only once in the final function matrix (as illustrated on the right-hand side of Fig. 6a).

– If an output variable level y_i is skipped (more precisely: the high or low edge of a vertex labeled by x_i point to a vertex labeled by $l \neq y_i$), this implies the skipped y_i vertex would be redundant (both children would be the same). This case can easily be handled by setting $f_{00} = f_{01} = f_0$ or $f_{10} = f_{11} = f_1$, respectively, before applying the general transformation rule. For instance, the case of a skipped variable on the low edge is illustrated in Fig. 6b.

Example 9. Consider again the characteristic BDD shown in the center of Fig. 4. Here, the single x_1 vertex and the leftmost x_2 vertex can be transformed to their QMDD equivalent by applying the general transformation rule. For the remaining x_2 vertices, the methodology for skipped y_2 output variables is to be applied. Overall, this yields the QMDD shown on the right-hand side of Fig. 4.

Overall, following this procedure yields a QMDD representing the function matrix (in case of a reversible function, a permutation matrix) of any Boolean function f originally provided in terms of an SOP.

4   Constructing QMDDs for Quantum Functionality

In this section, we describe how to efficiently construct a QMDD representing desired quantum functionality. General quantum functionality is usually either given (a) in terms of an abstract *quantum algorithm* which describes a series of computational steps or complex quantum operations (modules) to be conducted or (b) in terms of a *quantum circuit* consisting of a cascade of elementary quantum operations (so-called *quantum gates*) that form a more complex operation.

Example 10. Consider the 3-qubit quantum circuit shown in Fig. 7a. Horizontal lines represent qubits. Quantum gates, i.e. $\boxed{H}$ (a Hadamard operation) and

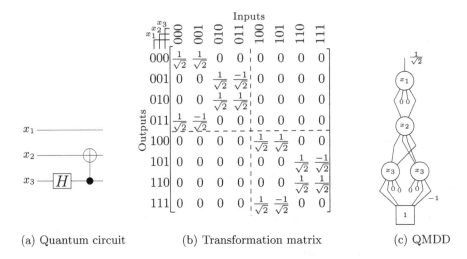

(a) Quantum circuit   (b) Transformation matrix   (c) QMDD

Fig. 7. Different representations of quantum functionality.

$\bullet\oplus$ (a controlled NOT, $CNOT$), are applied successively from left to right. The corresponding transformation matrix is depicted in Fig. 7b. As for any matrix of a linear transformation, columns denote input basis vectors and rows denote output basis vectors. In the quantum domain, the basis vectors are called *basis states* and are commonly denoted as $|x_1 x_2 x_3\rangle$ using the so-called *ket-notation*. For instance, the basis state $|001\rangle$ is mapped to the linear combination (*superposition*) $\frac{1}{\sqrt{2}}|000\rangle - \frac{1}{\sqrt{2}}|011\rangle$. Note that there is a strong relationship between the partitioning of the matrix with respect to a variable x_j and the input/output mapping of the corresponding qubit. More precisely, the top-left sub-matrix of a partitioning represents the mapping $|0\rangle \mapsto |0\rangle$, the top-right sub-matrix represents the mapping $|1\rangle \mapsto |0\rangle$, and so on. This transfers to the corresponding QMDD vertices such that the outgoing edges represent the mappings $|0\rangle \mapsto |0\rangle$, $|1\rangle \mapsto |0\rangle$, $|0\rangle \mapsto |1\rangle$, and $|1\rangle \mapsto |1\rangle$ from left to right and are denoted by $e_{00}, e_{10}, e_{01}, e_{11}$ in the following. Finally, the corresponding QMDD is depicted in Fig. 7c.

For quantum algorithms as well as circuits, the representation/description of the overall functionality is successively built from functional descriptions/representations of the individual parts (modules or gates). More precisely, for a cascade of modules/gates $g_1 g_2 \ldots g_l$ where the transformation for module/gate g_i is defined by matrix $\mathbf{M}_i$, the transformation for the complete algorithm/circuit is given by the direct matrix product $\mathbf{M}_l \cdot \mathbf{M}_{l-1} \cdot \ldots \cdot \mathbf{M}_1$. Note that the order of the matrices has to be reversed to achieve the correct order of applying the modules/gates (first g_1, then g_2, etc.). To construct this matrix product, the QMDDs for the single modules/gates simply have to be multiplied using the QMDD-based algorithm for matrix multiplication. Consequently, for the remainder of this section we focus on how the QMDD representations for elementary quantum gates can be constructed efficiently.

A gate g is specified by the 2×2 base transition matrix $\mathbf{B}$, the target qubit x_t and a possible empty set of control qubits $C \subset \{x_1, \ldots, x_n\}$ (with $x_t \notin C$) together with a map $\alpha \colon C \to \{|0\rangle, |1\rangle\}$ which describes the activating values, i.e. qubit basis states, of each control qubit.

Example 11. The base transition matrix of the first gate of the quantum circuit in Fig. 7a (Hadamard gate) is given by $\mathbf{H} = \frac{1}{\sqrt{2}}\begin{pmatrix} 1 & 1 \\ 1 & -1 \end{pmatrix}$. This gate has a target x_3 and no controls, i.e. $C = \emptyset$. The second gate of the circuit is a controlled NOT gate with the base transition matrix $\mathbf{X} = \begin{pmatrix} 0 & 1 \\ 1 & 0 \end{pmatrix}$, a target x_2, and one positive control, i.e. $C = \{x_3\}$ with $\alpha(x_3) = |1\rangle$. This gate effectively swaps the basis states $|0\rangle$ and $|1\rangle$ on qubit x_2 if, and only if, qubit x_3 is in the $|1\rangle$-state.

The QMDD for a quantum gate is built variable by variable (qubit by qubit) in a bottom-up fashion from the terminal to the root vertex. To this end, we assume the variable order $x_1 \succ x_2 \succ \ldots \succ x_n$ from the root vertex towards the terminal vertex. In order to indicate which set of variables has been processed so far, we use the notation $\mathbf{M}_{\{x_k, \ldots, x_n\}}$. Moreover, for the sake of an easier reference, we term those edges of a QMDD vertex *diagonal* that correspond to a $|i\rangle \to |i\rangle$ mapping ($i = 0, 1$), i.e. e_{00} and e_{11}, and the remaining edges *off-diagonal*.

Although it is possible to construct the QMDD for the gate in a single run as roughly sketched in [8], for a better understanding we follow [13] and construct two QMDDs representing the cases that the gate is active (all control qubits are in their activating state) or inactive (at least one control qubit is not).[3] By adding these QMDDs, the actual QMDD for the gate results.

Case "gate is active", i.e. the base transition $\mathbf{B}$ is performed on qubit x_t if, and only if, all controls are in their activating state. All other qubits preserve their original state.

Consequently, the QMDD for the active case contains all (non-zero) paths of the final QMDD for which all decision variables (qubits) except for the target have an activating assignment.

In order to have a valid starting point, we begin at the terminal level with an edge pointing to the terminal vertex with weight 1, i.e. $\mathbf{M}_\emptyset = [1]_{1 \times 1}$.[4] Afterwards, the qubits are processed in a bottom-up fashion. If the current qubit x_c

- is neither a control nor the target, i.e. $x_c \neq x_t, x_c \notin C$, the gate is active regardless of the qubit's state. Consequently, at the matrix level the result is $\mathrm{id}_{2 \times 2} \otimes \mathbf{M}_{\{x_{c+1}, \ldots, x_n\}}$ which corresponds to a QMDD vertex labeled x_c where all diagonal edges point to the existing QMDD and all remaining edges are 0-edges.

---

[3] Without loss of generality, we consider only basis states of the underlying quantum system, i.e. each qubit is assumed to be in one of its basis states. Due to the linearity of quantum operations, these are sufficient to construct the corresponding transformation matrix which yields the correct behaviour also for the case of superposed input states.

[4] The appropriate weights of the base transition will be incorporated later.

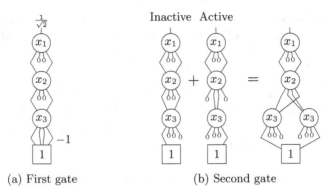

Fig. 8. QMDD representations for the gates from the quantum circuit in Fig. 7a.

- is a control, i.e. $x_c \in C$, the gate is only active for one control value $|i\rangle = \alpha(x_c)$. Consequently, the result is a vertex labeled x_c with only 0-edges except from the edge $|i\rangle \rightarrow |i\rangle$ which points to the existing QMDD.
- is the target, i.e. $x_c = x_t$, the base transition is performed. Consequently, the result is $\mathbf{B} \otimes \mathbf{M}_{\{x_{c+1},...,x_n\}}$, i.e. a vertex labeled x_t with all edges pointing to the existing QMDD with the corresponding edge weight taken from the base transition matrix $\mathbf{B}$ (if a weight is zero, the corresponding edge is a 0-edge directly pointing to the terminal).

During this construction, the QMDD is normalized as described in Example 4.

Example 12. Consider the QMDD in Fig. 8a which represents the first gate of the quantum circuit shown in Fig. 7a. As this gate does not have any controls, it is always active and, thus, it suffices to build the QMDD representing the active part. We start with an edge to the terminal vertex with weight 1. As the bottom-most qubit is already the target qubit, all edges of the x_3-vertex point directly to this terminal with the appropriate weight of the Hadamard transformation matrix $\mathbf{H} = \frac{1}{\sqrt{2}} \left(\begin{smallmatrix} 1 & 1 \\ 1 & -1 \end{smallmatrix} \right)$. Note that normalization will propagate the common multiplier $\frac{1}{\sqrt{2}}$ of this matrix to the root edge. The remaining qubits are neither control nor target. Thus, vertices representing an identity mapping of these qubits are inserted.

The QMDD for the inactive case is constructed similarly.

Case "gate is inactive", i.e. the identity transition is performed on qubit x_t since at least one control is not in its activating state. All qubits preserve their original state, i.e. none but diagonal edges are populated at all.

Consequently, the QMDD for the inactive case contains all (non-zero) paths of the final QMDD for which at least one decision variable (qubit) does not have an activating assignment.

However, when constructing the QMDD in a bottom-up fashion, we always use the hypothesis that all controls above the current qubit are in their activating states and at least one control below is not.

To make sure that this hypothesis gives the correct result even for the bottom-most control (for which no inactive control may exist below), we start at the terminal level with an edge pointing to the terminal vertex with weight 0, i.e. $\mathbf{M}_\emptyset = [0]_{1\times1}$. This ensures that all edges corresponding to the activating value of this bottom-most control are 0-edges.

The remaining qubits are processed as follows. If the current qubit x_c

- is neither a control nor the target, i.e. $x_c \neq x_t, x_c \notin C$, the gate is inactive regardless of the qubit's state. Consequently, at the matrix level the result is $\mathrm{id}_{2\times2} \otimes \mathbf{M}_{\{x_{c+1},...,x_n\}}$ which corresponds to a QMDD vertex labeled x_c where all diagonal edges point to the existing QMDD and all remaining edges are 0-edges.
- is a control, i.e. $x_c \in C$, the gate is definitely inactive for all but one control value $|i\rangle = \alpha(x_c)$. For the latter, the activity of the gate depends on the remaining qubits. Consequently, the result is a vertex with all diagonal edges pointing to the k-fold tensor product $\mathrm{id}_{2\times2}^{\otimes k}$ (nothing happens to all k qubits below the current one) except from the edge $|i\rangle \rightarrow |i\rangle$. The latter handles the case that the qubit is in its activating state and is pointing to the existing QMDD $\mathbf{M}_{\{x_{c+1},...,x_n\}}$.[5] All off-diagonal edges are 0-edges.
- is the target, i.e. $x_c = x_t$, the identity transformation is performed on the target. Consequently, the result is $\mathrm{id}_{2\times2} \otimes \mathbf{M}_{\{x_{c+1},...,x_n\}}$ like in the unconnected case.

Example 13. The QMDDs for the circuit's second gate is shown in Fig. 8b.

For the inactive part, we start with a 0-edge. For the control on x_3, we construct a vertex which uses this 0-edge as e_{11} and for which the other diagonal edge e_{00} represents the identity $\mathrm{id}_{2\times2}^{\otimes0} = [1]_{1\times1}$, i.e. it points to the terminal vertex with weight 1. As x_3 is the only control, we simply add vertices representing an identity mapping for the remaining qubits.

For the active part, we start with an edge to the terminal vertex which becomes the e_{11} edge of the x_3-vertex, as the activating state of x_3 is $|1\rangle$. For the target qubit x_2 with the base transition matrix $\mathbf{X} = \left(\begin{smallmatrix} 0 & 1 \\ 1 & 0 \end{smallmatrix}\right)$, an x_2-vertex is added. For this vertex, both off-diagonal edges point to the x_3-vertex constructed before (with weight 1 as the corresponding entry in $\mathbf{X}$ is 1) and both diagonal edges are 0-edges (as the corresponding entry in $\mathbf{X}$ is 0). Last, but not least, for the unconnected qubit x_1 a vertex representing its identity mapping is added. Finally, by adding the QMDDs for the inactive and active part, we obtain the actual QMDD for the CNOT gate.

Overall, the resulting QMDDs for the active as well as the inactive part of the gate are linear in the number of variables—regardless of the complexity of the gate under consideration. Both QMDDs can be constructed in parallel while

---

[5] If there is no further control below the current qubit, the gate inactivity is ensured by choosing a 0-edge as the initial QMDD.

iterating through the variables in a bottom-up fashion. In addition, they describe disjoint parts of the gate matrix, while they are padded with zeros outside of that particular part. Consequently, their sum can be computed in linear time and will also be linear in size. In fact, there are only trivial additions where at least one of the summands is a 0-matrix and, as already recognized in [8], the addition could be saved entirely, such that the whole construction could be performed in a single pass from the terminal to the root vertex with no backtracking or recursion. Either way, QMDD representations for single gates can be computed very efficiently and the potentially rather expensive part of constructing a QMDD representation for quantum algorithms or quantum circuits (as well as any other quantum logic representation) is given by the (QMDD-based) matrix multiplication that is required to concatenate the representations of single modules/gates.

5   Feasibility Study

In this section, we demonstrate the applicability of the discussed methods for QMDD construction. To this end, we implemented them in C++ on top of the QMDD package (provided together with [13]) and the BDD package *CUDD* [18]. As benchmarks for the construction of QMDDs representing Boolean functions, we considered functions from *RevLib* [19]. For quantum benchmarks, we considered quantum realizations of the Boolean functions from RevLib, realizations of the Quantum Fourier Transformation and Grover's search algorithm (cf. [9]), implementations of error-correcting codes (taken from [7]) as well as randomly generated Clifford group circuits. All experiments have been conducted on a 4 GHz processor with 32 GB of memory running Linux 4.4.

Table 1a lists the results for the QMDD construction for Boolean functions (reversible as well as non-reversible ones). The first three columns list the name of the benchmark as well as the number of primary inputs and primary outputs (denoted by PI and PO, respectively). Note that the number of variables of the resulting QMDD is accordingly given by $n = \max(PI, PO)$. The remaining two columns of Table 1a list the run-time (in CPU seconds) required for constructing the QMDD and the size of the resulting QMDD (i.e. its number of vertices).

The numbers show that the QMDDs construction could either be conducted in negligible run-time (i.e. in less than a second) or fails by running into a timeout of 10 000 s (denoted by TO). However, the latter case was only observed for two benchmarks with more than 100 QMDD variables. The limiting factor in these cases was the construction of the characteristic function, since the variables in the BDD have to adhere to a certain order. More precisely, the variables representing primary inputs and primary outputs are interleaved – allowing that the transformation of the characteristic function into a QMDD can be conducted as described in Sect. 3.3. While certainly a limitation, this is in line with the characteristic matrix partitioning of QMDDs, i.e. QMDDs eventually employ a similar order (only with the difference that corresponding PIs and POs are jointly considered in a single vertex). That is, the QMDD data-structure itself is the limiting factor for these two functions; not the proposed construction method.

Table 1. Feasibility study

(a) Boolean functions

Benchmark	PI	PO	t	size
5xp1_90	7	10	0.10	342
sao2_199	10	4	0.11	138
urf3_75	10	10	0.15	1001
urf4_89	11	11	0.22	2774
add6_92	12	7	0.11	309
alu1_94	12	8	0.12	189
apla_107	10	12	0.12	288
cycle10_2_61	12	12	0.13	66
sqr6_204	6	12	0.11	112
0410184_85	14	14	0.26	38
alu4_98	14	8	0.16	1471
cu_141	14	11	0.10	165
misex3c_181	14	14	0.13	522
table3_209	14	14	0.12	934
tial_214	14	8	0.14	1503
ham15_30	15	15	0.50	2021
in0_162	15	11	0.10	492
urf6_77	15	15	0.53	2312
cmb_134	16	4	0.11	86
decod_137	5	16	0.12	111
apex4_103	9	19	0.16	1189
cm151a_129	19	9	0.11	141
mux_185	21	1	0.15	145
cordic_138	23	2	0.11	132
bw_116	5	28	0.11	432
frg1_160	28	3	0.12	417
apex2_101	39	3	0.22	1797
pdc_191	16	40	0.29	1800
seq_201	41	35	0.35	1881
spla_202	16	46	0.25	1538
ex5p_154	8	63	0.20	1139
e64_149	65	65	0.22	1161
cps_140	24	109	0.92	3763
apex5_104	117	88	TO	–
frg2_161	143	139	TO	–

(b) Quantum functionality

Benchmark	n	|G|	t	size
QFT-3	3	9	0.11	21
QFT-4	4	16	0.10	85
QFT-5	5	21	0.11	341
QFT-6	6	30	0.11	1365
7-qubit-code	7	18	0.11	29
Grover-3	7	83	0.10	209
hwb6_56	7	1153	0.15	87
QFT-7	7	37	0.11	5461
5-qubit-code	9	24	0.11	83
9-qubit-code-A	9	11	0.11	25
Grover-4	9	106	0.12	1075
rd73_252	10	660	0.18	42
9symml_195	11	2945	0.49	53
dc1_221	11	290	0.11	64
Grover-5	11	131	0.18	2816
cycle10_2_110	12	722	0.13	66
adr4_197	13	426	0.18	174
dist_223	13	3544	2.42	284
radd_250	13	327	0.16	151
co14_215	15	1290	0.29	65
dc2_222	15	1218	0.67	360
ham15_107	15	1101	0.25	4521
Clifford-15	15	100	1.43	22697
5xp1_194	17	931	0.36	719
9-qubit-code-B	17	40	0.11	1075
Clifford-18	18	100	0.84	21609
Clifford-20	20	100	10.21	76473
decod_217	21	845	0.15	187
pcler8_248	21	289	0.26	1083
apla_203	22	2051	1.43	421
cu_219	25	752	1.28	525
Clifford-25	25	100	284.16	580992
cm151a_211	28	639	45.13	6408
cm163a_213	29	575	3.44	1205
add64_184	193	576	0.14	701

Table 1b shows the obtained results for constructing QMDDs for quantum computations. The first three columns of the table list the name of the benchmarks, the number of qubits n as well as the number of gates of the quantum circuit $|G|$. The remaining two columns list the run-time required to construct the QMDD and its number of vertices. Here, the numbers show that a QMDD can be constructed for quantum circuits composed of more than one thousand gates quite efficiently. Indeed, we observe a run-time of less than one second for most cases. However, there are also a few benchmarks for which the time to construct the QMDD takes longer (e.g. *Clifford-20* or *Clifford-25*), but these are exactly the cases where the size of the resulting QMDD is large.

6   Conclusions

In this work, we considered how to efficiently construct a QMDD representation for Boolean functions, reversible and non-reversible ones, as well as quantum functionality. These representations are essential for the efficiency of various approaches in reversible/quantum logic design, but are usually not the originally provided description means. For the Boolean case, we developed a methodology to obtain and transform the BDD of the characteristic function which is structurally already very similar to the desired QMDD. For the quantum case, we focused on the construction of QMDD representations for elementary quantum gates from which the representation of the entire circuit or algorithm can be obtained using (QMDD-based) matrix multiplication. The feasibility of the proposed methods has been confirmed on several examples. In fact, the obtained results showed that the construction can be conducted in negligible run-time when the characteristic matrix partitioning of QMDDs allows for an efficient representation. Overall, this work closes an important gap for several design solutions based on QMDDs e.g. for embedding, synthesis, or verification.

Acknowledgements. This work has partially been supported by the European Union through the COST Action IC1405.

References

1. Athas, W., Svensson, L.: Reversible logic issues in adiabatic CMOS. In: Proceedings of the Workshop on Physics and Computation, PhysComp 1994, pp. 111–118 (1994)
2. Berut, A., Arakelyan, A., Petrosyan, A., Ciliberto, S., Dillenschneider, R., Lutz, E.: Experimental verification of Landauer's principle linking information and thermodynamics. Nature **483**, 187–189 (2012)
3. Bryant, R.E.: Graph-based algorithms for Boolean function manipulation. IEEE Trans. Comput. **35**(8), 677–691 (1986)
4. Grover, L.K.: A fast quantum mechanical algorithm for database search. In: Theory of Computing, pp. 212–219 (1996)
5. Houri, S., Valentian, A., Fanet, H.: Comparing CMOS-based and NEMS-based adiabatic logic circuits. In: Conference on Reversible Computation, pp. 36–45 (2013)
6. Merkle, R.C.: Reversible electronic logic using switches. Nanotechnology **4**(1), 21 (1993)
7. Mermin, N.D.: Quantum Computer Science: An Introduction. Cambridge University Press, New York (2007)
8. Miller, D.M., Thornton, M.A.: QMDD: a decision diagram structure for reversible and quantum circuits. In: International Symposium on Multi-Valued Logic, p. 6 (2006)
9. Nielsen, M., Chuang, I.: Quantum Computation and Quantum Information. Cambridge University Press, New York (2000)
10. Niemann, P., Wille, R., Drechsler, R.: On the "Q" in QMDDs: efficient representation of quantum functionality in the QMDD data-structure. In: Conference on Reversible Computation, pp. 125–140 (2013)

11. Niemann, P., Wille, R., Drechsler, R.: Efficient synthesis of quantum circuits implementing Clifford group operations. In: ASP Design Automation Conference, pp. 483–488 (2014)
12. Niemann, P., Wille, R., Drechsler, R.: Equivalence checking in multi-level quantum systems. In: Conference on Reversible Computation, pp. 201–215 (2014)
13. Niemann, P., Wille, R., Miller, D.M., Thornton, M.A., Drechsler, R.: QMDDs: efficient quantum function representation and manipulation. IEEE Trans. CAD **35**(1), 86–99 (2016)
14. Ren, J., Semenov, V., Polyakov, Y., Averin, D., Tsai, J.S.: Progress towards reversible computing with nSQUID arrays. IEEE Trans. Appl. Supercond. **19**(3), 961–967 (2009)
15. Shor, P.W.: Algorithms for quantum computation: discrete logarithms and factoring. In: Foundations of Computer Science, pp. 124–134 (1994)
16. Soeken, M., Wille, R., Hilken, C., Przigoda, N., Drechsler, R.: Synthesis of reversible circuits with minimal lines for large functions. In: ASP Design Automation Conference, pp. 85–92 (2012)
17. Soeken, M., Wille, R., Keszocze, O., Miller, D.M., Drechsler, R.: Embedding of large Boolean functions for reversible logic. J. Emerg. Technol. Comput. Syst. **12**(4), 41:1–41:26 (2015)
18. Somenzi, F.: Efficient manipulation of decision diagrams. Softw. Tools Technol. Transf. **3**(2), 171–181 (2001)
19. Wille, R., Große, D., Teuber, L., Dueck, G.W., Drechsler, R.: RevLib: an online resource for reversible functions and reversible circuits. In: International Symposium on Multi-Valued Logic, pp. 220–225 (2008). RevLib is available at http://www.revlib.org
20. Zulehner, A., Wille, R.: Make it reversible: efficient embedding of non-reversible functions. In: Design, Automation and Test in Europe, pp. 458–463 (2017)

Improving Synthesis of Reversible Circuits: Exploiting Redundancies in Paths and Nodes of QMDDs

Alwin Zulehner[(⊠)] and Robert Wille

Institute for Integrated Circuits, Johannes Kepler University Linz, Linz, Austria
{alwin.zulehner,robert.wille}@jku.at

Abstract. In recent years, reversible circuits have become an established emerging technology through their variety of applications. Since these circuits employ a completely different structure from conventional circuitry, dedicated functional synthesis algorithms have been proposed. Although scalability has been achieved by using approaches based on decision diagrams, the resulting circuits employ a significant complexity measured in terms of quantum cost. In this paper, we aim for a reduction of this complexity. To this end, we review QMDD-based synthesis. Based on that, we propose optimizations that allow for a substantial reduction of the quantum costs by jointly considering paths and nodes in the decision diagram that employ a certain redundancy. In fact, in our experimental evaluation, we observe substantial improvements of up to three orders of magnitudes in terms of runtime and up to six orders of magnitudes (a factor of one million) in terms of quantum cost.

1 Introduction

In the recent years, reversible circuits – circuits that additionally allow to compute the inputs from the outputs – have become an established field in research due to their characteristics regarding low power design (based on the seminal work of Landauer [5] and Bennett [3]) and their application in quantum computations [10] – a new computation paradigm that allows for solving certain tasks substantially faster. Most recently, reversible circuits also found their application in the design of on-chip interconnects [18,20], encoders [21], and verification [1].

Reversible circuits employ a completely different structure compared to conventional circuits, because not only the outputs are determined by the inputs, but also vice versa. This leads to a structure where circuits consist of a set of circuit lines that are passed through a cascade of reversible gates and, hence, disallow direct feedback and fanout. Consequently, dedicated synthesis approaches that establish the desired unique mapping from inputs to outputs are required. Although a variety of synthesis approaches exist, functional synthesis approaches are of special interest, since they result in a circuit where the number of circuit lines is minimal. Over the years, several such synthesis approaches have been proposed, ranging from exact ones (i.e. the number of gates is minimal) [4] to

© Springer International Publishing AG 2017
I. Phillips and H. Rahaman (Eds.): RC 2017, LNCS 10301, pp. 232–247, 2017.
DOI: 10.1007/978-3-319-59936-6_18

heuristic ones based on truth tables [6,12]. However, since their underlying data structure is exponential they suffer from limited scalability. Therefore, methods based on a more compact representation of the function to be synthesized such as decision diagrams [15,16] or Boolean satisfiability [13] have been proposed. They, in contrast, yield rather costly circuits.

In this paper, we focus on QMDD-based synthesis [16], one of the scalable synthesis approaches listed above. This synthesis approach is based on *Quantum Multiple-Valued Decision Diagrams* (QMDDs [7,11]), a decision diagram introduced for the compact representation of reversible and quantum computations. The main premise of QMDD-based synthesis is to employ reversible gates which transform each QMDD node to the identity. By doing that for all nodes of a QMDD (representing the function to be synthesized) in a breadth first fashion, a circuit realizing the given function results. However, during this process often equal cases are considered iteratively; for each, the same cascade of gates are applied – leading to a large number of redundant steps and, hence, gates.

In this work, we introduce a new QMDD-based synthesis approach which aims to consider those redundant cases only once. To this end, a scheme is employed which considers all paths to the currently considered node together and performs logic minimization to reduce their number. Furthermore, nodes which can be transformed to the identity with the same cascade of gates are considered jointly. This allows for a substantial reduction of gates. Experimental evaluations show that the proposed scheme improves the current state of the art QMDD-based synthesis by several orders of magnitudes in terms of runtime as well as in terms of quantum cost (an abstract measure of the complexity of the resulting circuit).

This paper is structured as follows. In Sect. 2, we briefly review reversible functions and their representation as well as reversible circuits. Based on that, we review QMDD-based synthesis in Sect. 3 and discuss the proposed optimizations in Sect. 4. In Sect. 5, we discuss the improvement that can be achieved by the proposed optimization, whereas Sect. 6 experimentally confirms these improvements. Section 7 concludes the paper.

2   Background

In this section we briefly recapitulate reversible functions including their efficient representation as well as reversible circuits.

2.1   Reversible Functions

A Boolean function is reversible if the mapping from inputs to outputs establishes a bijection, i.e. the inputs can also be computed from the outputs.

Definition 1. *A Boolean function $f : \mathbb{B}^m \to \mathbb{B}^n$ is reversible iff $n = m$ and there exists a unique mapping from inputs to outputs and vice versa.*

Besides truth tables, reversible functions can also be represented by means of a permutation matrix.

Definition 2. *Consider a reversible Boolean function* $f : \mathbb{B}^n \to \mathbb{B}^n$. *Then, the permutation matrix of* f *is a* $2^n \times 2^n$ *matrix with entries* $m_{i,j}$, $0 \le i, j < 2^n$ *such that*

$$m_{i,j} = \begin{cases} 1 & if\ f(j) = i \\ 0 & otherwise. \end{cases}$$

A 1-entry in the permutation matrix means that an input (column) is mapped to an output (row) by f. All other entries of the permutation matrix are zero. Since a permutation represents a unique mapping (i.e. a reversible function), it contains exactly one 1-entry in each column and in each row.

Example 1. Consider the reversible function depicted in Fig. 1a. The function is reversible because the number of inputs is equal to the number of outputs and each output pattern occurs exactly once. Consequently, the input can be uniquely determined having the output only. The permutation matrix of this reversible function is shown in Fig. 1b. Here, reversibility can easily be seen since each column as well as each row contains exactly one 1-entry.

x_1 x_2 x_3	x_1' x_2' x_3'
0 0 0	0 1 0
0 0 1	0 1 1
0 1 0	1 0 0
0 1 1	0 0 1
1 0 0	1 1 0
1 0 1	1 0 1
1 1 0	0 0 0
1 1 1	1 1 1

(a) Truth table

Inputs

Outputs	000	001	010	011	100	101	110	111
000	0	0	0	0	0	0	1	0
001	0	0	0	1	0	0	0	0
010	1	0	0	0	0	0	0	0
011	0	1	0	0	0	0	0	0
100	0	0	1	0	0	0	0	0
101	0	0	0	0	0	1	0	0
110	0	0	0	0	1	0	0	0
111	0	0	0	0	0	0	0	1

(b) Permutation matrix

Fig. 1. Representation of reversible functions

2.2   Quantum Multiple-Valued Decision Diagrams (QMDDs)

The description means for reversible functions discussed in the previous section is rather limited. Since the size of truth tables as well as the size of permutation matrices grows exponentially with the number of variables, a more scalable representation is desirable in order to represent large functions. However, permutation matrices can be represented more compactly – and with non-exponential space in many relevant cases – using so called *Quantum Multiple-Valued Decision*

Diagrams (QMDDs [7,11]). QMDDs were initially introduced to represent the unitary matrices of quantum computations. Since quantum computations are reversible and the matrices are also of dimension $2^n \times 2^n$, QMDDs are perfectly suited for representing permutation matrices. For simplicity, we discuss only those aspects of QMDDs that are relevant for this paper and omit all quantum related issues.

The main idea of QMDDs is a recursive decomposition of a permutation matrix M over its variables. A variable x_i represents a mapping from the ith input to the ith output of the function. There exist four possible mappings of a variable, since an input may be mapped from 0 to 0, from 0 to 1, from 1 to 0, or from 1 to 1. Considering the most significant variable x_1 of the permutation matrix, these four different mappings exactly describe the four quadrants of the matrix, which we denote $M_{0 \to 0}$, $M_{1 \to 0}$, $M_{0 \to 1}$, and $M_{1 \to 1}$. This decomposition can be represented by a decision diagram node labeled x_1 with four outgoing edges, describing exactly those quadrants $M_{0 \to 0}$, $M_{1 \to 0}$, $M_{0 \to 1}$, and $M_{1 \to 1}$ from left to right.

This decomposition is recursively applied until a single entry is reached. Such an entry is then represented by a terminal. The compactness of QMDDs results – as for other types of decision diagrams – from sharing equal nodes (and thus representing equal sub-matrices). For simpler graphical visualization, we represent 0-matrices (i.e. matrices containing 0-entries only) with a 0-stub, independent of their dimension.

Example 2. Consider again the permutation matrix depicted in Fig. 1b. The decomposition over its variables x_1, x_2, and x_3 yields the QMDD shown in Fig. 2. Note that the path highlighted in bold traverses the third edge of the node labeled x_1, the second edge of the node labeled x_2 and the first edge of the node labeled x_3. Consequently, this path describes a mapping of variable x_1 from 0 to 1, a mapping of variable x_2 from 1 to 0, and a mapping of variable x_3 from 0 to 0, i.e. a mapping from input $x_1 x_2 x_3 = 010$ to output $x_1 x_2 x_3 = 100$.

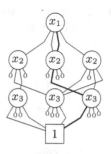

Fig. 2. QMDD of the permutation matrix shown in Fig. 1b

For a formal definition of QMDDs, as well as manipulation algorithms such as matrix multiplication we refer to [11].

2.3   Reversible Circuits

The structure of reversible circuits is completely different to classical circuitry, because fanout and feedback are not directly allowed. A reversible circuit rather consists of a set of circuit lines (one for each variable of the realized reversible function) which are passed through a cascade of reversible gates. The values of the circuit lines may be changed in a reversible fashion by these gate or passed through unaltered. In this paper, we focus on Toffoli gates – a reversible gate that has been proven to be universal (i.e. all reversible functions can be realized using Toffoli gates only).

Definition 3. *Consider a set* $X = \{x_1, x_2, \ldots, x_n\}$ *of* n *circuit lines and a sequence* $G = g_1, g_2, \ldots, g_k$ *of* k *reversible gates. Then, the pair* $C = (X, G)$ *describes a reversible circuit. A Toffoli gate* $g_i = TOF(C_i, t_i)$ *consists of a set* $C_i \subseteq \{x_i^- | x_i \in X\} \cup \{x_i^+ | x_i \in X\}$ *of negative and positive control lines, and a target line* t_i. *The Boolean value of the target line is inverted iff the Boolean value of all positive and negative control lines is 1 and 0, respectively. All circuit lines except the target line are passed unaltered through the gate.*

Toffoli gates as defined above are self-inverse, i.e. applying a Toffoli gate twice results in the identity. For graphical visualization we use the symbols ●, ○, and ⊕ to represent a positive control line, a negative control line, and a target line, respectively.

Example 3. Consider the reversible circuit shown in Fig. 3. The circuit is composed of three Toffoli gates and is labeled with the intermediate values resulting when the input lines are assigned $x_1 x_2 x_3 = 010$. The first gate $g_1 = TOF(\{x_1^-, x_2^+\}, x_3)$ inverts the value of target line x_3, because the negative control line x_1 is assigned 0 and the positive control line x_2 is assigned 1. Similarly, the second gate $g_2 = TOF(\{x_3^+\}, x_1)$ is activated, because the value of circuit line x_3 is now 1. Consequently, the value of target line x_1 is changed to 1. The last gate $g_3 = TOF(\{x_2^+, x_3^-\}, x_1)$ does not change the value of target line x_1, because the negative control line x_3 is assigned 1. Therefore, all three circuit lines are passed through the gate unaltered in this case. Eventually, the circuit maps input $x_1 x_2 x_3 = 010$ to output $x_1' x_2' x_3' = 111$.

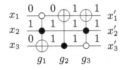

Fig. 3. Reversible circuit

The complexity of reversible circuits is usually measured in terms of quantum cost. These cost result from mapping the circuit to specific libraries of quantum gates. Two commonly used libraries for determining the quantum cost of a reversible circuit are the *NCV* library [8] and the *Clifford+T* library [2]. Here, the quantum cost are determined by the overall number of gates (*NCV-cost*) or the length of the sequence of *T-gates* (and, therefore, denoted *T-depth*), respectively. As shown in Table 1, the *NCV-cost* as well as the *T-depth* of a Toffoli gate depends on the number of control lines. The quantum costs listed in Table 1 were determined using RevKit [14].

Table 1. Quantum cost of Toffoli gates

Control lines	*NCV-cost*	*T-depth*
1	1	0
2	5	3
3	20	12
4	40	24
5	60	36

Example 3 (continued). The *NCV-cost* and the *T-depth* of the circuit shown in Fig. 3 are 11 and 6, respectively.

3 QMDD-Based Synthesis

In this section, we review QMDD-based synthesis (originally proposed in [16]). As discussed in Sect. 1, QMDD-based synthesis is a functional synthesis approach which yields a circuit with the minimal number of circuit lines. The main idea behind the algorithm is described as follows.

Assume the function to be synthesized is described by a permutation matrix M. Then, due to reversibility its inverse M^{-1} exists, and their product $M \circ M^{-1} = I$ is the identity matrix. Consequently, if we find a cascade of reversible gates G that transforms M to the identity, we implicitly found a reversible circuit for M^{-1}. Reversing G yields a reversible circuit that realizes M (because the Toffoli gates are self-inverse). Therefore, an algorithm is required that transforms the QMDD representing M to the identity. Since the identity matrix only maps input 0 to output 0 and input 1 to output 1, the identity QMDD imposes the structure depicted in Fig. 4.

To obtain the desired identity QMDD, we traverse the QMDD in breadth-first manner and transform each node we encounter to the identity structure shown in Fig. 5 by applying Toffoli gates. To this end, the paths to the 1-terminal (called 1-paths in the following) through the second and third edge of the currently considered node have to be moved to the first and fourth edge, respectively. These 1-paths refer to the input of the encountered variables and therefore contain a negative literal $\overline{x}_j$ (positive literal x_j) whenever the first or third (second or fourth) edge of a node labeled x_j is traversed.

In the following, we denote the sets of 1-paths through the first, second, third and fourth edge of the currently considered node by P_1, P_2, P_3, and P_4,

Fig. 4. Identity QMDD with n variables

Fig. 5. Identity structure

respectively. Similarly, we refer to the sets of 0-paths (i.e. paths that terminate in a 0-stub) with $\overline{P}_1$, $\overline{P}_2$, $\overline{P}_3$, and $\overline{P}_4$. Since the QMDD represents a permutation matrix, each column and each row of the matrix contains exactly one 1-entry. Therefore, the number of 0-paths in $\overline{P}_1$ ($\overline{P}_4$) is equal to the number of 1-paths in P_2 (P_3), i.e. $|\overline{P}_1| = |P_2|$. Moreover, $\overline{P}_1 = P_3$ and $\overline{P}_4 = P_2$.

Example 4. Consider the QMDD shown in Fig. 2 and assume that the root node is currently considered. The sets of 1-paths are $P_1 = P_4 = \{\overline{x}_2\overline{x}_3, \overline{x}_2x_3, x_2x_3\}$ and $P_2 = P_3 = \{x_2\overline{x}_3\}$.

To obtain the identity structure for the currently considered node labeled x_i, we swap the 1-paths in P_2 with the 0-paths in $\overline{P}_1$. This inherently swaps the 1-paths in P_3 with the 0-paths in $\overline{P}_4$. Swapping paths can be accomplished by applying Toffoli gates, since applying a Toffoli gate $TOF(C, x_i)$ inverts the input of variable x_i for all paths that are represented by C.

Example 4 (continued). The path $p = x_2\overline{x}_3$ is contained in the set P_2 of 1-paths through the second edge as well as in the set $\overline{P}_1$ of 0-paths through the first edge. These two paths can be swapped by applying the Toffoli gate $TOF(\{x_2^+, x_3^-\}, x_1)$. This automatically swaps the 1-path in P_3 with the 0-path in $\overline{P}_4$. The resulting QMDD is depicted in Fig. 6.

For a more formal description of how the currently considered node can be transformed to the desired identity structure we refer to [16], because understanding the main idea of QMDD-based synthesis (the breadth-first traversal of the nodes) is sufficient for the purpose of this paper.

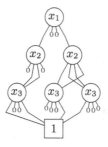

Fig. 6. QMDD resulting from transformation of the root node of the QMDD in Fig. 2

If the currently considered node is not the root node of the QMDD, we have to ensure that no other node is affected by the applied gates. To this end, we add further control lines that describe the path to the currently considered node to each Toffoli gate that is applied. More precisely, if the path to the currently considered node traverses the first edge of another node (representing a mapping from 0 to 0), we add a negative control line for the corresponding variable. Analogously, we add a positive control line for the corresponding variable if the path traverses the fourth edge of that node[1]. If there exist k such paths to the currently considered node, we have to replicate each Toffoli gate for each of those k paths in order to eventually transform the currently considered node to the identity structure.

Example 5. Consider the QMDD depicted in Fig. 7 and assume that the node highlighted in blue is currently considered. This node can be transformed to the desired identity structure by applying a Toffoli gate with target line x_3. Since there exist two paths to this node, namely $\overline{x}_1 x_2$ and $x_1 \overline{x}_2$, we have to apply two gates $TOF(\{x_1^- x_2^+\}, x_3)$ and $TOF(\{x_1^+ x_2^-\}, x_3)$ to eventually transform this node to the desired identity structure. The resulting circuit is shown in Fig. 8a.

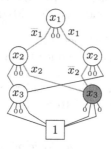

Fig. 7. Paths to the currently considered node

---

[1] A path to the currently considered node can only traverse the first or the fourth edge of other nodes, because they already establish the identity structure.

(a) Without optimization   (b) ESoP-minimized

Fig. 8. Gates required to transform the currently considered node from Fig. 7

4   Improving QMDD-Based Synthesis

In the synthesis scheme originally proposed in [16] and reviewed above, the overall number of paths to the nodes of a certain variable grows exponentially with the number of variables above. This leads to a substantial number of gates with (partially) redundant sets of control lines. This poses a significant drawback to QMDD-based synthesis since

– a significant number of gates is applied to transform each single node of the considered QMDD to the identity structure and
– the applied gates usually include rather large sets of control lines.

More precisely, the number of gates is heavily influenced by the number of paths to the currently considered node, because each gate that is required to transform the currently considered node to the identity has to be replicated for each path. Furthermore, the number of control lines of these Toffoli gates depend on the number of literals of the path from the root node to the currently considered node (because these literals are added to the Toffoli gates in form of control lines to ensure that no other node is affected). Since the overall costs of a reversible circuit depend on both, the total number of gates as well as the respective number of control lines, this makes circuits generated using QMDD-based synthesis rather expensive.

In order to address the problem, we propose two optimization techniques to reduce the cost of the circuits generated by QMDD-based synthesis, namely

1. a straightforward solution which performs logic minimization on the paths to the currently considered node to reduce the number of paths as well as the number of their literals and
2. a more elaborate approach which considers nodes that require the same sequence of Toffoli gates in order to get transformed to the identity structure jointly.

The straight forward solution utilizes logic minimization techniques to reduce the overall number of paths to the currently considered node as well as to reduce the overall number of literals in the paths. To this end, each path to the currently considered node is described as a product (conjunction) of its literals. Then, the exclusive sum (exclusive disjunction) of all these products is formed. The sum has to be exclusive, because applying a Toffoli gate an even times does not have any effect (since a Toffoli gate is self-inverse). The resulting *Exclusive Sum of Products* (ESoP) can be minimized using techniques such as proposed in [9]. Such a minimization reduces the overall number of products (and, hence, the number of paths and gate replications) as well as the number of literals in these products (and, hence, the number of control lines that have to be added to each gate).

Example 6. Consider again the QMDD depicted in Fig. 7 and assume that the node highlighted in blue is currently considered. There exist two paths to the currently considered node, namely $x_1\overline{x}_2$ and $\overline{x}_1x_2$. The ESoP of the two paths is then $x_1\overline{x}_2 \oplus \overline{x}_1x_2$. Minimizing this ESoP yields $x_1\overline{x}_2 \oplus \overline{x}_1x_2 = x_1 \oplus x_2$. Consequently, also the two paths x_1 and x_2 can be used to describe all paths to the currently considered node. The resulting gates are shown in Fig. 8b. Although the number of paths (and therefore the number of gates) did not change, the *NCV-cost* and *T-depth* are reduced from 10 to 2 and from 6 to 0, respectively.

The more elaborated optimization approach aims to further reduce the cost of the circuits considering more than one node simultaneously. The general idea is based on the key observation that sometimes different QMDD nodes require the same sequence of Toffoli gates in order to get transformed to the identity. As described in Sect. 3, this sequence of Toffoli gates depends on the set P_1 of 1-paths through the first edge and the set P_2 of 1-paths through the second edge only. From these two sets, the other sets of 1-paths ($P_3 = \overline{P}_1$, $P_4 = \overline{P}_2$) as well as the set of 0-paths can uniquely be determined. Cases frequently occur where nodes in the QMDD have equal sets of 1-paths P_1 and P_2, even though they are structurally different.

Example 7. Consider the QMDD depicted in Fig. 9. The root node already establishes the desired identity structure and the two nodes labeled x_2 (highlighted in blue) are structurally different. However, their sets of 1-paths are equal, i.e. $P_1 = \{\overline{x}_3\}$ and $P_2 = \{\overline{x}_3\}$ for both nodes. Consequently, both nodes can be transformed to the identity structure with the same sequence of Toffoli gates. One possible sequence is $TOF(\{x_2^+\}, x_3), TOF(\{x_3^+\}, x_2)$.

Without applying this scheme, the sequence of Toffoli gates has to be replicated twice – once for each node (including control line x_1^- for the left node and control line x_1^+ for the right node). This resulting in the circuit shown in Fig. 10a. The gates g_1 and g_2 thereby transform the left node to the identity, whereas the gates g_3 and g_4 transform the right node to the identity.

Since QMDD nodes that employ an equal characteristic regarding their sets of 1-paths P_1 and P_2 can be transformed to the identity structure with the same sequence of Toffoli gates, they can considered jointly for synthesis purposes and thus processed together. To this end, we form the ESoP of the paths to all nodes with equal sets P_1 and P_2 and apply the logic minimization as described in the straight forward approach.

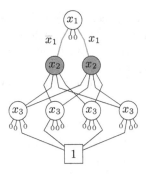

Fig. 9. QMDD nodes with equal sets P_1 and P_2 (Color figure online)

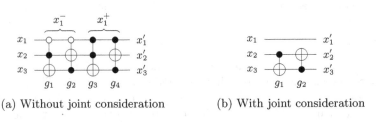

(a) Without joint consideration   (b) With joint consideration

Fig. 10. Gates required to transform the nodes labeled x_2

Example 7 (continued). Since both nodes labeled x_2 have equal sets of 1-paths P_1 and P_2, they can be considered jointly and processed together. The minimized ESoP of all paths to these nodes is $x_1 \oplus \overline{x}_1 = 1$, a sum consisting of a single product without any literals. Therefore no additional control lines are required (all nodes labeled x_2 can be considered jointly). The resulting circuit that transforms all nodes labeled x_2 to the identity structure is shown in Fig. 10b. Compared to the gate sequence depicted in Fig. 10a we observe a reduction of the *NCV-cost* from 20 to 2 and a reduction of the *T-depth* from 12 to 0.

5   Discussion

In this section, we briefly analyze the potential of the optimization scheme described above, i.e. we discuss how many nodes might be considered together in the best case. To this end, we assume that the nodes of n variables are left to be processed, i.e. the currently considered nodes are sub-QMDDs with height n, and that the sequence of Toffoli gates that transforms these nodes to the identity structure is uniquely determined by the set of 1-paths P_1 and P_2.

First, we determine how many different sequences of Toffoli gates exist. Since we assume that the sequence of Toffoli gates is uniquely determined by P_1 and P_2, we analyze how many combinations of sets P_1 and P_2 exist: The QMDD of the currently considered node represents a $2^n \times 2^n$ permutation matrix (since all nodes above already employ the identity structure). Consequently, there must be exactly one 1-entry in each of the 2^n rows and in each of the 2^n columns. This means, that there must be exactly 2^{n-1} 1-entries in the upper half of the matrix, i.e. $|P_1| + |P_2| = 2^{n-1}$. These 2^{n-1} 1-entries (1-paths) are arbitrarily distributed in the 2^n columns (in the sets P_1 and P_2). Consequently, there exist $\binom{2^n}{2^{n-1}}$ possibilities in which rows the 1-entries are located, i.e. possible different pairs of sets (P_1, P_2). If we assume $n = 2$, there exist $\binom{2^2}{2^2-1} = 6$ different sequences that transform a currently considered node to the identity. These sequences as well as their corresponding sets P_1 and P_2 are depicted in Fig. 11.

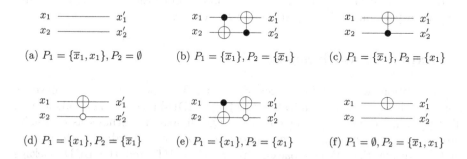

(a) $P_1 = \{\overline{x}_1, x_1\}, P_2 = \emptyset$ (b) $P_1 = \{\overline{x}_1\}, P_2 = \{\overline{x}_1\}$ (c) $P_1 = \{\overline{x}_1\}, P_2 = \{x_1\}$

(d) $P_1 = \{x_1\}, P_2 = \{\overline{x}_1\}$ (e) $P_1 = \{x_1\}, P_2 = \{x_1\}$ (f) $P_1 = \emptyset, P_2 = \{\overline{x}_1, x_1\}$

Fig. 11. Sequences of Toffoli gates for $n = 2$

As a second step, we analyze how many different sub-QMDDs with n variables exist. Recall, that a QMDD composed of n variables represents a permutation matrix of dimension $2^n \times 2^n$, i.e. a matrix that represents a permutation of 2^n elements. Since 2^n elements can be permuted in $2^n!$ ways, there exist $2^n!$ structurally different QMDDs with n variables. Considering again that $n = 2$, there exist $2^2! = 4! = 24$ structurally different QMDDs.

Having an arithmetic expression for the number of sequences as well as for the number of QMDDs allows one to analyze the potential of the proposed optimization. The resulting numbers for several values of n are provided in Table 2. As one can easily see, there are many more different QMDDs than sequences, because $\binom{2^n}{2^{n-1}} \ll 2^n!$. Consider the case that the $n = 3$ variables of the QMDD are not yet processed. In the worst case, the QMDD has 40 320 nodes labeled with the currently considered variable. For each of those nodes, a sequence of

Table 2. Potential of the proposed optimization

n	No. sequences $\binom{2^n}{2^{n-1}}$	No. QMDDs $2^n!$
2	6	24
3	70	40 320
4	12 870	$2 \cdot 10^{13}$
5	$6 \cdot 10^8$	$2.6 \cdot 10^{35}$

Toffoli gates has to be determined. If we apply the proposed optimization (i.e. if we jointly consider nodes with equal sets of 1-paths), the number of nodes that have to be processed drops to 70 – reducing the computational effort by a factor of 576. Furthermore, the logic minimization used to reduce the paths to the currently considered nodes is applied to a larger set of paths, which makes it more likely to obtain a more compact ESoP.

Obviously, it is more likely that many nodes can be processed together if their currently considered variable is the label for a large number of nodes. Therefore, this optimization has a higher impact on large QMDDs than on small ones. Since we observed that large QMDDs tend to yield circuits with rather high quantum cost, we expect higher improvements for these cases.

6   Experimental Results

In this section, we evaluate the reduction of the quantum cost we achieve by applying the proposed optimizations to the QMDD-based synthesis algorithm. To this end, we have reimplemented the QMDD-based synthesis as originally proposed in [16] (including some minor optimizations regarding performance) in C++ using the QMDD package provided in [11] and the BDD package CUDD [17]. This implementation represents the current state-of-the-art and serves as baseline. Based on that, we have implemented the optimizations discussed in Sect. 4. In the following, Scheme A denotes the optimization where the paths to the currently node are reduced using logic minimization[2] and Scheme B denotes the case if we additionally process nodes with equal sets of 1-paths jointly. As benchmarks served the reversible circuits provided at RevLib [19]. All experiments were conducted on a 4 GHz processor with 32 GB of memory running Linux 4.4.

Table 3 summarizes the experimental results. The first two columns list the name of the benchmark and the number of circuit lines n. Then, for each synthesis scheme, the runtime, the *NCV-cost* as well as the *T-depth* is listed. Finally, we list the reduction of the quantum cost for Scheme A with respect to the baseline and for Scheme B with respect to Scheme A. Since the improvement rates observed for *NCV-cost* and for *T-depth* are almost identical for each of the benchmarks (they deviate in a fraction of a percent only), we only list the improvement regarding *T-depth* in the last two columns of Table 3.

The obtained results clearly show a significant improvement in terms of runtime. While the original approach requires a significant amount of runtime for some benchmarks (e.g. more than 1000 s for benchmarks *sym9*, *rd84*, and *cycle10*), the optimizations proposed in this paper allowed to synthesize all benchmarks within a few seconds (Schemes A and B). Only one benchmark (*cordic*) required slightly more than a minute.

Furthermore, a substantial improvement in terms of quantum cost can be observed for the benchmarks. For all benchmarks that result in a circuit with

---

[2] We utilized the methods available at RevKit [14] for logic minimization.

Table 3. T-depth improvements compared to the state-of-the-art

Benchmark	n	Baseline (original QMDD-based synth.)			Scheme A			Scheme B			Improvement	
		t	NCV	T-depth	t	NCV	T-depth	t	NCV	T-depth	Base/A	A/B
alu1	20	0.02	319	180	0.03	319	180	0.04	319	180	1.00	1.00
cmb	20	0.00	1462	864	0.01	1462	864	0.00	1462	864	1.00	1.00
cycle17_3	20	0.00	50270	30105	0.01	50270	30105	0.01	46513	27852	1.00	1.08
ex1010	20	1.91	139558	83724	1.76	140282	84156	1.64	136098	81648	0.99	1.03
C7552	21	0.01	963	576	0.00	963	576	0.01	963	576	1.00	1.00
decod	21	0.00	963	576	0.00	963	576	0.01	963	576	1.00	1.00
dk17	21	0.01	2308	1371	0.00	2308	1371	0.01	2308	1371	1.00	1.00
ham7	21	0.06	2528008	1516800	0.03	165254	99147	0.03	1169	696	15.30	142.45
pcler8	21	0.00	509	300	0.00	509	300	0.00	509	300	1.00	1.00
alu4	22	6.66	193546	116109	1.89	204945	122946	1.95	196765	118038	0.94	1.04
apla	22	0.02	4442	2652	0.02	4442	2652	0.03	4442	2652	1.00	1.00
cm150a	22	0.19	1302	768	0.19	1302	768	0.19	1302	768	1.00	1.00
f51m	22	1.48	61066	36630	1.46	61066	36630	1.49	61066	36630	1.00	1.00
mux	22	0.19	1284	768	0.19	1284	768	0.18	1284	768	1.00	1.00
tial	22	1.26	107806	64665	1.21	107806	64665	1.30	98646	59169	1.00	1.09
plus63mod4096	23	5.71	174926090	104955648	0.59	1822510	1093500	0.32	465	276	95.98	3961.96
add8	25	7.92	753638	452175	3.90	252538	151512	4.00	252538	151512	2.98	1.00
cordic	25	76.91	747026	448080	72.43	747026	448080	73.42	747026	448080	1.00	1.00
cu	25	0.01	1535	915	0.02	1535	915	0.01	1535	915	1.00	1.00
plus127mod8192	25	21.83	588787850	353272704	1.78	4054830	2432892	1.24	510	303	145.21	8029.35
plus63mod8192	25	21.91	588787850	353272704	1.85	4054830	2432892	1.23	510	303	145.21	8029.35
rd73	25	39.61	1047169928	628301952	0.65	1184798	710868	0.12	13899	8334	883.85	85.30
in0	26	0.44	25117	15057	0.46	25117	15057	0.44	25117	15057	1.00	1.00
sym9	27	1572.09	42859993608	25715996160	2.75	6353079	3811839	1.13	531033	318615	6746.35	11.96
apex4	28	2.25	97777	58641	2.12	97777	58641	2.22	96717	58005	1.00	1.01
cm151a	28	0.03	1246	744	0.04	1246	744	0.06	1246	744	1.00	1.00
hwb5	28	88.62	1761636344	1056981792	2.41	2895078	1737033	1.91	19298	11556	608.50	150.31
misex3	28	2.22	155005	92991	2.24	155005	92991	2.29	154905	92931	1.00	1.00
misex3c	28	2.26	155006	92991	2.27	155006	92991	2.32	154906	92931	1.00	1.00
table3	28	2.22	98535	59112	2.16	98535	59112	2.15	98755	59244	1.00	1.00
cm163a	29	0.02	1144	678	0.01	1144	678	0.02	1144	678	1.00	1.00
in2	29	0.15	32177	19296	0.16	32257	19344	0.15	32177	19296	1.00	1.01
frg1	31	2.50	25384	15219	2.62	25384	15219	3.06	25384	15219	1.00	1.00
mod5adder	32	446.53	10236860020	6142116000	1.72	1746181	1047696	1.30	20789	12453	5862.50	84.13
rd84	34	MO	–	–	1.25	1699111	1019451	0.92	28039	16794	–	60.70
cycle10	39	MO	–	–	6.24	11338986	6803379	5.71	2520	1500	–	4535.59

a *T-depth* of more than half a million using the original approach, substantial improvements of several orders of magnitudes were determined. Consider for example the benchmarks *plus127mod8192* and *plus63mod8192*. Performing logic optimizations on the paths to the currently considered node (i.e. Scheme *A*) already result in a reduction of the quantum cost by a factor of 145.21. If we additionally transform nodes together that have equal sets of 1-paths (i.e. Scheme *B*), we get another improvement by a factor of 8029.35 and, hence, an overall improvement of six orders of magnitudes. On average, we observe an improvement by a factor of 4.22 for Scheme *A* with respect to the original approach and an improvement by a factor of 5.35 of Scheme *B* with respect to Scheme *A*. This results in an overall improvement by a factor of 22.57.

7   Conclusion

In this paper, we reviewed the QMDD-based synthesis algorithm (proposed in [16]) for reversible circuits. Based on that review, we discovered cases that result in the same sequence of Toffoli gates, but are considered iteratively – leading to a substantial overhead in the number of gates. To reduce the costs of the resulting circuits, we proposed optimizations that consider such redundant cases jointly during synthesis. Experimental evaluations show that substantial improvements to the current state-of-the-art can be achieved. More precisely, improvements of up to three orders of magnitudes were observed for the runtime and improvements up to six orders of magnitudes were observed regarding the quantum cost of the resulting circuits.

Acknowledgements. This work has partially been supported by the European Union through the COST Action IC1405.

References

1. Amarù, L.G., Gaillardon, P., Wille, R., Micheli, G.D.: Exploiting inherent characteristics of reversible circuits for faster combinational equivalence checking. In: Design, Automation and Test in Europe, pp. 175–180 (2016)
2. Amy, M., Maslov, D., Mosca, M., Roetteler, M.: A meet-in-the-middle algorithm for fast synthesis of depth-optimal quantum circuits. IEEE Trans. CAD Integr. Circ. Syst. **32**(6), 818–830 (2013)
3. Bennett, C.H.: Logical reversibility of computation. IBM J. Res. Dev. **17**(6), 525–532 (1973)
4. Große, D., Wille, R., Dueck, G.W., Drechsler, R.: Exact multiple control Toffoli network synthesis with SAT techniques. IEEE Trans. CAD **28**(5), 703–715 (2009)
5. Landauer, R.: Irreversibility and heat generation in the computing process. IBM J. Res. Dev. **5**(3), 183–191 (1961)
6. Miller, D.M., Maslov, D., Dueck, G.W.: A transformation based algorithm for reversible logic synthesis. In: Design Automation Conference, pp. 318–323 (2003)
7. Miller, D.M., Thornton, M.A.: QMDD: a decision diagram structure for reversible and quantum circuits. In: International Symposium on Multi-Valued Logic, p. 6 (2006)

8. Miller, D.M., Wille, R., Sasanian, Z.: Elementary quantum gate realizations for multiple-control Toffolli gates. In: International Symposium on Multi-Valued Logic, pp. 288–293 (2011)
9. Mishchenko, A., Perkowski, M.: Fast heuristic minimization of exclusive-sums-of-products. In: International Workshop on Applications of the Reed-Muller Expansion in Circuit Design, pp. 242–250 (2001)
10. Nielsen, M., Chuang, I.: Quantum Computation and Quantum Information. Cambridge University Press, New York (2000)
11. Niemann, P., Wille, R., Miller, D.M., Thornton, M.A., Drechsler, R.: QMDDs: efficient quantum function representation and manipulation. IEEE Trans. CAD **35**(1), 86–99 (2016)
12. Shende, V.V., Prasad, A.K., Markov, I.L., Hayes, J.P.: Reversible logic circuit synthesis. In: International Conference on CAD, pp. 353–360 (2002)
13. Soeken, M., Dueck, G.W., Miller, D.M.: A fast symbolic transformation based algorithm for reversible logic synthesis. In: Devitt, S., Lanese, I. (eds.) RC 2016. LNCS, vol. 9720, pp. 307–321. Springer, Cham (2016). doi:10.1007/978-3-319-40578-0_22
14. Soeken, M., Frehse, S., Wille, R., Drechsler, R.: RevKit: a toolkit for reversible circuit design. In: Workshop on Reversible Computation, pp. 69–72 (2010). RevKit is available at http://www.revkit.org
15. Soeken, M., Tague, L., Dueck, G.W., Drechsler, R.: Ancilla-free synthesis of large reversible functions using binary decision diagrams. J. Symb. Comput. **73**, 1–26 (2016)
16. Soeken, M., Wille, R., Hilken, C., Przigoda, N., Drechsler, R.: Synthesis of reversible circuits with minimal lines for large functions. In: ASP Design Automation Conference, pp. 85–92 (2012)
17. Somenzi, F.: CUDD: CU decision diagram package release 3.0. 0. (2015)
18. Wille, R., Drechsler, R., Osewold, C., Ortiz, A.G.: Automatic design of low-power encoders using reversible circuit synthesis. In: Design, Automation and Test in Europe, pp. 1036–1041 (2012)
19. Wille, R., Große, D., Teuber, L., Dueck, G.W., Drechsler, R.: RevLib: an online resource for reversible functions and reversible circuits. In: International Symposium on Multi-Valued Logic, pp. 220–225 (2008). RevLib is available at http://www.revlib.org
20. Wille, R., Keszocze, O., Hillmich, S., Walter, M., Ortiz, A.G.: Synthesis of approximate coders for on-chip interconnects using reversible logic. In: Design, Automation and Test in Europe (2016)
21. Zulehner, A., Wille, R.: Taking one-to-one mappings for granted: Advanced logic design of encoder circuits. In: Design, Automation and Test in Europe (2017)

Design of Efficient Quantum Circuits Using Nearest Neighbor Constraint in 2D Architecture

Leniency Marbaniang[1], Abhoy Kole[2], Kamalika Datta[1],
and Indranil Sengupta[3(✉)]

[1] National Institute of Technology Meghalaya, Shillong, India
leniencym06@gmail.com, kdatta@nitm.ac.in
[2] B.P. Poddar Institute of Management and Technology, Kolkata, India
abhoy.kole@gmail.com
[3] Indian Institute of Technology Kharagpur, Kharagpur, India
isg@iitkgp.ac.in

Abstract. With the development in quantum computing, nearest neighbor constraint has become important for circuit realization. Various works have tried to make a circuit nearest neighbor compliant (NNC) by using minimum number of SWAP gates. To this end, an efficient qubit placement strategy is proposed that considers interaction among qubits and their positions of occurrence. Experimental results show that the proposed method reduces the number of SWAP gates by 3.3% to 36.1% on the average as compared to recently published works.

Keywords: Nearest neighbor · Qubit · 2D architecture · Quantum gate

1 Introduction

Quantum computing has drawn the attention of researchers over several decades. Unlike conventional binary logic systems that manipulate bits, quantum systems manipulate qubits that can exist as a state of superposition: $\phi = \alpha|0\rangle + \beta|1\rangle$, where $|\alpha|^2 + |\beta|^2 = 1$. Qubits can be implemented using technologies like ion-trap [1], photonics [4], nuclear magnetic resonance [3], etc. In some technology like ion-trap, the operation requires that the interacting qubits must be adjacent to each other known as the *Nearest Neighbor Constraint*. This is achieved by inserting an appropriate number of SWAP gates for nearest neighbor compliance. Several works have been proposed for arranging qubits in 1D [2,5,6] and 2D [7–9] architectures where the main aim is to minimize the number of SWAP gates. 2D architectures require fewer number of SWAP gates for NNC. In this paper, a heuristic procedure for mapping qubits to a 2D grid is proposed, which considers gate position, degree of lookahead and strength of interaction among qubits.

The paper is organized as follows. Section 2 explains the proposed method and steps of algorithm using examples. In Sect. 3, experimental results and comparison with previous works have been presented followed by concluding remarks in Sect. 4.

© Springer International Publishing AG 2017
I. Phillips and H. Rahaman (Eds.): RC 2017, LNCS 10301, pp. 248–253, 2017.
DOI: 10.1007/978-3-319-59936-6_19

2   Proposed Method

This section presents a qubit placement and SWAP gate insertion approach to make a quantum circuit NNC. This is based on a lookahead strategy that considers the frequency of occurrence of gates and their relative positions. Given the lookahead value LA, a window of LA gates $C = g_i g_{i+1} g_{i+2} \cdots g_{(i+LA-1)}$ is analyzed to determine the most interactive and frequently occurring qubits in the block. A data structure as shown in Fig. 1 is constructed for each qubit consisting of their interacting qubits, number of interactions and gate numbers. Using this structure, an interaction table is created as shown in Tables 1(a) and (b), from which the priority of the qubits is determined. Having the qubit priority list as in Table 1(g), qubit placement in the 2D grid as explained by Algorithm 1 is carried out such that the highest priority qubit is placed at the center and its interacting qubits are placed around it in the order <bottom, right, top, left>. Using the 2D grid, appropriate number of SWAP gates are inserted before the gate to bring the interacting qubits adjacent to each other and the new position of the qubit is retained. Finally, the total number of SWAP gates is counted and recorded. The same process is repeated for the next block of LA gates and also for the pair of blocks combined. This method is applied to other blocks of the same circuit and for different values of LA, and the configuration with minimum SWAP gate count is chosen as the best.

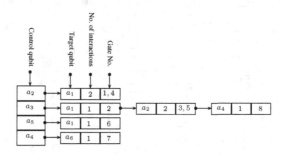

Fig. 1. Data structure of 1st block

2.1   The Proposed Algorithm

Knowing the LA value, different blocks of the circuit are defined by scanning the circuit from left to right. For each block, data structure and priority table are constructed and placement of the qubits in the 2D grid is performed (see Algorithm 1). Firstly, a qubit from the qubit priority table is selected and placed in the grid followed by its interaction qubits as shown in Fig. 2. If the qubit is already present, nothing is done. Initially it checks if the cell is empty; if not, it checks the next cell for space availability. This process is repeated until it finds an empty cell and inserts the qubit. Next SWAP gates are inserted as needed. Lastly the number of SWAP gates is calculated and recorded.

Algorithm 1. Qubit Placement

```
Input:    Qubit Priority Table PT, Interaction Table IT
Output:   Qubit placement GD in 2D grid
begin
    for qᵢ ∈ PT do
        if (qᵢ ∉ GD) then
            x = mid_x(GD);
            y = mid_y(GD);
            if (GDₓ,ᵧ is NOT empty) then
                Find (x, y) such that GDₓ,ᵧ is empty and adjacent to maximum number of empty cells;
            enddif
            Place qᵢ at GDₓ,ᵧ;
        else
            Retrieve location (x, y) of qᵢ ∈ GD;
        endif
        for ((qⱼ ∈ IT) and (ITqᵢ,qⱼ ⩾ 1)) do
            Place qⱼ in one of the empty cell from GDₓ±ᵣ,ᵧ±c where r, c = 1, 2, . . . ;
        endfor
    endfor
    return GD;
end
```

Table 1. Illustration for the first block. (a) Random Interaction Table, (b) Interaction Table (after sorting), (c) Qubit Table, (d) Qubit Table (after sorting based on maximum interactions), (e) Qubit Table (after sorting the gate numbers), (f) Qubit Table with time interval, (g) Qubit Priority Table

Control	Target	Interactions	Gate no
a2	a1	2	1,4
a3	a1	1	2
a3	a2	2	3,5
a3	a4	1	8
a5	a1	1	6
a4	a6	1	7

(a)

Control	Target	Interactions	Gate no
a2	a1	2	1,4
a3	a2	2	3,5
a3	a1	1	1
a3	a4	1	8
a5	a1	1	6
a4	a6	1	7

(b)

Qubit	Interactions	Gate no
a2	4	1,4,3,5
a3	4	3,5,2,8
a5	1	6
a4	2	8,7
a1	4	1,4,2,6
a6	1	7

(c)

Qubit	Interactions	Gate no
a2	4	1,4,3,5
a3	4	3,5,2,8
a1	4	1,4,2,6
a4	2	8,7
a5	1	6
a6	1	7

(d)

Qubit	Interactions	Gate no
a2	4	1,3,4,5
a3	4	2,3,5,8
a1	4	1,2,4,6
a4	2	7,8
a5	1	6
a6	1	7

(e)

Qubit	Interactions	Gate no	Time Interval
a2	4	1,3,4,5	4
a3	4	2,3,5,8	6
a1	4	1,2,4,6	5
a4	2	7,8	1
a5	1	6	0
a6	1	7	0

(f)

Qubit	Interactions	Gate no	Time Interval
a2	4	1,3,4,5	4
a1	4	1,2,4,6	5
a3	4	2,3,5,8	6
a4	2	7,8	1
a5	1	6	0
a6	1	7	0

(g)

2.2 Illustrative Example

Consider the benchmark circuit *4gt4-v0_80* that consists of 6 qubits and 44 gates. We illustrate the steps of qubit mapping for $LA = 8$. In the first invocation of the lookahead mechanism the block will consist of the first 8 gates. In the second call it will consist of the next 8 gates, and in the last call it will consist of all the 16 gates. In the first invocation a data structure as shown in Fig. 1 is constructed to find out the interacting qubits, the number of interactions and gate numbers where they interact within this block. Then a random interaction table is created by filling it randomly as shown in Table 1(a).

This random priority table is then sorted based on the interactions to get Table 1(b). If there is more than one gate with the same interacting qubits then we keep a record of just one gate, sum up the interactions, append the gate numbers and sort it again. Using the modified priority table, for each qubit, we calculate the total interactions and record all the gate numbers as shown in Table 1(c) followed by sorting as in Table 1(d). Next, the gate numbers of each qubit are sorted in ascending order as in Table 1(e). From this table, the qubits, their total interactions, the gate numbers, and the interval between the gates of each qubit is calculated as shown in Table 1(f). It is seen that qubits $a2$, $a3$ and $a5$ have four interactions but their frequencies of interaction are different. So qubit with the least time interval gets the highest priority, viz. $a2$, as seen in Table 1(g). Lastly, the circuit is scanned again to check if any qubit not in the block is left unfilled in the qubit priority table. If so, the qubit is appended in the table. Using this priority table, qubit placement is done as Algorithm 1 and illustrated in Fig. 2.

After qubit placement is completed in a 2D grid, SWAP gates insertion is performed. The process is illustrated for a benchmark *4gt11_84* that have five qubits, one of which (viz. a_4) is not involved in any gate interactions. The steps are shown in Fig. 3 which requires 2 SWAP operations.

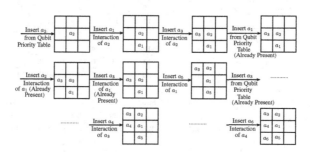

Fig. 2. Qubit placement of 1st block

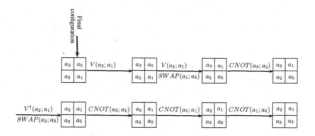

Fig. 3. Swap gate insertion

3   Experimental Results

The proposed method has been implemented in C and run on a core-i5 based desktop with 4 GB of RAM. Experiments have been carried out on NCV benchmarks that was used in [7–9] and results are shown in Table 2 along with previous results. The first two columns represent the benchmark name and number of qubits (n). SWAP gates count ($swap$) observed in [8] is presented next followed by number of SWAP gates for joint lookahead ($swap_\triangle$) and iterative lookahead ($swap_\triangledown$) reported in [9] in the next two columns respectively. After this, SWAP

Table 2. Improvements in SWAP gates of 2D qubit placement over [7–9]

Benchmark		[8]	[9]		[7]	Proposed 2D			Impr. (%)			
Name	n	$swap$	$swap_\triangle$	$swap_\triangledown$	$swap$	$swap$	l	grid	[8]	[9]$_\triangle$	[9]$_\triangledown$	[7]
QFT5	5	5	–	–	5	4	2	3 × 2	20.0	–	–	20.0
QFT7	7	14	13	22	18	14	7	3 × 3	0	−7.7	36.4	22.2
QFT8	8	23	17	25	18	20	4	3 × 3	13.0	−17.6	20	−11.1
QFT9	9	36	22	27	34	32	11	4 × 3	11.1	−45.5	−18.5	5.9
QFT10	10	51	37	43	53	43	2	4 × 3	15.7	−16.2	0	18.9
Shor3	10	1770	1010	1485	1710	828	16	3 × 4	53.2	18	44.2	51.6
Shor4	12	–	2757	3807	4264	2118	20	3 × 4	–	23.2	44.4	50.3
Shor5	14	–	6344	8504	8456	5566	15	4 × 4	–	12.3	34.5	34.2
Shor6	16	19980	12468	15970	20386	12905	25	4 × 5	35.4	−3.5	19.2	36.7
3_17_13	3	3	5	8	6	5	2	2 × 2	−66.7	0	37.5	16.7
4gt4-v0_80	6	15	–	–	17	10	8	2 × 3	33.3	–	–	41.2
4gt10-v1_81	5	15	15	22	16	14	4	2 × 3	6.7	6.7	36.4	12.5
4gt12-v1_89	6	18	–	–	19	14	4	3 × 4	22.2	–	–	26.3
4mod5-v1_23	5	7	–	–	11	6	6	3 × 3	14.3	–	–	45.5
aj-e11_165	5	22	16	37	24	11	3	3 × 4	50.0	31.3	70.3	54.2
alu-v4_36	5	11	–	–	10	8	5	3 × 3	27.3	–	–	20.0
cycle10_2_110	12	588	483	824	839	635	11	4 × 3	−8.0	−31.5	22.9	24.3
ham7_104	7	45	37	53	48	29	9	3 × 4	35.6	21.6	45.3	39.6
ham15_108	15	280	233	355	328	199	8	4 × 4	28.9	14.6	43.9	39.3
hwb4_52	4	9	–	–	9	5	6	3 × 2	44.4	–	–	44.4
hwb5_55	5	49	37	64	45	35	3	3 × 3	28.6	5.4	45.3	22.2
hwb6_58	6	76	59	85	79	52	5	3 × 3	31.6	11.9	38.8	34.2
hwb7_62	8	1500	1050	1703	1688	1093	6	4 × 4	27.1	−4.1	35.8	35.2
hwb8_118	9	7877	6316	11096	11027	5892	6	3 × 4	25.2	6.7	46.9	46.6
hwb9_123	10	11233	8522	14459	15022	8661	10	4 × 3	22.9	−1.6	40.1	42.3
mod5adder_128	6	36	33	45	41	30	6	3 × 3	16.7	9.1	33.3	26.8
mod8-10_177	6	43	–	–	45	36	4	3 × 4	16.3	–	–	20
plus63mod4096_163	13	13316	11764	22160	22118	15180	17	4 × 4	−14.0	−29.0	31.5	31.4
plus63mod8192_164	14	18987	15484	29939	29835	15931	20	4 × 4	16.1	−2.9	46.8	46.6
plus127mod8192_162	14	33299	27549	52333	53598	28520	30	5 × 4	14.4	−3.5	45.5	46.8
rd53_135	7	40	30	47	39	29	6	4 × 3	27.5	3.3	38.3	25.6
rd73_140	10	43	–	–	37	25	5	4 × 4	41.9	–	–	32.4
urf1_149	9	37722	29252	41058	38555	22358	10	3 × 4	40.7	23.6	45.5	42
urf2_152	8	16755	12872	18101	16822	9098	10	3 × 4	45.7	29.3	49.7	45.9
urf3_155	10	93558	69693	95485	94017	67034	30	3 × 4	28.4	3.8	29.8	28.7
urf5_158	9	34416	25887	36813	34406	19050	15	4 × 3	44.6	26.4	48.3	44.6
urf6_160	15	42910	31540	43100	43909	28147	15	5 × 4	34.4	10.8	34.7	35.9

gate count of [7] is presented. In the next three columns, SWAP gate count of proposed approach (*swap*), *LA* value and 2D configuration (*grid*) are reported. The last four columns show the % improvement of the proposed approach over [7–9]. On an average improvements of 22.4% (53.2% in the best case) over [8], 3.3% and 36.1% (31.3% and 70.3% in the best case) over joint and iterative lookahead strategy from [9], and 32.4% (54.2% in the best case) over [7] are observed.

4   Conclusion

In this work, a new lookahead approach for qubit placement in a 2D grid to minimize the number of SWAP gates for NN-compliance is proposed. Prioritization of the qubits has been worked out to determine which qubit should be placed earlier by considering the qubit's number of interactions and position in the circuit. The most frequent qubit with less interval gets a higher priority. The results obtained are found to be better than those reported in existing works.

Acknowledgement. This work was partially supported by Department of Science and Technology, Government of India under Grant No. YSS/2015/001461.

References

1. Blatt, R.: Quantum information processing with trapped ions. In: Quantum Information and Measurement, p. Th1.1 (2013)
2. Chakrabarti, A., Sur-Kolay, S., Chaudhury, A.: Linear nearest neighbor synthesis of reversible circuits by graph partitioning. arXiv preprint (2011). arXiv:1112.0564
3. Lu, D., Brodutch, A., Park, J., Katiyar, H., Jochym-O'Connor, T., Laflamme, R.: NMR quantum information processing. In: Takui, T., Berliner, L., Hanson, G. (eds.) Electron Spin Resonance (ESR) Based Quantum Computing. BMR, vol. 31, pp. 193–226. Springer, New York (2016). doi:10.1007/978-1-4939-3658-8_7
4. Nemoto, K.: Photonic architecture for scalable quantum information processing in diamond. Phys. Rev. X **4**(3), 031022 (2014)
5. Rahman, M.M., Dueck, G.W., Chattopadhyay, A., Wille, R.: Integrated synthesis of linear nearest neighbor ancilla-free MCT circuits. In: 46th International Symposium on Multiple-Valued Logic (ISMVL), pp. 144–149, May 2016
6. Shafaei, A., Saeedi, M., Pedram, M.: Optimization of quantum circuits for interaction distance in linear nearest neighbor architectures. In: 50th ACM/EDAC/IEEE Design Automation Conference (DAC), pp. 1–6, May 2013
7. Shafaei, A., Saeedi, M., Pedram, M.: Qubit placement to minimize communication overhead in 2D quantum architectures. In: 2014 19th Asia and South Pacific Design Automation Conference (ASP-DAC), pp. 495–500, January 2014
8. Shrivastwa, R.R., Datta, K., Sengupta, I.: Fast qubit placement in 2D architecture using nearest neighbor realization. In: IEEE International Symposium on Nanoelectronic and Information Systems, pp. 95–100, December 2015
9. Wille, R., Keszocze, O., Walter, M., Rohrs, P., Chattopadhyay, A., Drechsler, R.: Look-ahead schemes for nearest neighbor optimization of 1D and 2D quantum circuits. In: 21st Asia and South Pacific Design Automation Conference (ASP-DAC), pp. 292–297, January 2016

Erratum to: Designing Parity Preserving Reversible Circuits

Goutam Paul[1]([✉]), Anupam Chattopadhyay[2], and Chander Chandak[3]

[1] Cryptology and Security Research Unit (CSRU),
R.C. Bose Centre for Cryptology and Security,
Indian Statistical Institute, Kolkata 700 108, India
goutam.paul@isical.ac.in
[2] School of Computer Engineering,
Nanyang Technological University (NTU), Singapore, Singapore
anupam@ntu.edu.sg
[3] Liv Artificial Intelligence Pvt. Ltd., Bengaluru, India
chandar.chandak@gmail.com

Erratum to:
Chapter "Designing Parity Preserving Reversible Circuits" in:
I. Phillips and H. Rahaman (Eds.),
Reversible Computation, LNCS 10301,
DOI: 10.1007/978-3-319-59936-6_6

The 6th and 7th row of Table 2 (starting with 101 and 110 respectively) must have "0" in their last column instead of "1".

The updated online version of this chapter can be found at
http://dx.doi.org/10.1007/978-3-319-59936-6_6

© Springer International Publishing AG 2017
I. Phillips and H. Rahaman (Eds.): RC 2017, LNCS 10301, p. E1, 2017.
DOI: 10.1007/978-3-319-59936-6_20

Author Index

Printed in the United States
By Bookmasters